Clinical Applications of Rational-Emotive Therapy

Clinical Applications of Rational-Emotive Therapy

Edited by

Albert Ellis

Institute for Rational-Emotive Therapy
New York, New York

and

Michael E. Bernard

University of Melbourne
Parkville, Victoria, Australia

Plenum Press • New York and London

Library of Congress Cataloging in Publication Data

Main entry under title:

Clinical applications of rational-emotive therapy.

Includes bibliographies and index.
1. Rational-emotive psychotherapy. I. Ellis, Albert. II. Bernard, Michael Edwin, 1950– . [DNLM: 1. Mental Disorders—therapy. 2. Psychotherapy. WM 420 A6515]
RC489.R3A66 1985 616.89′14 85-3709

ISBN-13: 978-1-4612-9506-8 e-ISBN-13: 978-1-4613-2485-0
DOI: 10.1007/978-1-4613-2485-0

Softcover reprint of the hardcover 1st edition 1985
Plenum Press is a Division of Plenum Publishing Corporation
233 Spring Street, New York, N.Y. 10013

Contributors

MICHAEL E. BERNARD • Department of Education, University of Melbourne, Parkville, Victoria, Australia

MICHAEL S. BRODER • Philadelphia Institute for Rational-Emotive Therapy, Philadelphia, Pennsylvania. Clinical psychologist in private practice, Philadelphia, Pennsylvania

IAN M. CAMPBELL • Department of Psychology, University of Melbourne, Parkville, Victoria, Australia

RAYMOND A. DIGIUSEPPE • Institute for Rational-Emotive Therapy, New York, New York

ALBERT ELLIS • Executive Director, Institute for Rational-Emotive Therapy, New York, New York

VINCENT GREENWOOD • Washington Center for Cognitive Therapy, 5525 Connecticut Avenue, N.W., Washington, D.C.

PAUL A. HAUCK • Clinical psychologist in private practice, Rock Island, Illinois

WILLIAM J. KNAUS • Psychologist in private practice, Longmeadow, Massachusetts

ROSE OLIVER • Clinical psychologist in private practice, New York, New York. Staff psychotherapist, Institute for Rational-Emotive Therapy, New York, New York

HARRY SOBEL • Department of Psychiatry, Harvard Medical School, Boston, Massachusetts

SUSAN R. WALEN • Baltimore Center for Cognitive Therapy, Baltimore, Maryland. Department of Psychology, Towson State University, Towson, Maryland

GARY WITKIN • Behavior Modifiers, Valley Stream, New York

JANET L. WOLFE • Associate Executive Director, Institute for Rational-Emotive Therapy, New York, New York

CYNTHIA ZEEVE • Stanford University, Stanford, California

Preface

Since its launching in 1955, rational-emotive therapy (RET) has become one of the most influential forms of counseling and psychotherapy used by literally thousands of mental health practitioners throughout the world. From its beginnings, RET has dealt with problems of human disturbance. It presents a theory of how people primarily disturb themselves and what they can do, particularly with the help of a therapist or counselor, to reduce their disturbances (Ellis, 1957a,b, 1958a,b, 1962). Almost immediately after the creation of RET, it became obvious that the methodology could be used in many other fields—especially those involving human relations (Ellis & Harper, 1961a), and in love, sex, and marital relationships (Ellis, 1958a, 1960, 1963a,b; Ellis & Harper, 1961b). The evident popularity and clinical utility of RET in different cultures and its increasing application to contemporary problems of living indicate that rational-emotive therapy continues to be vital and dynamic.

The growing appeal of RET may be due in part to its essentially optimistic outlook and humanistic orientation; optimistic because it provides people with the possibility and the means for change. Showing to people how their attitudes and beliefs are responsible for their emotional distress and interpersonal problems (and not some out-of-conscious early childhood experience), awakens in them the hope that, in reality, they have some control over their destiny. Providing people with a scientific method of rational thought enables them to foresee how they can achieve emotional self-control and, as a consequence, how they can lessen their own distress so that their personal goals can be achieved. RET with its emphasis on total self- and other-acceptance, irrespective of performance shortcomings and/or social disapproval, also encourages people to become more completely self-actualized. The fullest development of human potential—one of the basic aims of RET—is further encouraged in RET by helping people judge the rightness and wrongness of their own actions as well as the actions of others in terms of how these actions effect the achievement of personal and work goals.

One of the recognitions that Albert Ellis is most proud of is the award of Humanist of the Year, bestowed in the early 1970s, by the American Humanist Association.

Today RET is being applied to a myriad of personal problems and issues, some but certainly not all of which are written about in this book and include: addiction and substance abuse (Drake, 1964; Ellis, 1974a, 1982; Maultsby, 1978; Silverstain, 1977; Wolfe, 1979), adolescent and child problems (Bernard & Joyce, 1984; Ellis & Bernard, 1983; Kranzler, 1974; Tosi, 1974), anger and rage (Ellis, 1977a; Hauck, 1974), assertion training (Alberti & Emmons, 1982; Jakubowski & Lange, 1978; Lange & Jakubowski, 1976; Lee-Gilmore, 1981; Paris & Casey, 1983; Wolfe, 1977; Wolfe & Fodor, 1975), children's literature (Bedford, 1974; Garcia & Pellegrini, 1974; Merrifield & Merrifield, 1980; Waters, 1981), communication (Crawford, 1982; Garner, 1981; Lacey, 1982; Martin, 1983), education (Bingham, 1982; Gerald & Eyman, 1981; Knaus, 1974), executive leadership and management (Ellis, 1972, 1985), health and medicine (Ellis & Abrams, 1978; Greenwood & Bernstein, 1982; Johnson, 1981), humor and fun (Ellis, 1977b,c, 1981; Little, 1977), law and criminality (Church, 1975; Ellis & Gullo, 1972), love, marriage, and sex (Araoz, 1982; Ard, 1974; Ellis, 1958b, 1960, 1963a,b, 1976, 1979, 1982b; Grossack, 1976; Hauck, 1981, 1984), philosophy (Ellis, 1968; Shibles, 1974), parenting (Ellis, 1978; Ellis, Wolfe, & Moseley, 1966; Hauck, 1967; McMullin, 1978), religion (Dougherty, 1979; Grau, 1977; Hauck, 1972; Lawrence & Huber, 1982; Powell, 1976), self-discipline and high-frustration tolerance (Ellis & Knaus, 1977; Hauck, 1975; Knaus, 1979, 1982, 1983), and sports psychology (Bell, 1980; Ellis, 1982c; Gologar, 1979; Nardi, 1980; Orlick, 1980; Simek & O'Brien, 1981; Wessler, 1980).

In addition to these publications, which describe how RET can be applied to many important areas of human life, a variety of general self-help books have been written that show how rational-emotive principles and techniques can help to solve almost any emotional problem. Some of these books have been bestsellers: *Your Erroneous Zones* (Dyer, 1977); *A New Guide to Rational Living* (Ellis & Harper, 1975); *Feeling Good* (Burns, 1980); *Overcoming Depression* (Hauck, 1973); *Help Yourself to Happiness* (Maultsby, 1975); and *A Rational Counseling Primer* (Young, 1974).

Audio cassettes have also brought RET messages to the general public and some of them, too, have been bestsellers—including *How to Stubbornly Refuse to Be Ashamed of Anything* (Ellis, 1973a), *Twenty-one Ways to Stop Worrying* (Ellis, 1973b), *Rational Living in an Irrational World* (Ellis, 1974b), *A Garland of Rational Songs* (Ellis, 1977c), *Twenty-two Ways to Brighten Up Your Love Life* (Ellis, 1982b), *Self-hypnosis: A Rational-Emotive Approach* (Golden, 1982), *Rational-Emotive Therapy and Women's Problems* (Wolfe, 1974), and *Assertiveness Training for Women* (Wolfe, 1977).

Despite all of this material on the applications of RET to people's emotional problems and to many areas of life, no one book shows how RET can be applied to important and vital aspects of human existence. Therapists, counselors, and mental health practitioners who want to adapt RET to a particular kind of problem now have to search through considerable resources, some of which are no longer up-to-date. Consequently, the editors of this book decided to invite a number of outstanding RET specialists to devote a chapter to how RET is used in their speciality. All the authors have extensive experience in rational-emotive therapy and cognitive-behavior therapy; several of them are pioneers in these areas.

The book's first chapter, by the editors, provides a background for the applications of RET to clinical problems by introducing its basic theory, philosophy, and practice. The second, third, and fourth chapters of the book deal with love, marriage, and divorce, respectively. In Chapter 2, Ellis—who for over 35 years has been a leading authority on problems of love, sex, and marriage—writes about the diagnosis and treatment of love problems. He describes the romantic myths of our culture and highlights the treatment of obsessive-compulsive love, jealousy and possessiveness, problems in encountering suitable partners, and loss of love. Ellis includes in his chapter suggestions for keeping love alive. In Chapter 3, Raymond DiGiuseppe, Director of Training and Research at the Institute for Rational-Emotive Therapy, and Cynthia Zeeve, of Stanford University, provide new insights into how RET can be combined with social-exchange theory in the practice of helping couples who have relationship problems. The irrational beliefs that underlie relationship difficulties are discussed. Michael Broder's chapter on divorce and separation stems from his innovative program known as R.O.A.D.S. (Rational Options in Adjusting to Divorce and Separation), which encourages the establishment of support groups to help treat the addiction to a terminated love relationship. As well as describing his program, Broder also pinpoints the irrationalities that contribute to problems in divorce and separation.

Janet L. Wolfe, Associate Executive Director of the Institute for Rational-Emotive Therapy, has pioneered the use of RET with women to help them cope with the practical and emotional problems of their transition into more expanded roles. The past 10 years has seen the development at the Institute in New York of one of the broadest-based therapy programs in the United States that addresses women's issues. Chapter 5 not only describes the work of Wolfe and her colleagues at the Institute but also surveys a wide range of issues that will be of interest to practitioners seeking to update their knowledge in this area.

The sixth and seventh chapters of this book directly concern different aspects of human sexuality. In Chapter 6, Susan R. Walen, a leading RET author, reviews the latest trends in sex therapy and provides rational perspectives concerning different sexual behaviors and concerns. Her cognitive-behavioral feedback model of sexual arousal, which details the important role of perceptual and evaluative cognitions, represents an important new contribution in this area. Ian M. Campbell, in Chapter 7, presents an extended theory of human psychological functioning, based on RET, which leads to the conclusion that sexual pathology is independent from the issue of sexual preference. Chapter 7 is recommended for those who are interested in the chain of irrational thought processes (demandingness-awfulizing-low-frustration tolerance-globalizing) that is hypothesized to underlie an emotional disturbance.

The next two chapters deal with problems associated with establishing healthy living patterns. Gary Witkin, an RET therapist with a great deal of experience in helping people to lose weight, to give up smoking, and to exercise, shares in Chapter 8 his insights into the cognitive distortions that interfere with those people who are trying to maintain newly acquired positive health habits. A discussion of the self-defeating nature of fanatical and excessive adherence to principles of healthy living breaks new ground in this area. Vince Greenwood illustrates in Chapter 9 how RET can be used to help people stop or significantly reduce substance abuse (e.g., alcohol, tobacco, barbiturates, amphetamines, heroin, and cocaine) and to maintain the desired change. An important contribution of his chapter is the description of disputational strategies that can be used to zero in on the substance abuser's core irrational assumptions.

Paul Hauck has written extensively on RET over the past 20 years and is conversant on many issues of concern to RET practitioners. In Chapter 10, he describes the compatibilities and incompatibilities between RET and religion. William Knaus, a leader in the field of rational-emotive education (REE), demonstrates in Chapter 11 how the phenomenon of student burnout can be treated with the use of REE. The application of REE to the treatment of a 10-year-old learning-disabled boy reveals the ways in which RET can be simplified for use with younger clients. In Chapter 12, Michael E. Bernard presents a rational-emotive mental training program that he employed with a group of professional football players. After a discussion of the ABC's of the mind and body as well as the typical stresses that football players encounter, Bernard presents material on how to teach different mental skills and attitudes (relaxation, mental practice, disputation of irrational thinking, positive thinking, goal-setting, concentration training) to professional athletes.

The final two chapters of the book round out the life span. In Chapter 13, Rose Oliver writes about the problems of middle age and discusses how RET is used to treat midlife problems related to work, to the end of parenting, and to a declining body image. Harry Sobel is a recognized authority in helping patients cope with terminal illness. In Chapter 14, he discusses his belief concerning the importance of regarding dying and death as normal dimensions of the life process and illustrates how RET is a most humanistic and pragmatic approach for clinicians and for the families of the dying.

RET celebrates its thirtieth birthday this year. As editors, we believe that this book—which demonstrates the wide range and distinctive value of RET—will provide a solid foundation for the application of RET over the coming years. We hope that clinicians, educators, pastoral counselors, and other professionals will gain appreciably from their reading of the book and thus learn how to apply RET in theory and in practice.

ALBERT ELLIS
MICHAEL E. BERNARD

REFERENCES

Alberti, R. E., & Emmons, M. L. (1982). *Your perfect right* (4th ed.). San Luis Obispo, CA: Impact.
Araoz, D. L. (1982). *Hypnosis and sex therapy*. New York: Brunner/Mazel.
Ard, B. N. (1974). *Treating psychosexual dysfunction*. New York: Aronson.
Bedford, S. (1974). *Instant replay*. New York: Institute for Rational-Emotive Therapy.
Bell, K. F. (1980). *The nuts and bolts of psychology for swimmers*. Austin, TX: Keith Bell.
Bernard, M. E., & Joyce, M. (1984). *Rational-emotive therapy with children and adolescents*. New York: Wiley.
Bingham, T. R. (1982). *Program for affective learning*. Blandint, UT: Metra.
Burns, D. (1980). *Feeling good*. New York: Morrow.
Church, V. A. (1975). *Behavior, law and remedies*. Dubuque, IA: Kendall/Hunt.
Crawford, T. (1982). *The personal revolving discussion sequence package*. Rosemead, CA: Ted Crawford.
Dougherty, D. (1979). *A psychological handbook for Christian pastoral counselors*. St. Joseph, MO: Benedictine Counseling and Consulting Institute.
Drake, W. (1964). *Guidebook for alcoholics*. New York: Exposition.
Dyer, W. (1977). *Your erroneous zones*. New York: Funk & Wagnalls.
Ellis, A. (1957a). Outcome of employing three techniques of psychotherapy. *Journal of Clinical Psychology, 13*, 334–350.
Ellis, A. (1957b). *How to live with a neurotic*. New York: Crown.
Ellis, A. (1958a). Rational psychotherapy. *Journal of General Psychology, 59*, 35–49.
Ellis, A. (1958b). *Sex without guilt*. New York: Lyle Stuart.
Ellis, A. (1960). *The art and science of love*. New York: Lyle Stuart.

Simek, T. C., & O'Brien, R. M. (1981). *Total golf.* Garden City, NY: Doubleday.
Tosi, D. (1974). *Youth: Toward personal growth.* Columbus, OH: Merrill.
Waters, V. (1981). *Rational stories for children.* New York: Institute for Rational-Emotive Therapy.
Wessler, R. (1980). How to play golf under pressure. *Rational Living, 15,* 21–24.
Wolfe, J. L. (Speaker). (1974). *Rational-emotive therapy and women's problems.* (Cassette recording).
Wolfe, J. L. (1976). *How to be sexually assertive.* New York: Institute for Rational-Emotive Therapy.
Wolfe, J. L. (Speaker). (1977). *Assertiveness training for women.* (Cassette recording). New York: BMA Audio Cassettes.
Wolfe, J. L. (1979). A cognitive-behavioral approach to working with women alcoholics. In V. Burtle (Ed.), *Women who drink* (pp. 197–216). Springfield, IL: Thomas.
Wolfe, J. L., & Fodor, I. G. (1975). A cognitive/behavior approach to modifying assertive behavior in women. *Counseling Psychologist, 5*(4), 45–52.
Young, H. (1974). *A primer of rational counseling.* New York: Institute for Rational Emotive Therapy.

Contents

Freud, Bertrand Russell, and John B. Watson—and began to work determinedly on himself to overcome what he conceived of as his needless emotional problems. From the age of nineteen onward (in 1932), he adopted a cognitive-behavioral approach to overcoming his public speaking and social anxiety difficulties (Ellis, 1972a).

In 1939, Ellis started to do research in sex, love, marriage, and family problems, mainly because he was interested in writing in those fields, and accidentally discovered that he could effectively counsel his friends and relatives who were anxious and depressed in those areas. He consequently received his M.A. in clinical psychology from Columbia University in 1943 and his Ph.D. in 1947; and he began to practice formal psychotherapy and sex and marital therapy in 1943. Although he had some doubts about the unscientific manner in which psychoanalysis was usually practiced, he still believed that it was a deeper form of therapy and therefore started his personal analysis and training analysis in 1947 with a training analyst of the Karen Horney Institute. He practiced classical analysis and psychoanalytically oriented therapy until 1953, when he became increasingly disillusioned with its theory and its efficacy and began to call himself a "psychotherapist" rather than a "psychoanalyst." Up to this time, he vainly tried to reformulate psychoanalysis in scientific terms (Ellis, 1949a,b, 1950, 1956a); but he then abandoned it, concluding that it often does more harm than good (Ellis, 1962, 1968; Ellis & Harper, 1961a).

At first, rational-emotive therapy was called rational therapy (RT) because Ellis emphasized its cognitive and philosophic aspects and wanted to differentiate it clearly from the other therapies of the 1950s (Ellis, 1958). But many people wrongly identified RT with eighteenth-century rationalism (to which it was opposed). It always had very strong evocative-emotive and behavioral components and from the start favored activity-oriented, therapeutic homework assignments, *in vivo* desensitization, and skill training (Ellis, 1956b, 1962). It was also highly confronting, quite unlike classical analysis and Rogerian client-centered therapy. So Ellis, in collaboration with his first associate in this new mode of treatment, Dr. Robert A. Harper, decided in the early sixties to change its name to rational-emotive therapy (RET).

From the beginning, RET was highly philosophic and disputational because Ellis, at the age of sixteen, took as his main interest and hobby the pursuit of philosophy and held that if people acquired a sane philosophy of life they would rarely be emotionally disturbed. RET was influenced by the writings of many philosophers, especially Epictetus, Marcus Aurelius, Baruch Sprinoza, John Dewey, Bertrand Russell, A.J. Ayer, Hans Reichenbach, and Karl Popper. Psychologically, it incor-

Freud, Bertrand Russell, and John B. Watson—and began to work determinedly on himself to overcome what he conceived of as his needless emotional problems. From the age of nineteen onward (in 1932), he adopted a cognitive-behavioral approach to overcoming his public speaking and social anxiety difficulties (Ellis, 1972a).

In 1939, Ellis started to do research in sex, love, marriage, and family problems, mainly because he was interested in writing in those fields, and accidentally discovered that he could effectively counsel his friends and relatives who were anxious and depressed in those areas. He consequently received his M.A. in clinical psychology from Columbia University in 1943 and his Ph.D. in 1947; and he began to practice formal psychotherapy and sex and marital therapy in 1943. Although he had some doubts about the unscientific manner in which psychoanalysis was usually practiced, he still believed that it was a deeper form of therapy and therefore started his personal analysis and training analysis in 1947 with a training analyst of the Karen Horney Institute. He practiced classical analysis and psychoanalytically oriented therapy until 1953, when he became increasingly disillusioned with its theory and its efficacy and began to call himself a "psychotherapist" rather than a "psychoanalyst." Up to this time, he vainly tried to reformulate psychoanalysis in scientific terms (Ellis, 1949a,b, 1950, 1956a); but he then abandoned it, concluding that it often does more harm than good (Ellis, 1962, 1968; Ellis & Harper, 1961a).

At first, rational-emotive therapy was called rational therapy (RT) because Ellis emphasized its cognitive and philosophic aspects and wanted to differentiate it clearly from the other therapies of the 1950s (Ellis, 1958). But many people wrongly identified RT with eighteenth-century rationalism (to which it was opposed). It always had very strong evocative-emotive and behavioral components and from the start favored activity-oriented, therapeutic homework assignments, *in vivo* desensitization, and skill training (Ellis, 1956b, 1962). It was also highly confronting, quite unlike classical analysis and Rogerian client-centered therapy. So Ellis, in collaboration with his first associate in this new mode of treatment, Dr. Robert A. Harper, decided in the early sixties to change its name to rational-emotive therapy (RET).

From the beginning, RET was highly philosophic and disputational because Ellis, at the age of sixteen, took as his main interest and hobby the pursuit of philosophy and held that if people acquired a sane philosophy of life they would rarely be emotionally disturbed. RET was influenced by the writings of many philosophers, especially Epictetus, Marcus Aurelius, Baruch Sprinoza, John Dewey, Bertrand Russell, A.J. Ayer, Hans Reichenbach, and Karl Popper. Psychologically, it incorporated some of the views of important cognitive therapists, such as Adler (1927, 1929), Coué (1923), Dubois (1907), Frankl (1959), Herzberg (1945), Johnson (1946), Horney (1939), Kelly (1955), Low (1952), and Rotter (1954), although Ellis did not read some of these cognitivists (such as Dubois, Frankl, Kelly, and Low) until after he had already originated the basic theory and practice of RET.

Uniquely, RET was highly experiential (and experimental) from the start and became even more so when it began using, in the early sixties, some of the encounter methods originated by Perls (1969), Schutz (1967), and others. Since that time, it has developed its own experiential exercises—such as its famous shame-attacking exercise (Ellis, 1969, 1971a; Ellis & Abrahms, 1978). Just as RET has adopted certain experiential methods, so has the experiential movement also been influenced by RET and has adopted some of its basic cognitive-behavioral orientation (S. Emery, 1978; Erhard, 1976; Goulding & Goulding, 1979).

For a good many years, Ellis was remarkably alone in writing major treatises on RET but in recent years a good number of other authors have published clinical texts applying RET to various kinds of emotional problems. These RET texts have included books by Bard (1980), Bernard and Joyce (1984), Church (1975), Diekstra and Dassen (1976), Grieger and Boyd (1980), Grieger and Grieger (1982), Ellis and Abrahms (1978), Ellis and Bernard (1983), Ellis and Grieger (1977), Hauck (1972, 1980), Kessler and Hoellen (1982), Lange and Jakubowski (1976), Lembo (1976), Maultsby (1984), Morris and Kanitz (1975), D. Schwartz (1981), Tosi (1974), Walen, DiGiuseppe, and Wessler (1980), Wessler and Wessler (1980), and Wolfe and Brand (1977).

RET has always specialized in self-help procedures and Ellis pioneered in this respect by publishing a good many popular books on rational-emotive procedures that have been designed for self-actualization purposes. These books have included *How to Live with a "Neurotic"* (Ellis, 1957a), *Sex Without Guilt* (Ellis, 1958b), *The Art and Science of Love* (Ellis, 1960), *A Guide to Rational Living* (Ellis & Harper, 1961), *A Guide to Successful Marriage* (Ellis & Harper, 1961b), *Sex and the Liberated Man* (Ellis, 1976a), *Overcoming Procrastination* (Ellis & Knaus, 1977), *The Intelligent Woman's Guide to Dating and Mating* (Ellis, 1979), and *A Guide to Personal Happiness* (Ellis & Becker, 1982).

In addition to these, many other popular books have been written to help members of the public benefit from RET, including those by Bedford (1980), Blazier (1975), Burns (1980), Butler (1981), G. Emery (1982), Garner (1980), Goodman and Maultsby (1974), Grossack (1971, 1974), Hauck (1973, 1974, 1975, 1976, 1979, 1981, 1984), Jakubowski and Lange (1978), S. Johnson (1977), Knaus (1982), Kranzler (1974), Lazarus and Fay (1975), Lembo (1974, 1977), Garcia and Blythe (1977), Lacey (1982), Little (1977), Losoncy (1980), Maleske (1976), Maultsby (1975, 1978), Maultsby and Hendricks (1974), McMullen and Casey (1975), J. Miller (1983), T. Miller (1983), Nash (1981), Paris & Casey (1983), Powell (1976), Thoresen (1975), Silverstein (1977), and Young (1974).

Furthermore, RET has been almost astoundingly successful in that many writers have incorporated its philosophy and practice into their work even though they may have failed to acknowledge doing so; and some of these writers have published immensely successful and influential books—including L. S. Barksdale (1972), Wayne Dyer (1977), William Glasser (1965), Haim Ginott (1965), Ken Keyes (1979), and Manuel Smith (1976).

Finally, several studies appearing in the professional literature have shown the enormous influence of Ellis and RET on today's psychotherapists and counselors. Thus, D. Smith (1982) found that Ellis was second to Carl Rogers and ahead of Sigmund Freud when 800 clinical and counseling psychologists ranked the psychotherapists whom they consider to be most influential today. Smith also noted that "cognitive behavioral and/or rational therapy was the predominant representation among the ten most influential therapists. These findings suggest quite clearly that cognitive behavior therapy is one of the major trends in counseling and psychotherapy" (Smith, 1982, p. 807). Heesacker, Heppner, and Rogers (1982) did a frequency analysis of approximately 14,000 references cited in three major counseling psychology journals for the years 1980 and 1981 and found Ellis to be the most frequently cited author of works published after 1957. Sprenkle, Keeney, and Sutton (1982) questioned 310 members of the American Association of Marital and Family Therapy as to whom they considered the ten most influential theorists in the field of marriage and family therapy and they chose Virginia Satir as No. 1. Sigmund Freud as No. 2, Carl Rogers as No. 3, and Albert Ellis as No. 4.

In view of the profound effect that RET has had on the mental health profession and the public during the last two decades, it seems reasonable to say that it has been, and still is, one of the most influential systems of psychotherapy (and of marriage and family therapy) of the twentieth century.

Ellis was practically alone in practicing and promulgating rational-emotive therapy from 1955 to 1963. But thereafter, largely as a result of his strong advocacy of cognitive-behavior therapy and because of the work of therapists whom he had trained in RET, this form of therapy began to take hold among professionals and to be adopted or modified by a number of outstanding practitioners and researchers. Most of the leading cognitive-behavior therapists have directly followed in the pioneering pathways marked by Ellis; but a few, such as Beck (1967, 1976) and Bandura (1969, 1977) have independently arrived at principles and practices that significantly overlap with RET. Some of the professionals who have been most influential in the cognitive-behavior area and have helped make this form of therapy perhaps the most popular form today include Goldfried and Davison (1976), Greenwald (1973), A. Lazarus (1971, 1981), R. Lazarus (1966), Mahoney (1977), Masters and Rimm (1974), Meichembaum (1977), and Raimy (1975).

Values and Goals of RET

RET does not pretend to be entirely objective and value free. Quite the contrary. It is a system of psychotherapy designed to help people live longer, minimize their emotional disturbances and self-defeating behaviors, and actualize themselves so that they live a more fulfilling, happier existence. Once these goals are chosen, and RET sees them as matters of choice rather than as absolute givens, then subgoals of the "best" ways for people to think, feel and behave seem to follow from these main purposes; and whether or not the subgoals really work and actually result in longer and happier lives for most of the people most of the time can be scientifically (that is, logically and empirically) determined. Also, RET holds, the scientific (logical-empirical), method so far appears to be the best (most efficient) way of discovering what techniques of psychotherapy are most workable for which people under what conditions in order for their main goals and subgoals to be achieved (Ellis, 1962, 1971b, 1973, 1974, 1984a, 1984b, in press-a, in press-b; Ellis & Grieger, 1977; Ellis & Whiteley, 1979).

The main subgoals of RET consist of helping people to think more rationally (scientifically, clearly, flexibly); to feel more appropriately; and to act more functionally (efficiently, undefeatingly) in order to achieve their goals of living longer and more happily. Consequently, RET defines rationality, appropriate feeling, and functional behavior in terms of these basic goals; and it tries to be as precise as it can be about these definitions. In particular:

Rational thoughts (or rational ideas or beliefs) are defined in RET as those thoughts that help people live longer and happier, particularly by (1) setting up or choosing for themselves certain (presumably) happiness-producing values, purposes, goals, or ideals; and (2) using effiriences. When overly upset, people are prone to seek out and respond ineffectually to these As (and to block the fulfilment of their goals) because of (1) their biological or genetic predispositions; (2) their constitutional history; (3) their prior interpersonal and social learning; and (4) their innately predisposed and acquired habit patterns (Ellis, 1976b, 1979b, in press-a, in press-b).

According to RET theory, people have almost innumerable beliefs (Bs), or cognitions, thoughts, or ideas, about their activating events (As); and these Bs importantly and directly tend to exert strong influences on their cognitive, emotional, and behavior consequences (Cs) and on what we often call their "emotional" disturbances. Although activating events (As) often seem to directly cause or contribute to Cs, this is rarely true, because Bs normally serve as important mediators between As and Cs and therefore more directly cause or create Cs. This RET theory of human action and of disturbance is firmly held by rational-emotive therapists (Bard, 1980; Bernard & Joyce, 1984; Ellis, 1957a, 1958a, 1962, 1977a; Grieger & Boyd, 1980; Grieger & Grieger, 1982; Walen, DiGiuseppe & Wessler, 1980; Wessler & Wessler, 1980). RET holds that people largely bring their beliefs to A; and they subjectively and idiosyncratically view or experience As in the light of these beliefs (expectations, evaluations) and also in the light of their emotional consequences (Cs) (desires, preferences, wishes, motivations, tastes, disturbances). Therefore, humans virtually never experience A without B and C; but they also rarely experience B and C without A.

The term *belief* can be used to refer to various characteristics of thinking activity that are seen to cause dysfunctional emotions and patterns of behavior. The unique properties of beliefs can be summarized as follows (Bernard, 1981; Bernard & Joyce, 1984):

1. Belief may be viewed as a very broad hypothetical construct that embraces at least three distinct subclasses of cognitive phenomena: (1) thoughts that an individual is thinking and is aware of at a given time; (2) thoughts that the individual is not immediately aware of; and (3) more abstract beliefs that the individual may hold in general.

2. The more abstract beliefs that people hold are unspoken and constitute the assumptive framework by which they appraise and form conclusions about what they observe to be happening to themselves, to others, and in the world around them.

3. Abstract beliefs can be differentiated on the basis of whether they reflect absolute and imperative qualities (irrational) or relativistic and conditional qualities (rational).

4. The main irrational beliefs that people tend to hold can be categorized under three major ones, each with many derivatives: (a) "I must

do well and win approval, or else I rate as a rotten person," (b) "Others must treat me considerately and kindly in precisely the way I want them to treat me; if they don't, society and the universe should severely blame, damn, and punish them for their inconsiderateness," (c) "Conditions under which I live must be arranged so that I get practically all I want comfortably, quickly, and easily, and get virtually nothing that I don't want."

5. There are four common forms of self-defeating thinking which derive from these irrational beliefs and which lead to psychological disturbance: (a) *awfulizing* ("It is *awful*, or *terrible*, or *horrible* that I am not doing as I must"); (b) *I can't stand-it-itis* ("I *can't stand, can't bear* the things that are happening to me that must not happen!"); (c) worthlessness ("I am a worthless person if I don't do as well and win as much approval as I must"); (d) allness or unrealistic overgeneralization ("Because I failed at this important task, as I must not, I'll *always* fail and *never* succeed!").

6. Abstract beliefs are often an expression of the values of people and as such play an important role in explaining the basic goals and purposes of people's behavior.

7. Beliefs refer to people's appraisals and evaluations of their interpretations, expectations, and inferences concerning reality. For example, consider Bill, who is sitting at home feeling depressed because his woman friend has not called when she was supposed to. Bill interprets the situation as follows: "She is not going to call, and if she doesn't, that will really show that she doesn't like me any more." While these interpretations may be true or false, they are in and of themselves (even if they are true) insufficient to trigger Bill's extreme upsettedness. For Bill to become really upset, it would be necessary for him to appraise (make an affective judgment about) his interpretations. His belief that he needs (must have) Jane's love and his appraisal that he could not stand it (or himself) without it are irrational and lead to depression. One of RET's distinctive contributions to psychotherapy is the separation of interpretations of reality from appraisals and the systematic delineation of irrational beliefs that lead to emotional upset.

8. Irrational beliefs can be distinguished from expectations, inferences, and conclusions insofar as the latter can be considered *assumptions* about reality that are capable of being proven true or false, whereas beliefs are judged to be irrational when they express unconditional and absolutistic demands that do not help the individual remain happy and goal achieving.

People sometimes learn irrational beliefs and erroneous assumptions from their parents and teachers (Bernard & Joyce, 1984); for example, "I must have good luck, but now that I have broken this mirror more incapacitating than their primary symptom and that may actually prevent them from understanding and working against this primary disturbance (Ellis, 1962, 1979c, 1980a).

RET assumes that people often use their cognitive processes in this self-defeating manner, because this is the way they naturally, easily tend to think. RET therefore routinely looks for secondary symptoms and treats them prior to or along with dealing with clients' primary symptoms. The clinical observation that people tend to spy on themselves and condemn themselves when they have primary symptoms, and that they thereby frequently develop crippling secondary symptoms, tends to support the RET hypothesis that cognition is enormously important in the development of neurotic feelings and behaviors and that efficient psychotherapy had better include considerable rational-emotive methodology.

When people develop secondary symptoms, for example, feel very anxious about their anxiety, as agoraphobics tend to do, their secondary feelings strongly influence their cognitions and their behaviors. Thus, they feel so badly that they tend to conclude, "It really *is* awful that I am panicked about open spaces!" and they tend to behave more self-defeatingly than ever (e.g., they withdraw even more from open spaces). This again demonstrates that A (activating events), B (beliefs), and C (cognitive, emotive, and behavioral consequences) are interactive, that thoughts significantly affect feelings and behaviors, that emotions significantly affect thoughts and feelings, and that behaviors significantly affect thoughts and feelings (Ellis, 1962, 1984a, in press-a,b).

In RET, we are mainly concerned with people's "emotional" disturbances. But the ABC theory also is a personality theory that shows how people largely create their own "normal" or healthy (positive and negative) feelings and how they can change them if they wish to work at doing so (Ellis, 1978b).

Disputation of Irrational Beliefs

A fundamental theory of RET is that when people seriously disturb themselves they almost always implicitly or explicitly accept or invent strong, absolutistic, "musturbatory" irrational beliefs (iBs); and that one of the very best methods of helping them diminish or remove their emotional disturbances is to show them how to actively dispute these iBs at point D and to encourage them to do so, during therapeutic sessions and on their own, until they arrive at E, a new effective philosophy that enables them to think and behave more rationally and selfhelpingly. As Phadke (1982) has shown, D can be divided into three important sub-Ds: (1) Detecting irrational beliefs and clearly seeing that they are illogical and unrealistic. (2) Debating these iBs and showing oneself exactly how and why they do not hold water. (3) Discriminating irrational beliefs (iBs) from rational beliefs (rBs) and showing oneself how the former lead to poor and the latter to much healthier results.

Disputing of irrational beliefs may also be effected in a number of other ways. Cognitively, they can be replaced by rational beliefs or sensible coping statements; they can be undermined by practicing some of the teachings of general semantics (Korzybski, 1933); they can be contradicted by being replaced by positive imagery (Maultsby, 1975; Maultsby & Ellis, 1974); they can be combatted by focusing on the distinct disadvantages they create and the advantages of giving them up; they can be supplanted by alternative problem solving methods; can be put out of mind by cognitive distraction and by thought stopping; and they may be alleviated by the use of many other kinds of thinking methods (Ellis & Abrahms, 1978; Ellis, 1984a, 1984b, in press-a, in press-b).

RET theory and practice also hold that the best techniques for disputing people's irrational beliefs and of helping them to change their feelings and behaviors in directions they consider more desirable are frequently emotive and behavioral in character. Emotively, therefore, it employs a number of selected experiential methods, including rational-emotive imagery (Maulsby, 1975; Maultsby & Ellis, 1974), shame-attacking exercises (Ellis, 1969, 1971a), role playing (Ellis & Abrahms, 1978), unconditional acceptance by the therapist of her or his clients (Ellis, 1962, 1972c, 1976c), the use of forceful self-statements and self-dialogues (Ellis, 1979d), and other evocative-dramatic techniques (Ellis, 1984a; Ellis & Abrahms, 1978). Behaviorally, it also uses a variety of selected methods, including reinforcement, penalizing, activity homework assignments, implosive assignments, and skill training (Bernard & Joyce, 1983; Ellis, 1962, 1977c, 1978a, 1984a; Ellis & Abrahms, 1978; Ellis & Becker, 1982; Ellis & Bernard, 1983).

To demonstrate a typical method in which RET helps clients to actively dispute their irrational beliefs and arrive at a new effective philosophy, Figure 1 consists of a filled-out version of the recently revised Rational Self-Help Report Form, devised by Sichel and Ellis (1983) and commonly distributed to the regular individual and group therapy clients seen at the Institute for Rational-Emotive Therapy in New York City. We have filled in this form using some of the material mentioned previously in this chapter in connection with the irrational beliefs (iBs) an individual might well have if (let us say) he observed at point A (activating events) that people were laughing and if he felt anxious and

RET SELF-HELP FORM

Institute for Rational-Emotive Therapy
45 East 65th Street, New York, N.Y. 10021
(212) 535-0822

(A) ACTIVATING EVENTS, thoughts, or feelings that happened just before I felt emotionally disturbed or acted self-defeatingly:

I noticed that people were laughing

(C) CONSEQUENCE or CONDITION—disturbed feeling or self-defeating behavior—that I produced and would like to change:

I felt anxious and depressed. I started to stay away from people.

(B) BELIEFS—Irrational BELIEFS (IBs) leading to my CONSEQUENCE (emotional disturbance or self-defeating behavior). Circle all that apply to these ACTIVATING EVENTS **(A)**.	**(D) DISPUTES** for each circled IRRATIONAL BELIEF. Examples: "*Why* MUST I do very well?" "*Where is it written* that I am a BAD PERSON?" "*Where is the evidence* that I MUST be approved or accepted?"	**(E) EFFECTIVE RATIONAL BELIEFS (RBs)** to replace my IRRATIONAL BELIEFS (IBs). *Examples: "I'd* PREFER *to do very well but I don't* HAVE TO." *"I am a* PERSON WHO *acted badly, not a BAD PERSON." "There is no evidence that I* HAVE TO *be approved, though I would* LIKE *to be."*
1. I MUST do well or very well!		
2. I am a BAD OR WORTHLESS PERSON when I act weakly or stupidly.	How does it make me a bad person if people dislike me?	It doesn't! It only makes me a person who is less liked than I wish to be.
3. I MUST be approved or accepted by people I find important!	Why must I?	I don't have to be, though that would be desirable.
4. I am a BAD, UNLOVABLE PERSON if I get rejected.	In what way am I a bad person?	I am not! I am just a person who got rejected.
5. People MUST treat me fairly and give me what I NEED!		
6. People who act immorally are undeserving, ROTTEN PEOPLE!		
7. People MUST live up to my expectations or it is TERRIBLE!		
8. My life MUST have few major hassles or troubles.	Where is this law written?	Only in my head! Life <u>will</u> have major hassles. Tough!
9. I CAN'T STAND really bad things or very difficult people!		

(OVER)

FIGURE 1. RET Self-Help Form, completed.

depressed about this observation. Guided by an RET practitioner and by reading some of the RET pamphlets and books, especially *A New Guide to Rational Living* (Ellis & Harper, 1975) and *A Guide to Personal Happiness* (Ellis & Becker, 1983) and *Overcoming Procrastination* (Ellis & Knaus, 1977), this person might well fill out the Rational Self-Help Report Form as it is filled out in Figure 1.

Unlike most other systems of cognitive-behavior therapy, RET em-

RET SELF-HELP-FORM (Continued)

10. It's AWFUL or HORRIBLE when major things don't go my way!		
11. I CAN'T STAND IT when life is really unfair!		
12. I NEED to be loved by someone who matters to me a lot!		
13. I NEED a good deal of immediate gratification and HAVE TO feel miserable when I don't get it!		
Additional Irrational Beliefs:		
14. These people must be laughing at me. If so, that makes me a fool!	Where is the evidence that they are laughing at me? If they are, how does that make me a fool?	There is none. They may be laughing for many other reasons! Even if I am acting foolishly, that doesn't make me a fool.
15. If they are laughing at me it's awful!	Why would it be awful if they were?	It wouldn't be. It would only be inconvenient!
16. They only despise me and see I am an undeserving person	Is this likely to be true?	No. A few of them may despise me but even if they do I can still accept myself.
17. They will talk badly about me and make me lose all my friends.	How do I know that this will happen?	I don't. They may not talk badly about me; and if they do I'll hardly lose all my friends.
18. Even if they are not laughing at me now, they will find me out and see how ridiculous I am later.	Where is the evidence that this will happen?	Nowhere! If they do later find me ridiculous, I can still see myself as a person with some foolish behavior but not a bad person.

(F) FEELINGS and BEHAVIORS I experienced after arriving at my EFFECTIVE RATIONAL BELIEFS: Disappointment at people's laughing. Happy about overcoming my anxiety and depressions.

I WILL WORK HARD TO REPEAT MY EFFECTIVE RATIONAL BELIEFS FORCEFULLY TO MYSELF ON MANY OCCASIONS SO THAT I CAN MAKE MYSELF LESS DISTURBED NOW AND ACT LESS SELF-DEFEATINGLY IN THE FUTURE.

Joyce Sichel, Ph.D. and Albert Ellis, Ph.D.

phasizes the use of active disputing as the most elegant, though hardly the only, way of helping people to surrender their irrational beliefs (iBs). Rational-emotive therapists preferably, with clients who are able to do disputing, show them: (1) How to look for and detect their irrational beliefs, particularly their absolutistic shoulds and musts, their awfulizing, their I-can't-stand-it-itis, their can'ts, and their self-downing. (2) How to logically and empirically question and challenge their iBs and to vigorously argue themselves out of believing them. (3) How to replace them with alternate, rational beliefs (rBs) and coping statements. (4) How to think about these rational beliefs and show themselves why they are rational and in what ways they are different from irrational beliefs. (5) How to internalize the scientific method, and steadily, for the rest of their lives, see that their irrational beliefs are hypotheses, not facts, and strongly challenge and question these hypotheses until they give them up. As noted above, RET uses many other cognitive, emotive, and behavioral methods of helping people to combat and to surrender their irrational beliefs. But it prefers, with many individuals, to use active-directive disputing.

Unique Features of RET

As already noted, RET has a number of unique features that make it differ significantly from most of the other popular forms of therapy. To conclude this introductory chapter, let us briefly note (and in some cases repeat) some of its main uniquenesses.

Innate Predispositions to Disturbance

Although RET uses social learning theory and holds that external and external events and environmental influences significantly affect humans and contribute to their emotional disturbances, it stresses biological tendencies and innate predispositions to disturbance more than do most other forms of psychotherapy, including the cognitive therapies. Because it holds that people naturally and easily, as well as through cultural teaching, imbibe and create irrational beliefs, RET stresses the importance of the therapist's vigorously and forcefully disputing these iBs and encouraging clients to do so steadily and powerfully themselves (Ellis, 1976b, 1979d, 1983a, in press-a,b).

Secondary Disturbances

RET especially emphasizes the human disposition first to disturb oneself over some failure or frustration and secondarily to disturb oneself over one's disturbances. It assumes that secondary disturbances often exist, particularly with individuals who have had strong primary disturbances for a period of time; looks for these secondary symptoms; and usually deals with them first, before it then goes on to deal with their primary disturbances (Ellis, 1962, 1979c, 1980a, 1984a, in press-a,b).

Assessment Procedures

RET at times employs many different assessment procedures associated with other forms of cognitive-behavior therapy; but it also favors rational-emotive therapy itself as an important means of assessment. It holds that in many (not all) cases the therapist can quickly zero in on some of the client's irrational beliefs (iBs), and make this therapeutic procedure highly diagnostic, that is, see how and under what conditions the client is likely to react to therapy (Ellis, 1984a, in press-a).

Appropriate and Inappropriate Feelings

As indicated above, RET clearly defines inappropriate feelings, separates them from appropriate ones, and focuses (especially with new clients) on discovering what people's inappropriate feelings are, how they can learn to discriminate them from appropriate ones, and how they can work on changing them (Ellis, 1971b, 1973).

Absolutistic and Anti-Empirical Irrational Beliefs

RET holds that although many kinds of human irrationalities and illogicalities exist and produce poor results, what we call "emotional disturbance" most importantly is a concomitant of absolutistic and unconditional shoulds, oughts, musts, demands, commands, and expectations. It hypothesizes that the awfulizing, I-can't-stand-it-itis, damning, personalizing, all-or-nothing thinking, overgeneralizing, and other kinds of crooked thinking that disturbed individuals do and that lead to their emotional problems largely stem from explicit or implicit dogmatizing and absolutism; and that therefore if we therapeutically dispute clients' derivative inferences and illogicalities alone, they will not tend to make as profound and healthy a philosophic change as when we show them their intolerant demands and commands and induce them to surrender these, too. Preferential RET usually deals with absolutistic *and* unrealistic Beliefs, and not merely with one or the other (Ellis, 1980b, 1984a, in press-a,b).

Evaluative and Nonevaluative Dogmas

Although RET discloses and argues against all kinds of dogmas and unscientific postulates, it particularly looks for and opposes people's absolutistic evaluative judgments about themselves, about others, and about the world, as it holds that these are closely related to cognitive, emotive, and behavioral dysfunctioning that accompanies disturbed symptoms (Ellis, 1984b, in press-b).

Relationship Processes

RET favors the building of a good rapport with clients, uses empathic listening and reflection of feeling, and emphasizes unconditional acceptance by the therapist of the client as well as strong encouragement by the therapist to help clients look at themselves and to change (Ellis, 1973, 1976c, 1984c). But it takes a cautious attitude toward both therapists' and clients' dire need for each others' approval and continually explores the irrational beliefs (iBs) that they may tell themselves about needing this approval, which interferes (1) with the clients' really working to change themselves and (2) with therapists' being firm enough with clients to help them change (Ellis, 1977b). RET also notably tries to induce clients to refuse to rate themselves poorly whether or not they do well in therapy and win their therapist's approval; and it shows therapists how to unconditionally accept themselves whether or not they are successful with various clients. While RET tries to show clients that they are equal and active collaborators with the therapist in changing themselves, it also encourages the therapist to be a highly active-directive teacher who had often better take the lead in explaining, interpreting, and disputing clients' iBs and to come up with better solutions to their problems (Ellis, 1984b, in press-a, b).

Multimodal and Comprehensive Use of Techniques

RET has a distinct theory of human disturbance and of how it probably can most efficiently be ameliorated. But its theory is interactive and multimodal, and sees emotions, thoughts, and behaviors as transacting with each other and including one another. Hence it has always been multimodal in its use of many cognitive, emotive, and behavioral methods. Because it emphasizes the biological as well as social sources of disturbance, it frequently favors the use of medication and of physical techniques—including diet, exercise, and relaxation techniques. At the same time, RET is selective in its methods and only occasionally uses a technique (such as positive thinking or religious conversion) just because it works. Instead, RET looks at the long range as well as the short range effects of various techniques; considers many methods (such as cognitive distraction) as more palliative than curative; and tries to emphasize those that tend to produce a profound philosophic change that helps clients not merely *feel* but *get* better (Bernard & Joyce, 1984; Ellis, 1972b, 1974, 1977a, 1983b). As noted above, RET is famous for its cognitive and philosophic approaches to psychotherapy but it also heavily emphasises the use of many selective emotive and behavioral methods.

The Use of Force and Vividness

The theory of RET holds that when they are emotionally disturbed, people tend to forcefully, vividly, and vigorously, with profound conviction, hold on to their main irrational beliefs (iBs); and that even when they have "insight" into these beliefs, they may still strongly believe them and refuse to give them up. Therefore, RET not only often emphasizes quite active-directive disputing of irrationalities but also stresses those emotive techniques (such as its shame-attacking exercises and such as rational-emotive imagery) and those behavioral techniques (such as implosive *in vivo* desensitization) that powerfully contradict and work against people's disturbed thoughts, feelings, and behaviors (Dryden, 1984; Ellis, 1979d, 1984a, 1984b).

Ego Anxiety and Discomfort Anxiety

RET holds that people have two basic kinds of emotional disturbance that often significantly overlap and reinforce each other: (1) ego anxiety (or ego depression) arising from their absolutistic and perfectionistic demands that they personally perform well and be approved by others and leading to feelings of severe inadequacy when they perform poorly and are disapproved by significant others; and (2) discomfort anxiety (or discomfort depression) arising from their absolutistic and perfectionistic demands that others do their bidding and that conditions be arranged so that they easily and quickly get what they demand. RET almost invariably looks for both these kinds of disturbance, reveals them to clients, and shows people various methods of effectively overcoming them (Ellis, 1979c, 1980a).

Humanistic Aspects

RET does not pretend to be "purely" objective, scientific, or technique-centered but takes a definite humanistic-existential approach to human problems and their basic solutions. It primarily deals with disturbed human evaluations, emotions, and behaviors. It is highly rational and scientific but uses rationality and science in the service of humans in an attempt to enable them to live and be happy. It is hedonistic, but espouses long-range instead of short-range hedonism: so that people may achieve the pleasure of the moment and that of the future, may arrive at maximum freedom *and* discipline. It hypothesizes that nothing superhuman probably exists and that devout belief in superhuman agencies tends to foster dependency and increase emotional disturbance (1983c). It assumes that no humans, whatever their antisocial or obnoxious behavior, are damnable nor subhuman. It particularly emphasizes the importance of will and choice in human affairs, even though it accepts the likelihood that some human behavior is partially determined by biological, social, and other forces (Ellis, 1973, 1984c; Bandura, 1978).

Views of Self-Esteem and Self-Acceptance

Where most other psychotherapies attempt to help people achieve self-esteem, RET is skeptical of this concept and tries, instead, to help them achieve what it calls self-acceptance, or better, to refuse to rate their selves, their being, or their essence at all but only to rate their acts, deeds, and performances (Ellis, 1972c, 1973, 1976c, 1977a, 1984c). RET shows people that no matter what criteria they rate themselves on, whether it be external (e.g., success or approval), or internal (e.g., character or emotional stability), or supernatural (e.g., acceptance by Jesus or by God), they really *choose* these criteria. Therefore, they can more elegantly accept themselves, without any intervening variables, merely because they *choose* to do so (Ellis, 1983c, in press-a, b).

Views of Efficient and Elegant Psychotherapy

RET especially strives for efficient and elegant forms of psychotherapy. It aims not merely for symptom removal but also for a profound change in people's basic philosophy. It tries to alleviate or remove most symptoms of disturbance permanently, not transiently, though it acknowledges that people have a strong tendency to retrogress and reinstitute their symptoms once they have originally overcome them. It tries to develop methods of elegant therapy that require relatively little therapeutic time and that produce maximum results quickly and efficiently (Ellis, 1980c, in press-b). It specializes in psychoeducational methods (such as bibliotherapy, audiotherapy, videotherapy, workshops, and other media presentations) in the course of which some of the main RET teachings can be effectively used with large groups of individuals for self-help purposes (Ellis, 1978a; Ellis & Abrahms, 1978).

Views on Behavioral Methods

RET favors *in vivo* rather than purely imaginative modes of systematic desensitization and it often encourages implosive instead of gradual-activity homework assignments. It uses reinforcement procedures but takes a somewhat different attitude toward them than do other cognitive-behavioral schools: (1) It is wary of using love or approval as a reinforcer, because that may help make people more suggestible and less autonomous and self-thinking. (2) It strives, in the last analysis, to help people choose their own goals and think for themselves and hence become less suggestible and less reinforceable by external influences. It encourages some clients who are not easily reinforceable to use stiff penalities when they resist changing their dysfunctional behaviors. But it tries to make very clear that penalties are not to be used as punishments and not to include any ideas of undeservingness or damnation (Ellis, 1983b).

Insight and Behavioral Change

RET particularly stresses cognitive or intellectual insight; but it also shows the difference between intellectual and emotional insight and indicates how clients can achieve the latter and can effect behavioral change through achieving it (Ellis, 1962, 1963, in press-b). Thus, it shows clients that when they have intellectual insight they usually believe something lightly and occasionally and that when they have emotional insight they usually believe this thing strongly and persistently, and therefore because of their powerful belief, feel and act on it. RET holds that before people can change their inappropriate feelings and behaviors they normally require three main kinds of insight: Insight No. 1 is the acknowledgment that disturbances mainly or largely stem not from past events but from the irrational beliefs (iBs) that people bring to such events. In RET terms, activating events (A's) may significantly contribute to disturbed consequences (Cs) but their more important and relevant contribution of cause comes from their irrational beliefs (iBs) about what happens at A. Insight No. 2 is the realization that no matter how we originally become (or make ourselves) disturbed, we feel upset today because we are still reindoctrinating ourselves with the same kinds of irrational beliefs that we originated (or took over from others) in the past. Insight No. 3 is the full acceptance of the idea that even if we achieve insights No. 1 and No. 2 and realize that we have created and keep carrying on our own disturbed feelings and behaviors, these insights will not automatically make us change ourselves. Only if we constantly work and practice, in the present and future, to think, feel, and act against our irrational beliefs are we likely to surrender them and make and keep ourselves less disturbed (Ellis, 1977a, in press-b; Ellis & Knaus, 1977).

Use of Humor

RET hypothesizes that people had better give significant meaning to their lives, as Frankl (1959) has ably shown, but that emotional disturbance easily arises when they give exaggerated or overly serious significance to some of their thoughts, feelings, and actions (Ellis, 1962, 1971a, 1973). RET therefore specializes in ripping up people's irrational beliefs (iBs)—and not, of course, the people themselves—in many humorous ways (Ellis, 1977d,e). Ellis has composed a number of rational humorous songs that he often employs with his clients and at his RET talks and workshops; and many other RET (and non-RET) therapists and leaders have also adopted his song techniques (Ellis, 1981). Here, for example, are three of his popular rational humorous songs:

Whine, Whine, Whine!

(To the tune of the Yale *Whiffenpoof Song*, originally
composed by Guy Scull—a Harvard man!)

I cannot have all of my wishes filled—
Whine, whine, whine!
I cannot have every frustration stilled—
Whine, whine, whine!
Life really owes me the things that I miss,
Fate has to grant me eternal bliss!
And since I must settle for less than this—
Whine, whine, whine!

Maybe I'll Move My Ass

(To the tune of *After the Ball*, composed by
Charles K. Harris)

After you make things easy, and you provide the gas;
After you squeeze and please me, maybe I'll move my ass!

Make my life soft and easy, fill it with sassafras!
And possibly, if things are easy, I'll move my ass!

I Wish I Were Not Crazy

(To the tune of *Dixie,* composed by Dan Emmett)

Oh, I wish I were really put together—
Smooth and fine as patent leather!
Oh, how great to be rated innately sedate!
But I'm afraid that I was fated
To be rather aberrated—
Oh, how sad to be mad as my Mom and my
  Dad!
Oh, I wish I were not crazy! Hooray, hooray!
I wish my mind were less inclined
To be the kind that's hazy!
I could agree to try to be less crazy,
But I, alas, am just too goddamned lazy!

(Lyrics to all songs by Albert Ellis.
Copyright 1977 by Institute for Rational-
Emotive Therapy)

Summary and Conclusion

RET was originally developed as a pioneering form of cognitive-behavioral therapy (CBT) to help clients overcome their emotional disturbances, including their primary and their secondary problems. But it also has developed into a personality theory that shows people how they largely create their own normal or healthy (positive and negative feelings and how they can change them if they wish to work at doing so (Ellis, 1978b). It is psychoeducational as well as therapeutic and is now being applied, as the various chapters of this book show, to a large number of fields of human endeavour. It is based on the assumption that survival and happiness are of great value to most people and that these values can be appreciably achieved and enhanced by the use of flexible, undogmatic, rigorous, scientific thinking. It has already made significant contributions to psychotherapy and to self-actualization and, as it changes and develops (as scientifically-based theories and practices almost invariably tend to do), it is hoped that it will have important and useful applications to still more fields of human striving.

References

Adler, A. (1927). *Understanding human nature.* New York: Greenberg.

Adler, A. (1929). *The science of living.* New York: Greenberg.

Bandura, A. (1969). *Principles of behavior modification.* New York: Holt, Rinehart & Winston.

Bandura, A. (1977). *Social learning theory.* Englewood Cliffs, NJ: Prentice-Hall.

Bandura, A. (1978). The self system in reciprocal determinism. *American Psychologist, 33,* 344–358.

Bard, J. A. (1980). *Rational-emotive therapy in practice.* Champaign, IL: Research Press.

Barksdale, L. S. (1972). *Building self-esteem.* Los Angeles: Barksdale Foundation.

Beck, A. T. (1967). *Depression.* New York: Hoeber-Harper.

Beck, A. T. (1976). *Cognitive therapy and the emotional disorders.* New York: International Universities Press.

Bedford, S. (1980). *Stress and tiger juice.* Chico, CA: Scott.

Bernard, M. E. (1981). Private thought in rational-emotive therapy. *Cognitive therapy and Research, 5,* 125–143.

Bernard, M. E., & Joyce, M. R. (1984). *Rational-emotive therapy with children and adolescents. Theory: Treatment strategies, preventative methods.* New York: Wiley.

Blazier, D. (1975). *Poor me, poor marriage.* New York: Vantage.

Burns, D. (1980). *Feeling good.* New York: Morrow.

Butler, P. E. (1981). *Talking to yourself.* New York: Stein & Day.

Church, V. A. (1975). *Behavior, law and remedies.* Dubuque, IA: Kendall, Hunt.

Coué, E. (1923). *My method.* New York: Doubleday.

Diekstra, R., & Dassen, W. F. (1976). *Rationele therapie.* Amsterdam: Swets & Zeitlinger.

Dryden, W. (1984). *Rational-emotive therapy: Fundamentals and innovations.* London: Croom Helm.

Dubois, P. (1907). *The psychic treatment of nervous disorders.* New York: Funk & Wagnalls.

Dyer, W. (1977). *Your erroneous zones.* New York: Funk & Wagnalls.

Ellis, A. (1949a). Towards the improvement of psychoanalytic research. *Psychoanalytic Review, 36,* 123–143.

Ellis, A. (1949b). Re-analysis of an alleged telepathic dream. *Psychiatric Quarterly, 23,* 116–126.

Ellis, A. (1950). *An introduction to the principles of scientific psychoanalysis.* Genetic Psychology Monographs. Provincetown, MA: Journal Press.

Ellis, A. (1956a). An operational reformulation of some of the basic principles of psychoanalysis. In H. Feigl and M. Scriven (Eds.), *Minnesota studies on the philosophy of science. Vol. I.: The foundations of science and concepts of psychology and psychoanalysis* (pp. 131–154). Minneapolis: University of Minnesota Press.

Ellis, A. (1956b). The effectiveness of psychotherapy with individuals who have severe homosexual problems. *Journal of Consulting Psychology, 20,* 191–195.

Ellis, A. (1957a). *How to live with a "neurotic".* New York: Crown. (Rev. ed., 1975.) North Hollywood, CA: Wilshire Books.

Ellis, A. (1957b). Rational psychotherapy and individual psychology. *Journal of Individual Psychology, 13,* 38–44.

Ellis, A. (1957c). Outcome of employing three techniques of psychotherapy. *Journal of Clinical Psychology, 13,* 344–350.

Ellis, A. (1958a). Rational psychotherapy. *Journal of General Psychology, 59,* 35–49.

Ellis, A. (1958b). *Sex without guilt.* Secaucus, NJ: Lyle Stuart. (Rev. ed., 1965.) North Hollywood, CA: Wilshire Books.

Ellis, A. (1960). *The art and science of love.* Secaucus, NJ: Lyle Stuart. (Rev. ed., 1965.) New York: Bantam.
Ellis, A. (1962). *Reason and emotion in psychotherapy.* Secaucus, NJ: Lyle Stuart & Citadel Press.
Ellis, A. (1963). Toward a more precise definition of "emotional" and "intellectual" insight. *Psychological Reports, 13,* 125–126.
Ellis, A. (1968). Is psychoanalysis harmful? *Psychiatric Opinion, 5*(1), 16–24. Reprinted: New York: Institute for Rational-Emotive Therapy.
Ellis, A. (1969). A weekend of rational encounter. In A. Burton (Ed.), *Encounter.* San Francisco: Jossey-Bass.
Ellis, A. (Speaker) (1971a). *How to stubbornly refuse to be ashamed of anything.* (Cassette recording). New York: Institute for Rational-Emotive Therapy.
Ellis, A. (1971b). *Growth through reason.* North Hollywood: Wilshire Books.
Ellis, A. (1972a). Psychotherapy without tears. In A. Burton (Ed.), *Twelve therapists.* San Francisco: Jossey-Bass.
Ellis, A. (1972b). Helping people get better rather than merely feel better. *Rational Living, 7*(2), 2–9.
Ellis, A. (1972c). *Psychotherapy and the value of a human being.* New York: Institute for Rational-Emotive Therapy.
Ellis, A. (1973). *Humanistic psychotherapy: The rational-emotive approach.* New York: McGraw-Hill.
Ellis, A. (1974). Cognitive aspects of abreactive therapy. *Voices, 10*(1), 48–56.
Ellis, A. (1976a). *Sex and the liberated man.* Secaucus, NJ: Lyle Stuart.
Ellis, A. (1976b). The biological basis of human irrationality. *Journal of Individual Psychology, 32,* 145–168.
Ellis, A. (1976c). RET abolishes most of the human ego. *Psychotherapy,* 1976, *13,* 343–348. Reprinted: New York: Institute for Rational-Emotive Therapy.
Ellis, A. (1977a). *How to live with—and without—anger.* Secaucus, NJ: Citadel Press.
Ellis, A. (1977b). Intimacy in psychotherapy. *Rational Living, 12*(2), 13–19.
Ellis, A. (1977c). Skill training in counseling and psychotherapy. *Canadian Counselor, 12*(1), 30–35.
Ellis, A. (1977d). Fun as psychotherapy. *Rational Living, 12*(1), 2–6.
Ellis, A. (Speaker) (1977e). *A garland of rational songs.* (Cassette recording and songbook). New York: Institute for Rational-Emotive Therapy.
Ellis, A. (1978a). Rational-emotive therapy and self-help therapy. *Rational Living, 13*(1), 2–9.
Ellis, A. (1978b). Toward a theory of personality. In R. J. Corsini (Ed.), *Readings in current personalities theories.* Itasca, IL: Peacock.
Ellis, A. (1979a). *The intelligent woman's guide to dating and mating.* Secaucus, NJ: Lyle Stuart.
Ellis, A. (1979b). The theory of rational-emotive therapy. In A. Ellis & J. M. Whiteley (Eds.), *Theoretical and empirical foundations of rational-emotive therapy* (pp. 33–60). Monterey, CA: Brooks/Cole.
Ellis, A. (1979c). Discomfort anxiety: A new cognitive-behavioral construct. Part 1. *Rational Living, 14*(2), 3–8.
Ellis, A. (1979d). The issue of force and energy in behavioral change. *Journal of Contemporary Psychotherapy, 10,* 83–97.
Ellis, A. (1980a). Discomfort anxiety: A new cognitive-behavioral construct. Part 2. *Rational Living, 15*(1), 25–30.
Ellis, A. (1980b). Rational-emotive therapy and cognitive behavior therapy: Similarities and differences. *Cognitive Therapy and Research, 4,* 325–340.

Ellis, A. (1980c). The value of efficiency in psychotherapy. *Psychotherapy, 17,* 414–419.
Ellis, A. (1981). The use of rational humorous songs in psychotherapy. *Voices, 16*(4), 29–36.
Ellis, A. (1983a). Failures in rational-emotive therapy. In E. F. Foa & P. M. G. Emmelkamp (Eds.), *Failures in behavior therapy* (pp. 159–171). New York: Wiley.
Ellis, A. (1983b). The philosophic implications and dangers of some popular behavior therapy techniques. In M. Rosenbaum, C. M. Franks, & Y. Jaffe (Eds.), *Perspectives on behavior therapy in the eighties* (pp. 138–151). New York: Springer.
Ellis, A. (1983c). *The case against religiosity.* New York: Institute for Rational-Emotive Therapy.
Ellis, A. (1984a). Introduction to Windy Dryden's *Rational-Emotive Therapy: Fundamentals and innovations* (pp. vii–xxvi). London: Croom Helm.
Ellis, A. (1984b). Rational-emotive therapy. In R. J. Corsini (Ed.), *Current psychotherapies* (pp. 196–238). Itasca, IL: Peacock.
Ellis, A. (1984c). *Intellectual fascism.* New York: Institute for Rational-Emotive Therapy.
Ellis, A. (1985). Expanding the *ABC*s of rational-emotive therapy. In M. Mahoney & A. Freeman (Eds.) *Cognition and psychotherapy* (pp. 313–323). New York: Plenum Press.
Ellis, A. (in press-a). *Rational-emotive therapy and cognitive-behavior therapy.* New York: Springer.
Ellis, A. (in press-b). *Overcoming resistance.* New York: Springer.
Ellis, A., & Abrahms, Ed. (1978). *Brief psychotherapy in medical and health practice.* New York: Springer.
Ellis, A., & Becker, I. (1982). *A guide to personal happiness.* North Hollywood: Wilshire Books.
Ellis, A., & Bernard, M. (Eds.) (1983). *Rational-emotive approaches to the problems of childhood.* New York: Plenum Press.
Ellis, A., & Grieger, A. (Eds.) (1977). *Handbook of rational-emotive therapy.* New York: Springer.
Ellis, A., & Harper, R. A. (1961a). *A guide to rational living.* Englewood Cliffs, NJ: Prentice-Hall.
Ellis, A., & Harper, R. A. (1961b). *A guide to successful marriage.* North Hollywood, CA: Wilshire Books.
Ellis, A., & Harper, R. A. (1975). *A new guide to rational living.* North Hollywood, CA: Wilshire Books.
Ellis, A., & Knaus, W. (1977). *Overcoming procrastination.* New York: New American Library.
Ellis, A., & Whiteley, J. M. (Eds.) (1979). *Theoretical and empirical foundations of rational-emotive therapy.* Monterey, CA: Brooks/Cole.
Emery, G. (1982). *Own your own life.* New York: New American Library.
Emery, S. (1978). *Actualizations.* New York: Doubleday.
Epictetus. (1899). *The works of Epictetus.* Boston: Little, Brown.
Erhard, W. (1976). *What is the purpose of the est training?* San Francisco: Erhard Seminars Training.
Frankl, V. (1959). *Man's search for meaning.* New York: Pocket Books.
Garcia, E., & Blyth, B. T. (1977). *Developing emotional muscle.* Atlanta: Georgia Center for Continuing Education.
Garner, A. (1980). *Conversationally speaking.* New York: McGraw-Hill.
Ginott, H. (1965). *Between parent and child.* New York: Macmillan.
Glasser, W. (1965). *Reality therapy.* New York: Harper & Row.
Goldfried, M. R., & Davison, G. (1976). *Clinical behavior therapy.* New York: Holt, Rinehart & Winston.
Goodman, D., & Maultsby, M. C., Jr. (1974). *Emotional well-being through rational behavior training.* Springfield, IL: Charles C Thomas.

Goulding, M. M., & Goulding, R. L. (1979). *Changing lives through redecision therapy*. New York: Brunner/Mazel.
Greenwald, H. (1973). *Decision therapy*. New York: Wyden.
Grieger, R., & Boyd, J. (1980). *Rational-emotive therapy: A skills based approach*. New York: Van Nostrand Reinhold.
Grieger, R., & Grieger, I. (1982). *Cognition and emotional disturbance*. New York: Human Sciences Press.
Grossack, M. (1974). *You are not alone*. Boston: Marlborough.
Grossack, M. (1971). *Love and reason*. New York: New American Library.
Hadas, M. (1912). *Essential works of stoicism*. New York: Bantam.
Heesacker, M., Heppner, P. P., & Rogers, M. E. (1982). Classics and emerging classics in counseling psychology. *Journal of Counseling Psychology, 29*, 400–405.
Hauck, P. A. (1972). *Reason in pastoral counseling*. Philadelphia: Westminster.
Hauck, P. A. (1973). *Overcoming depression*. Philadelphia: Westminster.
Hauck, P. A. (1974). *Overcoming frustration and anger*. Philadelphia: Westminster.
Hauck, P. A. (1975). *Overcoming worry and fear*. Philadelphia: Westminster.
Hauck, P. A. (1976). *How to do what you want to do*. Philadelphia: Westminster.
Hauck, P. A. (1979). *How to stand up for yourself*. Philadelphia: Westminster.
Hauck, P. A. (1980). *Brief counseling with RET*. Philadelphia: Westminster.
Hauck, P. A. (1981). *Overcoming jealousy and possessiveness*. Philadelphia: Westminster.
Hauck, P. A. (1984). *The three faces of love*. Philadelphia: Westminster.
Heidegger, M. (1962). *Being and time*. New York: Harper and Row.
Herzberg, A. (1945). *Active psychotherapy*. New York: Grune & Stratton.
Horney, K. (1939). *The neurotic personality of our time*. New York: Norton.
Jakubowski, P., & Lange, A. (1979). *The assertive option*. Champaign, IL: Research Press.
Johnson, S. M. (1977). *First person singular*. New York: Signet.
Johnson, W. (1946). *People in quandaries*. New York: Harper & Row.
Kelly, G. (1955). *The psychology of personal constructs*. New York: Norton.
Kessler, G., & Hoellen, B. (1982). Rational-emotive therapie in der klinischen praxis. Weinheim, Germany: Beltz Verlag.
Keyes, K. (1979). Handbook to higher consciousness. St. Mary, KY: Cornucopia Institute.
Knaus, W. J. (1982). *How to get out of a rut*. Englewood Cliffs, NJ: Prentice-Hall.
Korzybski, A. (1933). *Science and sanity*. San Francisco: International Society for General Semantics.
Lacey, L. A. (1982). *Effective communication with difficult people*. San Diego: Common Visions.
Lange, A., & Jakubowski, A. (1976). *Responsible assertive training*. Champaign, IL: Research Press.
Lazarus, A. A. (1971). *Behavior therapy and beyond*. New York: McGraw-Hill.
Lazarus, A. A. (1981). *The practice of multimodal therapy*. New York: McGraw-Hill.
Lazarus, A. A., & Fay, A. (1975). *I can if I want to*. New York: Morrow.
Lazarus, R. S. (1966). *Psychological stress and the coping process*. New York: McGraw-Hill.
Lembo, J. (1974). *Help yourself*. Niles, IL: Argus.
Lembo, J. (1976). *The counseling process*. New York: Libra.
Lembo, J. (1977). *How to cope with your fears and frustrations*. New York: Libra.
Little, B. L. (1977). *This will drive you sane*. Minneapolis, MN: Comp Care.
Losoncy, L. E. (1980). *You can do it*. Englewood Cliffs, NJ: Prentice-Hall.
Low, A. (1952). *Mental health through will training*. Boston: Christopher.
Mahoney, M. (1977). Personal science: A cognitive learning therapy. In A. Ellis & R. Grieger (Eds.), *Handbook of rational-emotive therapy*. New York: Springer.

Maleske, N. (1976). *Natural therapy*. Reseda, CA: Mojave Books.
Marcus Aurelius (1900). *The thoughts of the Emperor Marcus Aurelius*. Boston: Little, Brown.
Masters, J., & Rimm, D. (1974). *Behavior therapy*. New York: Academic Press.
Maultsby, M. C., Jr. (1975). *Help yourself to happiness*. New York: Institute for Rational-Emotive Therapy.
Maultsby, M. C., Jr. (1978). *A million dollars for your hangover*. Lexington, KY: Rational Self-Help Books.
Maultsby, M. C., Jr. (1984). *Rational behavior therapy*. New York: Wiley.
Maultsby, M. C., Jr., & Ellis, A. (1974). *Techniques of using rational-emotive imagery*. New York: Institute for Rational-Emotive Therapy.
Maultsby, M. C., Jr., & Hendricks, A. (1974). *Cartoon booklets illustrating basic rational behavior therapy concepts*. Lexington, KY: Rational Behavior Training Unit.
McMullen, R. E., & Casey, B. (1975). *Talk sense to yourself*. Champaign, IL: Research Press.
Meichenbaum, D. (1977). *Cognitive-behavior modification*. New York: Plenum Press.
Miller, J. (1983). *Headaches: The answer books*. Old Tappan, NJ: Revell.
Miller, T. (1983). *So you secretly suspect you're worthless*. Manlius, NY: Tom Miller.
Morris, K. T., & Kanitz, J. M. (1975). *Rational-emotive therapy*. Boston: Houghton Mifflin.
Morse, C., Bernard, M. E., Dennerstein, L., & Spencer-Gardner, C. (1984, May). *The effects of rational-emotive therapy on premenstrual tension*. Paper presented at the Fifth Annual Meeting of the Australian Behavior Modification Association. Perth, Australia.
Nash, J.D. (1981). *Taking charge of your smoking*. Palo Alto, CA: Bull.
Paris, C., & Casey, B. (1983). *Project you*. North Hollywood, CA: Wilshire Books.
Perls, F. S. (1969). *Gestalt therapy verbatim*. Lafayette, CA: Real People Press.
Phadke, K. M. (1982). Some innovations in RET theory and practice. *Rational Living, 17*(2), 25–30.
Powell, J. (1976). *Fully human, fully alive*. Niles, IL: Argus.
Raimy, V. (1975). *Misconceptions of the self*. San Francisco: Jossey-Bass.
Rotter, J. B. (1954). *Social learning and clinical psychology*. Englewood Cliffs, NJ: Prentice-Hall.
Schutz, W. (1967). *Joy*. New York: Grove.
Schwartz, D. (1981). *RE-therapie: So wird man sein eigener Psychologe*. Landsberg am Lech, Germany: Wolfgang Dummer.
Sichel, J., & Ellis, A. (1983). *RET self-help form*. New York: Institute for Rational-Emotive Therapy.
Silverstein, L. (1977). *Consider the alternative*. Minneapolis, MN: CompCare.
Smith, D. (1982). Trends in counseling and psychotherapy. *American Psychologist, 37*, 802–809.
Smith, M. (1977). *Why do I feel guilty when I say NO?* New York: Dell.
Sprenkle, D. H., Keeney, B. P., & Sutton, P. M. (1982). Theorists who influence clinical members of AAMFT: A research note. *Journal of Marital and Family Therapy, 8*, 367–369.
Thoresen, E. H. (1975). *Learning to think: A rational approach*. Clearwater, FL: Institute for Rational Living.
Tosi, D. J. (1974). *Youth: Toward personal growth*. Columbus, OH: Merrill.
Walen, S., DiGiuseppe, R., & Wessler, R. (1980). *A practitioner's guide to rational-emotive therapy*. New York: Oxford.
Wessler, R. A., & Wessler, R. L. (1980). *The principles and practice of rational-emotive therapy*. San Francisco: Jossey-Bass.
Wolfe, J. L., & Brand, E. (Eds.) (1977). *Twenty years of rational therapy*. New York: Institute for Rational-Emotive Therapy.
Young, H. (1974). *Rational counseling primer*. New York: Institute for Rational-Emotive Therapy.

2

Love and Its Problems

ALBERT ELLIS

Rational-emotive therapy (RET) is largely a theory and practice of interpersonal relationships and most probably would never have been created and developed had I not been absorbed, from childhood onward, with my own love and relating problems (Ellis, 1965, 1972a, 1983a). Because of my personal interest in love, I was motivated to do a considerable amount of pioneering research on the emotion of love (Ellis, 1949a, 1949b, 1949c, 1950, 1951, 1954). I also focused RET clinical work, from 1955 onward, on helping people with their love, marital, and sex problems (Ellis, 1957, 1958, 1960, 1962, 1963a, 1963b, 1963c, 1972b, 1973a; Ellis & Harper, 1961a, 1961b). Some of the early RET clinicians also devoted themselves to problems of love and interpersonal relations and made significant contributions to these areas (Ard, 1967; Ard & Ard, 1969; Blazier, 1975; Demorest, 1971; Grossack, 1976; Harper, 1960, 1963; Harper & Stokes, 1971; Hauck, 1973, 1974, 1977, 1981; Hibbard, 1975; Maultsby, 1975; McClellan & Stieper, 1973; Shibles, 1978).

As a result of this emphasis, RET has always been especially concerned with the diagnosis and treatment of love problems. I shall present in this chapter its theories and practices regarding some of the most common amative disturbances (and shall largely omit its treatment of sex and marriage problems, which are covered in other chapters of this book).

Because this chapter is largely concerned with love problems and their treatment, it emphasizes certain kinds and degrees of love—especially intense, romantic love. Actually, the feeling of love is normally healthy and gratifying. It frequently is altruistic and is socially oriented (rather than primarily self-absorbed and centered on egoism). It not only

---

ALBERT ELLIS • Executive Director, Institute for Rational-Emotive Therapy, New York, New York 10021.

vitalizes human life and happiness but it also helps to perpetuate and preserve the human race. Without love, who among us would dare to care for and to rear children? Or to extend our own lives?

What is love? It is a feeling that is so varied and pervasive that it is hard to define. *Webster's New World Dictionary* bravely starts off: "A strong affection for or attachment or devotion to a person or persons." But then it quite appropriately adds: "A strong liking for or interest in something: as her *love* of acting." Combining these two definitions, we come to my designation of love in *The American Sexual Tragedy:* "Any kind of more or less intense emotional attraction to or involvement with another. It includes many types and degrees of affection, such as conjugal love, parental love, familial love, religious love, love of humanity, love of animals, love of things, self-love, sexual love, obsessive-compulsive love, etc." (Ellis, 1954, p.117). Some of the many appropriate synonyms for love—and especially for healthy love—are: fondness, liking, regard, esteem, closeness, intimacy, friendship, caring, concern, tenderness, kindliness, and ardor.

Super-Romantic Love

Romantic, passionate love, or intense in-lovedness has existed from time immemorial but received an enormous boost in the Middle Ages and has become a near-requisite of mating or marriage in the twentieth century (Burgess & Locke, 1953; de Rougemont, 1956; Ellis, 1954; Ellis & Harper, 1961a, Finck, 1887; Hunt, 1959; Lucka, 1915; Murstein, 1974). It has enormous advantages, in that romantic lovers often experience extremely pleasurable feelings and are motivated to great efforts and outstanding performances.

Romantic love generally is acknowledged to include several strong factors, especially idealization of the beloved; a high degree of exclusivity; intense feelings of attachment, usually with a strong sexual component; the powerful conviction that the love will last forever; obsession with thoughts of the beloved; a strong desire to mate with the beloved; an urge to do and to sacrifice almost anything to win the beloved; the conviction that romantic love is the most important thing in the world; and the belief that one can practically merge with one's beloved and become one with him or her (Ellis, 1949a, 1949b, 1949c, 1950, 1951, 1954; Hunt, 1959; Katz, 1976; Kremen & Kremen, 1971; McDonald & McDonald, 1973; Stendhal, 1947; Tennov, 1979).

Devotees of romance tend to create and maintain a number of irrational beliefs (iBs) or myths that interfere with their intimate relationships and with their happiness. Here, for example, are some of the common romantic myths of our culture:

1. You can passionately love one, and only one, person at a time (Ellis, 1954).
2. True romantic love lasts forever.
3. Deep feelings of romantic love insure a stable and compatible marriage.
4. Sex without romantic love is unethical and unsatisfying. Sex and love always go together (Bach & Wyden, 1969; Ellis, 1954).
5. Romantic love can easily be made to develop and grow in marital relationships.
6. Romantic love is far superior to conjugal love, friendship love, nonsexual love, and other kinds of love, and you hardly exist if you do not experience it intensely.
7. If you lose the person you love romantically you must feel deeply grieved or depressed for a long period of time and cannot legitimately fall in love again until this long mourning period is over.
8. It is necessary to perceive love all the time to know someone loves you (Katz, 1976).

When people devoutly hold these kinds of myths they tend to put them into personal rules of behavior and to imbed them into absolutistic *shoulds* and *musts*. Thus, they tell themselves (or implicitly believe), "I *must* only romantically love one person at a time and am a phony if I love simultaneous persons." "I *have to* marry only a person I romantically love and will be desolate if he or she does not mate with me." "My romantic feelings *must* last forever and there is something very wrong with me if they fade after a relatively short time. That proves I did not *really* love." "If I do not experience enduring intense romantic love, I *cannot* be satisfied with other kinds of love feelings and will have, at most, only a mildly happy existence." "My partner *must* love me completely and passionately at all times or else he or she doesn't really love me."

RET, when faced with highly unrealistic romantics who make themselves anxious, depressed, hostile, or self-pitying because of their holding myths and irrational Beliefs like those just listed, uses two main modes of disputing:

1. It shows people how their Beliefs are anti-empirical or unrealistic and gives them evidence of their invalidity. Thus, it presents data that one can positively love two or more people simultaneously (Murstein, 1974); that romantic love usually fades, especially when the lovers live together (Finck, 1887); that deep feelings of love not only do not insure

a stable and compatible marriage but often interfere with it (de Rougemont, 1956); and that romantic love is by no means always superior to and more happiness-producing than other kinds of love (Lederer & Jackson, 1968).

2. RET, as it does with people's irrational beliefs about other aspects of their lives, particularly reveals and disputes their absolutistic shoulds and musts about romantic love. It shows them that no matter how much they legitimately prefer passionate involvements they do not have to achieve or maintain them; and that when they lose out in the early or later stages of romance, that it is highly inconvenient and very sad and deplorable but is not awful and terrible (Ellis, 1957, 1962, 1984a; Ellis & Becker, 1983; Ellis & Grieger, 1977; Ellis & Harper, 1961b, Ellis & Harper, 1975).

In addition to these cognitive techniques for helping people surrender their self-defeating myths and musts about romantic love, RET uses a number of other emotive and behavioral methods. Thus, it may show clients that their relationship with their therapist is nonromantic but still satisfying and helpful; it demonstrates that the therapist can respect and accept them whether or not they are romantically successful; it gives them *in vivo* homework assignments to allow themselves to become romantically involved with some "wrong" partners, and to see that they do not have to live with or marry these partners; and it may provide them with skill training or help them encounter, communicate with and win the love of romantic partners (Ellis, 1962, 1973b, 1976, 1979a, in press-a). It specifically deals with obsessive-compulsive love or limerence, as shown in the next section of this chapter.

Obsessive-Compulsive Love or Limerence

Extreme obsessive-compulsive love, or what Tennov (1979) has called limerence, is usually but not necessarily romantic. Thus, a mother can obsessively love her son or daughter, an entrepreneur may compulsively love his work, and an adolescent may obsessively-compulsively worship his or her same-sex friend without wanting to have sex with or to marry this friend. For the most part, however, limerence is an extreme form of romantic love that frequently includes: (1) disturbed behaviors such as obsessive and intensive thinking about the beloved; (2) the dire need for reciprocation; (3) mood swings dependent on the lover's interpretation of the beloved's reciprocation; (4) severe feelings of anxiety and depression when the beloved doesn't seem to requite one's love; (5) idealization of the beloved and refusal to see or abide by some of his or her deficiencies; (6) eagerness to do foolhardy things to win or keep the beloved's favor (Tennov, 1979).

According to RET, obsessive-compulsive love or limerence normally includes lovers' devoutly and absolutistically holding one or more of these irrational beliefs (iBs): (1) "I *must* have my beloved's reciprocation or else I am an undeserving, inadequate person!" (2) "It is *horrible* to lose my beloved. I *can't stand* it!" (3) "If my beloved does not care for me or if he or she dies, life has no value and I might as well be dead!" (4) "My beloved is the *only* one in the world for me, and his or her love *alone* can make me and my life worthwhile!" (5) "Because I *must* win my beloved's favor and *have to be* miserable without it, it is worth doing *anything*, including seriously risking my life, to win him or her!" (Ellis, 1962, 1973a, 1973b, 1979a, 1984a; Ellis & Grieger, 1977; Ellis & Whiteley, 1979).

RET employs a number of cognitive methods to help people overcome their obsessive-compulsive disturbances about love, including these:

1. It shows them how to actively and persistently dispute their irrational beliefs (iBs) and to change them for relativistic preferences (Ellis, 1957, 1962, 1973a, 1973b, 1984a, in press-a, b, c).

2. RET shows them how to use rational beliefs (rBs) or coping statements and how to think them through and keep repeating them until they truly feel them. Typical rational self-statements are: "I would like to have my beloved's reciprocation but I don't *need* it to live and be happy!" "It would be *unfortunate* if I lost my beloved but it wouldn't be *horrible* and I *could* stand it!" "My beloved is not the *only* one I could care for and I could have a worthwhile existence even if he or she did *not* love me!"

3. RET shows people how to use cognitive distraction techniques, such as Jacobsen's (1942) progressive relaxation method or Yoga or meditation techniques, to divert them from intrusive thoughts about their beloved (Ellis, 1984b).

4. RET shows obsessive-compulsive lovers how they can also focus on caring for other people besides their one "true" beloved and can thereby be less obsessive.

5. RET helps people to make out a list and steadily review several disadvantages of their overattachment to their beloved and several advantages of caring for some other people, interests, and involvements until they become less obsessed with one special beloved.

6. RET particularly shows obsessive-compulsive lovers (or limerents) how to work on their secondary symptoms of disturbance. On the primary level, they make themselves obsessed and compulsive; and then, secondarily, they note this and tell themselves irrational beliefs

(iBs) such as "I *must* not be obsessed! It's stupid of me to be irrationally in love, and I am therefore a stupid, worthless person!" RET shows them how to dispute these self-downing iBs by asking themselves "Why *must* I not be obsessed?" and "Where is the evidence that I am a stupid, worthless person for being compulsively in love?" By thereby helping them to accept themselves in spite of their foolish behavior, RET alleviates their secondary disturbances and gives them leeway to return to working against and surrendering their primary obsessive-compulsive attachments (Ellis, 1962, 1979b, 1980, in press-a; Ellis & Harper, 1975).

RET also employs a number of emotive and behavioral methods with obsessive-compulsive lovers. Thus, it has the RET practitioner accept them unconditionally, in spite of their crazy addiction to love; it shows them how, through role-playing methods, to resist the unreasonable demands of their partners; it gives them the homework assignments of resisting these demands, and shows them how to reinforce themselves for resisting; it shows them how to penalize themselves (e.g., by burning money) when they indulge in too much in thinking about their beloved or in phoning him or her too frequently (Ellis & Abrahms, 1978).

Jealousy and Possessiveness

We may distinguish between two forms of jealousy: rational and irrational jealousy. We are rationally jealous when we desire a continuing, and sometimes a monogamous, relationship with our beloved and when we are concerned about its being disrupted by his or her loving (or in paying too much attention to) someone else—thereby depriving us of the lover's presence and probably threatening us with complete loss. When we are rationally jealous, we feel frustrated and disappointed when our beloved pays "too much" attention to others but we are not severely disturbed.

We are irrationally (or insensately) jealous when we absolutistically demand or command that our beloved almost exclusively care for and pay attention to us and are horrified at the thought of his or her being emotionally intimate with and perhaps leaving us for another person. When irrationally jealous, we tend to feel seriously anxious, hostile and/or depressed, to ruminate obsessively about the grave danger of losing our beloved, to be very suspicious of her or his actions, to keep demanding tokens and words of affection from him or her, and to try to be with him or her practically all the time (Clanton & Smith, 1977; Ellis, 1972b, in press-b; O'Neill & O'Neill, 1972).

RET hypothesizes that insensately jealous and possessive people tend to dogmatically hold several irrational Beliefs (iBs) that create their jealousy, such as (1) "I must have a guarantee that you strongly love only me, and will continue to do so indefinitely!" (2) "If you do not love me as I love you, there must be something radically wrong with me, and I hardly deserve your affection." (3) "Because I love you intensely and keep being devoted to you, you have to always return my love, will cause me great suffering if you don't, and are then a rotten, damnable person." (4) "Unless I have the absolute certainty that you adore me and always will, my life is too disorganized and unpleasant, and it hardly seems worthwhile going on with it." (Ellis, 1972b; Harper, 1963; Hauck, 1981).

When people are irrationally jealous, RET particularly tries to help them recognize their irrational beliefs (iBs) and change them for rational beliefs (rBs). Thus, it shows them how to dispute their irrationalities and to wind up with these more realistic and undogmatic philosophies of love and life: (1) "I would very much like you to care for me as I care for you, but there is no reason you have to do so. I can still be happy, though not as happy, if you don't." (2) "You may well be the best love partner I am likely to find during my lifetime and I therefore highly value your love and companionship. But if I somehow lose you, I can almost certainly love others and achieve a satisfying loving relationship with one of them." (3) "Although I love you dearly and am quite willing to devote myself to you, my love does not oblige you to love me in return or to restrict yourself for me. You have a perfect right to your own feelings and behaviors regarding me and, since I cannot make you change them, I will try to accept them as best I can and still keeping loving you." (4) "If you lie to me or otherwise contradict the feelings of love you say you have for me and betray our relationship, I shall consider your behavior unloving and untrustworthy but I shall not damn you as a person for acting in this undesirable manner." (Ellis, 1972b, in press-b; Harper, 1963; Hauck, 1981).

RET uses several other cognitive methods to help people combat their self-defeating feelings of jealousy:

1. It encourages them to make a comprehensive list of the disadvantages of jealousy, possessiveness, and hatred and a list of the advantages of rational jealousy and feelings of concern and frustration. It also encourages them to make a list of the advantages of agreed-upon open relationships that allow both partners to engage in nonmonogamous activities and to solidly review these advantages when one of the partners feels jealous. Some of the advantages of open relationships are: (a) They lead to a greater variety of sex and love experiences and to the

to date partners who are also involved emotionally with other partners. And, at times, it encourages them to arrange an open relationship with a mate, in the course of which they can actively work through some of their jealous feelings. RET would tend to endorse the behavioral rules of Taylor (1982) who advises jealous lovers: (1) Do not spy or pry. (2) Do not confront or entrap. (3) When you think your partner is having an affair, stay out of it. Or, as we would add in RET, if you are determined to confront or get into a partner's affair, first get rid of your hostility and whining self-pity, and then, and then only, do your confronting.

Using, then, several cognitive, emotive and behavioral methods, RET helps people retain rational or appropriate feelings of jealousy but to minimize insensate, irrational jealousy and possessiveness (Ellis, in press-b).

Encountering Suitable Partners

Because satisfactory love relationships are often difficult to find, because most people are much more selective about love than they are about companionship and sex, and because long-term high-level love partnerships are hard to maintain, literally millions of would-be lovers rarely or never enjoy enduring intimacy. Social shyness, unassertiveness and fear of rejection are important blocks to encountering suitable love partners; and RET has always specialized in helping people overcome these blocks.

People who block themselves from meeting a good many potential partners and from eventually narrowing down their intimacies to one or a few almost always profoundly hold the same kind of irrational beliefs (iBs) as other self-defeating individuals hold, especially these three: (1) "I must win the approval of all the highly desirable lovers I encounter, and I am pretty worthless if I don't!" (2) "The partners I select must be considerate and loving to me and they are rotten people if they aren't!" (3) "Conditions must be arranged so that I fairly easily meet potential lovers; and it is *awful* and I *can't stand* it when these conditions are quite difficult and when they put real blocks in my way!" RET shows shy and procrastinating would-be lovers that they explicitly or implicitly hold these irrational beliefs (iBs) and teaches them active methods of disputing and overcoming such iBs (Ellis, 1957, 1962, 1971a, 1973a, 1973b, 1979a, in press-a,b,c).

Cognitively, an RET practitioner will often have the following kind of dialogue with a female client who wants to meet men she might relate to emotionally but who rarely does very much to initiate or facilitate encounters.

T: When you see what you consider to be an attractive and personable man at a dance, a party or other social situation and you want to talk to him but run away from doing so, what do you tell yourself to make yourself retreat?

C: I tell myself that he's not for me—that he already has a woman, or something like that.

T: Well, that's a rationalization. You're giving yourself an excuse, which seems to be plausible (but really isn't), so that you don't have to talk to him. But what's your *reason* behind your rationalization? What are you really telling yourself that makes you afraid to talk to him?

C: I don't know.

T: Yes, you do! "If I go over and talk to him . . . ?" What?

C: "He may not like me. He may reject me."

T: Right! That's what you're saying to yourself. "And if he doesn't like me, if he rejects me . . . ?" What?

C: "I'll never get anyone I want. No good man will want me."

T: Yes, that's what you're saying to yourself. But that's an antiempirical or unrealistic statement that follows from some absolutistic philosophy—from some should or must. What do you think that absolutistic philosophy is?

C: "I *must* not ever get rejected by a man I really want. I *should* win them all. Otherwise, I'm unlovable and will never get one."

T: Right. Now let's go over that set of irrational beliefs. At A, Activating Event, you encounter a man you really would like to talk to, probably date, and maybe eventually to mate with. At B, your irrational set of Beliefs, you tell yourself that you *must* not get rejected by him or any other decent man; that you *should* win every man who is good for you. Then, at C, emotional and behavioral Consequence, you feel anxious and you withdraw and refuse to talk to this man.

C: Yes, that's the way it always seems to go.

T: That's the way you *make* it go. But let's get you to make it go otherwise: help you approach many or most men you find desirable.

C: How?

T: First, by going on to D—Disputing. Let's you and I now do some active disputing. First of all, Why *must* you get all the desirable males you meet? Where is it written that you *should* not get rejected by them?

C: Uh—. Because it's so uncomfortable not to get what I want.

T: So it's uncomfortable! Why *must* you be comfortable?

C: Because I *want* to be.

T: Why *must* you get what you want?

C: Uh—. I guess I don't have to.

T: "But I really *should!*"

C: (laughs): Yes. I guess I feel I really should.

T: And where will that *should* and *must* get you?

C: Anxious—and withdrawing.
T: Exactly! But you'd better go over that—better show yourself, very carefully and in detail, that as long as you insist that you *must* do well and get what you want, you'll almost inevitably be anxious and withdrawing.
C: Mmm.
T: Yes—Mmm! Suppose you don't get this attractive man, you really try and you still don't get him. How would you feel about that?
C: Awful!
T: Why would it be *awful* to get rejected.
C: Because I wouldn't like it.
T: That's why it would be *bad*. Uncomfortable. A pain in the ass. But why would that badness be *awful?*
C: Well, I guess it really wouldn't be.
T: Why, *wouldn't* it be?
C: Well, uh, because it would only really be inconvenient. And there are other men available.
T: Right. And if it were *awful,* it would be *totally* bad or inconvenient—or 101% bad. And it hardly is that! No matter how inconvenient it is, you can probably always live and be happy—and then look for something *less* inconvenient.
C: Yes, I suppose so.
T: You'd better say that more enthusiastically!
C: Yes, I guess I could be happy without this one man. But suppose I *never* got a good lover or husband. Could I *then* be happy?
T: Why not? You wouldn't be *as* happy as if you did get one. But you could certainly be happy *at all,* couldn't you? In *some* way?
C: Oh, yes. I see what you mean. Even if I never succeeded in love I could still be happy in other ways, with other things.
T: Damned right!

In this manner, the therapist keeps cognitively, philosophically, showing the client that she can risk rejection, and that if she does not, she is likely to be much less happy than if she does. The RET practitioner takes her absolutistic views and her unrealistic derivatives of them, rips them up, and shows her how to dispute them herself. She learns to use the scientific method to keep proving to herself that (1) She does not have to find love; (2) it is hardly horrible if she doesn't find it; (3) she can stand males rejecting her; (4) her worth as a human does not decrease when she gets rejected; (5) men who treat her badly in encountering situations are behaving inconsiderately but are not total bastards; and (6) it would be nice if conditions made it easy and enjoyable for her to meet a good many men until she finally found a suitable love partner, but the world is hardly a terrible place if things are difficult and if she has to keep striving to get what she wants.

RET uses, with clients like this one, some of its other common cognitive techniques, such as: (1) She is shown how to make a list of all the advantages of taking risks and getting, probably, many rejections while doing so, and all the disadvantages of "comfortably" refusing to take such risks and waiting like a sitting duck for personable men to come to her. (2) She is given information on where are some of the best places to go to meet men and what methods of approach she can use to encounter them. (3) She is taught techniques of cognitive distraction, such as Jacobsen's (1942) relaxation techniques, when she makes herself quite anxious in an encountering situation. (4) She is shown how to imagine herself encountering men and talking to them in a sustained manner. (5) She is given bibliotherapy materials to read on RET and encountering, such as *The Intelligent Woman's Guide to Dating and Mating* (Ellis, 1979a) and *First Person Singular* (Johnson, 1977).

Emotively, RET again uses its common techniques with clients who are having trouble encountering others and finding love partners, such as: (1) *Forceful self-statements:* Helping clients to say to themselves, very forcefully, statements such as: "It's hard to encounter new potential partners; but it's much harder if I don't!" "If I fail in my encountering methods, too damned bad! It's better to have tried and lost than never to have encountered at all!" (2) *Rational-emotive imagery:* Showing clients how to imagine themselves failing miserably at encountering others and only feeling sorry, regretful, frustrated and annoyed, and not depressed or self-downing. (3) *Role playing:* Giving clients practice through role playing, in meeting partners they consider suitable, and showing them how they make themselves anxious, and need not do so, when they do encountering. (4) *Shame attacking exercises:* Inducing clients deliberately to do something they consider foolish or shameful in their encountering procedures: such as wearing outlandish clothing or deliberately saying the wrong thing; and showing them how to feel unashamed and self-accepting when they do so.

RET uses a number of behavioral methods in helping clients overcome their fear of encountering possible love partners: (1) *In vivo desensitization:* Helping them to take homework assignments of actually encountering potential partners at least several times a week, until they become desensitized to rejection. (2) *Implosive assignments:* Inducing clients to encounter potential partners many times in a row, say, twenty times a day, until they soon see that there is no "danger" in doing so. (3) *Reinforcement:* Showing clients how to reinforce themselves every time they carry out one of their encountering homework assignments. (4) *Penalization:* Showing clients how to penalize themselves every time they refuse to carry out an encountering homework assignment. (5) *Skill training:* Giving clients skill training (or sending them to someone who gives it) that will help them encounter others—for example, assertion training, communication training, and sex training.

Loss of Love

One of the main love problems is that of losing the love of a chosen partner: either at the beginning, when one first loves and is rejected by the beloved; or later, after one has experienced reciprocation for awhile but then loses it because one's partner rejects one's love or dies. In any of these instances, the loss of love may lead to anxiety, depression, self-pity, self-downing, rage, or even (in not a few cases) suicide or homicide. RET theory postulates that in most of the cases where people suffer greatly from loss of love, and are not merely extremely sorrowful or mournful but also self-hating and self-pitying, they tend to create and strongly maintain several irrational beliefs (iBs), such as:

1. "I must not be rejected by you, for if you reject me there is something radically wrong with me, and if that is so I am a quite inadequate person, most probably not worthy of winning any good person's love in the present or future."

2. "I would, if I were truly attractive and competent, be able to win the love of practically any person whom I really wanted; and since I have never gained or have lost the love of my beloved, I am gruesomely unattractive and incompetent!"

3. "I really am an excellent person, and you do not appreciate me and favor me as you *should!* You're mean and nasty for rejecting me, and I will have to get even with you if it's the last thing I do!"

4. "Conditions *should* be arranged so that I am always able to win the love of a person I really desire and so that I do not have to go to too much trouble to win it. When conditions are against me, life is perfectly *awful,* I *can't stand* it, and I can be nothing but perfectly miserable!"

5. "When someone whom I love and who loves me dies or is otherwise taken away from me it is totally unfair, and I *can't bear* a world that is that unfair and cruel! There is *no one* else in the world who can make up for me the kind of relationship I had with this person. I cannot be happy *at all* and I might as well kill myself!"

When people possess these irrational beliefs (iBs) and rigidly cling to them, they will tend to feel exceptionally upset emotionally; will do little to continue to win the love of a chosen partner; they will, when this partner is unavailable, sit on their rumps and refuse to look for other love partners; and they will frequently interfere with their work, school, and social lives and make themselves incompetent in these areas. They sometimes will be obsessed with the lost partner for many years; they will compulsively (and often foolishly) keep doing everything to try to get this partner back; and they will practically insure that they do not have any kind of a future intimate relationship with anyone else.

As usual, RET employs its most popular and effective cognitive methods with people who are not merely bereaved but are exceptionally anxious and depressed about the loss of love: (1) It shows them their major irrational beliefs (iBs) and it actively disputes these beliefs, and keeps teaching them how to do this kind of scientific disputing on their own. (2) It gives them coping or rational beliefs (rBs) to tell themselves and think about, over and over, such as: "My beloved was a fine partner but there are always other partners with whom I can have a good relationship." "The person whose love I lost has his or her own reasons (or prejudices) for rejecting me, and these reasons may have little to do with me or the ways in which I act." (3) RET shows clients many techniques of cognitive distraction when they have lost a beloved: such as, meditation, sports, creative activity, seeking for a new partner, absorption in work, etc. (4) RET may give clients considerable information about love and its myths (as noted above) and may help them with practical problem solving techniques to obtain new partners to replace lost ones. (5) RET helps clients do referenting: to focus on the disadvantages of the person whose love they have lost and the advantages of other possible partners. (6) It shows people how to reframe rejection and loss: to see it as a challenge instead of a horror and to see its benefits rather than only its disadvantages. (7) RET uses bibliotherapy to help clients overcome their dire need for another person. For example, it recommends books like *How to Break Your Addiction to a Person* (Halpern, 1982), *Letting Go* (Wanderer & Cabot, 1978) and *How to Survive The Loss of a Love* (Colgrove, Bloomfield & McWilliams, 1981), and tape recordings like *Conquering the Dire Need for Love* (Ellis, 1974), *Conquering Low Frustration Tolerance* (Ellis, 1975), and *Twenty-two Ways to Brighten Your Love Life* (Ellis, 1983b). (8) RET particularly shows clients how to accept themselves with their anxiety and horror over their loss of love, how to rid themselves of their depression over their depression, and their guilt about their anger at their lost beloved (Ellis, 1979b, 1980; Ellis & Whiteley, 1979).

Emotively RET uses the same kind of techniques for overcoming depression over loss of love as it uses with other love problems: rational emotive imagery (Maultsby, 1975; Maultsby & Ellis, 1974), rational role playing (Ellis & Abrahms, 1978), shame-attacking exercises (Ellis, 1969a, 1971b), forceful self-statements (Ellis, in press-c) and devotion to other pleasurable pursuits (Ellis & Becker, 1982). Behaviorally, it again uses the kinds of favored RET methods listed previously in this chapter, such as *in vivo* desensitization (Ellis, 1962; Ellis & Abrahms, 1978), reinforcement and penalization (Ellis, 1969b, 1973c), skill training (Ellis, 1956, 1962, 1977d), and self control methods (Ellis, 1982).

Keeping Love Alive

Lest it be thought that RET deals only with love problems and pathologies, I shall conclude this chapter with some of its applications to the "normal" human desire to keep love alive. RET is dedicated to helping humans to survive—and survive happily; and it focuses on an alleviation of emotional misery in order to abet happiness and self-fulfillment (Ellis, 1984a, 1984b, in press-a; Ellis & Whiteley, 1979). As part of its double-barreled emphasis, first, on abetting self-actualization and growth, and second, on therefore minimizing disturbance, it gives serious thought to devising methods of creating and enhancing feelings of love and of keeping these feelings alive once they have developed. Because space limitations preclude my discussing all the salient things that RET has to contribute in these applications of positive love-making, I shall conclude with some of its contributions to keeping love alive.

Several writers have recently written optimistic views of how people can infinitely perpetuate and deepen romantic love in marriage or in living together arrangements, but they tend to define romance in fairly unrealistic ways (Branden, 1982; Callahan, 1982). RET therapists, educators, and writers tend to take a quite realistic and unutopian view, leaving aside the dubious issue of indefinitely prolonging romantic attachments. RET makes the following recommendations to those who would enhance and perpetuate their intense love feelings:

1. Let your expectations be optimistic but do not let them run riot. Assume that you can steadily and continuingly but not always and ecstatically love.

2. Although you may spontaneously love or fall violently in love, realize that the continuation of your passions frequently requires unspontaneous *work*. Plot and scheme, yes, give some real thinking, emoting and believing *effort* to maintaining your love feelings, and to sometimes enhancing them.

3. Ask yourself, "What do I find and can I continue to find lovable about my partner? What are this partner's good traits that I can focus on? What are the things I can enjoy with him or her? What loving thoughts can I have and what caring things can I do for my beloved?"

4. Practice loving feelings. Remember and imagine situations that make you feel affectionate, caring, tender, ardent, and desirous. Spend some amount of time, perhaps each day, thinking about these situations and working up your amative feelings about them.

5. Deliberately act in loving ways to your beloved. Send flowers; buy gifts; write poems; say loving words; tell others how much you care. No matter how difficult you find saying "I love You!" say it! Again and again! (Ellis & Harper, 1961b; Hauck, 1977, 1984).

6. Plan and carry out mutually enjoyable pursuits with your beloved such as, reading aloud together, engaging in sports, attending movies and plays, visiting friends, having sex, camping out, etc. (Buscaglia, 1982).

7. Observe your feelings of anger, irritation, resentment, boredom, and frustration with your beloved. See when they spring from desires or preferences ("I wish my partner would be more attentive to me") or from absolutistic demands and commands ("My partner at all times *must* pay more attention to me!"). Keep your desires but scuttle your demandingness (Ellis & Becker, 1982).

8. If you mainly desire your beloved to think, act or feel differently, try to express your desire preferentially and unhostilely and warmly encourage her or him to fulfill it. If you cannot arrange this kind of fulfillment, work at accepting your frustration and refrain from making too much of it (Ellis, 1979a, in press-b).

9. If you feel resentful about your beloved's frustrating you, look for your authoritarian commandingness—your insistence that she or he absolutely must give you what you demand—and use RET disputing to surrender your demands. Vigorously tell yourself, "I would *prefer* very much to have my partner fulfill my desire but he or she never *has* to!" (Blazier, 1975; Ellis, 1977a, 1979a, 1983b; Hauck, 1974, 1977, 1984).

10. If you have low frustration tolerance about the conditions blocking you from fully enjoying yourself with your beloved, look for your musts and shoulds about these conditions and actively use RET to Dispute them. Strongly tell yourself "It would be nice if economic, social and other conditions helped me to enjoy myself more with my beloved, but if they are frustrating and sabotaging, tough! I can stand it!" (Ellis, 1975, 1979a).

11. Considerativeness is not the same as loving but it certainly helps. If you go out of your way to discover what your beloved likes and to abet those preferences; and if you especially go out of your way to discover what your beloved dislikes or hates and to avoid doing those things, you will go a long way toward keeping his or her love for you alive (Taylor, 1982).

12. Do not be compulsively honest about everything! Silence is often golden, especially when your partner keeps doing irritating things that you can well put up with. Do not think you have to speak up, express yourself, or be perfectly honest. But if she or he does something that is against your basic goals and values and that can be changed—then speak up.

13. Keep a good sense of humor! Reduce your own overly-serious ideas about your beloved's "obnoxious" behavior to absurdity. Learn some RET rational humorous songs about love and disturbance and lustily sing them to yourself on appropriate occasions (Ellis, 1977b, 1977c). Try, for example, these songs:

Love Me, Love Me, Only Me!

(To the tune of *Yankee Doodle*)

Love me, love me, only me or I'll die without you!
Make your love a guarantee, so I can never doubt you!
Love me, love me totally; really, really try, dear;
But if you must rely on me, I'll hate you till I die, dear!
Love me, love me all the time, thoroughly and wholly;
Life turns into slushy slime 'less you love me solely!
Love me with great tenderness, with no ifs or buts, dear:
For if you love me somewhat less I'll hate your goddamned guts, dear!

I Love You Unduly

(To the tune of *I Love You Truly,* by Carrie Jacobs Bond)

I love you unduly, unduly, dear!
Just like a coolie I persevere!
When you are lazy and act like a bore,
I am so crazy, I love you more!
I love you truly, truly, dear!
Very unduly and with no cheer!
Though you're unruly and rip up my gut,
I love you truly—for I'm a nut!

I Am Just a Love Slob

(To the tune of *Annie Laurie,* by Lady Scott)

Oh, I am just a love slob,
Who needs to have you say

That you'll be truly for me
Forever and a day!
If you won't guarantee
Forever mine to be,
I shall whine and scream and make life stormy,
And then la-ay me doon and dee!

(Lyrics to all songs by Albert Ellis. Copyright 1977 by Institute for Rational-Emotive Therapy)

14. Frankly acknowledge your own and your partner's sex desires and proclivities, recognize that sex does not equal intercourse but includes many noncoital enjoyments, and in collaboration with your mate arrange for your both achieving regular sex satisfaction (Ellis, 1960, 1976, 1979a).

15. Be with and share with your partner to a considerable degree, but try to arrange that you both also maintain appreciable individuality and personal identity (Ellis & Becker, 1982).

16. Make consistent efforts to communicate well with your beloved. Especially, use the RET method of facilitating communication developed by Ted Crawford (1982). This includes active listening to your partner, revolving discussion sequence (where you make sure you understand each other's views before you agree or disagree with them), and elimination of your shoulds and musts that block real communication (Brainerd, 1976; Ellis, 1983b).

17. Love requires some sacrifices, particularly of time and effort. You may legitimately love—be quite devoted to—your work (as Edison was) or to a cause (as Lenin was). But if you want to primarily love and be loved by another person, you had better be devoted, first, to accepting (and I could say, loving) yourself and to caring for that person. Let yourself be devoted to work and to a cause, yes—somewhat. But not too much. How about some compromise and some balance in this respect (Blazier, 1975; Ellis, 1979a; Ellis & Harper, 1961b; Fromme, 1965; Kelley, 1979; Murstein, 1974)?

Summary and Conclusion

RET has its own theories about love, its blockings, and its possibilities of fulfillment. It particularly has applications for individuals having serious love problems, such as people possessed by super-romantic love, limerents who are mired in obsessive-compulsive feelings, insensately jealous and possessive lovers, people who needlessly interfere with their encountering suitable partners, and those who suffer anguish and depression when they lose love. On the more positive side, it has important things to teach about normal human desires to enhance love and keep it alive. Naturally, RET does not have all the answers to love nor to anything else. But it is making significant contributions to this fascinating field of human endeavor and endearment.

REFERENCES

Ard, B. N., Jr. (1967). The A-B-C of marriage counseling. *Rational Living, 2*(2), 10–12.

Ard, B. N., Jr., & Ard, C. C. (Eds.) (1969). *Handbook of marriage counseling*. Palo Alto, CA: Science and Behavior Books.

Bach, G. R., & Wyden, P. (1969). *The intimate enemy*. New York: Morrow.

Blazier, D. C. (1975). *Poor me, poor marriage*. New York: Vantage.

Boylan, B. R. (1971). *Infidelity*. Englewood Cliffs, NJ: Prentice-Hall.

Brainerd, G. (1976). *Basic marriage communication training*. Pasadena, CA: Communication Marriage Training.

Branden, N. (1971). *The psychology of romantic love*. New York: Bantam.

Burgess, E. W., & Locke, H. T. (1953). *The family*. New York: American Book Company.

Buscaglia, L. (1982). *Living, loving and learning*. New York: Ballantine.

Callahan, R. (1982). *It can happen to you: The practical guide to romantic love*. New York: A & W Publishers.

Clanton, G., & Smith, L. (1977). (Eds.). *Jealousy*. New York: Holt, Rinehart & Winston.

Colgrove, M., Bloomfield, H. H., & McWilliams, P. (1981). *How to survive the loss of love*. New York: Bantam.

Crawford, T. (1982). *Communication and revolving discussion sequence*. Unpublished manuscript.

De Rougemont, D. (1956). *Love in the western world*. Greenwich, CT: Fawcett.

Demorest, A. F. (1971). Love, romance and neurosis. *ART in Daily Living. 1*(3), 6–7.

Ellis, A. (1949a). Some significant correlates of love and family behavior. *Journal of Social Psychology, 30*, 3–16.

Ellis, A. (1949b). A study of human love relationships. *Journal of Genetic Psychology, 75*, 61–76.

Ellis, A. (1949c). A study of the love emotions of American college girls. *International Journal of Sexology, 3*, 15–21.

Ellis, A. (1950). Love and family relationships of American college girls. *American Journal of Sociology, 55*, 550–556.

Ellis, A. (1951). *The folklore of sex*. New York: Boni.

Ellis, A. (1954). *The American sexual tragedy*. New York: Twayne. (Rev. ed., 1966.) New York: Lyle Stuart and Grove Press.

Ellis, A. (1957). *How to live with a "neurotic."* New York: Crown. (Rev. ed., 1975.) North Hollywood, CA: Wilshire Books.

Ellis, A. (1958). *Sex without guilt*. Secaucus, NJ: Lyle Stuart. Rev. ed., 1965.

Ellis, A. (1960). *The art and science of love*. Secaucus, NJ: Lyle Stuart. (Rev. ed., 1969.) New York: Bantam.

Ellis, A. (1962). *Reason and emotion in psychotherapy.* Secaucus, NJ: Lyle Stuart and Citadel Press.
Ellis, A. (1963a). *The intelligent woman's guide to mate-hunting.* New York: Lyle Stuart and Dell.
Ellis, A. (1963b). *Sex and the single man.* New York: Lyle Stuart and Dell Books.
Ellis, A. (1963c, April & May). Sick and healthy love. *Independent,* No. 132, pp. 1, 8–9; No. 133, pp. 4–6.
Ellis, A. (1965). *Suppressed: seven key essays publishers dared not print.* Chicago: New Classics House.
Ellis, A. (1969a). A weekend of rational encounter. In A. Burton (Ed.), *Encounter.* San Francisco: Jossey-Bass.
Ellis, A. (1969b). A cognitive approach to behavior therapy. *International Journal of Psychiatry, 8,* 896–900.
Ellis, A. (1971a). *Growth through reason.* North Hollywood, CA: Wilshire Books.
Ellis, A. (Speaker), (1971b). *How to stubbornly refuse to be ashamed of anything.* (Cassette recording). New York: Institute for Rational-Emotive Therapy.
Ellis, A. (1972a). Psychotherapy without tears. In A. Burton (Ed.), *Twelve therapists.* San Francisco: Jossey-Bass.
Ellis, A. (1972b). *The civilized couple's guide to extramarital adventure.* New York: Wyden.
Ellis, A. (1973a). Unhealthy love: its causes and treatment. In M. E. Curtin (Ed.), *Symposium on love* (pp. 175–198). New York: Behavioral Publications.
Ellis, A. (1973b). *Humanistic psychotherapy: The rational-emotive approach.* New York: Crown and McGraw-Hill.
Ellis, A. (1973c). Are cognitive behavior therapy and rational therapy synonymous? *Rational Living, 8*(2), 8–11.
Ellis, A. (Speaker) (1974). *Conquering the dire need to be loved.* (Cassette recording). New York: Institute for Rational-Emotive Therapy.
Ellis, A. (Speaker) (1975). *Conquering low frustration tolerance.* (Cassette recording). New York: Institute for Rational-Emotive Therapy.
Ellis, A. (1976). *Sex and the liberated man.* Secaucus, NJ: Lyle Stuart.
Ellis, A. (1977a). *How to live with—and without—anger.* New York: Reader's Digest Press & Secaucus, NJ: Citadel Press.
Ellis, A. (1977b). Fun as psychotherapy. *Rational Living, 12*(1), 2–6.
Ellis, A. (Speaker) (1977c). *A garland of rational humorous songs.* (Songbook and cassette recording). New York: Institute for Rational-Emotive Therapy.
Ellis, A. (1977d). Skill training in counseling and psychotherapy. *Canadian Counselor, 12*(1), 30–35.
Ellis, A. (1979a). *The intelligent woman's guide to dating and mating.* Secaucus, NJ: Lyle Stuart.
Ellis, A. (1979b). Discomfort anxiety: A new cognitive behavioral construct. Part 1. *Rational living, 14*(2), 3–8.
Ellis, A. (1980). Discomfort anxiety: A new cognitive behavioral construct. Part 2. *Rational Living, 15*(1), 25–30.
Ellis, A. (1982). Self-direction in sport and life. *Rational Living, 17*(1), 27–34.
Ellis, A. (1983a). My philosophy of work and love. *Psychotherapy in Private Practice, 1*(1), 43–49.
Ellis, A. (Speaker) (1983b). *Twenty-two ways to brighten your love life.* (Cassette recording). New York: Institute for Rational-Emotive Therapy.
Ellis, A. (1984a). Rational-emotive therapy. In R. J. Corsini (Ed.), *Current psychotherapies* (pp. 196–238). Itasca, IL: Peacock.

Ellis, A. (1984b). The place of meditation in cognitive behavior therapy and rational-emotive therapy. In D. H. Shapiro & R. N. Walsh (Eds.). *Meditation* (pp. 671–673). New York: Aldine.

Ellis, A. (in press-a). *Rational-emotive therapy and cognitive-behavior therapy*. New York: Springer.

Ellis, A. (in press-b). Jealousy: Its etiology and treatment. In D. C. Goldberg (Ed.), *Contemporary Marriage*. Homewood, IL: Dorsey.

Ellis, A. (in press-c). *Overcoming resistance*. New York: Springer.

Ellis, A. & Abrahms, E. (1978). *Brief psychotherapy in medical and health practice*. New York: Springer.

Ellis, A., & Becker, I. (1982). *A guide to personal happiness*. North Hollywood, CA: Wilshire Books.

Ellis, A., & Grieger, R. (Eds.) (1977). *Handbook of rational-emotive therapy*. New York: Springer.

Ellis, A., & Harper, R. A. (1961a). *A guide to rational living*. Englewood Cliffs, NJ: Prentice-Hall.

Ellis, A., & Harper, R. A. (1961b). *A guide to successful marriage*. North Hollywood, CA: Wilshire Books.

Ellis, A., & Harper, R. A. (1975). *A new guide to rational living*. North Hollywood, CA: Wilshire Books.

Ellis, A., & Whiteley, J. M. (1979). *Theoretical and empirical foundations of rational-emotive therapy*. Monterey, CA: Brooks/Cole.

Finck, H. T. (1877). *Romantic love and personal beauty*. New York: Macmillan.

Fromme, A. (1966). *The ability to love*. New York: Pocket Books.

Grossack, M. (1976). *Love and reason*. New York: New American Library.

Halpern, H. M. (1982). *How to break your addiction to a person*. New York: McGraw-Hill.

Harper, R. A. (1960). Marriage counseling as rational process-oriented psychotherapy. *Journal of Individual Psychology, 16*, 197–207.

Harper, R. A. (1963). Jealousy—its prevention and cure. *Sexology, 29*, 516–518.

Harper, R. A., & Stokes, W. R. (1971). *Forty-five levels to sexual understanding and enjoyment*. Englewood Cliffs, NJ: Prentice-Hall.

Hauck, P. A. (1973). *Overcoming depression*. Philadelphia: Westminster.

Hauck, P. A. (1974). *Overcoming frustration and anger*. Philadelphia: Westminster.

Hauck, P. A. (1977). *Marriage is a loving business*. Philadelphia: Westminster.

Hauck, P. A. (1981). *Overcoming jealousy and possessiveness*. Philadelphia: Westminster.

Hauck, P. A. (1984). *The three faces of love*. Philadelphia: Westminster.

Hibbard, R. W. (1975). A rational approach to treating jealousy. *Rational Living, 10*(2), 25–27.

Hunt, M. M. (1959). *The natural history of love*. New York: Grove.

Jacobsen, E. (1942). *You must relax*. New York: McGraw-Hill.

Johnson, S. M. (1977). *First person singular*. New York: New American Library.

Katz, J. M. (1976). How do you love me? Let me count the ways. *Sociological Inquiry, 46*, 17–22.

Kelley, H. H. (1979). *Personal relationships: Their structures and processes*. Hillsdale, NJ: Erlbaum.

Kremen, H., & Kremen, B. (1971). Romantic love and idealization. *American Journal of Psychoanalysis, 31*, 134–143.

Lederer, W. J., & Jackson, D. D. (1968). *The mirages of marriage*. New York: Norton.

Lucka, E. (1915). *Eros*. New York: Putnam.

Maultsby, M. C., Jr. (1975). *Help yourself to happiness*. New York: Institute for Rational-Emotive Therapy.

Maultsby, M. C., Jr., & Ellis, A. (1974). *Techniques for using rational-emotive imagery*. New York: Institute for Rational-Emotive Therapy.
McClellan, T. A., & Stieper, D. R. (1973). A structured approach to group marriage counseling. *Rational Living, 8*(2), 12–18.
McDonald, P., & McDonald, D. (1973). *Loving free*. New York: Ballantine.
Murstein, B. I. (1974). *Love, sex and marriage through the ages*. New York: Springer.
O'Neill, N., & O'Neill, G. (1972). *Open marriage*. New York: Evans.
Shibles, W. (1978). *Rational love*. Whitewater, WI: Language Press.
Stendhal (M. H. Beyle). (1947). *On love*. New York: Liveright.
Taylor, R. (1982). *Having love affairs*. Buffalo, NY: Prometheus.
Tennov, D. (1979). *Love and limerence*. New York: Stein & Day.
Wanderer, Z., & Cabot, T. (1978). *Letting go*. New York: Putnam.

3

Marriage

Rational-Emotive Couples Counseling

RAYMOND A. DIGIUSEPPE
AND CYNTHIA ZEEVE

INTRODUCTION

In this chapter, we will present an overview of the practice of rational-emotive couples therapy; outline some of its basic philosophical underpinnings and indicate their relationship to its general goals; discuss some of the distinctions between rational-emotive and other forms of marital or relationship therapy; and show how various principles from social exchange theory can be integrated into a rational-emotive approach to couples therapy that distinguishes between two basic types of relationship problems.

In addition to addressing these more theoretical or descriptive points, we also wish to offer recommendations that will be of concrete help to the therapist who wishes to do rational-emotive therapy with couples. In supervision, we find that one of the biggest problems encountered by such therapists is that of trying to pinpoint the irrational beliefs on which to concentrate their efforts: the difficulty appears to be more a matter of problem identification than of uncertainty as to technique—of what to dispute rather than how to go about disputing it. This chapter will accordingly focus more on helping therapists identify some of the irrational beliefs that are especially relevant to relationship difficulties

---

RAYMOND A. DIGIUSEPPE • Institute for Rational-Emotive Therapy, New York, New York 10021. CYNTHIA ZEEVE • Stanford University, Stanford, California 94305.

than on recommending specific intervention strategies, descriptions of which may readily be found elsewhere in the existing RET literature (see, for example, Ellis & Grieger, 1977; Grieger & Boyd, 1980; Walen, DiGiuseppe, & Wessler, 1980; Wessler & Wessler, 1980).

The Practice of Rational-Emotive Couples Therapy: A Brief Overview

As Dryden (1984) has shown, RET practitioners of couples therapy can make use of the best parts of psychoanalytic object relations theory, systems and strategic theory, and behavioral interventions. Ellis (1978, 1982) is more precise on this point, and indicates how all forms of RET—individual and group therapy as well as couples and family therapy—employ a large number of cognitive, emotive, and behavioral methods; and indicates that RET does so not merely for practical purposes but also because its theory holds that people rarely, if ever, experience pure feelings, have uncontaminated thoughts, or display unalloyed behaviors. Instead, their thinking includes emotional and behavioral components, their emotions embody thinking and action, and their behaviors incorporate thoughts and feelings (Ellis, 1962, 1984b, 1984c).

Following Ellis, R-E couples therapy generally employs a number of cognitive techniques such as the disputation of irrational beliefs, the use of rational or coping self-statements, several kinds of cognitive homework, the teaching of rational philosophies (especially those of tolerance, flexibility, humanism, and the unconditional acceptance of oneself and others), imaging methods, and the use of cognitive distraction or thought-stopping techniques. Second, R-E couples therapy uses a number of emotive-evocative methods such as rational-emotive imagery, shame-attacking exercises, role playing, forceful and vivid language, humor and paradoxical intention, and the unconditional acceptance of clients (no matter how badly they behave toward each other, or toward the therapist!). Third, R-E couples therapy, following its theory, almost always includes the use of several behavioral techniques. It stresses activity homework assignments, and favors their being done *in vivo* rather than only in imagination (as in systematic desensitization). It encourages clients, in many instances, to remain in couples situations that they may currently find unpleasant until they have worked on their thoughts and feelings and learned not to upset themselves. R-E couples therapy uses reinforcement methods that include having partners contract with each other, so that one agrees to help the other in some way (e.g., by communicating better) while the other agrees to do something the first one wants (e.g., keeping expenses under better control). It also does considerable skills training, such as teaching couples how to be more assertive or to have better sex relations.

General Philosophy and Goals of Rational-Emotive Couples Therapy

Much of the literature on marital and couples therapy focuses on how clients can best be helped to achieve good relationships. What, however, is a "good" relationship? Rather than attempting to reduce this elusive abstraction to any standard (and inevitably arbitrary) set of characteristics, rational-emotive theory simply defines a good relationship as one that provides long-range hedonistic satisfaction—that is, pleasurable experience—for the individuals in it.

This definition reflects a basic tenet of rational-emotive theory: that humans operate according to hedonistic principles. RET assumes that, in general, people want to experience pleasure and to avoid or terminate pain, and that they will conduct themselves in ways that they believe will allow them to achieve these goals. In line with this view, the theory suggests that people will be motivated to enter into relationships that promise or provide the most hedonistic satisfaction, and that they will be inclined to stay in relationships that continue to furnish it over the long run (Ellis, 1957, 1979a, 1982; Ellis & Becker, 1982; Ellis & Harper, 1961).

What is satisfying or pleasurable, however, is a highly individual matter; and one that, even for a single individual or couple, is subject to change over time. What one person or couple finds satisfying may be exactly what turns another off, and a given pattern of interaction may be experienced as more or less satisfying by any particular couple at different points in time. In light of these considerations, rational-emotive theory's definition of a good relationship is, intentionally, one that provides a great deal of inherent flexibility. Rational-emotive theory posits no absolute standards for what people should or should not do in relationships, just as it posits no such standards for what people should or should not do as individuals. Indeed, the entire thrust of RET involves attempting to reduce or eliminate the emotional and behavioral dysfunctions associated with absolutistic thinking of all kinds, and particularly with the *shoulds*, *oughts*, *musts*, and other forms of imperatives for human conduct that it classifies as irrational beliefs (Ellis, 1962, 1971, 1973; Ellis & Becker, 1982; Ellis & Harper, 1975).

In our experience, the basic idea that there are no absolute or uniform prescriptions for good relationships appears easier to accept in theory than to carry into practice; and we often find in supervision that the first beliefs that had better be addressed in discussing rational-emotive couples therapy are not those of the client(s), but of the therapist. Therapists, like other humans, have their own personal preferences and values about relationships; they may also, in the course of their training and professional practice, have developed various ideas as to what constitutes psychologically healthy relationships and interpersonal functioning. To the extent that such ideas actually do reflect rationally-held preferences, values, and theories, and to the extent that they are recognized and/or expressed as such by the therapist, they need not interfere with effective therapy. Unfortunately, however, therapists also share with their fellow fallible humans the tendency to escalate their rational beliefs into irrational ones, in which case a variety of problems can (and often do) arise.

When a therapist maintains irrational beliefs about relationships that coincide with those of one or both clients, therapeutic effectiveness can be seriously impaired. Difficulty in generating credible and forceful disputations can be expected, for example, if the therapist essentially shares a client's irrational belief that it *would* indeed be awful if some event occurred (e.g., if Mrs. X. engaged in extramarital affairs or if Mr. Y. attempted to thwart his wife's desires to develop her career interests). In such cases, it is extremely important that therapists learn to recognize and vigorously dispute their own irrational relationship beliefs as a first step toward more effectively helping clients do the same.

Another kind of problem can arise when therapists escalate their own preferences, values, and pet psychological theories about good relationships into absolutistic demands and prescriptions for client behaviors. The therapist who irrationally demands, for example, that "Mr. and Mrs. Z. learn to communicate openly and honestly" will probably experience undue and inappropriate anger and frustration when the couple persist in communicating "badly." Such feelings will probably, in themselves, tend to diminish the therapist's ability to perform effectively. Further, demands that clients adopt one's own views or behave as one irrationally believes they should can conceivably result in therapist behaviors that are questionable in terms of ethics as well as effectiveness. Therapists had therefore better work hard at accepting clients with their various irrationalities while at the same time trying to help them change; and at accepting clients' rights to maintain their own preferences and values for relationships, however different these may be from those of the therapist.

In line with this relativistic philosophy, the general aim of the rational-emotive therapist who works with couples is simply to assist the individuals in a relationship, via cognitive, emotive, and/or behavioral techniques, to become more rational and less disturbed, and therefore better able to pursue their own goals for long-range pleasure and satisfaction. This often involves helping clients to pursue these goals within the context of their existing relationship, but this is not necessarily so. In the course of counseling, it may become apparent (both to the therapist and, more important, to the clients themselves) that the long-range interests of both parties might better be served through separation or divorce. If this proves to be the case, then the focus of therapy might move to helping the individuals dissolve their relationship with a minimum of emotional disturbance and pain.

Rational-Emotive Couples Therapy versus Other Approaches

As the preceding statement of RET's general goals for couples therapy suggests, there are some distinct and, we think, advantageous differences between rational-emotive couples therapy and other approaches such as systems theory, purely behavioral couples therapy, and traditional marital counseling.

First of all, most other approaches tend to give what we consider inadequate attention to the role of cognition in relationship difficulties. As Ellis (1978) points out, "disturbed marital and family relationships stem not so much from what happens among family members as from the perceptions that these members have and the views they take of these happenings." This point reflects RET's general theoretical view of human disturbance: whether disturbance manifests itself most clearly as an intrapersonal problem, interpersonal problem, or both, rational-emotive theory holds that it can be traced back to individuals' irrational cognitive processes, and the interaction of disturbed cognition with related processes in the domains of sensing, feeling, and behavior (Ellis, 1962, 1984b,c). Although RET would certainly acknowledge that disturbed systems of interaction can evolve between or among individuals, it would argue that family systems approaches are simply not sufficiently clear in specifying the mechanisms whereby such systems develop and are maintained in disturbed homeostasis. Rational-emotive theory proposes that the cognitions (and associated feelings and behaviors) of the individuals in the system serve as these mechanisms, not influences that somehow arise mysteriously from the system itself. Thus, an individual may behave, and continue to behave, in accordance with some dysfunctional marital or family pattern because he or she holds irrational beliefs about events, people, or anticipated reinforcement contingencies in (or related to) the system; these beliefs lead to disturbed emotions and reduced behavioral flexibility.

Rational-emotive couples therapy does not suggest that the therapist overlook the ripple effects that changes in one partner may have on the other, or on other family members. In fact, the rational-emotive therapist would almost always seek to determine how a client's mate or other family members might think, feel, and behave in response to the individual's changes. If irrational responses by people close to the client appear to be impeding his or her progress, the therapist may attempt to work with the others, if this is feasible, in order to provide a more favorable interpersonal environment for the client's change efforts; and/or may concentrate on helping the client to cope more effectively with others' irrational responses, if these are unlikely to change substantially.

RET thus places clear emphasis on the individual as the focus of therapy, and provides an answer to the fundamental question, "Who is the client?" that is very different from that offered by other couples approaches, which tend to conceptualize the dyad, the system, or the relationship itself as the focal unit of study or intervention. This difference reflects both practical and philosophical considerations relevant to the conduct of couples therapy.

In our view, attempting to focus treatment efforts on the marriage, system, or relationship itself, instead of on the individuals in it, is often a misguided proposition that involves enormous, if not insuperable, practical problems. It is important to remember that *system* and *relationship* are words whose referents are really abstractions: properly used, they refer to patterns that observers or participants actively abstract, via their own cognitive processes, from ongoing flows of interaction, not to some objective, static entity that can be considered treatable *per se*. Instead of attempting to treat the abstraction as though it were an entity, with goals and interests of its own, we suggest that therapists had better define *clients* as the individuals who have come for help; and then focus on helping them modify disturbed cognitive, affective, and behavioral processes that interact with those of their partner to create what they see as problems.

Emphasis on the individual as the focus of therapy also reflects RET's roots in philosophical humanism (Ellis, 1962, 1973; Walen, DiGiuseppe, & Wessler, 1980). This philosphical school places the highest value on the pursuit of individual personal happiness, and conceptualizes relationships and larger social groups as valuable not so much for their own sakes as for their ability to contribute to the happiness of the individual. Seeing the continuation of a marriage, relationship, or larger social group as an end in itself, or valuing it above the interests of the individuals involved, would thus be inconsistent with humanistic philosophy and with a rational-emotive approach to couples therapy. The question asked in rational-emotive therapy with couples is not the proverbial, "Can this marriage (relationship) be saved?" but "How can the long-range interests of the individuals now in this relationship best be served?" It is important to keep this distinction clearly in mind when conceptualizing relationship problems, for as Harper (1981) points out, viewing human problems only on the level of the system or group can result in a subtle shift in the emphasis of therapy, towards the interests of the system and away from those of the individuals involved. Therapists had therefore better work to maintain a clear awareness of their values and priorities regarding individual and group interests, particularly in establishing goals for therapy.

It should be noted that in placing greater emphasis on the individual than on the relationship or group, proponents of RET do not mean to suggest that the interests of the group are unimportant, or that individuals should never be willing to consider group interests in the process of pursuing their own goals. Indeed, rational-emotive theory postulates that people had better learn to make compromises and to balance their own interests against those of the group, as many of life's pleasures are to be derived from successful functioning in social groups. Nor does RET suggest that the study of human functioning from a social-psychological or systems perspective is either scientifically unimportant or irrelevant to the practice of couples therapy; quite the contrary. At least one such model of relationships appears to be quite compatible with RET: that is, social exchange theory (Blau, 1964; Homans, 1961; Thibaut & Kelley, 1959). Later in this chapter, we will discuss various social exchange concepts in some detail, and show how they can be integrated into a rational-emotive approach to couples therapy. First, however, we will discuss rational-emotive couples therapy itself in greater detail.

An RET Classification of Relationship Problems

One of the most basic ideas in RET is that rational beliefs (which are usually expressed as preferences) lead to appropriate emotional responses and adaptive behaviors, whereas irrational beliefs (which are usually expressed as absolutistic demands or overly extreme evaluative statements) lead to inappropriate and dysfunctional ways of feeling and behaving (Ellis, 1962). In working with clients who have relationship problems, we find it helpful to use this fundamental idea as a basis for sorting those problems into two categories: relationship dissatisfaction, and relationship disturbance.

Relationship dissatisfaction problems reflect a rational preference, rather than an irrational demand, that a relationship be more rewarding than it is. Dissatisfaction with a relationship may occur for any number of reasons, none of which need have anything to do with psychopathology, deep-seated conflicts, or irrational demands by either partner. As we pointed out earlier in this chapter, people's notions about what is or is not satisfying may change over time, simply in the course of normal human development: a relationship that was considered very satisfying when a couple were in their twenties, for instance, may seem much less so once the partners, who will have developed new interests and pursuits over the years, move into their forties. It may also happen that a mate who was considered the best choice at one time may come to seem less satisfying if the person's available alternatives widen to include more desirable potential mates. A person's choice of mate may also have been recognizably less than satisfactory to begin with.

Whatever the cause of relationship dissatisfaction, it involves negative emotions that, though they might be quite intense, are nonetheless appropriate. People who are rationally dissatisfied because their partner does not provide what they want in a relationship will experience such emotions as sadness, disappointment, annoyance, regret, or concern about the relationship rather than feeling inappropriately and dysfunctionally depressed, angry, guilty, or panicked (Ellis, 1977a, 1977c, 1979a; Ellis & Harper, 1975). The person's behavior, too, will fall into the adaptive range: he or she may try to improve the relationship by various means; or if improvement is not feasible, may either attempt to make the best of an apparently bad bargain, or decide to leave the relationship.

Problems that involve *relationship disturbance,* on the other hand, reflect irrational needs or demands (on the part of one or both partners) that a relationship be other than it manifestly is, at any given point in time. Here, the couple's problems will be characterized by intense, inappropriate negative emotions like severe anxiety, rage, guilt, or depression; and by maladaptive behaviors that, in all probability, will tend only to escalate the couple's difficulties.

As the foregoing paragraphs suggest, relationship dissatisfaction need not lead to relationship disturbance. Partners may be quite dissatisfied with a relationship and still not become disturbed or neurotic about the situation unless they create and maintain irrational beliefs about it. On the other hand, we hypothesize that relationship disturbance problems will almost always have a negative impact on a couple's level of satisfaction.

A hypothetical case can be used to illustrate these points: let us assume that Mr. and Mrs. X. report a moderate level of satisfaction with their marriage in general. Let us now suppose that Mr. X. engages in a behavior of which Mrs. X. disapproves—for example, flirting with another woman at a party. Given this activating event, a number of different scenarios are possible.

Our first hypothetical scenario illustrates what we would consider a straightforward dissatisfaction problem. Here, both Mr. and Mrs. X. remain rational. Mrs. X., for example, rationally believes something like, "I'd much prefer it if my husband were interested only in me, and I really don't like it when he flirts with other women." We predict that if she stays with this rational belief, she will experience some appropriate negative affect, such as annoyance or sadness, in response to her husband's behavior, upon which she might then express her dissatisfaction to her husband and assertively request that he behave differently in future. In this scenario, Mr. X., too, stays with rational beliefs in responding to his wife's request. He might think, for example, "I'd much rather that she didn't object to a little flirting now and then, and I find it really unpleasant when she chastises me." He might then feel somewhat annoyed at her attempts to influence his behavior, and feel just as dissatisfied with the current state of the relationship as Mrs. X. does.

In this kind of scenario, both partners experience some negative feelings and a reduction in satisfaction with their relationship. Their dissatisfaction may be short-lived; or, if this type of situation recurs frequently in their marriage, the couple might experience chronic dissatisfaction and eventually seek therapy for their problem. Whether the couple's dissatisfaction is temporary or chronic, however, the important thing for the therapist to recognize is that irrational beliefs and concomitant emotional disturbance are not involved in the problem. We often find that, in such cases, novice therapists waste time in a fruitless search for irrational beliefs to dispute (believing, perhaps, that they must be present if the couple are having problems); and sometimes end up by trying to dispute irrational beliefs that the clients really do not maintain, or beliefs that are actually more or less rational in the first place.

Determining whether or not irrational beliefs are indeed involved in a couple's difficulties is therefore an important step in the initial assessment of relationship problems. If they are not, and the problem is essentially one of relationship dissatisfaction, then appropriate cognitive interventions might include helping clients make better use of the hedonic calculus in deciding how they might wish to behave in a given situation; while behavioral interventions usually involve some form of contracting that will allow the couple to negotiate reductions in negative behaviors and increases in positive ones (Ellis & Harper, 1961; Stuart, 1980; Jacobson & Margolin, 1979).

Our second hypothetical scenario illustrates what we would classify as a relationship disturbance problem, with both partners maintaining irrational beliefs in addition to their rational preferences: here, Mrs. X. might react to her husband's flirtation by thinking irrationally that he must not show interest in other women, and that she can't stand it if he does, and, further, that he is a horrible person for behaving as he did, and deserves to suffer extreme blame and punishment for his misdeeds. We predict that such beliefs will lead Mrs. X. to experience inappropriate and disturbed emotions, such as intense rage, in addition to the more appropriate annoyance or disappointment that she would feel if she stayed with her rational preferences about her husband's behavior; and that these disturbed emotions might then lead her to engage in dysfunctional aggressive behaviors like screaming insults at her husband, refusing to talk to him at all, or perhaps even attempting to do him physical harm. If Mr. X. responds in kind because he, in turn, maintains an irrational belief that his spouse should not behave so badly toward him, then the interaction will involve emotional upset and dysfunctional behavior on the part of both partners, and a full-fledged relationship disturbance problem will be underway.

In such cases, we predict that the couple's dissatisfaction with their relationship will almost always be intensified by the overlay of disturbance: first of all, each partner's emotional reaction to any given activating event will be more intense and more negative than it would be if they remained rational, making their subjective experience of the event more unpleasant and stressful than it would otherwise be. Second, each partner will be faced with both the activating event itself (which may be quite unpleasant enough) and the additionally aversive matter of dealing with an emotionally upset mate. Disturbance thus "turns up the volume" on whatever difficulties the couple are experiencing and becomes an additional potential source of dissatisfaction with the relationship.[1]

Where both dissatisfaction and disturbance are involved in a rela-

[1] This same reasoning would also apply to "mixed" scenarios, in which one partner remained consistently rational while the other did not: We would predict that even a steadfastly rational individual would find it more dissatisfying to deal with a disturbed mate than a non-disturbed one.

tionship problem, RET holds that the preferred therapeutic strategy is to work first on the relationship disturbance. There are several reasons for this: first, we hypothesize that it will be extremely difficult to clearly identify and operationalize dissatisfaction variables until the overlay of disturbance has been ameliorated; second, we believe that interventions helpful in addressing dissatisfaction problems are unlikely to be maximally effective when one or both partners are emotionally upset. (It is difficult, for example, to get angry couples to comply with behavioral contracting procedures: angry people see little reason to try to please those with whom they are angry, and see similarly little reason to stop engaging in behaviors designed to punish their offending mates. Further, angry people often construe—or misconstrue—their mate's compliance with a contract as mere manipulative attempts to win over the therapist and get him or her to take sides.) Initially, therefore, it will be important for the therapist to focus on eliciting and addressing the irrational beliefs that one or both parties are bringing to the relationship, and attempt to achieve, insofar as is possible, an elegant solution to the disturbance problem before going on to address whatever dissatisfactions the couple may be experiencing (Ellis, 1980b).

All of the irrational beliefs that operate in individual disturbance may also play a role in relationship disturbance problems; however, certain categories of irrational beliefs seem to be particularly relevant to relationship difficulties. These include (1) dire needs for love and approval; (2) perfectionistic demands for self, mate, and relationships in general; (3) a philosophy of blame and punishment; (4) beliefs that frustration and/or discomfort are catastrophic; and (5) beliefs that emotions are externally caused and therefore uncontrollable (Ellis & Harper, 1961).

Couples may, of course, develop their own idiosyncratic variations on these general irrational themes. For example, one couple may apply perfectionistic standards and demands only to sexual behavior, whereas another applies them only to child-rearing practices, whereas yet another applies them to virtually every aspect of their relationship. Similarly, dire needs for love and approval may reflect beliefs that the individual, and/or the spouse, and/or relationships in general are worthless unless love and approval are supplied. Discomfort anxiety—or low frustration tolerance (LFT) as we call it in RET (Ellis, 1980a)—often accompanies other irrational beliefs that a couple may maintain, intensifying a disturbance problem; or, if one or both people think in catastrophic terms about the discomfort of less-than-perfect satisfaction, LFT can transform a dissatisfaction problem into a disturbance problem.

The belief that emotions are externally caused and therefore uncontrollable is particularly pervasive in relationship problems, and often precedes or accompanies irrational beliefs in the other categories we have mentioned here. Statements like "He made me angry" or "She made me feel guilty" reflect this fundamental irrational belief, and are often ubiquitous in early sessions with couples. Teaching clients the ABCs is one of the first general steps in RET, and also a primary means of uprooting this particular pernicious belief. Once clients grasp the idea that they themselves largely determine the nature and extent of their emotional reactions, and may have a choice as to how they will feel and behave in response to any given activating event, they can then use the ABC model to challenge the various other irrational beliefs that they may maintain about themselves, their mates, and/or relationships in general.

The ABC model is also invaluable in helping the therapist identify and untangle the beliefs involved in couples' problems; for, in general, couples are just as creative in generating and combining irrational beliefs as individuals are, and often present the therapist with a chaotic welter of information about their thoughts, feelings, and behavior. The ABC model serves as a primary assessment tool, enabling the rational-emotive therapist to translate this welter of information into a manageable number of clearly-defined problems and corresponding therapeutic goals. Once this is accomplished, the therapist can use sessions to help the couple by using various cognitive, emotive, and behavioral techniques as described in the RET literature for practitioners (e.g., Ellis & Grieger, 1977; Grieger & Boyd, 1980; Walen, DiGuiseppe, & Wessler, 1980; Wessler & Wessler, 1980); and can assign the clients homework designed to help them challenge their irrational beliefs between sessions.

How best to handle sessions in terms of whether and/or when to see clients individually or conjointly is a question that is often raised in supervision. Although there are no hard-and-fast answers to this question in RET, we do have some observations that may serve as helpful guidelines in making decisions on this score.

In assessing dissatisfaction problems, it is often advisable to spend some time with each partner separately. This is often discouraged in the literature on couples therapy, partly because it may raise suspicions and/or fears in the clients as to what is going on in the individual sessions with their partners; however, we believe that the risks of not conducting such sessions can be substantial. Often, the information that clients are least likely to disclose in a conjoint session is much more important to a valid assessment of the problem (and, in turn, to its effective treatment) than what they will reveal in that setting; and by seeing the couple only in conjoint sessions, the therapist risks remaining ignorant of crucial requests, complaints, or individual agendas that the clients may be unwilling or afraid to disclose in the presence of their partners.

Differences in the degree of irrationality and emotional upset between the partners may also make it advisable to see the individuals separately, or to recommend more intensive individual work for one of the partners. Conjoint sessions tend to be most helpful when the therapist can spend approximately equal amounts of time working with the disturbance of each client. Among other things, this is important in assuring that the therapist is not perceived as singling out one partner as more disturbed, and as thereby somehow taking sides. When one partner clearly does seem to be more disturbed than the other, imbalanced conjoint sessions may create more resistance and defensiveness than they do positive change. In such cases, it may thus be preferable to see the clients separately, at least for a brief period, in order to minimize resistance and defensiveness, and allow the therapist to give more concentrated time and attention to disputing the more disturbed partner's irrational beliefs.

Separate individual sessions may also be preferable when both parties are so angry that they see conjoint sessions mainly as an opportunity to exchange barrages of verbal vitriol. In this, as in other situations we have described here, there is much to be gained by being flexible: though conjoint sessions might be considered a generally preferable means of conducting couples therapy, there is no reason why the rational-emotive therapist should not feel free to discontinue them in favor of individual sessions, if and when a specific case seems to call for it.

Rational-Emotive Couples Therapy and Social Exchange Theory

Therapists who work with couples may, of course, draw on the entire spectrum of rational-emotive theory and techniques. As we mentioned earlier in this chapter, however, social exchange theory offers a number of concepts that are consistent with RET and that we think can be quite helpful in conceptualizing relationship problems. In the pages that follow, we will describe some of these concepts and show how they can be integrated into a rational-emotive approach to couples therapy.

Relationships as Exchanges of Reinforcers

Social exchange theory, like RET, is based essentially on hedonistic assumptions. Quite simply, it proposes that people enter into and remain in relationships that provide a mutual exchange of positive reinforcers.[2]

Viewing relationships as systems of mutual reinforcers may seem less subjectively appealing than traditional views of romantic love; however, it is certainly more realistic. It is therefore, in our view, much less likely to lead to difficulty than the fairy-tale expectations about relationships that prevail in our popular culture. Further, the idea is not necessarily the cold-blooded proposition that it may initially seem to be. Enlightened self-interest need not preclude altruistic or loving behaviors. Indeed, as we noted earlier in this chapter, RET reflects the principles of ethical humanism; and the notion of "responsible hedonism" in RET suggests that truly rational self-interest incorporates a very real concern for the long-range consequences of one's behavior towards others (Ellis, 1973; Ellis & Becker, 1982; Walen, DiGuiseppe, & Wessler, 1980).

Equity in Social Exchange

One concept emphasized in social exchange theory that can be useful in understanding relationships is the notion of equity, or fair exchange. Alvin Gouldner (1960) observed that the idea of reciprocity appears to be universal; and the social exchange theorist George Homans (1961) asserted that fair exchange is a critical element in human relationships. Homans hypothesized that, given an opportunity to do so, people will almost always choose to leave relationships that do not provide an equitable exchange of reinforcers.

In looking at the concept of equity, the rational-emotive therapist will recognize that, like other aspects of relationships, equity is largely a matter of subjective judgment: what seems fair to one person may seem manifestly unfair to another, and individuals may hold widely different views as to how much or what kind of reinforcement it is fair to expect in a relationship. People's definitions of equity, and their consequent tendency to perceive given situations as fair or unfair, often reflect other aspects of their general belief system: for example, people with a dire need for love may consider it grossly unfair when their mates fail to provide it on a continuous basis, whereas those with more rational beliefs about love and approval might perceive the same situation as merely unfortunate or unpleasant. Similarly, individuals with low frus-

[2] The notion that organisms will "continue to perform" for reinforcers is, of course, a familiar proposition from behaviorism (Skinner, 1953). In developing his principles of Social Exchange, George Homans (1961), a sociologist, simply applied this fundamental concept to human relationships.

tration tolerance (LFT) may complain that their relationship is unfair whenever they do not get what they want, and especially when they do not get it immediately.

LFT, or discomfort anxiety, in our opinion, is a major source of perceived inequity in relationships. Most relationships are best (that is to say, rationally) evaluated as equitable or inequitable over the long haul rather than the short run. Temporarily "inequitable" situations may not be defined as such, and may be willingly tolerated by partners who perceive them, instead, as compromises that will enable the couple to eventually achieve various long-term goals. One partner, for example, might be willing to tolerate putting off his or her individual plans for starting a career or a family, in order to put the other through school; or a partner who is temporarily unable to give a great deal of attention to the relationship while completing an important work project may later give up some pleasure in order to help the other person in some way. In relationships like this, there is a long-term "accounting system" for balancing the couple's resources, and the partners generally trust each other to reimburse temporary withdrawals eventually, rather than (so to speak) absconding with the funds. Such arrangements reflect a high degree of frustration tolerance and a rational philosophy of long-term hedonism.

People with LFT, on the other hand, characteristically maintain an irrational philosophy of short-term hedonism, and tend to operate on a *quid-pro-quo* basis in their relationships. They typically demand that the equity of the relationship be evaluated immediately after every transaction, and insist that the books balance perfectly (or in their favor) every time. If at any given instant this is not the case, clients with LFT are likely to scream for an audit and start hurling accusations of foul play, which they often follow up with attempts to coerce their partner into immediately repaying whatever debt the client irrationally believes is "owed." These coercive behaviors usually result in diminished satisfaction for the person's mate, and may bring about reprisals which the client with LFT will define as even more unfair and intolerable than the initial situation.

In such cases, it is important for the therapist to help the client dispute the irrational beliefs associated with LFT (e.g., "I *must* not experience frustration or discomfort at any time, because frustration and discomfort are *awful;* and my spouse, and the world in general, must see to it that I do not, or they will be awful, too"). Helping clients to adopt a philosophy of long-term rather than short-term hedonism will generally aid them in reducing their LFT-related emotional upsets, and enable them to achieve more long-range benefits by better tolerating the compromises they now define as intolerable inequities.

A potential source of real, as opposed to arbitrarily defined, inequity in relationships is unassertive behavior, which often occurs when a person's irrational beliefs lead to feelings of fear or guilt that block appropriately assertive requests for fairer treatment.

Fear of asking for better treatment often reflects a client's dire need for love: for example, people may fear that assertive requests will prompt their partner to stop loving them, or even to leave them. Because they believe that this would be catastrophic, they tolerate exploitative behavior by their mates rather than risk losing them. In such cases, the quickest strategy is to empirically dispute the fearful person's inference that their mate will reject them or leave if they behave assertively; however, we consider it an inferior strategy because it leaves the client's underlying irrational belief system intact. Almost all spouses will get angry or annoyed at some point if asked to do something they consider inconvenient or unpleasant, and some may actually withdraw their affection or leave. Even if this is unlikely, it is certainly possible, and an empirical strategy leaves the client ill-prepared to cope with the situation. The preferred strategy, therefore, is to work for an elegant solution, challenging the client's belief that he or she desperately needs love and that it would be catastrophic to lose it. Once this is accomplished, the therapist can help the client more calmly evaluate the probability that assertive requests will lead to rejection, and encourage him or her to seek greater equity in the relationship.

Partners who feel guilty about asking for more equitable treatment often feel this way because they are chronic self-downers. People with serious self-rating problems often believe that they are totally unworthy and undeserving of good treatment. They consequently tend to believe that unfair treatment by their spouse is appropriate, that it would be inappropriate and shameful to ask for better treatment, and that doing so would therefore make them even wormier than they already believe themselves to be. In other words, chronic self-downers paradoxically manage to perceive unfair treatment as fair, given their own dismal opinion of themselves. In our experience, it often takes intensive individual RET to combat the self-downing problem before such individuals can begin to assertively negotiate for improved equity and satisfaction in their relationships.

As the preceding discussion indicates, people not only define equity differently, but they may also differ substantially in their beliefs and expectations about it. These beliefs may be either rational or irrational, with predictably different results. In RET, we predict that people who adhere quite rationally to a strong desire for equity in their relationships will feel appropriately dissatisfied, disappointed, or annoyed when perceived inequities occur, and will accordingly make active and constructive attempts to improve matters. Others, however, may go beyond the rational preference for equity and tack on irrational, absolutistic demands that they be treated fairly. When people with such beliefs encounter inequitable situations, as they almost inevitably will, rational-emotive theory predicts that their emotional responses will be disturbed and their behavior dysfunctional. Therapists had therefore better not only elicit and address clients' definitions of equitable exchange, but also their more general beliefs and expectations about equity in general.

Clients' cognitions about reinforcers and the equity of their exchange may have a powerful impact on their degree of relationship satisfaction, and therefore bear careful examination by the rational-emotive therapist working with distressed couples. Again, the basic ABC model (Ellis, 1962, 1977a) and recent expansions thereof, such as the eight-step model described by Wessler & Wessler (1980), provide a framework within which to explore these cognitions. What are the partners attending to in their exchanges, and how do they define and label what they perceive? What do they infer as to the probable causes, meaning, and consequences of a given exchange or exchange pattern? Having arrived at a specific interpretation of an event or events, how do they then evaluate what they think has happened? (Do they regard it as good? bad? indifferent? awful?) What evaluative criteria are they using, and are these expressed as preferences, or as absolutistic demands?

By eliciting specific answers to questions like these, the therapist can arrive at a detailed breakdown of the ABCs relevant to a particular couple's pattern of exchange, and can then proceed to develop an appropriate treatment plan. Cognitive restructuring efforts may be directed at faulty perceptions and inferences, if these are indeed factors contributing to the couple's difficulties. It should be noted, however, that preferential or "elegant" RET will differ from nonpreferential or "inelegant" RET—which Ellis (1980b) considers synonymous with general cognitive behavior therapy—in its strong, primary emphasis on helping clients revise their irrational evaluative cognitions; and particularly the absolutistic *shoulds* and *musts* that lead them to rate various activating events as utterly horrific or awful instead of relatively unpleasant or bad (Ellis, 1977b, 1978, 1982).

Equity and Reinforcement Cost

Counseling and therapy with couples often involves helping clients to identify patterns of exchange in their relationship, and helping them to assess the relative equity of exchanges according to rational criteria.

A useful conceptual tool in this endeavor is the social exchange notion of *reinforcement cost*. This concept is roughly analogous to the cost-benefit ratios used in business, and to the concept of the hedonic calculus often referred to in RET.

According to social exchange theory, continuing to receive reinforcers usually involves also furnishing them to the other person in a relationship. As Masters & Johnson (1970) once put it, when speaking of sexual exchanges, one had better "give to get." So long as both parties perceive that they are giving and getting in roughly equal amounts, they will tend to perceive the relationship as fair and desirable. However, if the perceived costs of furnishing reinforcement exceed what is viewed as an acceptable limit, or if they are perceived as far outweighing the value of reinforcers received in exchange, then the relationship will usually be seen as inequitable. Perceived inequity, in turn, generally becomes a source of dissatisfaction, and the individuals may think of terminating the relationship.

From the standpoint of social exchange theory, then, the relationships most likely to prove satisfying and enduring are those in which neither party profits (i.e., receives reinforcers in excess of the costs of obtaining them) nor loses (i.e., receives reinforcers that fall short of the costs of obtaining them), over the long run. In other words, the social exchange model suggests that, for relationships to be stable, they had better function essentially as non-profit corporations.

We can apply the concept of reinforcement cost to specific sets of reinforcers operating in a given relationship. Though in many cases a couple's most salient reinforcers may be idiosyncratic, several general classes of reinforcers can be identified as common sources of satisfaction, or dissatisfaction. These include such things as expressions of affection, sexual activities, money or other material rewards, and support of one's self-image. To take just two of these as examples:

Sex is generally considered an important and valuable reinforcer in most romantic relationships. If one person's desire for sex exceeds or falls far short of what the other party wants to furnish, then we can predict that dissatisfaction with the relationship, or at least with its sexual aspect, will occur as sex becomes a "cost" in the relationship. We can also predict that the dissatisfaction will increase as that "cost" grows higher, unless one or both parties can be persuaded to revise their definitions of an acceptable amount of sex.

The same kind of reasoning applies to support of one's self-concept. Some theorists hold this to be not only an important reinforcer but also, indeed, the very basis of relationships. This view suggests that we seek out people who will support our self-image; that is, people who will behave toward us as though we are the kind of person we think we are, or would like to be. Indeed, interactionist theory (e.g., Wegner & Vallacher, 1979) suggests that we work very hard at maneuvering people into behaving in ways that support not only our self-concept and our beliefs about how we want to be treated, but also our ways of construing the world in general. When such support is lacking, the relative cost of maintaining the relationship may be perceived as too high, and dissatisfaction can be expected to occur.

Exchanges involving any particular reinforcer do not necessarily determine the overall picture of reinforcement costs or equity in a given relationship, however. Sex, for example, is by no means the only source of reinforcement in romantic relationships; and even if people perceive themselves as being "cheated" with respect to sex, they may still feel compensated by an abundance of satisfiers in other areas. Hence, a relationship might be less than ideally satisfying (or even downright dissatisfying) in terms of particular sets of reinforcers; but, on balance, sufficiently rewarding that it is not perceived as inequitable on the whole, and is not disrupted significantly by its dissatisfying elements. Reinforcement costs are therefore best assessed in the context of any given couple's overall pattern of exchanges.

Interpersonal Attraction and the Concept of Market Value

In social exchange theory, people are thought to assign themselves a "market value"; that is, they make a subjective estimate of their own desirability and attractiveness that they weigh against the desirability of potential partners. The theory holds that people tend to actively pursue those potential partners whom they perceive as having a market value roughly equal to their own: they do not simply seek out the partner that they consider the most attractive in an absolute sense; rather, they seek out the most attractive (or richest or most powerful) person that they believe might feasibly be attracted to them, given their estimate of their own market value. Similarly, people will take relative market values into account when deciding whether to accept or reject others' attempts to interest them in a relationship. If a large discrepancy exists between the market values of any two people, the theory holds that they will be unlikely to establish a relationship.

The principle of market value would seem to regulate mate-seeking behavior in favor of maximal efficiency and species survival value, leading people to selectively approach prospective partners with whom their efforts will have a high probability of success, and limiting the time and energy that might otherwise be wasted in the pursuit of improbable choices. Certain complications, however, can and do arise—as they often do when subjective estimates are involved.

Individuals may, for example, consistently underestimate, overestimate, or otherwise distort their own market values; or they may tangle up the idea of their market value with irrational beliefs about more global self-worth issues—almost always with highly unfortunate results. Clients who are self-downers, for example, will almost always underestimate their market value, and frequently end up settling for mates that they really do not find attractive or satisfying. In general, the entire process of making market-value estimations is fraught with all the potential hazards and irrationalities involved in any person-rating procedure.

Even once a relationship has been successfully established, difficulties may arise as people's perceptions of their market values change. If an "ugly duckling," for example, comes to see himself or herself as a graceful swan, an ugly-duck spouse may come to be seen as a good deal less attractive and desirable than before. The swan may then tend to see the relationship as less satisfying and be more likely to seek out more attractive alternatives. However, the newly fledged swan may be willing to accept the relative costs of staying with the ugly duck if other values in the hedonic calculus outweigh attractiveness: when children are involved, for instance, maintaining the relationship might be seen as desirable, on balance, even if it involves enduring the company of a spouse who no longer provides much satisfaction as such.

Changes in self-image, then, can precipitate revised estimates of the relative market values in a relationship and, in turn, reevaluations of the degree of satisfaction or dissatisfaction one feels with a given choice of mate. As successful psychotherapy may be one reason why a person's self-image changes, therapists had better be aware of the effects that even positive changes can have on a client's relationship satisfaction. Former self-downers, for example, may find themselves quite dissatisfied with the mate they chose on the basis of their earlier, abysmal self-rating. In cases where successful therapy for a self-rating problem may well lead to the recognition or development of dissatisfaction problems, the therapist had better be prepared to help the client reevaluate his or her present relationship rationally, so that the new dissatisfactions do not escalate into irrational disturbance problems and precipitate unwise or overly hasty breakups.

Revised market value estimates and changes in satisfaction can also occur as time and familiarity lead individuals to adjust initial assumptions they may have made regarding their mate's characteristics. The literature on attribution theory and cognitive consistency (see Wegner

& Vallacher, 1977) suggests that we tend to attribute values and characteristics similar to our own to attractive persons, and to assume that the person we find attractive for some initial reason will prove equally attractive on a variety of other, as-yet-unexplored dimensions. Even in the unlikely event that our own values and self-perceived characteristics remained completely unchanged over time, increased familiarity with the other person may prove our initial attributions of similarity and consistency wrong. The attraction between people may thus diminish over time as they have opportunities to do some reality testing about the qualities they may initially have ascribed to their partners.

Power and Dependency in Romantic Relationships

In the social exchange view, power and dependency are interrelated, and are defined by the control of resources (read: "reinforcers") in a relationship. Where the reinforcers (e.g., material goods, affection, support for the self-concept) that each person provides for the other are roughly equal, the power balance in the relationship will assume a state resembling equilibrium. Where they are not, the partner who controls more resources desired by the other partner will have more power in the relationship, and the other will assume the dependent role. In any given relationship, the person with the greater power will tend to be the one who wants the relationship less, for he or she will have less to lose should the relationship fail. Ironically, this tends to mean that when difficulties arise, the person who wants the relationship more, and who will consequently try harder to save it, will not only have more to lose but also less power with which to defend it.

Rational-emotive theory adds to and refines this view of power in relationships. The value of any given resource in a relationship is determined not by its "supplier" but by its potential "consumer," who may magnify the power/dependency issue by irrationally defining the resources controlled by his or her partner as necessities, rather than as preferences. Thus, rational-emotive theory suggests that other people have undue power over us only insofar as our irrational thinking gives them mastery and makes us subservient. When we irrationally believe that we *must* have a certain resource (e.g., our partner's love and approval), and when we consequently believe that not getting it would be *awful,* we grant much greater power to our mates than they could otherwise conceivably possess (Ellis, 1979b, 1982, 1984a). People whose irrational neediness leads them to assume what Russianoff (1981) calls "desperately dependent" roles in their relationships are as much at the mercy of their own irrational beliefs as at the mercy of their partners. Ellis (1979b) has aptly coined the term "love slob" to describe such overly needy persons.

In RET, we thus view the relative proportion of resources controlled by one partner as a less important determinant of power dynamics than the relative value ascribed to various resources by the partners in a relationship. We would hypothesize that one partner could control 100% of the resources in a relationship (although such a situation is admittedly unlikely), but that the other partner could still remain psychologically undependent (Russianoff, 1981) by steadfastly refusing to evaluate any of those resources as a dire necessity (Ellis, 1957, 1979b; Ellis & Harper, 1961).

It is important for the therapist working with couples engaged in bitter power struggles (or with couples in which one partner's excessive dependence is creating problems) to assess not only their available resources, but also the extent to which the partners escalate their rational desires into irrational demandingness or dire need. Rational restructuring of needy and demanding philosophies is to be worked for in effectively defusing power and dependency issues. Once this is done, then other interventions (e.g., assertiveness training and behavioral contracting) can be used to help effect a more satisfactory distribution of resources in the relationship.

Absolute versus Relative Satisfaction

Earlier in this chapter, we drew a distinction between relationship problems involving dissatisfaction and those involving disturbance. In this section, we will draw on social exchange principles in further breaking down the category of satisfaction/dissatisfaction. Social exchange theory (Thibaut & Kelley, 1959) and rational-emotive theory (Ellis & Grieger, 1977) both distinguish between what we might call absolute and relative satisfactions in a relationship.

Absolute satisfaction refers to the degree of satisfaction or dissatisfaction one feels with an actual relationship when evaluating it against some ideal or absolute standard. *Relative satisfaction,* on the other hand, refers to the degree of satisfaction or dissatisfaction that one feels with a relationship when evaluating it against possible, real-world alternatives. Although partners may never achieve their standard of absolute or ideal satisfaction with their mates, they may choose partners whose resources they consider good relative to those of other mates they could conceivably have chosen. Clients seen in couples therapy are frequently crooked or dichotomous thinkers, however, and they often erroneously conclude that unless their relationship is utterly ideal, it must be utterly bad; and they believe that if they are not absolutely satisfied (as they frequently believe they must be), then they cannot be satisfied at all. Such all-or-nothing and demanding thinking omits relative satisfaction from the client's mental vocabulary, which makes it extraordinarily difficult to work toward as a goal. Indeed, the emotional upset experienced by clients as a result of this kind of irrational thinking is likely to interfere with any relative satisfactions that the relationship might actually be able to offer. RET practitioners can therefore help clients by building the concept of relative satisfaction into their cognitive repertoire, and helping them surrender their irrational demands for absolute satisfaction. This same strategy is also appropriate for single clients who enter therapy depressed over not being able to find the ideal mate.

Clients may also unrealistically demand more relative satisfaction than it is possible to achieve within a given relationship. Indeed, they may hold such high expectations for relative satisfaction that their chances of achieving it are almost as remote of their chances of achieving perfection. Such clients, if they wish to preserve a relationship, may find it in their best interests to revise their expectations (though not their preferences) downward, and learn to accept (though not necessarily to like) the limitations inherent in being involved with their particular partner. The objective here, in Ellis's inimitable language, is to teach clients how to "gracefully lump what they don't like,"—if in fact they cannot realistically expect to change it. Clients who hold unrealistic expectations for relative satisfaction in general, rather than just in relation to a particular partner, may also benefit from learning this particular strategy, whether or not they ultimately decide to stay with their current partner or to look for someone new.

The concepts of absolute and relative satisfaction can also help explain why people often remain in relationships that are either underreinforcing or even destructive. Here, an individual may not be locked into absolute standards that are unrealistically high, like the dichotomous thinkers mentioned earlier in this section; but, rather, into relative standards that are unrealistically low. Such people may remain in a poor or destructive relationship simply because they perceive it as the best, or perhaps the only, alternative open to them. A strategy often pursued profitably in such cases is to help clients realize that more or better alternatives may indeed be available to them (Ellis, 1982; Ellis & Abrahms, 1978; Ellis & Harper, 1961; Goldfried & Davison, 1976).

A case reported by one of our colleagues is a good example of this type of problem and corresponding therapeutic strategy. The client described in this case report was a woman whose marriage was apparently extremely unsatisfying. Her husband was abusive and took little interest in her other than for sex. The couple had, consequently, little to show for their relationship except a multitude of children, and the woman was manifestly unhappy. When asked why she was willing to stay in such a marriage, the client's reply was, "I have no choice. I have no alternatives. I have nowhere else to go. What would I do?" The therapist's intervention was to explore various alternatives with her, and to show her that in fact she had several choices open to her that would probably prove both feasible and more satisfying than remaining with her husband, including the possibility of leaving him and not mating with anyone else.

Fear may often restrict the number of alternatives that a person will perceive as feasible. In the case described above, the woman's fear of change, and of the uncertainty associated with leaving her husband made the idea of staying with him seem, to her, like the only alternative. It is important to recognize that, often, a person's decision to stay in an underreinforcing or destructive relationship may not reflect a failure to realize that the relationship is bad; but rather, the person's belief that the alternatives would be even worse. In such cases, the rational-emotive therapist can help the client discriminate between rational concern about some of the real social, emotional, financial, and other costs of leaving a relationship; and fears based on irrational beliefs that the client may hold about these potential costs. Once irrational fears have been disputed successfully, the therapist can go on to help the client identify various alternatives and evaluate them according to rational and informed criteria. Once the client has reached a decision among these, the therapist can turn to helping him or her carry it out effectively, with a minimum of upset.

Some Final Comments

In this chapter, we have discussed various aspects of rational-emotive couples therapy, including its philosophical roots and general goals, and the distinction which can be made between relationship dissatisfaction and relationship disturbance. We have also noted some of the irrational beliefs that are characteristically associated with couples problems. Our discussion of social exchange concepts here represents, we think, only one possible example of how a variety of non-RET constructs can be usefully integrated into a rational-emotive approach to couples therapy: no doubt other rational-emotive therapists have found, and will continue to find, other models that can be used within an RET approach—a fact that we think only serves to illustrate the tremendous flexibility that RET offers its practitioners, as well as the benefits that it offers to its clients.

Whereas rational-emotive couples therapy may often utilize the best elements and techniques of other types and models of couples counseling, it is important to emphasize that it does so within the unique, and uniquely powerful, framework of rational-emotive theory and practice. Within this framework, the RET couples therapist strives to help both partners in a close relationship to understand themselves better and increase their own individual happiness; and simultaneously tries to help them function better, and with greater enjoyment, in the relationships that they choose to establish and maintain. Rational-emotive couples therapy is thus, in sum, both a comprehensive approach to the practical and emotional problems that are frequently encountered in intimate relationships, and a powerful means by which most mates can be helped to enhance not only their love lives, but also their lives in general.

References

Blau, P. (1964). *Exchange and power in social life*. New York: Wiley.

Dryden, W. (1984). *Rational-emotive therapy: Fundamentals and innovations*. London: Croom Helm.

Ellis, A. (1957). *How to live with a "neurotic."* New York: Crown (Rev. ed., 1975.) North Hollywood, CA: Wilshire Books.

Ellis, A. (1962). *Reason and emotion in psychotherapy*. Secaucus, NJ: Citadel Press.

Ellis, A. (1971). *Growth through reason*. North Hollywood, CA: Wilshire Books.

Ellis, A. (1973). *Humanistic psychotherapy: The rational-emotive approach*. New York: McGraw-Hill.

Ellis, A. (1977a). The basic clinical theory of rational-emotive therapy. In A. Ellis & R. Grieger (Eds.), *Handbook of rational-emotive therapy* (pp. 3–34). New York: Springer.

Ellis, A. (1977b). *How to live with—and without—anger*. Secaucus, NJ: Citadel Press.

Ellis, A. (1977c). The nature of disturbed marital interaction. In A. Ellis & R. Grieger (Eds.), *Handbook of rational-emotive therapy*. New York: Springer. Reprinted: New York: Institute for Rational-Emotive Therapy.

Ellis, A. (1978). Family therapy: A phenomenological *and* active-directive approach. *Journal of Marriage and Family Counseling, 4*(2), 43–50. Reprinted: New York: Institute for Rational-Emotive Therapy.

Ellis, A. (1979a). The theory of rational-emotive therapy. In A. Ellis & J. M. Whiteley (Eds.), *Theoretical and empirical foundations of rational-emotive therapy* (pp. 33–60). Monterey, CA: Brooks/Cole.

Ellis, A. (1979b). *The intelligent woman's guide to dating and mating*. Secaucus, NJ: Lyle Stuart.

Ellis, A. (1980a). Discomfort anxiety: A new cognitive-behavioral construct. Part 2. *Rational Living, 15*(1), 25–30.

Ellis, A. (1980b). Rational-emotive therapy and cognitive-behavior therapy: Similarities and differences. *Cognitive Therapy and Research, 4*, 325–340.

Ellis, A. (1982). Rational-emotive family therapy. In A. M. Horne & M. M. Ohlsen (Eds.), *Family counseling and therapy* (pp. 302–328). Itasca, IL: Peacock.
Ellis, A. (1984a). Rational-emotive therapy. In R. J. Corsini (Ed.), *Current psychotherapies.* (3rd ed.). (pp. 196–238) Itasca, IL: Peacock.
Ellis, A. (1984b). Is the unified-interactions approach to cognitive-behavior modification a reinvention of the wheel? *Clinical Psychology Review, 4*, 215–218.
Ellis, A. (1984c). The essence of RET—1984. *Journal of Rational-Emotive Therapy, 2*(1), 19–25.
Ellis, A., & Abrahms, E. (1978). *Brief psychotherapy in medical and health practice.* New York: Springer.
Ellis, A., & Becker, I. (1982). *A guide to personal happiness.* North Hollywood, CA: Wilshire Books.
Ellis, A., & Grieger, R. (Eds.). (1977). *Handbook of rational-emotive therapy.* New York: Springer.
Ellis, A., & Harper, R. A. (1961). *A guide to successful marriage.* North Hollywood, CA: Wilshire Books.
Ellis, A., & Harper, R. A. (1975). *A new guide to rational living.* North Hollywood, CA: Wilshire Books.
Goldfried, M. R., & Davison, G. C. (1976). *Clinical behavior therapy.* New York: Holt, Rinehart & Winston.
Gouldner, A. (1960). The norm of reciprocity: A preliminary statement. *American Sociological Review, 25*, 161–179.
Grieger, R., & Boyd, J. (1980). *Rational-emotive therapy: A skills-based approach.* New York: Van Nostrand Reinhold.
Harper, R. A. (1981). Limitations of marriage and family therapy. *Rational Living, 16*(2), 3–6.
Homans, C. G. (1961). *Social behavior: Its elementary forms.* New York: Harcourt Brace & World.
Jacobsen, N., & Margolin, G. (1979). *Marital therapy: Strategies based on social learning and behavior exchange principles.* New York: Brunner/Mazel.
Masters, W., & Johnson, V. (1970). *Human sexual inadequacy.* Boston: Little, Brown.
Russianoff, P. (1981). *Why do I think I am nothing without a man?* New York: Bantam Books.
Skinner, B. F. (1953). *Science and human behavior.* New York: Gree Press.
Stuart, R. (1980). *Helping couples change.* New York: Guilford Press.
Thibaut, J., & Kelley, H. (1959). *The social psychology of groups.* New York: Wiley.
Walen, S. R., DiGiuseppe, R. A., & Wessler, R. L. (1980). *A practitioner's guide to rational-emotive therapy.* New York: Oxford University Press.
Wegner, D., & Vallacher, R. (1977). *Implicit psychology: An introduction to social cognition.* New York: Oxford University Press.
Wessler, R. A., & Wessler, R. L. (1980). *The principles and practice of rational-emotive therapy.* San Francisco: Jossey-Bass.

4

Divorce and Separation

MICHAEL S. BRODER

Over the past few decades, divorce has reached epidemic proportions in the United States. At this moment, over fifty percent of those now getting married can expect their marriage to end in divorce. In fact, some trend analysts have predicted a divorce rate in the range of eighty to ninety percent should the upward trend prove to be a linear one! In addition, although there are few statistics to bear this out, it is believed that there is an even greater termination rate of long-term, nonmarried relationships. Therefore, it makes a great deal of sense that as societal norms make both divorce and nonmarried cohabitation more "acceptable," emotional disentanglement from a former mate is a skill that many people had better learn at some point in their lives.

Divorce and marital separation, respectively, have been found to represent the second and third most severe forms of stress one can undergo (Holmes & Rohe, 1967). Only the death of a spouse is considered to have a more stressful impact, and the latter will be considered elsewhere in this book. Divorce, separation, and grieving over the death of a mate are all variations of the same theme—ending love relationships. The crises that people often go through when they end love relationships have created a glut of work for a variety of professionals, including attorneys, physicians, clergymen, and mental health professionals at all levels. (Kessler, 1978). This has even inspired the publication of *The Journal of Divorce,* which addresses research done and procedures developed to handle matters for professionals who are involved with helping this population. In addition, several popular books (Fisher, 1978; Gardner, 1970; Kessler, 1975; Krantzler, 1973; Phillips, 1978; Sheresky

MICHAEL S. BRODER • Philadelphia Institute for Rational-Emotive Therapy, Philadelphia, Pennsylvania 19107. Clinical psychologist in private practice, Philadelphia, Pennsylvania 19107.

& Mannes, 1972) have been published recently that have attempted to address the problem of this new "special interest group."

Pioneering efforts were made by Sheresky and Mannes (1972) in their book, *Uncoupling: The Act of Coming Apart*. The following year Krantzler (1973) wrote *Creative Divorce* and attempted to show how divorce could be a unique opportunity to break through the many barriers to personal growth that an unhappy marriage helps to perpetuate. He hypothesized that adjusting to divorce often involves the resolution of intense negative feelings that one generally experiences. He described the "mourning period" as one similar to that of overcoming the death of a spouse.

A more behavioral approach is described by Debora Phillips (1978) in *How To Fall Out of Love*. Her approach consists mainly of behavioral methods designed to neutralize one's feelings toward an ex-partner. Kessler (1975, 1977, 1978), Fisher (1976, 1978), Hyatt (1977), Gardner (1970), Hunt and Hunt (1977) and Weiss (1976) have all emerged with approaches to helping people emotionally disentangle from love relationships and to move on with their lives.

This chapter will deal with issues of emotionally ending love relationships—whether or not they are marriages—using an RET approach. The first issue may be whether to actually end it. The final one is often entering a new relationship. In between, there are numerous opportunities to disturb oneself and multiple potential pitfalls. A rational approach can address them all with the use of vigorous disputation and a healthy support system. Models and methods that incorporate all of this will be presented.

A Rational Approach to Divorce and Separation

The concept that marriage or other relationships are forever is thousands of years old. However, in ancient times one who lived through his or her thirties was considered to have led a long life. Today we have a more modular society. People change careers and for various reasons outgrow certain relationships. The idea that one can change an unpleasant situation, such as a relationship that is not working, is not a result of decadence, but of progress in our civilization. Remember, it was not so long ago that those who were locked into relationships that no longer fulfilled their desires simply denied those desires, and although they may have stayed together for 50 or 75 years, missed a great deal of the human experience as a result of complying with what were then the norms of the society.

When a decision is reached by one or both partners that their relationship will be terminated, they frequently experience strong and intense feelings. It is perfectly rational to be extremely sad at the loss of a loved one or extremely annoyed when someone causes you great inconvenience. However, during times of crisis we are most likely to lose control of our emotions and not only react to the apparent desperateness of the situation but additionally to our panic about the situation. This is basically what an emotional crisis is all about; and an ended love relationship can surely be an emotional crisis. Although RET views an emotional crisis as an extreme reaction to an objectively stressful event, it does not consider all expressions of emotional intensity as irrational. It is only when a person perpetuates his or her emotional crisis long into the future so that it *prevents* the person from achieving goals of personal happiness that RET defines the crisis as irrational and offers suggestions for how one can stop indoctrinating oneself with those irrational ideas, which, RET hypothesizes, maintain the emotional crisis. Also, people who experience excruciating and debilitating levels of depression or anger can be helped to reduce the intensity of their emotional reactions through an examination of their irrational ideas surrounding separation and their partner.

During such emotional times, it is most helpful for a person to accept the loss of control of one's emotions and to allow the process of grieving to go through its natural stages. Many theorists (Fisher, 1978; Kessler, 1975; Krantzler, 1977; Kübler-Ross, 1969; Weiss, 1975) have developed stage theories about the ending of a love relationship. To summarize, there are essentially two stages. Stage one involves accepting the end of a love relationship and letting go of past and absolute expectations about what "should" have been. The second stage involves rebuilding and redesigning, or becoming the architect of one's new life. The intense sadness, extreme disappointment, and other acute reactions to the shock of such a situation will purge themselves out of one's system if both the appropriateness and potential short-term nature of grief is accepted. Emotional disturbance arises when a demand is made that the situation that *has* occurred, *not* occur. Demanding that the world should be fair and just and that bad things such as divorce should never happen is one of the major irrationalities that underlie the anger which frequently accompanies separation. With such demandingness people continue to cling to the belief that what happened should not have happened and that the world (especially their partner) is horrible and damnable, and they thereby make themselves chronically angry with the world. Such magical thinkers damn themselves and others for being unable to control the past or predict the future. This is often referred to as crying over spilled milk.

An emotional crisis following divorce and separation will be resolved if it is allowed to run its course. It can stay for an indefinite period of time and involve a severe emotional crisis, however, if people continue to demand that reality always conform to their wishes, (I had one woman in a divorce group whose husband had left 35 years before, who still considered his leaving an emotional crisis).

THE ISSUES OF ENDING LOVE RELATIONSHIPS

There are basically two kinds of issues that people face when ending a love relationship:

1. *Practical issues.* Examples include finance, learning and replacing certain skills and tasks that the former mate provided, child rearing and visitation issues, legal issues, finding a new place to live, and meeting new people. In RET terms these are Activating events (As) that have the potential for creating emotional distress if not resolved.

2. *Emotional issues.* These are the feelings that are experienced and attributed to the ordeal of divorce or separation, such as loneliness, anger, depression, jealousy, fear, longing, and grief. In RET terms, these generally are the emotional Consequences (Cs) which those who seek help about ending love relationships present as their problems.

A common therapeutic error made by therapists who first meet clients is to diagnose the intense emotional state of a client as inappropriate or irrational without taking into consideration the potentially short-term nature of these emotions and why they are experienced as being so difficult and severe.

What often makes the period of separation especially difficult is that separated people do not put their emotional problems into perspective. I constantly show clients that if only practical issues were present, they would probably have little trouble resolving them. Unfortunately, they are so enveloped in the emotional turmoil accompanying separation that they have difficulty solving the easiest of problems. This, of course, only compounds their feelings of helplessness. But when I objectively discuss with them their practical issues and ask them to pretend they were advising me, their best friend, or even a total stranger, in almost every case they surprise themselves by coming up with adequate solutions. The emotional disturbances that clients find difficult to separate from their practical problems often make practical issues seem too difficult to resolve. This is frequently because of their irrational beliefs (iBs) about the practical issues. Once these iBs are put in perspective and disputed, the practical issues are easily resolved or appropriate help (such as attorneys, bankers, or career counseling) is sought to help resolve them without the confounding variables of the emotional disturbance behind them. For example, take a couple with one child who is separating. Let us further say that the separation is the woman's choice. The man would like them to stay together, but the woman has made an irrevocable decision to leave. A misguided but common reaction on his part might be to act out anger toward his wife by seeking custody of their child when he is not prepared to assume the responsibility that custody would require. If you, as an RET-oriented therapist, were to discuss his situation and to use another separating family as an example, he would probably not suggest that his counterpart take custody of the child. With his blinding emotion of anger, he cannot see the self-defeating nature of his act and may persist in acting out his anger at the expense of everyone involved. If the practical issue (who gets custody of the child) and the emotional problem (his rage at his spouse) were separated, you might show him that his anger stems from his demand that his wife not leave him, even though she is not happy in the relationship. Once his absolute damnation of her for choosing to leave is disputed and his anger changes to, first, disappointment, and finally acceptance, he will probably not engage in a foolish and expensive custody battle.

Thus, the RET approach to divorce and separation is first to resolve the emotional problems by finding and Disputing (D) people's irrational beliefs (iBs). Then they can directly tackle the practical issues of crisis situations. One of the most important applications of this principle can be made to the question of whether or not to end a relationship.

Situations that Make the Ending of a Love Relationship Imminent

A love relationship often ends when one partner for some reason decides to leave and consistently refuses to try any available means of working things out (e.g., with help from an outside party). This condition often exists when one mate finds in the other certain unacceptable traits or characteristics (or lack thereof). Either partner refuses to (or cannot) work on changing those traits, or either refuses to live with the discomfort that the traits produce.

The one who is struggling with making the decision about whether or not to leave may well be referred to Ellis's (1962; Ellis & Becker, 1982) method of hedonic calculus that involves helping the person examine the positive and negative short- and long-term consequences of leaving. It is helpful for people to look at the pros and cons of leaving, perhaps by listing them on opposite sides of a sheet of paper. Once all of the pros and cons have been listed, they take a quick look at the list. Is the answer bluntly obvious? If not, assign each item a score from one to ten. Add up the scores and consider the side with the highest score to be closest to the probable "right choice" of a decision to make. That sounds simple, does it not? Why, then, is there so much ambivalence about whether or not to leave a relationship that is perceived as no longer working?

The most common irrational belief (iB) that keeps unworkable relationships together is the demand for certainty that there will be no regrets once a relationship (no matter how lacking in fulfillment) is ended. Included in this demand for certainty is the highly irrational idea that an important decision must not be made if any shades of gray whatsoever exist and that perfect solutions can always be found if you look hard enough. Disputing this belief consists of correcting this misconception and realizing that certainty does not, never has, and probably never will exist with respect to anything, let alone something as subject to change as whether or not one's relationship will get better or worse. Experience has shown that people often later regret making decisions no matter how "sure" they were when first making them. Therefore, it is advisable to accept uncertainty from the start.

In working with a couple struggling with the question of whether to split or stay together, there are many factors to consider:

1. Are both partners willing to work on (by whatever means) the issues that have caused either or both to consider a breakup? As long as their answer is yes, the relationship may still be viable.

2. Are they willing to sacrifice unmet emotional desires for the practical things that the relationship provides, (e.g., financial stability, companionship or help in raising the children)? Or is it likely that they lack the motivation or resources to find a more emotionally fulfilling partner once the current relationship ends? If the answer to either one of these questions is yes for both partners, then it is possible that the relationship may be able to continue for practical reasons.

3. Is the relationship lacking practical compatibility and have the partners stayed together, thus far, for emotional, romantic, or sexual reasons? If so, can they learn to work together to help find solutions to these practical issues of day-to-day living and continue the relationship for emotional reasons? When this is the case, both partners can work at accepting the practical inconvenience in the marriage. This will help reduce feelings of anger, sadness, and general upset that each partner experienced toward the other as a result of what can often be described as mutual damnation. They can then concentrate on enjoying the emotional rapport that brought them together in the first place.

These questions ask whether the relationship can possibly continue with an acceptable amount of contentment and happiness for each partner. If it does continue, whether it will provide these things is another story. This depends on how hard the couple works to resolve their conflicts. When they agree to work together toward change or acceptance, they had better leave no stone unturned in their efforts to do so.

However, if either partner is dissatisfied with the relationship and does not have the desire to either work with the other person in changing or accepting those things with which he or she is dissatisfied, the relationship had often better terminate. Once the relationship is, in fact, ending, RET tries to help the partners become undisturbed as quickly as possible by changing their iBs that block the natural healing process. Ellis (1957, 1962; Ellis & Grieger, 1977; Ellis & Harper, 1961, 1975) has outlined the main irrational beliefs that people acquire and invent and that especially lead to their sex, love, and marital problems. He has also indicated, in an extensive series of articles and books, some of the main things that can be done to actively-directively dispute these iBs and to replace them with rational self-statements or philosophies (Ellis, 1962, 1976, 1977a, 1979). Following his lead, I shall outline in the next section of this chapter some of the main self-defeating ideas related to divorce and separation and some of the important rational beliefs (rBs) or affirmations that separatees can employ to change and replace their iBs.

Irrational Ideas Related to Divorce and Separation from Love Relationships

The following list of irrational Beliefs and their rational counterparts constitutes the blood and guts of the emotional problems mentioned previously. Instead of thinking of this list as exhaustive, consider it as some of divorced and separated people's most frequently reported difficulties.

Irrational Beliefs	*Rational Beliefs* (Affirmations)
1. "I need him/her (or another *ideal* relationship) *right now.*" Another version: "I must have a good mate to make me feel happy." *Associated Feelings:* panic, loneliness, depression, desperation, craving, and anxiety.	1. "I would prefer (as does practically every other person) a good relationship, but I do not *need* it right now in order to be undisturbed. Furthermore, completely ideal relationships rarely exist."
2. "Taking charge of my life without a partner is *too hard,*" and furthermore, "I shouldn't have to put up with these hassles at my age."	2. "While this is a very difficult time for me, calling it '*too hard*' implies impossible, which it isn't, rather than difficult, which it is."

Irrational Beliefs	*Rational Beliefs* (Affirmation)
Associated Feelings: discomfort, anxiety, (low frustration tolerance).	
3. "It's *impossible* to go through this period without feeling extremely depressed, angry, lonely or jealous, etc. ("evidence": 'everyone says it's perfectly normal to feel this way.')." *Associated Feelings:* helplessness, depression, anger, loneliness and jealousy.	3. "While it is expected for me to feel *somewhat* depressed, angry, lonely, or jealous, it is not inevitable for me to feel horribly upset. Let me admit that I am creating these extreme feelings through my irrational beliefs. I can choose *not* to feel so upset by keeping level-headed and refusing to blow things out of proportion."
4. "After all I did for him/her all of these years, he/she *owes* me a lifetime of happiness," or "I deserve better!" *Associated Feelings:* self-righteous anger.	4. "While I truly gave a great deal in the relationship and would prefer to have lived happily ever after, I realize that giving a lot does not guarantee anything."

Note: Concepts such as deservingness (Ellis, 1977), cause much disturbance in the world, including wars between nations. I do not know one indisputable example of a partner doing anything solely for another. *This is one of the most difficult concepts to get across.* When I try, people often give an example of someone who donates a tremendous amount of money to charity. However, we know that such donations are usually motivated by such *unaltruistic* things as tax deductions, the relief of guilt, and the good feelings that donors get when they do something substantial for others. It is healthy, positive, and desirable to please another person. The problem is when the donor demands something not necessarily forthcoming in return.

5. "He (or she) *should/must* change his/her tune, treat *me* better, or at least be *fair*." *Associated Feelings:* anger.	5. "It is unlikely that my mate will change his (or her) behavior towards me *merely* because I want him/her to do so. Changes that a person makes 'for' another person generally are not only temporary, but packed with ulterior motives. True change comes because of one's *own* desire to change. So, by working on my own anger, it is possible, but hardly necessary that my mate's attitude will change. Therefore I had better give up my demands and get on with my own life."

Note: There is no way (legally or by brute force), to make another person love you, want to treat you better, or want to be fair to you.

Irrational Beliefs	*Rational Beliefs* (Affirmation)
6. "I *have* failed," or "I *am* a failure." *Associated Feelings:* shame, guilt, and depression.	6. "I have probably failed in this relationship, but I am hardly a *failure*. Believing I am worthless for failing will only serve to make me depressed."

Note: The emphasis here is on the fact that the relationship has simply run its course; and though this may be highly disappointing it does not mean that either partner has poor traits, or is a failure for having them.

7. "*All* men/women are alike." *Associated Feelings:* hopelessness (about getting involved again) and generalized anger.	7. "I cannot accurately generalize the psychological traits of one man/woman to others. By overgeneralizing the traits of one person to all other members of the same sex, I will sabotage my becoming involved in another relationship, which may be more appropriate than the one from which I am separating."

Note: To make a point, emphasize how overgeneralizing about members of one sex is like the client being seen as a mass murderer because he, say, is a male and some other male has committed mass murder.

8. "There will *never* be another like him/her." *Associated Feelings:* depression, grief, and panic.	8. "There are many other fish in the sea."

Note: I have yet to meet a person separating from another who really wanted the other person back in his or her entirety. Usually the separator will pick certain positive traits of the separatee and fantasize he or she did not have the negative traits that led to their breakup. For example; a woman who describes her former mate as an "ideal man in every aspect" now wants him back without his need to run off with other women.

9. "I have ruined *everyone's* (including our children's) life	9. "Yes, it will be hard for others (such as our children) who

Irrational Beliefs	*Rational Beliefs* (Affirmations)
by leaving and I am a horrible person for doing so and for acting so selfishly." *Associated Feelings:* guilt.	depended on us being together. However, I believe I acted responsibly by leaving even though others will suffer from time to time. I will not put myself down because my actions contributed to others' discomfort.

Note: Studies have shown that children who come from divorced families where the individual parents are described as being generally happy, fare better emotionally than those who have come from unhappy, but intact homes (Berg & Kelly, 1979). Furthermore, when children are disturbed as a result of their parents separating, they are disturbed because of their own self-devaluation and low frustration tolerance about what happened, not by the separation itself.

10. "I made the wrong choice! Now, I have really ruined my life." *Associated Feelings:* depression, hopelessness, and jealousy.	10. "Well, I may have chosen wrongly, but at the time I chose my partner, I was acting on the facts and desires I had then. Too bad! Since foresight is rarely better than hindsight, it's now time to stop my own self-downing for my poor choice and then get on with my life."

Note: Clients often bring up a situation where they parted from their mates, are now sorry, but it is too late to go back since the former mate is perhaps remarried or indifferent. Here they can be helped to accept, but still not like, this grim reality.

11. "I am terrified of a future without my former mate. What will become of me!" *Associated Feelings:* panic, hopelessness, and depression.	11. "I am *not* sure what will become of me, but I don't *have* to be sure. If I think of other situations where I felt like I were a fish out of water, I realize that I was able to adjust, and I will adjust to this one too—as long as I do not convince myself that it is *too* hard, and that I can't adjust."

Note: Because anxiety about an uncertain future is frequently painful, it is important for the client to imagine growing and gaining through pain, and beginning to arrive at a more confident sense of self-acceptance, not solely defined in terms of a relationship with a mate.

Irrational Beliefs	*Rational Beliefs* (Affirmations)
12. "Others will reject me if I carry the 'stigma' of divorce. I will lose my family and friends and that will be awful." *Associated Feelings:* panic, depression, and shame.	12. "Yes, it is possible that some people will judge me harshly and perhaps be nasty and rejecting, but hopefully people whom I value the most will eventually accept what has happened as an unfortunate reality. Some may never accept it and that will be disappointing, but since I am powerless to change *their* thinking, I'd better refuse to agree with them and to put myself down. After all, whose life is it anyway?"

A Model to Treat the Addiction to an Ended Love Relationship

In 1974, two years into my own marital separation but while still in the process of obtaining a divorce, I observed that my three weekly therapy groups, each consisting of 12 members (36 in all) who simply registered for group therapy and randomly selected a night of the week, included 30 who were dealing with some issue concerning the ending of a love relationship. I noticed that people in that situation were very eager therapy group members. This made sense because therapy groups offered a form of social contact and, in the case of my three groups, much more homogeneity than I had previously thought. So I started the first groups in the Philadelphia area that were designed specifically for men and women who were ending love relationships. I named these groups "Breaking the Tie." They were open-ended, with group member turnover of course, and ran for about four years. While studying and observing the progress of group members, I incorporated the elements of "Breaking the Tie" into a more compact process by emphasizing what seemed to help members of this population the most. My new design, based on RET, became known as *Rational Options in Adjusting to Divorce and Separation* or R.O.A.D.S.

R.O.A.D.S. was designed as a short-term process that combined the best elements of the experiments of the previous four years into a four-week program that consisted of a workshop and follow-up session (both led by me) as well as in-between self-help meetings of members of the support groups we formed during the workshop meeting.

There are two major assumptions of R.O.A.D.S.:

First, members of a divorce group represent a spectrum of diverse backgrounds, talents, strengths, and weaknesses brought together only by their difficulty in adjusting to the ending of a love relationship. This puts them in an ideal position to help each other—with little hands-on help from a therapist, but a generous amount of guidelines as to how to help each other.

Second, people struggling with the issues of divorce and separation and trying to disentangle from an ended love relationship almost always suffer from a phenomenon resembling *addiction.*

Addicts generally have two things in common: (1) They strongly believe they cannot happily survive without that to which they are addicted. (2) They realize that whatever they crave is bad for them. The addicting substance in divorce is either the person being separated from or the lifestyle with that person to which they are accustomed and which is now ending.

I then developed a model of treatment for love addiction, loosely based on those used by Alcoholics Anonymous (A.A.), Synanon, Smoke Enders, Overeaters Anonymous, and other groups where addicts help each other, after a leader gives them careful and ample instructions as to how to do so.

Thus, in the R.O.A.D.S. daylong workshop, which may be attended by a large group of people, I gave a great deal of information about the cognitive, behavioral, and affective issues of disentanglement. Using RET principles, I showed the participants how they largely created their own emotional upset and how to stop doing so. All participants were given an opportunity

1. to identify disturbances;
2. to establish goals for the resolution of these problems;
3. to develop a plan to reach their goals of emotional health; and
4. most importantly, to establish support groups.

The support groups were designed to serve two purposes. First, they would serve as a source of support and encouragement for members to carry out their own self-designed plan that they took home from the workshop. Second, they would provide members with a number of people who could be called on at times when intense disturbed feelings (such as anger, grief, loneliness, etc.), emerged. Rather than panicking about such feelings, members could get help from someone who had been taught, via the eight-hour workshop and printed guidelines, how to provide support during acute crisis.

In between the workshop and follow-up session (four weeks later) support groups would meet at least once a week and devote about 30 minutes to each member. Support groups were composed of four to six same-sexed members who selected each other from among the entire workshop population. Usually, the criteria for selection was the ability to meet at a given time and place on a weekly basis. Early on, I learned that same-sexed groups worked much more efficiently without a professional present than did mixed groups. I always made arrangements with each support group to get a weekly report on the group and each member's progress, so that I could be alerted to any special issues that might have arisen. In this way, my presence could still be felt in the support group even though I rarely attended one of its sessions. At the end of four weeks, we would have a follow-up session where members would update their goals, deal with any other issues that arose, and make further arrangements for whatever help any member requested.

My own research (Broder, 1981) shows that at the end of four weeks, significant improvement in regard to disentanglement was made by the vast majority of members who attended their groups. Most members reported, at the end of this time, that what was previously described as constant need or addiction was now reduced to occasional desire, however intense. Many of the support groups continued on their own after the end of the formal program and some continue to meet years later, not as a divorce and separation support group, but as a group of friends who met each other at a point in their life when they were very open to new friendships.

R.O.A.D.S. members had to meet certain criteria. They had to either be physically separated from their former mate or have set a date to arrange physical separation. Those who were trying to determine whether they wanted to end their relationship were not admitted to R.O.A.D.S. Instead, they would be referred to couples counselling or individual therapy (when their partner refused to attend couple sessions). The R.O.A.D.S. groups only included those who made a decision to definitely leave or had it made for them by their former mate.

Use of Healthy Support Systems in Breaking the Addiction to an Ended Love Relationship

Research, as well as practice, has shown social support is often the most important ingredient in overcoming addiction. As I pointed out earlier, support groups are the power tool in the R.O.A.D.S. process. By *support,* I mean resourceful help in resolving practical issues in challenging the irrational beliefs (iBs) leading to emotional problems and replacing them with internalized new affirmations or rational beliefs (rBs).

Support for separatees can come from family, friends, peer support groups (such as those set up during the R.O.A.D.S. program), or from professionals (such as psychotherapists, psychotherapy groups, attorneys, mediators, or clergymen). In short, it is unwise for separatees to deny the potential impact of help from others during this time, since most people find that separation means dealing with some of the most difficult issues they may ever have to face.

Counselors or advisors who try to provide the kind of support that will be most helpful had better keep the following in mind:

1. We rarely help another person when we insist that they adopt our values. However, being supportive often involves helping people clarify and reassess certain values they hold.

2. Support persons or groups can keep the separatee's goals in mind. If you are unclear as to what those goals are, ask and probe until you are clear. How can you get any place if it is not clear where you are going?

3. Support is impeded when a separatee's vulnerability is exploited. In setting up support groups, I found it essential to separate work and socialization among members, in order for the group to do its work. Keeping the support groups homogeneous with respect to sex was learned from experience. At the beginning, the leaderless support groups consisted of members of both sexes. But often "help" given by one member to another turned out to be disguised seduction. Same-sexed groups served to protect members from this kind of seduction and allowed for more work to take place. A supportive person does not take advantage.

4. A good support group includes people who can be reached whenever a member experiences intense feelings of anger, grief, depression or loneliness, etc.—that is, undergoes an emotional crisis. These acute moments accompany withdrawal from the addiction. When empathetic help is available immediately, disturbed feelings pass. I have found that addictive "attacks" or cravings become less and less frequent. Within a short period of time (in R.O.A.D.S. programs about four weeks or less), the frequency became so significantly less, that we soon considered the addiction, *per se,* conquered. However, R.O.A.D.S. group members were strongly encouraged to accept the fact that occasional cravings can return at any time and are not to be inaccurately seen as complete relapse.

5. When giving support, do not confuse *sympathy* with *empathy.*

Sympathy (except perhaps during the most acute phases of a shock reaction to the most unfortunate of circumstances) is often counter-supportive. When sympathizing, one usually validates an irrational Belief. Example: "Yes, he is such a beast you should not let him see the children." To the naked ear, does this not sound like helpful support? When polled, 80% of R.O.A.D.S. group members initially thought it was. Empathy, on the other hand, involves knowing and understanding what the people feel, accepting them with their feelings, but trying to help them to feel differently by reminding them of their own self-chosen affirmations.

When giving support, it is best to say nothing that will help to perpetuate the irrational beliefs that lead to negative, self-defeating emotions. Finally, support involves constantly helping to set new goals that will make life more positive. A peer group of separatees will require that each give similar support to other members as they themselves find useful. That is how emotional problems are brought under control.

Scenario of a Separation without Irrational Beliefs

John and Mary have been married 14 years. They have two children, Bill, eleven, and Jane, eight. Let us forget the reasons why they are separating and just say that the relationship has run its course. So both have agreed that it would be in everyone's best interest for the relationship to no longer continue as they have known it, that is, living together as an exclusively married couple. They agree that it would serve no one in the long run for the children to be caught in the middle of whatever issues have brought the marriage to a close. They agree on joint custody of both children, but the children will still live on a day-to-day basis in their old home with Mary (since John agrees that they would be better off living together and Mary's part-time work schedule allows for more availability). This way there will be less transition for the children, since they will not have to deal with new schools, new friends, etc. John will move to an apartment that he can afford, but that is large enough to accommodate both children when they stay with him.

Mary realizes that it is time for her to give her future some thought, and so, she decides to go back to school and pursue a graduate degree in special education. This will involve her attending some night classes. John and Mary work out a schedule in which he can be with the children and allow Mary the opportunity to handle her schedule of classes. They divide up the marital property on the basis of what John really needs to set up his new home comfortably. John realizes that items that he would not mind having, but agrees to leave behind are not only for Mary's benefit, but also for the benefit of the children. They agree that each will want a night during the weekend for social purposes and agree to schedule that as well.

Even the most rational of individuals may disagree and John and Mary decide that disagreements will be brought before an impartial third-party, such as a marriage counselor, who in their case acts as a mediator. When all issues are resolved, they will go to an impartial attorney who, for a reasonable fee, will put their agreements on every issue to writing. John and Mary agree to pursue a divorce in as expedient and as inexpensive a way as possible. The purpose of the written agreement is to handle any misunderstandings later on, as well as to control the influence of any parties who may later enter the scene (such as an irrational future spouse of either partner). John and Mary acknowledge that any inconvenience caused by their separation is the lesser of two undesirable situations. The alternative, of course, would be staying in a relationship for a prolonged length of time, when it is serving neither of them adequately. They agree on a method of solving any future conflicts that arise. Neither puts him or herself or the other person down for not wanting the relationship to continue. Neither sees their new and different lifestyle as being too hard or impossible, but both acknowledge that until they get used to their new lifestyles, many aspects of it may be seen at times as extremely inconvenient.

Special Issues: Resistent Clients and Those Who "Relapse"

When working with separatees, several common types of resistance arise. They include the following:

1. Some separatees have extreme disturbances, unrelated to or merely triggered by the loss of a love relationship. Their symptoms may include the entire range of psychopathology.

2. Some resistances are traceable to extreme religiousity and beliefs, such as that of being "damned to hell" if an unworkable marriage ends in divorce.

3. Clients may fear their former partner physically, may be verbally intimidated, or may feel intimidated by their former partner's financial resources or sphere of influence and refuse to believe that, with proper help, they can overcome any retaliation threatened by their partner.

4. Clients may have such a strong degree of love slobbism that their addiction to being loved makes them sidestep healthy support and to needfully turn back to their former inappropriate mate during a period

of intense craving. This may even happen with those separating from abusive mates, who claim to be "sorry" for the chronic verbal or physical abuse and "promise that it will never happen again." Often such couples separate many times. Some of these relationships go on indefinitely and perpetuate this pattern. However, some end with consequences as extreme as homicide.

5. Separatees may lack emotional strength and have such low frustration tolerance and/or tendencies toward self-downing, that they refuse to accept any adaptive long-range solution to their crisis and consistently go for the type of short-range solutions that will almost inevitably make the situation worse or prolong it indefinitely.

Clients who fit the above descriptions are predictably inappropriate for peer support groups or other short-term interventions. Their disturbances go so far beyond those attributable to divorce and separation, so that longer-term psychotherapy with an experienced professional is recommended.

Rationally Replacing an Unhealthy Relationship

When it is all said and done, the final step for most separatees is to learn from the past and engage in new, better relationships. It is hoped that this will come with time (I have found the average to be a year or two), but you can often help your clients from avoiding or ruining new matings by helping them acquire these RET-oriented attitudes:

For clients who fear they will be too vulnerable in new relationships: The "worst" has already happened, you lived through it. Do not blow it now by telling yourself you could never go through it again. You will foolishly avoid new relationships by demanding a guarantee that if you get involved again, there will never be pain. Now is a time to have fun, meet lots of people, and remember—it is better to have loved and lost. . . .

For clients who tend to naively get involved with an inappropriate partner: If someone tells you, "I don't want to get involved," "I could never leave my present or previous partner," or "I just don't see this relationship going anywhere"—believe them!

For clients who overgeneralize about the past: Do not take certain similarities between your former mate and a new prospect to indicate that that is all there is to the new person. Someone can easily have similarities with your old mate, but not present the same problems. Keep this in mind. After all, where is it written that you cannot still be attracted to certain traits that turned you on about your former mate? Remember, despite what some "Gurus" say, desire is healthy!

For clients who tend to fall in love with the first person (or even second or third) they meet: Just as many separatees err in avoiding relationships, others get involved too quickly, more out of a fear of never meeting anyone than out of true desire. Imagine yourself hiring someone for an important position. Would you take the first person who comes through the door and assume he or she will have all of the necessary qualifications? Or would you interview as many qualified candidates as feasible before choosing? Make your next relationship a true choice. Avoid rationalizing yourself into a "Lesser of two evils" (this new person versus nobody) situation.

Conclusion

I have presented in this chapter an overview of how RET can be applied to the ending of a love relationship. Ironically, it seems so obvious, except for separatees' irrational beliefs. If you find yourself going through a divorce or separation, avoid demanding that this period of your life not be stressful. Because even in the ideal case of John and Mary, presented above, they both will feel distinct, and appropriate, sadness, disappointment, and frustration. However, if separatees refuse themselves with shoulds, musts, and other absolutistic demands, breaking up can be one of the most unique opportunities for personal growth they will ever have. If they learn and work at using a good amount of RET!

References

Berg, B., & Kelly, R. (1979). The measured self esteem of children broken, rejected and accepted families. *Journal of Divorce, 2* (4).

Broder, M. (1980). A descriptive study of a program designed to help participants to deal with issues related to divorce and separation from long-term relationships. (Doctoral dissertation, Temple University, 1980). *Dissertation Abstracts International*, 1981, *42*, 12.

Ellis, A. (1957). *How to live with a "neurotic."* North Hollywood, CA: Wilshire Books. rev. ed., 1975.

Ellis, A. (1962). *Reason and emotion in psychotherapy.* Secaucus, NJ: Citadel Press.

Ellis, A. (1976). *Sex and the liberated man.* Secaucus, NJ: Lyle Stuart.

Ellis, A. (1977). *How to live with—and without—anger.* Secaucus, NJ: Citadel Press.

Ellis, A., (1977) *The intelligent woman's guide to dating and mating.* Secaucus, NJ: Lyle Stuart.

Ellis, A., & Becker, I. (1982). *A guide to personal happiness.* North Hollywood, CA: Wilshire Books.

Ellis, A., & Grieger, R. (Eds.). (1977). *Handbook of rational-emotive therapy.* New York: Springer.

Ellis, A., & Harper, R. A. (1961). *A guide to successful marriage.* North Hollywood, CA: Whilshire Books.
Ellis, A., & Harper, R. A. (1975): *A new guide to rational living.* North Hollywood, CA: Wilshire Books.
Fisher, B. F. (1976). Identifying and meeting needs of formerly married people through a divorce adjustment seminar. *Dissertation Abstracts International, 37,* 11A, 7036.
Fisher, B. F. (1978). *When your relationship ends.* Boulder: Family Relations Learning Center.
Gardner, R. (1970). *The boys and girls book about divorce.* New York: Bantam Books.
Holmes, T. H., & Rohe, R. H. (1976). Social readjustment rating scale. *Journal of Psychosomatic Research, 11,* 213.
Hunt, M., & Hunt, B. (1977). *The divorce experience.* New York: McGraw-Hill.
Hyatt, J. R. (1977). *Before you marry . . . again.* New York: Random House.
Kessler, S. (1975). *The American way of divorce: Prescriptions for change.* Chicago: Nelson-Hall.
Kessler, S. (1977). *Beyond divorce: Leader's guide.* Atlanta: National Institute for Professional Training.
Kessler, S. (1978). Building skills in divorce adjustment groups. *Journal of Divorce, 2,* 2.
Krantzler, M. (1973). *Creative divorce.* New York: Evans.
Krantzler, M. (1977). *Learning to love again.* New York: Crowell.
Kübler-Ross, E. (1969). *On death and dying.* New York: Macmillan.
Phillips, D. (1978). *How to fall out of love.* Boston: Houghton Mifflin.
Sheresky, N., & Mannes, N. (1972). *Uncoupling: The art of coming apart.* New York: Viking.
Weiss, R. (1976). *Marital separation.* New York: Basic Books.

5

Women

Janet L. Wolfe

Women have long been the primary consumers of psychotherapeutic services, outnumbering males at a ratio of two to one (Chesler, 1972; Worrell, 1980). The changing nature of male and female roles in the past 15 years, along with the mental health community's emerging awareness of the overrepresentation of women in certain emotional disorders, has pointed to a need for a therapy better geared to helping women with the practical and emotional problems they face as they attempt the exciting but difficult transition into more expanded roles. Rational-emotive therapy, combined with a critical examination of female sex-role socialization messages, a "primordial soup" in which irrational beliefs abound, is seen as a particularly effective approach for helping this therapy population.

Women's Issues: An Update

Women have been traditionally overrepresented in the therapy population (Rothblum, 1983). We know these women well. They flood therapy offices and clinics, most frequently with psychological disorders linked to powerlessness—feelings of inadequacy, chronic low self-esteem, guilt, passivity, depression, and anxiety. These symptoms are a natural by-product of women's being steeped from childhood in the idea that their worth and happiness should derive from living for and through others (Heriot, 1983). Among the predominantly female disorders are depression (Weissman & Klerman, 1977), agoraphobia (Fodor, 1974),

---

Janet L. Wolfe • Associate Executive Director, Institute for Rational-Emotive Therapy, New York, New York 10021.

obesity (Stuart, 1979; Fodor, 1982), and anorexia (Wooley & Wooley, 1980). Despite the significant overrepresentation of women in these disorders (e.g., anorexics are 75%–85% women), few clinicians have attempted to try to understand the importance of sex-role learning when treating women with these types of disorders (Berzins, 1975).

In addition to dealing with these more conventional disorders, therapists are treating women clients whose conflicts are related to significant changes in economic, political, and legal areas that have occurred during the past 15 years. The women's movement, the changing composition of American families, and the 1979 Title IX Amendment of the Civil Rights Act are all sources of cultural change that have motivated individuals to alter their life-styles, expectations, and value systems (Worell, 1980).

Women are now single-parenting more frequently, marrying later, and having fewer children, as they enter the ranks of the labor force at a very high rate (Block, 1979). Typical conflicts with which they are struggling include:

- Do I have to be a superwoman?
- Will I miss out on life if I don't have children?
- How can I be happy and fulfilled if I don't have a relationship with a man?
- How can I get my mate to share more responsibility at home?
- How can I break into positions of power in my male-dominated field?
- Where can I find a role model if I don't want to be like my mother or like a driven male executive?
- Can I risk marriage without losing it all?
- Can I really be myself with a man? Does he actually want an equal?

Changing Directions in Therapy for Women

Society's discrimination against women is reflected in the way women's disturbances have been traditionally treated in therapy. In psychoanalytically oriented therapy, for example, striving for autonomy or fulfillment outside the traditional roles of wife and mother have been interpreted as penis envy or masculine protest.

Data from clients and therapists involved in nearly all types of therapy show that there is differential treatment of men and women. For example, when male and female neurotic depressives who are equally distressed are compared with regard to length of treatment and prescription of medications, females are seen for more therapy sessions and given more potent medications than males (Stein, DelGaudio, & Ansley, 1976). In studies comparing traditional and feminist therapists, most women thought of their nonfeminist therapist as manipulating them into the role of "proper" women and as being impersonal and paternalistic (Levine, Camin, & Levine, 1974).

Stimulated by writings in the women's movement criticizing a traditional therapeutic treatment of women (Chesler, 1972; Wyckoff, 1977), the therapeutic literature on the etiology of emotional stress in women and on potentially effective therapeutic procedures has expanded (Franks, 1979; Brodsky & Hare-Mustin, 1980b; Robbins & Siegel, 1983). The importance of developing specialized skills and knowledge in treating women was underscored by an American Psychological Association task force, which recommended that mental health professionals would do better to develop greater sensitivity to women's mental sets and socioeconomic realities, and develop special psychological service delivery models tailored to them (American Psychological Association, 1975, 1978).

Despite these recommendations, attention to sex-role issues appears to be restricted to a small group of mental health professionals (mainly women with a feminist orientation, who typically make up 95% or more of the audiences at convention panels dealing with "women's issues"). Traditional clinical psychology training reinforces stereotyped views of women (Weisstein, 1971), and sexism continues to rear its head in the mental health community. Findings of the "grandmother" of a number of studies on sex-role stereotypes and mental health problems demonstrate a double standard of mental health (Broverman, Broverman, Clarkson, Rosenkrantz, & Vogel, 1970). Clinicians rated healthy women as being more submissive, less independent, less competent, less adventurous, more easily influenced, less aggressive, less competitive, more excitable and emotional, and less objective than men. This negative assessment, which reflects stereotyped societal standards of sex behavior, puts women in a double bind. If they adopt the healthier, more socially desirable behaviors of the "competent, mature adult," they risk censure for being unfeminine. If they adopt the less healthy and less socially desirable behaviors of a female, they are seen as "incompetent" and "immature." (Franks, 1982; Kelly, Kern, Kirkley, Patterson, & Keane, 1980).

A feminist outlook holds that therapists should help both men and women to realize individual potential rather than adjustment to existing restrictive sex roles. This has been supported by a small but growing body of literature that supports the linkage between psychological androgyny (having a repertoire of both masculine and feminine behaviors) and positive mental health. Psychological androgyny has been found to be associated with greater maturity in our moral judgments (Block, 1973) and a higher level of self-esteem, while extreme femininity is correlated with high anxiety, high neuroticism, and low self-acceptance (Spence, Helmreich, & Stapp, 1975). Bem and Lenney (1976) found that psychologically androgynous people felt comfortable in a broader range of activities, while masculine men and feminine women were uncomfortable when they engaged in activities that they perceived as belonging to the opposite sex.

Feminist therapists have emphasized the conflict between women's early training to become childlike, helpless, submissive, and dutiful as daughters, wives, and mothers, and their current hopes and expectations to become self-sufficient, autonomous, fully functioning, valued adult members of society (Robbins & Siegel, 1983). They point out that the active supporting of "deviance"—the freedom to choose alternative life-styles—may be precisely what is needed to effect a more healthy behavioral pattern and social identity for today's woman (Rice & Rice, 1973; Barrett, Berg, Eaton, & Pomeroy, 1974).

Herstory

The last 12 years have seen the Institute for Rational-Emotive Therapy in New York develop one of the broadest-based therapy programs addressed to women's issues in the country (Wolfe, 1980a). This includes six-session women's assertiveness, effectiveness, and sexuality groups; women's ongoing therapy groups; workshops dealing with life-cycle change and career entry, habit control (weight and stress management), and mother–daughter communications. Institute staff have also conducted workshops for professionals in sex-role issues in therapy and engaged in collaborative projects with various women's organizations, including the National Organization for Women (N.O.W.) and a program to train minority women in the building trades. Leading rational-emotive therapists specializing in sex-role issues include Drs. Ingrid Zachary (1980), Penelope Russianoff (1982), Susan Walen (1983), Rose Oliver (1977), and Janet Wolfe (1975).

Rapprochement between Rational-Emotive Therapy and Feminist Therapy

The therapy goal agreed on by most feminist therapists is the development of an autonomous individual having personal strength, independence, and trust in self and in other women (Brodsky & Hare-Mustin, 1980b; Loeffler & Fiedler, 1979). Feminist therapists also see the therapist as an agent of societal change, increasing the client's awareness of sociopolitical pressures and helping her to recognize her choices and to change the context of her life (Hare-Mustin, 1983).

Rational-emotive therapy provides an effective and well-defined self-help system for facilitating personal growth and emotional well-being in women (Ellis, 1957, 1962, 1973, 1974, 1979; Ellis & Becker, 1982; Ellis & Harper, 1975). Those practicing "feminist RET" do not support a standard of mental health for women different from that of men. They view RET as a humanistic, nonsexist vehicle for helping women work through their emotional and practical problems via a realistic, logical examination of their beliefs and philosophies (Ellis, 1974; Zachary, 1980). RET teaches a woman how to define her problems, identify the variables which influence her present feelings and actions, and to alter both her behavior and her environment in positive ways.

More than any other school of therapy, RET seems to come closest to meeting the criteria for effective feminist therapy: (1) It deals with the *shoulds, musts,* self-rating, and love-slobbism inherent in sex-role messages, and provides a concrete method for disputing them; (2) It helps women to stop condemning themselves for their emotional disturbances and their ineffective behaviors; (3) It encourages autonomy, through client involvement in goal setting and doing self-therapy, and via its behavioral component, which teaches more effective behaviors; (4) It does not label assertiveness as masculine striving; (5) It shows women how to stop depressing themselves about their frustrations with a society that is not sex-fair, and with people who act in sexist ways, and also to fight determinedly for A-changes (alterations in their environment). For no matter how successfully women anti-awfulize or reduce self-downing, they still wind up with the short end of the stick unless they also work to improve their chances of increasing power, economic resources, and other elements involved in self-actualization (Wolfe, 1980).

All-Women's Therapy Groups: Rationale

Being involved with others who endorse their therapeutic successes is especially important for women, who may receive considerable negative reinforcement for departures from feminine behaviors from such significant others as a lover, husband, or parents (Krumboltz & Shapiro, 1979). Dependence on others' approval and poor self-acceptance may make it extremely difficult for women to accept themselves and persist in new behaviors in the face of heavy flak. Consequently, when a member of a women's group receives cheers from other members for moving toward autonomy, she is provided an important transition from dependency on male validation to self-reinforcement.

Recognizing the environmental context of their problems also facilitates change. A woman who sees her helplessness and dependency as caused by some personal failure may tell herself, "I have no skills. I'm totally dependent on others. I'm a weak, sick person." But as she discovers the enculturated aspects of feminine helplessness, this same woman may make an entirely different set of self-statements: "These feelings of helplessness I have are very normal. I'm not a helpless person, but my society has taught me to play a helpless role" (Krumboltz & Shapiro, 1979; Gornick & Moran, 1971).

Key Ingredients in RET Women's Groups

What is the more expanded RET approach to working with women at the Institute for Rational-Emotive Therapy? Whether done individually or in women's groups, the ingredients are essentially the same.

Consciousness raising. Showing women, through discussion, how the culture has helped shape and maintain their faulty belief systems. To aid in this process, members are from time to time assigned feminist literature on marriage, sexuality, and other topics.

Goal setting. As is commonly the case, RET women clients, collaborating with the therapist, learn to set their own goals. They thereby receive practice in counteracting passivity and dependency, in defining their own life plans instead of waiting for "white knights" to come along and plan for them. Women are asked to set up and review three-month plans, and are encouraged to project their future plans up to the age of 90.

RET. This involves "psyche-strengthening" work, namely, helping women change an "I'm helpless" belief system to one of optimism and self-acceptance. This phase also involves helping women develop better coping responses to the real world by teaching them to strengthen frustration tolerance and especially to handle their anxiety and rage.

Therapist role modeling. Because of the dearth of self-accepting and achieving female role models in women's lives, modeling and self-disclosure by the female therapist can provide an important coping model. For example, a client struggling to achieve greater autonomy and independence from her husband may benefit from a description of how the therapist and her spouse handle their finances.

Participants as role models. Additional role modeling is provided by encouraging group members, who share how they have achieved mastery of previous problem areas. This offers an additional source of effective role modeling and also helps the group members to give themselves credit for their successes as an antidote to their usual overfocusing on their flaws.

Assertiveness training. This constitutes a major remediation for female's passive and dependent behaviors. Cognitive and behavioral assignments are given to help women combat their fears of taking risks and of being disapproved of by others and to replace their habits of learned helplessness with those designed to increase personal effectiveness. An important part of assertiveness training is helping women to evaluate and cope with the possible negative consequences that may occur as a result of their assertions.

Positive self-messages. A large percentage of women have especially well-developed "flaw-detecting kits" and are practically addicted to self-downing (Russianoff, 1982). Women are regularly given assignments to write, or recite to a mirror, three positive traits or behaviors each day, or to "brag" aloud, first to the therapist and other group members and then to do so to others in their outside environment.

Self-pleasuring assignments. These are designed to combat cognitively and behaviorally the "put others first" and "I must not be selfish" sex-role messages. Homework assignments, such as taking time for a long bubble bath, buying oneself flowers, getting a massage, or having caviar and cognac in front of a fire by oneself are useful means for reinforcing the idea that "I have the right to do nice things for myself." At the same time, group members learn to give themselves the kind of stroking often expected only from males.

Encouragement of female friendships. Women frequently use the term *relationship* as synonymous with heterosexual sex-love relationships (e.g., "I haven't had a relationship for years!"), and in so doing, negate or minimize the value and importance of female friendships. Friendships with women are encouraged as fine ways for women to get loving, caring, sharing, support, intimacy, and nurturance into their lives, whether or not they are involved in a primary sex-love relationship.

Focus on environmental resources and societal change. RET women's groups go beyond the traditional boundaries of therapy and include all efforts and resources that we can muster to provide women with corrective socialization experiences and tools for environmental change. Unlocked from her paralyzing rage at discrimination on the job, for example, a woman may be encouraged to contact an organization that handles problems of sex discrimination. Extensive lists of resources, including battered women's shelters, women's professional organizations, and nonsexist gynecologists are kept by feminist rational-emotive therapists to help women work at changing some of the societal conditions they have successfully anti-awfulized.

The remainder of the chapter will deal with two different clusters of problems for which rational-emotive feminist therapy appears to provide help: (1) *High prevalence disorders,* which include the more apparent casualties of sex-role socialization: depression, phobias, and weight disorders. (2) *Relationship and work issues,* including marriage, sexuality, mothering, and career. In both these areas, RET promotes emotional and behavioral competencies which help women transcend their early sex-role programming.

Depression and Low Confidence

Women have twice as many depressive disorders as men (Weissman & Klerman, 1977). Seligman (1979) notes that the ratio between female and male depression may be as high as 10:1. Increasing numbers of researchers have found that depression is associated with the stress women experience from low social status, legal and economic discrimination, and learned helplessness (Hare-Mustin, 1983; Guttentag & Salasin, 1976).

NIMH statistics (Radloff, 1975) indicate that depression is higher in married women. In an attempt to account for the high depression rates, research has focused on the married woman's role (Franks, 1982). Homemakers are given a considerable amount of hard work but are rarely recognized or rewarded for their work. When homemakers also take on a paying job, they still wind up with few reinforcements in either area.

Although the cognitive process is the same for both depressed women and men, society tends to reinforce especially the negative messages that women tell themselves. Understanding the ecology of depression in terms of sex role is important in treating depression (Franks, 1982). From their training to be submissive, dependent, and passive, women may indeed find that they have less control over their environment, so that the perception of the relationship between their efforts and any significant results in their lives could result in learned feelings of helplessness (Seligman, 1975). Believing themselves to be helpless, they fail to attempt the things that might help them achieve some success and mastery over their environment. They then feed themselves still more messages about their helplessness and worthlessness, thus perpetuating the vicious cycle (Ellis, 1962, 1974). These early themes of helplessness get expressed over and over in women clients' beliefs that they are stupid, helpless, inadequate, and incompetent, and in their limited ability to focus on what they can do because of their overfocus on what they do not do.

The rational-emotive therapist's goal is to help a woman riddled with hopeless/helpless cognitions and consequent self-downing to vigorously dispute them in a world where in fact she has a low status, and where higher achieving people than she vigorously reinforce the idea of her helplessness and worthlessness. It is therefore especially helpful for the societal roots of women's role prescriptions to be unearthed and analyzed. In helping a depressed single parent dispute her ideas, "I am a rotten mother" and "I am a reject because I don't have a mate," the therapist helps her challenge not only her own, but the societal view.

Training in environmental mastery becomes an important adjunct to RET in working with the depressed woman. The therapist may inform the client of community and other resources, including vocational training, women's business organizations, financial aid, and day-care centers (Grieger, 1982).

PHOBIAS

Recent theoretical research and clinical writing have characterized clinical phobias as primarily female disorders (Fodor, 1974; Brehony, 1983). In spite of the overrepresentation of females and the underrepresentation of males in the phobia literature, there have been few attempts to explore the variables relevant to this sex difference.

Anxiety is a natural by-product of people whose sense of worth is highly dependent on pleasing others (Ellis, 1962, 1974, 1979). Agoraphobia, generally the most incapacitating of the phobias, is characterized by extreme fearfulness and panic in open situations that require independent behavior. It usually leads to a housebound lifestyle, feelings of helplessness, and feelings of being trapped. Agoraphobia is far more common among females (Fodor, 1982); more than a million American women find their lives restricted by agoraphobic syndromes (Agras, Sylvester, & Oliveau, 1969). As Fodor (1974) suggests, female agoraphobics are often traditionally feminine and rigidly sex typed. With few goals of their own, they passively wait for others to take care of or direct them. Resentment, depression, restricted activity, non-assertiveness, and low self-esteem frequently follow (Jasin, 1983). These fearful behaviors are then reinforced by significant others in the woman's life (e.g., their husbands) as consonant with her sex role (Goldstein & Chambless, 1980).

Fear of the outside world makes sense when we realize that women have systematically been denied access (and have denied themselves access) to skills that would enable them to cope with common adult situations: travelling alone, buying a car, taking out a loan, or applying for a job (Heriot, 1983). They especially lack adequate assertiveness skills, a behavioral deficit that correlates with and is significantly included in agoraphobia.

Other phobias also tend to reflect women's tendency to see themselves as helpless and powerless. Their alleviation may mean the removal of important blocks to personal growth and educational or vocational achievement. Test anxiety, for example, is higher in women than in men. If testing is required to enter a profession, change careers, or rise to a higher level in a job, a woman's ambition may be undermined by fear. Public-speaking anxiety has also been shown to be higher among women (Moulton, 1977), and may be one of the most important factors limiting women's vocational advancement.

Women also outnumber men in social phobias, which keep them from such goals as meeting new males, business networking, and meeting new women friends. Their task then becomes more difficult than that of their male counterparts. In addition to the usual fears of rejection, women confront the societal prejudice that a woman is defective or "hard up" if she initiates social contact with a man. In terms of business networking, it may be more difficult to approach a potential male contact because so much business dealing occurs mainly between men (the "old boy" network).

Weight Disorders

A billion-dollar weight reduction, medical, pharmaceutical, and publishing industry is supported by 20 million overweight women, or roughly one-quarter to one-third of the American female population (Fodor, 1983).

Sex roles and sex-role stereotypes are correlated with weight problems (Stuart, 1979). In a culture where a woman's self-worth is seen as depending on her body image, the media feature skinny prepubescent girls as sexy, an ideal difficult to attain by adult women, for whom it is biologically realistic to have more body fat than do men or teenage girls. The Victorian female's shape, including luxuriant bosoms, full and voluptuous thighs, is far more in accordance with women's natural body-build.

In contrast are the standards for men: The portly, cigar-smoking male is seen as attractive, or surely less stigmatized than a comparably built woman, despite the fact that overweight is far riskier for males than for females.

So distorted do women's body self-images become, that behavior therapists report as many as one-third of the applications for behavioral control programs are by women of normal weight (Fodor, 1983). The cultural prescriptions for ideal weight have an obsessional nature that has encouraged many women to be miserable every time they pass a mirror or to camouflage their thighs during sex. Therapists had better try to understand the role of sex-role stereotypes in treating the anorexic or the bulimic client, who is extremely obsessed with food, staying slim, and confusion about body image. The incidence of these disorders is appallingly high. Estimates of the rate of anorexia in teenage girls range from 0.4% to 4.0%. In a bulimia program conducted at Cornell University, an ad in the student paper drew 62 responses in two weeks (Boskind-White & White, 1983).

An effective rational-emotive program for working with women with weight disorders consists of helping clients to highlight some of the cultural irrational beliefs about overweight, and to recognize how they have made them into personal irrational beliefs (Fodor, 1982).

Cultural Message	*Personal Irrational Belief*
The ideal woman should look like (teenage model) Brooke Shields.	If my body doesn't look like a model's, then I'm fat and disgusting. It is horrible to be fat.
Fat people are lazy and undisciplined.	I should be able to lose weight on my own, and if I don't, I'm a lazy, worthless person.
Thin women are more worthwhile.	I cannot possibly have a sex-love relationship, self-acceptance, or life-enjoyment until I'm thin.

Many health professionals also hold society's prejudice against overweight women, and, rarely considering other alternatives, set up behavioral and cognitive programs designed to shape the woman into the thin mold defined in our culture. Such therapists would do well to challenge the assumptions that there is a standard weight for each person, that moderate overweight is unhealthy and deadly (Metropolitan Life, 1980), that self-control is easy, and that women are unattractive and undesirable when moderately overweight. In doing consciousness raising with clients, the therapist can point out that the prejudices against overweight women can be viewed as "fatism" or "weightism" akin to sexism or racism. Clients can be encouraged to bring in their own examples from magazines, TV, and shopping experiences, of societal messages relevant to thinness, sexual desirability, health, and self-control. Readings such as Orbach (1978) may be assigned. The focus is on helping clients to accept themselves unconditionally, no matter their body size. Disputes include: "Where is the evidence that I don't deserve to enjoy life as a fat person?" "Why can't fat people be happy?" Ultimately, clients begin to understand that the problem is not "overweight" but their negative evaluations about it and themselves, e.g., "I can't stand to be overweight" or "I am a horrible person for being overweight." These irrational beliefs perpetuate misery and preoccupation with dieting.

Marriage, Divorce, and Relationship Problems

Studies suggest that the social institution of marriage raises the risk of disorder for women but offers protection for men (Bernard, 1972). Married women who are not employed outside the home are the highest risk for psychological disorder: they have the highest rates of entry into psychiatric treatment of any occupational group; they request (and receive) the greatest quantity of prescribed mood-modifying drugs (New York Narcotic Addiction Control Commission, 1971); they report the highest incidence of psychogenic symptoms, such as nervousness, nightmares, dizziness, headaches, and related symptoms (Lief, 1975).

RET specializes particularly in helping women (and men) with marital and relationship problems (Ellis, 1957, 1977, 1979, 1982; Ellis & Harper, 1961, 1975)—in showing people their irrational beliefs about relating and how to dispute these beliefs. Typical irrational beliefs of the woman in marital conflict are: "If the relationship ends, *I'm* to blame." "I wasn't beautiful enough, interesting enough." "I was too smart, too dumb, too demanding, inadequate, crazy, not sexy enough, too sexually demanding." The woman with marital problems damns herself if she does, and damns herself if she doesn't, governed by the societal rule that the woman is responsible for the success or failure of the relationship. It takes a good deal of rational restructuring to help her see that there are two people involved.

Therapist Caveats for Couples' Counseling

1. Check out your own beliefs about women's roles:
   —Do you believe that a woman should stay home and take care of the children?

—Do you believe that working couples should equally divide the housework and other related tasks?
—In helping couples brainstorm options, would you bring up the possibility of the male becoming the homemaker while the wife went back to school or advanced her career?

2. Caveats for therapists
   —Do you tend to see the more overtly upset partner (usually the woman—since it's O.K. for women to cry) as more disturbed than the calmer, quieter, and emotionally constipated partner? Do you view emotional excess as a higher-order disturbance than emotional constipation?
   —Are you colluding with the husband, either because you are more sympathetic to his views (e.g., that wives should do most of the housework) or because you may yourself have a nagging wife at home?
   —Are you using extra energy to engage the male partner in an alliance—perhaps because you sense his reluctance to come in—or because you accept the male partner as the person who holds the power in the relationship, and the power to keep the couple in therapy?
   —Are you collaborating with the husband to cure the wife's passivity, neurosis, lack of assertiveness, and overdependence?
   —Are you overemphasizing the woman's and overlooking the male's anger? It is common for male therapists to be reactive to female "bitchiness" in that they see the active female as angry and the active male as appropriately reacting to his wife's anger (Haan & Livson, 1973).
3. Caveats for feminist therapists
   —Are you colluding too much with the wife, perhaps sensing her passivity and wanting to help support her, and thereby reinforcing her passivity and dependency?
   —Do you get angry with males and lose touch with your ability to be a sensitive reflector of what's happening when men become evasive and deny feelings?
4. Having some facts at your fingertips may often aid in consciousness raising and developing new options. A couple may be informed, for example, that men usually do one-third as many household tasks as their wives do, whether or not the wives work (Baruch & Barnett, 1983), and that employed wives do nearly as much daily work around the house as homemakers do,

while only 23% of the employed married men report a similar activity (Radloff, 1975).

Few areas are more poignant than the situation of a battered wife. Contemplating leaving her alcoholic husband after her fourth beating, one client (who was actually the larger breadwinner) said, "If he treats me this way, I must be a terrible person. The kids need him, and so do I." This woman is a particularly sad example of the lack of self-confidence and of problem-solving and goal-setting skills common in women who have resigned themselves to living out their marriages. Such a woman's thinking may be directly derivative of the confining stereotypes reinforced by our culture. She may be totally unable to imagine herself in another role (Martin, 1976). With her husband, she is battered and bruised, but at least coupled; without him, she sees herself as nothing.

The lot of the divorced or widowed woman is similarly grim. The woman contemplating divorce may suffer from an accumulation of disadvantages that severely limit the options she has for the rest of her life. Her earning capacity is usually much lower than her husband's. She has not had the same educational or vocational opportunities, and her career, if she has one, has generally been secondary and interrupted by family needs.

One of the biggest problems facing newly single women is that of raising children alone. The 1970 United States Census reports that more than 85% of single parents are women (Block, 1979). Single mothers face loneliness, insufficient funds, as well as the problems of developing new relationships, dependency, autonomy, and legal issues.

The job of the rational-emotive therapist is a monumental one: (1) How to counter self-blame in a society that teaches us that it is the woman who is primarily responsible for the success of her marriage and her children's mental health. (2) How to build self-acceptance when everything that she tends to equate with worthwhileness—being married, having a happy home, being vocationally successful—is no longer there. (3) How to help her with the myriad tasks of supporting herself and reconstructing her life, when she has been fed messages of helplessness from early childhood onward.

Motherhood

To many women, regardless of their other interests, relationships, and accomplishments, mothering is the function that is central to their perceptions of themselves (Oliver, 1977). Yet in the process of undertaking this enormously difficult task of growing a child, they are frequently pinned between two difficult alternatives. If they have the economic means not to work outside the home, they risk entering the ranks of the group with one of the highest rates of depression: women with young children who are full-time homemakers. However, the option of being a full-time homemaker and mother is a "privilege" available to fewer and fewer women. Today, 37% of women with children under five work, as compared with only 13% in 1948. Many working women must deal with prejudices from society and themselves: for example, that they are damaging their children permanently by working and that if they decide to work, they must be superwomen—hold down a job, attend to the physical and emotional needs of their children, and do all of these things perfectly—to the point of physical and psychological exhaustion (Zachary, 1980).

The option of remaining childless is also fraught with difficulties. There is still a stigma attached to the woman without children; she tends to be labeled deviant, infantile, or unwilling to accept the "feminine role."

Caveats in Working with Mothering Issues

1. In helping a woman dispute the irrational belief that she is a failure or a rotten person if she imperfectly mothers, works at a job, or housecleans, a therapist should have some additional facts handy to counter societal myths. For example: studies show that whether or not a mother is employed does not appear to be a determining factor in causing juvenile delinquency: it is the quality of a mother's care rather than the time consumed in such care which is of major significance (Block, 1979).

2. Assign some women's liberation readings (e.g., chapters on marriage and motherhood) from the anthologies *Woman in Sexist Society* (Gornick & Moran, 1972) or *Sisterhood Is Powerful* (Morgan, 1970).

3. Place the client in a woman's therapy and/or support group, to help her see that she is not alone with her problems and for practical help in dealing with mothering problems.

Sexual Dysfunctions

Approximately 10% of American women never experience orgasm, and well over half of sexually active women do not regularly reach orgasm in their coital experiences (Kinsey, Pomeroy, Martin, & Gebhard,

1953; Hunt, 1974; Hite, 1976). Numerous women have problems of arousal and of low sexual interest.

It is widely agreed that feelings and beliefs are the cause of many sexual dysfunctions (Barbach, 1980; Lieblum, 1980). A good number of these beliefs are derivative of sex-role *shoulds*. Women grow up with highly conflicting messages about their sexuality. They are indoctrinated in a romantic philosophy which dictates that they save themselves for their one true love; yet at the same time, they are encouraged to dress, walk, and talk seductively. Romanticism leads to an emphasis on beauty, as women's bodies become products to be improved for greatest marketability. Sexuality then becomes equated with beauty and ability to lure, rather than with pleasure and consummation. The result is that many women feel "like a woman" only when a man is around. The inability of some women to see themselves as having sexual feelings and desires other than those that have been male initiated makes it difficult for them to become initiators of or even active participants in sex.

Both sexes are victims of sexual ignorance; but in our culture, it is the female who has been forbidden to accept herself as a sexual being. Too often, both arousal and nonarousal are viewed as "bad" or "wrong" and encourage anxiety. In heterosexual relations, sex is frequently over before women even become aroused. By focusing on their appearance, comparing themselves to younger women, and worrying about pleasing their men, women lock themselves into a cycle of frustration that further exacerbates their inability to become aroused and to enjoy sex.

Consciousness-Raising Exercise: "Nasty Names"

This exercise is used both with women clients and mixed sexuality groups in order to illustrate sexual attitudes toward women.

Clients are asked to call out all the names they can think of for sexually active women (*slut, whore, tramp*); for sexually selective women (*frigid, uptight, women's libber*); and for sexually active men (*swinger, don juan, playboy*). Finally, clients are asked to brainstorm the nastiest names that men can be called (*pussywhipped, henpecked, bastards, sons-of-bitches, faggots*, etc.). The exercise demonstrates dramatically how women are globally labelled for their sexual behavior; how they are damned if they do, and damned if they don't; how a double standard exists for sexually active females and males; and how misogynism is so pervasive that the worst thing a man can be called is something that derogates him by associating him with a woman. Women tend to make themselves anxious over these words and behave in such a way as to avoid these "awful" labels. If not uncovered, these attitudes remain as schemata through which women perceive themselves and are perceived, and which interfere with pleasurable sex.

A highly effective modality for treating women with sexual dysfunctions has been found to be all-women's groups (Barbach, 1980; Kuriansky, Sharpe, & O'Connor, 1976; Walen & Wolfe, 1983). In RET women's sexuality groups, the teaching of a general disturbance-combatting cognitive self-help approach often leads to a fairly rapid elimination of the target problem (90%–100% orgasm after only six two-hour sessions) and for the generalization to other areas of the women's lives (Walen & Wolfe, 1983). In addition to sexual reeducation and behavioral assignments, other cognitive foci in RET women's sexuality groups (and individual therapy) include unveiling and debunking erroneous sexual myths and sex-role programming that interfere with autonomy and self-determination in sexual and nonsexual areas (Walen & Wolfe, 1983).

Cultural Message	*Personal Irrational Belief*
Only Freud and men know how a woman's body works.	I should be able to orgasm through intercourse, and I'm a sexual failure if I can't.
Sexy = beautiful and young.	I must have a trim and firm body to enjoy sex. It would be awful if he sees my cellulite. Menopause and hysterectomy end my ability for sexual enjoyment.
If you're in love, sex should automatically be terrific.	If he loves me, he should know what turns me on without my having to tell him. If I love him, I should want to have sex as much as he, enjoy swallowing his semen, etc.
Women are responsible for making relationships work.	If he's having trouble getting erections, I'm to blame. I must not hurt his feelings, make him feel emasculated. Sex is my obligation if I'm married.
It's wrong and selfish to put my interests first, or be sexually assertive.	I shouldn't take too long to come. It's selfish or unfeminine to ask for 20 minutes of clitoral stimulation; he must never feel uncomfortable or inconvenienced.
Liberated women should be sexually active and sexually assertive.	I should not say no to sex on the first date. I should initiate sex more, enjoy just about anything, and if I don't, I'm a prude. I should be having multiple orgasms.

Bibliotherapy includes the following recommended readings: *Intelligent Woman's Guide to Dating and Mating* (Ellis, 1979); *The Great Orgasm Robbery* (Tepper, 1977); *Our Bodies, Ourselves* (Boston Women's Health Collective, 1976); *The Hite Report on Female Sexuality* (Hite, 1976); and *How to Be Sexually Assertive* (Wolfe, 1976).

Sexual Abuse: Harrassment, Incest, and Rape

Given that one out of every three females now alive in the United States will be raped at least once in her lifetime, and that one out of every four girls in the U.S. will be sexually abused in some way before she reaches the age of 18 (Weber, 1980), the topic of sexual assault is one of great urgency for anyone working with women or children.

The effects of sexual victimization may not become apparent until months or years after the event. At times the event itself may be suppressed (common in incest). In other cases, there may be anger at the abuser or the judicial system, as well as guilt, shame, and sexual inhibition or dysfunction (Zachary, 1980). Because of the tremendous shame and secrecy surrounding the topic, professionals often fail to do the flushing-out required to open the topic with clients who do not present it as a complaint.

Better understanding of the cultural processes involved in sexual abuse may be achieved by viewing sexual assault as the extreme enactment of "male" and "female" roles as they are learned in this culture (Colao, 1983; O'Hare & Taylor, 1983). For example, a rape victim is likely to focus on exaggerated perceptions of her inadequacy, powerlessness, and incompetence, and on thoughts such as "Being raped was my own fault," or "I am worthless now that I've been raped."

Professionals, as members of this society, may have internalized some of these myths and unconsciously perpetuate them in their work with clients. Some of these myths, or irrational beliefs, include the following:

Incest

- It is usually a child's fantasy.
- It happens only among social outcasts or the psychiatrically disturbed.
- A bad mommy is responsible for the abuse.
- It may be O.K. because the child is at least getting sexual education at home and receiving affection.

Rape

- Women provoke or incite attack (e.g., "I'm to blame for being in the wrong place or for wearing sexy clothes").
- Women never get raped by men they know.
- Women invent stories of rape to get men in trouble.
- Women secretly desire rape—they only say "no" because they're playing hard-to-get.
- "I'm devalued, soiled; it would be awful if people knew I was raped; I can't stand facing them."
- "I'll never be able to enjoy sex again."

RET is particularly well-suited to the treatment of sexually abused clients. It shows them how to unconditionally accept themselves, no matter what has transpired. It provides a coping method that they can use to control their feelings and actions, and that can have a powerful therapeutic effect.

Therapist Caveats for Dealing with Victims of Sexual Abuse

- In helping to dispute the client's anger cognitions, don't move in too quickly before empathizing with her upset feelings. If you do, the client may continue to self-blame, or leave the therapist!
- Don't reinforce (inadvertently) the idea that the abused woman did something to provoke the abuse.
- Be aware of self-help groups in your community for incest and rape victims, as well as the address of any organizations dealing with sexual harrassment on the job.

Work

We live in a time when 52% of the women in this country work outside the home, when one out of six families is being maintained by women, and when the bulk of young families depend on two workers to survive. In order to deal with women's feelings as they try to cope with new and often unfamiliar roles, let us look at society's attitudes toward working women, and at the consequences of these attitudes on women's occupational patterns.

This is the age of the woman worker. But what do women find? They find that the gap in income between men's and women's wages has actually increased in the last generation, and that women still earn 60¢ to every dollar that men earn (Reskin, 1984). They find that sex stereotyping in jobs is rampant, and that women still work in a few familiar categories of jobs (clericals, service workers, and private household workers), while men work in dozens. In 1958, 53% of all women worked in these three female-dominated categories. By 1975, 58% of all women worked in these same categories. In 1958, 30% of all women worked as clerks and secretaries. By 1975, this had increased by five percentage points (Norton, 1981).

Societal prejudices against the working woman abound. Competence in women is seen as a deviation from the social norms of the feminine stereotype. If women try to succeed or exercise power, everyone, including they themselves, undervalues their accomplishments. The career-oriented male is considered a "go-getter," "assertive," "on the ball." His female counterpart is called "pushy," a "ball-breaker," or a "dyke," and is frequently ignored or penalized for her assertive behavior. In the traditional hierarchical structure of most workplaces, women, in the low ranks, rarely are given the right or the power to question, criticize, or make suggestions to men who have authority over them.

The reality of a 40% divorce rate, the fear of looking for security in marriage and ending up alone and desperate, has made many young women today, married and unmarried, seek security in careers. In so doing, they are expected to meet standards of performance in the workplace set in the past by and for men who had wives to take care of the details of living and, at the same time, were expected to perform as well at home and with children as women who are fulltime homemakers and mothers. Their struggle to do so is exacerbated by a dearth of good dual-career role models, by magazine articles on superwomen who marvelously balance home, career, mothering, and social activities; by low sense of competence; by fears of both failure and success (Horner, 1969) and by a tendency to go for a series of jobs rather than a planned career.

Typical Self-Messages Leading to Low Career Aspirations

- If I'm good, someone will come along and take care of me.
- I must not be too smart or assertive, lest I be seen as a castrating female.
- I must not speak too affirmatively of my abilities, lest I be thought "unfeminine," "bragging."
- It's O.K. to make commitments to other people, but not to myself.

Self-Messages Leading to Lack of Assertiveness and Minimal Efforts at Career Advancement

- There's no use in approaching my boss. Why bother—he's hopelessly sexist (depression, anger).

- Things are unfair; they shouldn't be. I can't stand it (low frustration tolerance).
- It's too late to change jobs, to get what I want, to be retrained (depression, low frustration tolerance).

Negative Self-Messages of Dual-Career and Re-Entry Women

- I must be young and beautiful (or more skilled) to get this job; and it's awful if I can't get it.
- I must be approved of by others (who criticize me for neglecting my kids), and if not, I'm a failure, a bad person.
- I shouldn't have to be starting at entry-level; I should be beyond this stage already (low frustration tolerance).

Negative Self-Statements

- I slipped into this job by a fluke. Any day they'll find out what an incompetent phony I am (self-downing, catastrophizing).
- Even though I work 10 hours a day without even stopping for meals, I feel inadequate—I should be doing more (perfectionism, self-downing).

Suggestions for Dealing with Work Issues in Therapy

1. Encourage women to:
   (a) Look for good role models; possibly join a professional organization.
   (b) Concentrate on the excitement (and not just the difficulties) of "pioneering."
   (c) Develop a support network.
2. Advise dual-career women to:
   (a) Adopt different standards (e.g., less neat house and kids, less time with mate).
   (b) See that their kids may not be ruined, but rather that their mother's being at work is a valuable educational experience and helpful in learning independence.

3. Have available a list of resources for helping women combat some of the inequities in the work-world: for example, Title VII of the Equal Employment Act of 1972, names of agencies dealing with sex discrimination, lists of nonstereotypic educational and vocational options, and lists of professional women's organizations.

4. Be alert to the reduced expectations women have of themselves, and brainstorm options other than their stated goal of getting a $15 a week raise on their secretarial job (e.g., ask if they have thought of applying for managerial-level positions).

5. Do lots of assertiveness training to help change habits (e.g., failing to respond effectively to put-downs or sexual innuendos; and competitiveness). It is not uncommon for a $50,000-a-year executive to break down in tears when her boss criticizes something she has done, or to act cute and seductive when her plan is rejected, or to sulk because she has been given a poor assignment. It is crucial that women learn how to ask for and get things without being manipulative or indirect.

6. Encourage covert and overt confidence building. Have clients log self-put-downs and replace them with comments like "I did that really well," "I handled that criticism much better than I did last time." To boost confidence and help increase their self-marketing skills, ask clients to write a letter of recommendation about themselves.

7. Encourage women to develop skills they may have told themselves they "can't understand" (e.g., suggest they take a financial management course).

Case Study

Nancy was a 28-year-old nurse whose presenting problems were depression, low self-acceptance, and difficulties in her relationship with a married doctor. Therapy focused on helping her change her emotional overreactions, as well as on ways to deal with a social system that made her daily work difficult and gave her limited opportunities for career advancement. Her problems at work included dealing with other nurses who were in fierce competition for the male doctors and coping with sexist behavior of doctors. (During open heart surgery, a surgeon had kept backing up against her.)

Problems	*RET Work*	*Adjunctive Therapy and Resources* • *Consciousness Raising/Education*
1. Anger and hurt at lover's inconsiderate behavior	Anti-awfulizing about his behavior	Read articles on women in the workplace. Go to N.O.W. (National Organization for Women) meeting. Record instances of sexism at work.
2. Anger and hurt at nurses' backbiting	Anti-awfulizing about their behavior	Contact Sexual Harrassment organization for information on filing complaints.

Problems	*RET Work*	• *Skill Building*
3. Poor assertiveness skills with boyfriend and people at work	Dispute idea that "I cannot effectively respond" and "I am a weak, wimpy person."	Take assertiveness training workshop. Read article on assertiveness for nurses (Herman, 1977). Practice assertiveness with friends. Do life-planning projection up to age 90.
4. Low self-acceptance, helplessness, hopelessness, anger at herself for her financial dependence on lover.	Dispute ideas that "I must be a worthless person if people treat me so badly." "There is nothing I can do about my situation." "I'm a bad person for having gotten myself into this situation." Give self 3 positive self-messages each day.	• *Social Support* Look for new friends not preoccupied with men. Observe and talk to good female role models. • *Economic Support* Investigate loan opportunities to replace financial dependence on lover. Consider part-time job. Consider possibility of training to become a nurse-anaesthesiologist.

Conclusion

American Psychological Association Task Forces (1975, 1978) have urged that psychologists promote concepts of equality as part of their practice, and concluded that psychologists have a responsibility to examine their personal roles in perpetuating the sex-bias and sex-role stereotyping that can be so destructive to the mental health of their women clients. RET, done within the framework of examining women's social context and the *should*s about social roles, offers a practical tool for helping women make broad cognitive and behavioral changes and develop their potential as full human beings.

References

Agras, S., Sylvester, D., & Oliveau, D. (1969). The epidemiology of common fears and phobias. *Comprehensive Psychiatry, 10,* 151–156.

American Psychological Association Task Force (1975). Report of the Task Force on Sex Bias and Sex Role Stereotyping in Psychotherapeutic Practice. *American Psychologist, 30,* 1169–1175.

American Psychological Association Task Force (1978). Report of the Task Force on Sex Bias and Sex Role Stereotyping in Psychotherapeutic Practice: Guidelines for therapy with women. *American Psychologist, 33,* 1122–1133.

Barbach, L. G. (1980). *Women discover orgasm: A therapist's guide to a new treatment approach.* New York: Free Press/Macmillan.

Barrett, C. J., Berg, P. I., Eaton, E. M., & Pomeroy, E. L. (1974). Implications of women's liberation and the future of psychotherapy. *Psychotherapy: Theory, Research and Practice, 11*(1).

Baruch, G., & Barnett, R. (1983). *Correlates of fathers' participation in family work: A technical report.* Wellesley, MA: Wellesley College Center for Research on Women.

Bem, S. L., & Lenney, E. (1976). Sex-typing and the avoidance of cross-sex behavior. *Journal of Personality and Social Psychology, 33,* 48–54.

Bernard, J. (1972). *The future of marriage.* New York: World.

Berzins, J. I. (1975, June). *Sex roles and psychotherapy: new directions for theory and research.* Paper presented at the 6th Annual Meeting, Society for Psychotherapy Research, Boston, MA.

Block, J. (1973). Conceptions of sex role: Some cross-cultural and longitudinal perspectives. *American Psychologist, 28*(6), 512–526.

Block, J. (1979, March). *The changing American parent: Implications for child development.* Paper presented at meeting of the Society for Research in Child Development, San Francisco, CA.

Boskind-White, M., & White W. (1983). *Bulimarexia: The binge/purge cycle.* New York: Norton.

Boston Women's Health Collective (1976). *Our bodies, ourselves.* New York: Simon & Schuster.

Brehony, K. (1983). Women and agoraphobia: A case for the etiological significance of the feminine sex-role stereotype. *In V. Franks & E. Rothblum (Eds.), Sex role stereotypes and women's mental health* (pp. 112–128). New York: Springer.

Brodsky, A. M., & Hare-Mustin, R. T. (Eds.) (1980a). *Women and psychotherapy: An assessment of research and practice.* New York: Guilford Press.

Brodsky, A. M., & Hare-Mustin, R. T. (1980b). Psychotherapy and women: Priorities for research. In A. Brodsky & R. Hare-Mustin (Eds.), *Women and psychotherapy: An assessment of research and practice* (pp. 385–409). New York: Guilford Press.

Broverman, C., Broverman, D., Clarkson, F., Rosenkrantz, P., & Vogel, S. (1970). Sex role stereotypes and clinical judgments of mental health. *Journal of Consulting and Clinical Psychology, 34,* 1–7.

Chesler, P. (1972). *Women and madness.* Garden City, NY: Doubleday.

Colao, F. (1983). Therapists coping with sexual assault. In J. Robbins & R. Siegel (Eds.), *Women changing therapy* (pp. 205–214). New York: Haworth Press.

Ellis, A. (1957). *How to live with a "neurotic."* New York: Crown. (Rev. ed., 1975.) North Hollywood, CA: Wilshire Books.

Ellis, A. (1962). *Reason and emotion in psychotherapy.* Secaucus, NJ: Citadel Press.

Ellis, A. (1973). *Humanistic psychotherapy: The rational-emotive approach.* New York: McGraw-Hill.

Ellis, A. (1974). Treatment of sex and love problems in women. In V. Franks & V. Burtle (Eds.), *Women in therapy* (pp. 284–306). New York: Brunner/Mazel.

Ellis, A. (1977). *How to live with—and without—anger.* Secaucus, NJ: Citadel Press.

Ellis, A. (1979). *The intelligent woman's guide to dating and mating.* New York: Lyle Stuart.

Ellis, A. (1982). Rational-emotive family therapy. In A. M. Horne & M. H. Ohlsen (Eds.), *Family counseling and therapy* (pp. 381–412). Itasca, IL: Peacock.

Ellis, A., & Becker, I. (1982). *A guide to personal happiness.* North Hollywood, CA: Wilshire Books.

Ellis, A., & Harper, R. A. (1961). *A guide to successful marriage.* North Hollywood, CA: Wilshire Books.

Ellis, A., & Harper, R. A. (1975). *A guide to rational living.* North Hollywood, CA: Wilshire Books.

Fodor, I. (1974). The phobic syndrome in women: Implications for treatment. In V. Franks & V. Burtle (Eds.), *Women in therapy* (pp. 132–168). New York: Brunner/Mazel.

Fodor, I. (1982). Toward an understanding of male/female differences in phobic anxiety disorders. In I. Al-Issa (Ed.) *Gender and psychopathology* (pp. 179–195). New York: Academic Press.

Fodor, I. (1983) Behavior therapy for the overweight woman. In M. Rosenbaum & C. Franks (Eds.), *Perspectives on behavior therapy in the eighties* (pp. 378–394). New York: Springer.

Franks, V. (1979). Gender and psychotherapy. In E. Gomberg & V. Franks (Eds.), *Gender and disordered behavior: Sex differences in psychopathology.* New York: Brunner/Mazel.

Franks, V. (1982, April). *Psychotherapy and women:* Letter No. 79. Belle Mead, NJ: Carrier Foundation.

Glaser, K. (1976). Women's self-help groups as an alternative to therapy. *Psychotherapy: Theory, Research and Practice. 13,* 77–81.

Goldstein, A. J., & Chambless, D. L. (1980). The treatment of agoraphobia. In A. J. Goldstein & E. G. Foa (Eds.), *Handbook of behavioral interventions* (pp. 322–415). New York: Wiley.

Gornick, V. & Moran, B. (1971). *Woman in sexist society.* New York: Basic Books.

Gornick, V. & Moran, B. (Eds.) (1972). *Woman in sexist society.* New York: Signet.

Grieger, I. Z. (1982). The cognitive basis of women's problems. In R. Grieger & I. Z. Grieger (Eds.), *Cognition and emotional disturbance* (pp. 197–211). New York: Human Sciences Press.

Guttentag, M. & Salasin, S. (1976). Women, men and mental health. In Cates, Scott & Martyna (Eds.), *Women and men: Changing roles and perceptions* (pp. 33–49). Aspen, CO: Aspen Institute for Humanistic Studies.

Haan, N., & Livson, N. (1973). Sex differences in the eyes of expert personality assessors: Blind spots? *Journal of Personality Assessment, 37,* 486–492.

Hare-Mustin, R. (1983). An appraisal of the relationship between women and psychotherapy: 80 years after the case of Dora. *American Psychologist, 38,* 593–602.

Heriot, J. (1983). The double bind: healing the split. In J. Robbins & R. Siegel (Eds.), *Women changing therapy* (pp. 11–28). New York: Haworth Press.

Herman, S. (1977). Assertiveness: One answer to job dissatisfaction for nurses. In R. Alberti (Ed.), *Assertiveness: Innovations, applications, issues.* San Luis Obispo, CA: Impact.

Hite, S. (1976). *The Hite report.* New York: Macmillan.

Horner, M. (1969). Women's motive to avoid success. *Psychology Today, 62,* 36–38.

Hunt, M. (1974). *Sexual behavior in the 1970's.* Chicago, IL: Playboy Press.

Jasin, S. (1983). Cognitive-behavioral treatment of agoraphobia in groups. In A. Freeman (Ed.), *Cognitive therapy in couples and groups* (pp. 199–220). New York: Plenum Press.

Kelly, J. A., Kern, J. M., Kirkley, B. G., Patterson, J. N., & Keane, F. M. (1980). Reactions to assertive versus nonassertive behavior: Differential effects for males and females, and implications for assertive training. *Behavior Therapy, 11,* 670–682.

Kinsey, A. C. Pomeroy, W. B., Martin, C. E., & Gebhard, P. H. (1953). *Sexual behavior in the human female.* New York: Simon & Schuster, Pocket Books.

Krumboltz, H. B. & Shapiro, J. (1979). Counseling women in behavioral self-direction. *Personnel & Guidance Journal, 4,* 415–418.

Kuriansky, J., Sharpe, L., & O'Connor, D. (1976, October). *Group treatment for women: The quest for orgasm.* Paper presented at the American Public Health Association of Washington, DC.

Levine, S. V., Camin, L. E., & Levine, E. L. (1974). Sexism and psychiatry. *American Journal of Orthopsychiatry, 44,* 327–336.
Lieblum, S. (Speaker). (1980). *Sexual problems of women.* Cassette recording. New York: SMA Audio Cassettes.
Lief, H. (1975). Sexual counseling. In S. Romney, *The health care of women* (pp. 171–193). New York: McGraw-Hill.
Loeffler, D. & Fiedler, L. (1979) Woman—a sense of identity: A counseling intervention to facilitate personal growth in women. *Journal of Counseling Psychology, 26*(1), 51–57.
Martin, D. (1976). *Battered wives.* San Francisco: Glide.
Metropolitan Life Insurance Company. (1980). Mortality differentials favor women. *Statistical Bulletin, 61,* 2–3.
Morgan, R. (1970). *Sisterhood is powerful.* New York: Vintage.
Moulton, R. (1977). Some effects of the new feminism. *American Journal of Psychiatry, 134*(1), 3.
New York Narcotic Addiction Control Commission (1971). Differential drug use within New York State labor force: *An assessment of drug use within the general population.* Albany, NY: New York Narcotic Addiction Control Commission.
Norton, E. (1981). Remarks at First Annual Women in Crisis Conference. In P. Russianoff (Ed.), *Women in crisis* (pp. 24–31). New York: Human Sciences.
O'Hare, J. & Taylor, K. (1983). The reality of incest. In J. Robbins & R. Siegel (Eds.), *Women changing therapy* (pp. 215–230). New York: Haworth Press.
Oliver, R. (1977). The 'empty nest syndrome' as a focus of depression: A cognitive treatment model, based on Rational-Emotive Therapy. *Psychotherapy: Theory, Research and Practice, 14*(1), 87–94.
Orbach, S. (1978). *Fat is a feminist issue.* New York: Paddington Press.
Radloff, L. (1975). Sex differences in depression: the effects of occupation and marital status. *Sex Roles, 1,* 249–265.
Reskin, B. (1984). Sex segregation in the work place. In *Gender at work: Perspectives on occupational segregation in comparable worth.* Washington, DC: Women's Research and Education Institute of the Congressional Caucus for Women's Issues.
Rice, J. K., & Rice, D. (1973). Implications of the women's liberation movement for psychotherapy. *American Journal of Psychiatry, 130,* 191–196.
Robbins, J. H., & Siegel, R. J., (Eds.) (1983). *Women changing therapy: New assessments, values and strategies in feminist therapy.* New York: Haworth Press.
Rothblum, E. (1983). Sex role stereotypes and depression in women. In V. Franks & E. Rothblum (Eds.), *Sex role stereotypes and women's mental health* (pp. 83–111). New York: Springer.
Russianoff, P. (1982). *Why do I think I'm nothing without a man?* New York: Bantam.
Seligman, M. (1975). *Helplessness.* San Francisco, CA: W. H. Freeman.
Seligman, M. (1979). Conference on learned helplessness. Charlottesville, Virginia.
Spence, J., Helmreich, R., & Stapp, J. (1975). Ratings of self and peers on sex-role attributes and their relation to self-esteem and conceptions of masculinity and femininity. *Journal of Personality and Social Psychology, 32,* 29–39.
Stein, L., DelGaudio, A., & Ansley, M. (1976). A comparison of male and female neurotic depressives. *Journal of Clinical Psychology, 32,* 19–21.
Stuart, R. B. (1979). Sex differences in obesity. In E. Bomberg & V. Franks (Eds.), *Gender and disordered behavior: Sex differences in psychopathology.* New York: Brunner/Mazel.
Tepper, S. (1977). *The Great orgasm robbery.* Denver, CO: RMPP Publications.
Walen, S. & Wolfe, J. (1983). Sexual enhancement groups for women. In A. Freeman (Ed.), *Cognitive therapy with couples and groups* (pp. 221–260). New York: Plenum Press.

Weber, E. (1980). Sexual abuse begins at home. *Ms Magazine.*
Weissman, M. M., & Klerman, G. L. (1977). Sex differences and the epidemiology of depression. *Archives of General Psychiatry, 34,* 98–111.
Weisstein, N. (1971). Psychology constructs the female, or the fantasy life of the male psychologist. In M. Garskof (Ed.), *Roles women play: Readings toward women's liberation.* Belmont, CA: Brooks-Cole.
Wolfe, J. (1975, September). Rational-emotive therapy as an effective feminist therapy. Paper presented at the American Psychological Association Convention, Chicago.
Wolfe, J. (1976). *How to be sexually assertive.* New York: Institute for Rational-Emotive Therapy.
Wolfe, J. (1980a, June). *Helping women change.* Paper presented at the 25th Anniversary Rational-Emotive Therapy Conference, New York.
Wolfe, J. (1980b, September). *Rational-emotive therapy women's groups: New model for an effective feminist therapy.* Paper presented at the American Psychological Association Annual Convention, Montreal, Canada.
Wooley, S., & Wooley, O. (1980). Eating disorders: Obesity and anorexia. In A. Brodsky & R. Hare-Mustin (Eds.), *Women and psychotherapy: An assessment of research and practice* (pp. 135–158). New York: Guilford Press.
Worrell, J. (1980). New directions in counseling women. *Personnel and Guidance Journal, 58,* 477–484.
Wyckoff, H. (1977). *Solving women's problems.* New York: Grove Press.
Zachary, I. (1980). RET with women. Some special issues. In R. Grieger & J. Boyd (Eds.), *Rational-emotive therapy: A skills based approach* (pp. 249–264). New York: Van Nostrand.

6

Rational Sexuality

Some New Perspectives

SUSAN R. WALEN

THE GOOD NEWS

In thinking about what is *new* in the field of sex therapy it seems to me that there are at least five major shifts in focus over recent years. First, there has been a reemergence of interest and research in biologic factors in sexuality along with an increased recognition of biological causes of sexual dysfunctions (e.g., Brody, 1982). In the 1960s and 70s, in the flurry of psychological enthusiasm that greeted the work of behavioral strategists such as Annon (1973) Wolpe (1969), and Masters and Johnson (1970), there was a rather glib assumption in the field that practically all sexual problems were psychological in origin, mostly rooted in anxiety. While anxiety and depression may certainly precede, accompany or be sequelae to sexual difficulties, more contemporary estimates suggest that about 40% of these problems have a biological etiology (Spark, White, & Connolly, 1980; Nolen, 1981).

In concert with the renewed emphasis on physiological factors has come a renewed stress on scientific validity, and the need for empirical verification of accepted dogma. An illustration of an increasing "hard-headedness" on the part of sexologists has been the reevaluation of the seminal work of Masters and Johnson. Although initially viewed as unquestionable and unimpeachable, their research and writings have

SUSAN R. WALEN • Baltimore Center for Cognitive Therapy, Baltimore, Maryland 21209. Department of Psychology, Towson State University, Towson, Maryland 21204.

more recently come under increasing scrutiny and critical reappraisal (e.g., Zilbergeld & Evans, 1980). In the field of human sexuality, perhaps more than in some others, myths and misconceptions seem to perennially surface and flourish. A recent example might be the dubious G-spot, said to be the site of a deep (and presumably better) vaginal orgasm and associated with female ejaculation (Kahn-Ladas, Whipple, & Perry, 1982). Rather swiftly and despite immense public popularity, this anatomic/physiologic concept has been debunked (Hoch, 1983). Science is truly beginning to blossom in sexology.

Another trend in the field seems to have been an increasing recognition of the impact of social-sexual roles. The women's liberation movement and the growth of men's consciousness raising has greatly expanded the boundaries of accepted sexual behaviors and life styles for both sexes. We have seen increasing study not only of the differences between the sexes, but of the similarities as well. Perhaps most importantly, women's sexuality, long neglected because of prejudice, mystery, and lack of appropriate measuring instrumentation, has come into the laboratory for study. For example, until very recently a review of the medical literature on the sexual impact of certain disease states (e.g., diabetes) or certain drugs (e.g., hypertensive medications) revealed data only on males. Although this deficit thankfully is being reversed, much remains to be done.

Yet another trend in the literature on sexuality has been a return to acknowledging the central role of love and relationship issues in sexual functioning. Sager (1976) points out that the vast majority of couples, whether the presenting complaint is marital or sexual, suffer both. For a time, however, it seemed as if researchers in the area were compartmentalizing issues so completely that they not only treated along one dimension, but assessed only one dimension. Changes are appearing, however; recent studies investigate the impact of sex therapy on marital functioning (e.g., Foster, 1978) as well as marital therapy on sexual satisfaction (e.g., O'Leary & Arias, 1983).

Finally, I see a shift in the field of sex therapy toward acknowledging the important role of cognitive factors and the value of an active-directive approach to treatment. The early treatment of sexual problems was done by psychoanalysts or client-centered therapists who dealt in the world of cognitions, but without sufficient clarity or directness and without a here-and-now focus. The more recent therapeutic vogue was behavioral, a model which was often mechanical and devoid of attention to the cognitive-affective world of the patient. RET therapists, on the other hand, combine the methodologies of various schools of therapy and use them within a systematic cognitive theory. "As a general system of psychotherapy, RET envisions most serious sex problems within a framework of prevailing emotional upsetness and it strives for reduced *general* disturbability along with minimizing of specific *sexual* malfunctioning" (Ellis, 1975, p. 11).

Rational-Emotive Theory and Sexuality

Sex therapists have shared a number of "bon mots" that will be immediately appreciated by an RET therapist. For example:

- Sex is perfectly natural, but rarely naturally perfect.
- Our greatest sex organ is not between our legs, but between our ears.

The common ingredient in these witticisms is that which acknowledges the primary role of cognitions in sexuality and sexual functioning. Cognitions can serve to augment or inhibit a sexual response cycle; in the latter case, the negative effect can be an incredibly powerful one that no amount of candlelight, romantic music, or satin sheets can contravene.

Recently I outlined a cognitive-behavioral feedback model of sexual arousal which details the important role of perceptual and evaluative cognitions (Walen, 1980; Wolfe & Walen, 1980). Let me briefly review this model, seen in Figure 1.

Perception, one major class of cognitive factors in arousal, can be viewed as a combination of three subprocesses: (a) *detection:* noting the presence of a stimulus or discriminating it from other stimuli; (b) *labeling:* applying descriptors to classify or categorize a stimulus; (c) *attribution:* finding an explanation for a stimulus event. For example, as I glance at an attractive man at a cocktail party, I become aware of a peculiar sensation in my chest (detection). I say to my companion, "My heart just

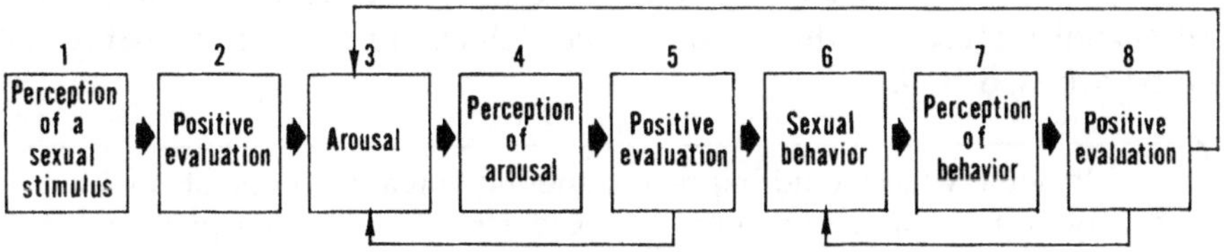

FIGURE 1. Proposed feedback loop of a positive sexual experience.

skipped a beat" (labeling). I think to myself, "could this be what true love feels like" (attribution). Why choose "true love" rather than "indigestion" as the attribution? Probably a number of factors contribute to this selection, including present situational cues, current motivational factors, and past learning experiences. Perception is a process of gathering data and drawing conclusions from that data. In the sexual arena, an inability to detect sexual stimuli, incorrect labeling of them, or misattribution of them may significantly impair sexual performance.

Evaluation, the other major class of cognitive events, is of primary focus in RET, and involves a rating process along a good-bad continuum. Obviously, evaluating a sexual stimulus as positive may enhance sexual feelings, just as a negative evaluation may diminish them. When evaluations become exaggeratedly negative—what Ellis (1977) refers to as "awfulizing"—the probability of sexual problems soars. For example, by exaggerating the negative evaluation of a flaccid penis, a man (as well as his partner) may set up such an intense cycle of anxiety and guilt that they may block present as well as future sensual pleasures.

In the feedback model, arousal and sexual behavior are linked by both perceptual and evaluative cognitions. A sexual cycle may begin, at Step 1, with the individual perceiving a sexual stimulus. At this first juncture we can see the impact of learning on our cognitions, for what we perceive as sexy is very much a function of the culture in which we live, the vocabulary with which we express ourselves, and conditioning experiences we may have had, a conclusion that seems inescapable on studying cross-cultural sexuality.

> In our language there are many words to describe the male sexual organ, the penis; we have a rich technical and slang vocabulary. However, there are virtually no synonyms for the female sexual organ, the clitoris. Is it possible that there is a relationship between this language deficit and the relatively high percentage of sexually dysfunctional women in our society?

Merely observing an erotic stimulus is not sufficient for arousal to occur, however. For example, an individual evaluating a sexual approach or sexual picture as "dirty," or worse, "disgusting," will probably fail to be aroused by it.

> Imagine what would happen to the individual who operates within a very narrow range of acceptable sexual stimuli or sexual signals; what would the impact be on probability of sexual arousal? On the extent of the sexual repertoire?

If a sexual stimulus is noted and positively evaluated, arousal, Step 3, will typically follow. Early stages of arousal are quite generalized, often indistinguishable from autonomic events that accompany physical exertion or other affective states (i.e., increases in heart rate, blood pressure, muscle tension). According to Schachter's classic model of emotional arousal, two elements are necessary for the experience of an emotion: (a) the physiologic state of arousal, and (b) situational cues that enable the individual to label the arousal as a specific emotion (Schachter, 1964). Thus, we presume that appropriate environmental cues can help us to label our arousal as sensations of love or sexual excitation. Because arousal is nonspecific, however, inaccurate labeling can occur.

Amy has been dating Martin off and on for months. He doesn't like to plan ahead, so often he phones her just before he wants to come pick her up. They often do exciting, adventuresome activities together, and Martin can be very romantic on their dates. He brings her surprises, dances in the street with her under the light of the moon, and yet comments on pretty girls that go by. Sometimes he doesn't call for weeks at a time, and Amy occasionally sees him walking across the campus with other women. Whenever she sees him or even thinks about him, Amy feels her heart pounding, she gets a knot in her stomach, and her knees tremble. Amy tells her best friend she's never been so much in love. Is she right?

At Step 4, perception of arousal, a noteworthy difference between men and women arises; men often seem to be better attuned to their bodies.

Research such as that conducted by Julia Heiman (1977) points to a significant sex difference. If male subjects are presented with erotic auditory stimuli and are asked if these are arousing, their answers agree virtually 100% with physiologic measures of genital vasocongestion. When female subjects are similarly engaged, there is frequently a discrepancy between what they say and what the machines are registering as arousal. Can you generate at least *two* plausible explanations for these discrepant data?

Recognizing and responding to arousal cues is partly a function of the individual's criteria for arousal. How full must an erection be before the man identifies it as a "sure" sign of arousal? How much lubrication is needed by the woman? Are these the only legitimate signs? How quickly must they be evidenced in order to "count"? If the individual uses only genital signals as criteria, two errors may intrude in an arousal sequence: (a) if the signal is delayed or does not match rigid criteria, the individual may despair and abandon further attempts at a sexual pursuit, or (b) the individual may erroneously conclude that he or she is maximally aroused based on minimal cues and may experience either an anhedonic orgasm or none at all.

> We make attributions about our arousal. Situational cues may play an important role in the interpretation we make about a physiological state of arousal. A young man encountering a coed while walking across a swaying suspension bridge is more likely to report feeling sexy than he is if he met a male or met the same coed while walking along the sidewalk (Dutton & Aron, 1974). Is it possible that such misattribution may be involved in the establishment of problematic or unusual sexual behavior?

At Step 5 in the model, arousal is evaluated. If an individual has learned to label arousal as bad, the subsequent negative emotional reactions may block further arousal. Thus, the woman who thinks of her vulva as dirty or smelly, and evaluates her own lubrication as merely "sticky" or worse, as "disgusting," may end up feeling embarrassed by her arousal and thus suppress it. Similarly, the man who decides that he "shouldn't" have erections in certain situations may find himself consumed with guilt rather than further arousal. It is for these reasons that much of the work of RET sex counseling consists of instilling a new set of sex-positive attitudes.

> We not only evaluate our own arousal, we tend to evaluate our partner's arousal as well. The significance of this step is nicely illustrated in a study by Beck, Barlow and Sakheim (1983), who compared groups of sexually functional and dysfunctional males. Nondistressed men consistently reported that high levels of arousal in their partner facilitated their own responding, while the reverse was so for a number of the dynsfunctional men. For the latter, partner arousal was evaluated negatively; these men interpreted it as increased pressure to perform, a belief which decreased their own arousal.

Once aroused, we begin or continue to behave sexually (Step 6). However, at this juncture, differences between the sexes again tend to emerge. Women, more than men, tend to block themselves cognitively (see box), and therefore often do not "lose themselves" in the sexual encounter. Her partner is much more likely to time his movements and behaviors to his state of arousal than she is. She may even repeatedly engage in sexual contact when she is at a low or even zero level of arousal, a pastime that one could easily imagine leading to resentment and further sexual difficulties.

Cognitive blockades in women may sound something like this:

- I can't take control.
- I couldn't ask for that!
- As long as he's happy, I'm happy.
- It's not nice to do that.
- What *would* he think?
- That doesn't look very ladylike.

At Step 7 in the feedback model, we observe ourselves observing our behavior. It is probably impossible for us to completely stop observing ourselves, and as long as our perceptions and labels are accurate and positive, they may further augment arousal. However, there is an important distinction between mere observation and what Masters and Johnson (1970) labeled "spectatoring." The latter implies a self-rating focus superimposed on a goal-oriented process. When we spectate on our performance, the here-and-how experience of pleasure will be lost, and sex becomes work rather than play. When the self-rating of the individual is critical, the results can certainly be a troublesome distraction from the arousal cycle.

Here's a sample of some troublesome perceptual comments that might be overheard at Step 7:

- Lord, I've just been lying here like a piece of lox.
- I must sound like a rutting hog!
- I just know I'm not making as much noise as I should.
- I bet I'm not doing this right.
- I wonder if I'm as good as her last lover.

Finally, and perhaps most importantly, at Step 8, we evaluate our sexual behaviors. At this juncture, as Ellis (1976) has forcefully pointed out, there is an important distinction to be made between a sexual *dysfunction* and a sexual *disturbance.* We may—in fact, in all probability, we *will*—experience a dysfunction (e.g., erectile difficulty), and yet we can choose to be relatively undisturbed about it emotionally. If disturbed, of course, the emotional turmoil will further inhibit good sexual functioning. In RET, the disturbance is assumed to be a direct result of the individual's evaluation of the sexual difficulty.

> Let's work out an example. Tom and Margaret have been dating, and he's finally gotten her to agree to go to bed with him. Once there, however, his penis fails to rise to the occasion. To turn this fact into a problem, Tom and Margaret could begin by evaluating the situation as "awful." If they go on to attribute the failure to some enduring characteristic of themselves and evaluate this characteristic as horrid, they will not only impede their performance at the moment, but will be making dire and probably self-fulfilling prophesies of the future. For example, he could say to himself, "Oh, no! This is the worst thing that could have happened. I'm impotent!" While she might be thinking, "Oh, no! I just knew that once he saw my stretch marks he'd be turned off forever. My body is disgusting!"
>
> On the other hand, if Tom and Margaret are able to conclude that the erectile failure is not catastrophic, that they can still function as good sex partners using other techniques, and that their "self" is still intact even if the erection is not, the erection may very well be recovered, or at least the couple may go on to their next sexual encounter unencumbered by fear, anxiety, or self-downing. Can you think of sample cognitions for Tom and Margaret that would help them cope?

What follows is a discussion of how a rational-emotive theory of sexuality can be applied to some contemporary concerns of sexologists:

Unusual Sexuality: The Paraphilias

The *DSM-III* defines a paraphilia as encompassing: (1) preference for use of a non-human object for sexual arousal, (2) repetitive sexual activity with humans involving real or simulated suffering or humiliation, or (3) repetitive sexual activity with non-consenting partners. Thus, sexual arousal or performance is dependent on unconventional imagery that may push aside or even totally replace erotic thoughts involving a partner (Money, 1977). Deviant fantasy is presumed to lead to deviant arousal, which in turn leads to deviant behavior, a conceptualization that follows the feedback model of Figure 1.

How is it that deviant cognitions acquire erotic potential for the individual? A variety of explanations has been offered, ranging from prenatal to contemporary events.

Some researchers suggest that there may be a genetic predisposition to paraphilia (Schwartz & Masters, 1983). Clues to this hypothesis come from studies of patients with temporal lobe disorders, chromosomal disorders, and disorders of prenatal hormonal environments. In addition, recent research at Johns Hopkins Hospital suggests that paraphiliacs suffer a surprising number of physiologic abnormalities, including elevated levels of testosterone and pituitary hormones, and possible cortical atrophy (McAuliffe, 1983).

Early learning experiences may play an etiologic role. Paraphiliacs tend to come from sexually repressive homes in which normal sexuality was considered highly taboo and was harshly punished. Because sexual rehearsal play seems to be essential to the development of normal sexuality, the assumption can be made that cognitive rehearsal is equally important. Yet many paraphiliac patients report that during their puberty, masturbation was done without fantasy, leading Schwartz, Money, and Robinson (1981) to conclude that this void may "leave the door open for the unusual to intrude or displace."

In addition, it is possible that reinforcement for unusual sexual fantasies or behaviors may be provided from either outside the patient or by orgasmic conditioning. For example, adult males who cross-dress frequently recall being dressed in girl's clothes by their mothers or sisters, with much delight or amusement being expressed by the women. Similarly, the adult cross-dresser may recall earlier episodes of masturbation in which the fetish objects were incorporated. One patient, for example, grew up in a home in which he shared the bathroom with his mother and numerous sisters. For years, his masturbation pattern had been to achieve arousal and orgasm while surrounded by drying pantyhose and undergarments.

Although we do not know the frequency of fetishistic fantasy in the nonclinical population, individuals who have common sexual dysfunctions frequently disclose that their fantasy life is fetishistic (Schwartz & Masters, 1983). The presumption in RET is that it is not the erotic fantasy that causes the dysfunction, but rather the strong feelings of guilt or shame that accompany these fantasies and that block arousal. It may be hypothesized that it is at this very link (Step 3 in our model) that we find a discrepancy between this population and the true paraphiliac.

A crucial aspect of the paraphilias is the compulsive, driven nature of the sexual response. Listening to such patients describe the course of an arousal cycle, one is impressed with the intensity of the building crescendo of sexual energy that they experience. They seem to be compelled to engage in the deviant behavior with the same sort of impulsive force that drives the obsessive-compulsive patient, and that seems to be quite different in nature from the more normative excitement and plateau stages of arousal described by Masters and Johnson (1966).

Theoretically, this perception of "drivenness" may in part be a misreading of their arousal. What the paraphiliac interprets as a welling-up of lust may, in part, be a welling-up of distress. Presumably, deviant behavior is even more ego-dystonic than deviant fantasy, and the resulting negative evaluation by the patient will merely serve to fuel the fires of shame, guilt, and self-loathing.

Like the obsessive-compulsive patient, the paraphiliac describes a dramatic lessening of tension when the behavioral chain is completed, particularly if there is orgasmic release. The sexual aspect of the arousal is now eliminated, but the patient continues to feel negative and uncomfortable affective states which may result in a sudden destruction of the fetish objects or vows of penitance and change. The inhibition of these negative emotions seems to weaken over time, while sexual energy begins to build, and soon the compulsive cycle begins anew.

Deviant sexual activity is often preceded by marital conflict, difficulties on the job, and similar life stresses. One of the worst stressors, however, may be the internal strife of the paraphiliac engendered by his own self-hate. The extent to which the paraphiliac regards his own sexual behavior as loathsome is perhaps most evident in the repeated denials of his acts. For example, one exhibitionist, with more than a 20-year history of multiple arrests, completely convinced a new therapist that he had merely been zipping his fly after urinating by the side of a highway when he was last arrested. Such denial may continue during treatment as a therapeutic alliance is constructed; the patient may not want to disappoint his hard-working therapist. In addition, many paraphiliacs believe that talking about the problem may unleash their minimal control over it and precipitate another immediate episode. Such cognitions, obviously, had better be therapeutically challenged (Walen & Roth, in press).

RET treatment starts with a decision: Is the behavior in question "benign" or "noxious" (harmful to the self or others)? Many paraphiliacs are married, and reactions of the spouse can run the gamut from acceptance to disgust. If the fetish is harmless and the spouse is tolerant, there may be no need to treat it directly. In many instances, however, the partners can use assistance in understanding and accepting the unusual behavior. In fact, helping the wife to avoid damning herself and her mate may often be a first step. At the other extreme, of course, is the noxious paraphilia which can benefit from forceful treatment and rigorous follow-up.

> An example of a benign paraphilia may be the middle-aged executive who goes to work in a three-piece suit, bowler, umbrella, and pantyhose. It might be a useful exercise to review the *DSM-III* for paraphiliac behaviors that could be classed as "benign."

As Ellis (1962, 1984) has repeatedly pointed out, the first therapeutic focus in RET is often on the second-level problem: the patient's distress about the presenting symptom. Thus, even in severely noxious paraphilias in which the patient may need immediate institutionalization or incarceration, the initial therapeutic foray had better be aimed at helping the client to stop beating on himself psychologically by learning to separate rating his "self" from rating his behavior. I would not want to underestimate either the importance or the difficulty of this therapeutic step.

With benign paraphilias the therapist may merely give permission to use the deviant fantasy. After all, probably most human beings engage in sexual thoughts that they may never act on; thinking something does not mean one must do it. An open climate may reduce the guilt and thereby lower the "drivenness" in the compulsive sexual chain. Schwartz and Masters (1983) have used such a procedure:

> For example, if the woman says, "I'll use my *Playgirl* pictures and you use your fetish," illicitness is immediately decreased and the fetish loses some of its addictive quality. (p. 13)

When the goal is to decrease arousal to non-normative stimuli, techniques such as *covert sentization* may be used, in which aversive imagery is paired with the deviant fantasy (see Davison, 1968; Harbert, Barlow, Hersen, & Austin, 1974; Hughes, 1977). To heighten arousal to more appropriate fantasies, *orgasmic reconditioning* may be useful (see Marquis, 1970; Annon, 1973). With extremely noxious or destructive paraphilias, the treatment of choice may be a biological one; for example, research on the use of the antiandrogen, Depo Provera, indicates great promise (c.f., Money, 1970).

When the shame about the paraphilia has kept the man from developing satisfactory relationships, other RET interventions would be prescriptively employed. Among the strategies that might be needed would be social skills training, communication/assertiveness training, sex education, sexual/intimacy skill training, and empathy training. Schwartz and Masters (1983) report that "when all is well in a love relationship, the paraphiliac's desire to act out usually is markedly diminished or completely alleviated." (p. 17) For this reason, couple counseling may often be an important ingredient in reducing the stress-compulsion-stress cycle.

Homosexuality

Or would it be more appropriate to speak of "homosexualities?" In cognitive therapy we are on the lookout for dichotomous thinking—

putting ideas in terms of black or white—and attempting to define sexual preference in such terms would often be erroneous. As long ago as the report of Alfred Kinsey and his colleagues (1948), the concept of a continuum of preference has been recognized. Kinsey used a 6-point scale incorporating behaviors as well as feelings, ranging from exclusive heterosexuality to exclusive homosexuality. Even this concept is clearly insufficient, however, for it cannot take into account variations that occur within an individual at different times and different circumstances and with differing intensities.

The concept of sexual preference also needs to take into account the element of love. It is not merely a genital fetish that we are discussing, but the person with whom one falls in love and toward whom one feels erotic attraction. In addition, life-style choice may be involved; individuals may privately or publicly identify themselves as homosexual. They may have one long-term, monogomous love affair, be active "cruisers" in the gay nightlife scene, be politically active for gay rights, live under the guise of a heterosexual marriage, etc. Each of these choices may present psychological issues and conflicts for the individual.

Is homosexuality a choice? Why do people become homosexual? At present the answer to that question is not available. We know that homosexual behavior occurs extensively throughout the animal kingdom. We know that it occurs across various cultures and historical eras; in some places homosexual behavior is expected of all young men (Money & Ehrhardt, 1972). Prenatal hormonal influences on the brain have been suggested as an etiologic factor in homosexual object choice (Money, 1980); pathological family dynamics are also commonly cited (Bieber *et al.*, 1962). We do know that almost all homosexuals have heterosexual parents! Most recently, Storms (1980) has suggested yet another explanation, one that could explain heterosexual preference as well. Briefly, his suggestion is that if one's sexual maturation is early, at a time when socialization is mainly with same-sex friends, these will become incorporated into the fantasy and erotic life of the individual. When strong sexual feelings begin to occur at 13 years or later, the social world of the adolescent is more likely to be composed of both genders and may be more likely to lead to heterosexual or bisexual fantasies.

> Many sexologists believe that all of us are basically born bisexual. Sol Gordon, a noted sex educator, suggests that some of us are lucky enough to be born *trisexual*. What does he mean by this? Why, simply that we're willing to try anything once!

What is the clinical issue in the homosexualities? The answer to that question will vary from case to case. What is *not* the clinical issue is clear, however; the sexual preference itself is not the elegant target. Rather, the fears, guilts, self-doubts, sexual concerns, and relationship issues are where the focus of the RET therapist lies. Living as a member of a discriminated minority group within a majority culture presents stresses and hassles, and coping with these may be part of the work in cognitive therapy. Resisting family distress may be a target in therapy. The key point is that the "problem" is not in the genital signature of the person one takes to bed, but in the cognitive-affective domain of the client who presents him or herself for help.

Educational counseling may be important, since myths about homosexuality abound. The following are a sampling of myths collected and disputed by Sol Gordon:

1. One, or even a few homosexual experiences do not make one "gay for life." Homosexual encounters are a common experience among teens, and most of these adopt a heterosexual pattern as adults.
2. A fantasy involving a member of the same gender does not mean that you're gay. Homosexual fantasies are common, especially among women.
3. Gay fantasies don't mean that you're a latent homosexual. What does latent mean? In fact, we're all latently everything.
4. Fear of homosexuality doesn't mean you are a latent homosexual. After all, says Dr. Gordon, a fear of dogs doesn't mean you're a latent dog!

AUTOSEXUALITY: THE JOYS OF MASTURBATION

In old, not to say antique, medical and sexual manuals, masturbation was listed under vices, debaucheries, illnesses, bad habits, or sin. An earlier Ellis—Havelock Ellis—writing at the turn of the century, was one of the first sexologists to challenge the theories that linked masturbation to insanity. His work transformed masturbation from a "malignant vice into a benign inevitability" (Robinson, 1976, p. 13). With the passing of that era came a more "enlightened" story: masturbation is fine . . . as long as you don't do it too much. Another generation of worries arose with such thinking: How much is too much? At last, even that mixed message passed away with the knowledge that we do not need to worry about that question; our bodies will know when they've had enough. Perhaps the last remaining bugaboo about masturbation is the notion that it is fine, but never, of course, as soul and body satisfying as the Real Thing (whatever that is).

Well, what *do* we know about masturbation? Actually, quite a lot of facts, including the following:

1. The overwhelming majority of adults masturbate, at least occasionally.
2. Women reach orgasm more easily and quickly by masturbation than by any other sexual modality.
3. Women who masturbate have a considerably better chance of achieving orgasm with a partner than those who do not.
4. Our most intense and focused orgasms often occur in masturbation.

Masturbation can allow us to experience our power as a person, to develop a positive relationship with ourselves and our bodies, and to take responsibility for our own orgasms. As Ellis (1958) concludes:

> It is difficult to conceive of a more beneficial, harmless, tension-releasing human act than masturbation that is spontaneously performed without (puritanically-inculcated and actually groundless) fears and anxieties. (p. 30)

A major RET focus in recent years has been to spread this good news, particulary to women, and in that most helpful modality of a women's sexual-enhancement group or workshop (Walen & Wolfe, 1983). In fact, it is often necessary to liberate womens' thinking in a more general way, toward a hedonic philosophy. The impact of sex role socialization is seen clearly in this arena, and is often particularly strong in women with strict religious upbringing or those who are deeply embedded in their roles as wives and mothers. Such women define their role as that of taking care of other people, and often have grossly neglected the habit of doing nice things for themselves. Work in therapy, therefore, is not merely sexual, but more broadly self-pleasuring, designed to reinforce the idea that "I have a right to have pleasure." Until a woman adopts this broader notion, without guilt or thoughts of unacceptable "selfishness," she will often have difficulty allowing herself pleasure in sexuality.

A group format is often the most facilitative one for such growth. The timid group member is often comforted by the thought that "between sessions there are at least six other women in my community who are masturbating." Back in the group she is provided with abundant reinforcement for self-pleasuring, a message which is often the reverse of what she gets in the "outside world." In contrast to the impatience or blame she may have gotten from her spouse or lover, she receives hugs and cheers from the group members for experiencing her tiniest genital tingles or for her first stumbling attempts at asserting herself.

> A plain-looking unpartnered woman in her 50s, often not seen as a sexual person on the outside (by others and herself), experiences herself for the first time as an envied sexpot and is complimented on her new "glow" when she reports to the group her sexual experimentation with water massagers and new masturbation positions. Group members are reinforced and supported in a new belief system that is the basis of their sexual self-determination: that they have a right to get satisfaction for their own wants (sexual and nonsexual), rather than merely taking care of others, and that they are in charge of their lives and their sexuality. And finally, in a group whose members all have the same kinds of genitals and essentially the same longtime freeze on sexual discussion, they receive much-needed practice in sharing sexual feelings and communicating these feelings to their partners with greater facility and comfort. (Walen & Wolfe, 1983).

One of the important homework assignments used in these women's sexual-enhancement groups, then, is permission giving and instruction in masturbation. The following excerpt is used by us as a handout to group members, usually after the second group meeting; we reproduce it here to illustrate clearly the kind of messages the RET therapist will be teaching:

Why Masturbate?

Masturbation or self-stimulation for sexual pleasure is liberating for men and women. It's a most natural function—children do it—developing guilt mainly when others start telling them it's wrong. Looking at and touching your genitals helps you gain greater comfort and acceptance of your sexuality and your body. And it helps you become more attuned to what feels good and better able to enjoy your sexual response—both with your most reliable sex partner (yourself!) as well as with others. It is the best way to learn about your own sexual reponses so that you can more clearly and effectively communicate them to your partner.

Masturbation can, if you so choose, be your primary sexual outlet. It's a great way to relieve sexual and other tensions (and a good nightcap to help you sleep!). With a partner, it can take the pressure off your partner (and you) to perform. It is one of many ways to share sexual experiences and techniques, and to develop greater sexual honesty with your partner. It can be a tremendous turn-on to see someone you care about give themselves pleasure. Finally, people who feel good about pleasuring themselves and who take responsibility for their sexual responses are less likely to have sexual problems. So . . .

Welcome to Masturbation Week!

Remember—it's important to make an agreement with yourself that if improving your sex life is important, you'll have to set aside enough time for you to work on it. A minimum of four separate 20-minute to 45-minute sessions this week is recommended.

Pick a time of day when you're relaxed and feeling reasonably good about yourself. Find a place (your bed, in front of the fireplace, in the bathtub, wherever) that's quiet, comfortable, and where you won't be interrupted. Turn off the phone! Create a sensuous atmosphere; turn down the lights, turn on background music if you wish. Feel free to do whatever may help you get in a more sensuous mood and arouse your sexual fantasies. This may include looking at sexy pictures in a magazine, reading an erotic book, thinking up sexy experiences or fantasies.

Remember some of the places that felt particularly good when you touched them last week. Remember, too, that masturbation is a natural body function and is *good* for you; give yourself permission, out loud if you wish, to enjoy it.

Now all you need is a little perseverence. You might not get excited for quite a while, or might not have any orgasm. These kinds of responses take practice. *Don't worry.*

Using some oil (or secretions) for lubrication, find an enjoyable place to stroke; when you've found one, keep rubbing, alternating the pressure and the rate. Try stroking up and down; try stroking sideways, in circles, back and forth. Try rubbing as though you were massaging yourself to reach the parts below the skin. Don't worry if you temporarily lose the pleasurable feeling. If a place becomes tender or numb, switch to a new place. Stop when you want, start when you want. Do what feels OK for you. Try whatever positions, movements, stimulation you want (with pillow, objects, whatever). Use one hand or both. Touch yourself elsewhere on your body—your breasts, inside of legs and arms, face. Experiment. Find what feels good. Make as much or as little noise as you want. And try to remember that there is no "right" or "best" way to masturbate—there's *your* way. And finding your way takes trying out lots and lots of different things. *You have the right to pleasure* . . . but even pleasure takes practice!

Among the books that are particularly fun for women to use in an autoerotic growth program are the following:

Liberating Masturbation by Betty Dodson. New York: Bodysex Designs, 1974.

Good Vibrations by Joani Blank. Burlingame, CA: Down There Press, 1976.

My Playbook for Women About Sex by Joani Blank. San Francisco: Multi-Media Resource Center, 1976.

The Cunt Coloring Book by T. Corinne. San Francisco: Pearlchild Productions, 1975.

UNEQUAL SEXUALITY: PARTNER DIFFERENCES

A common and often troublesome issue for couples is differences in the partners' sexual drive, including interest levels, timing preferences, behavior preferences, frequency preferences, and so forth. In most cases, the differences are not astonishing, and both partners are functioning within "normal limits." For example, he likes sex in the morning when he feels most refreshed, and she finds the problems of "morning mouth," a full bladder, and stirring children a turn-off then. Or, she would like to have sex almost any night of the week since it relaxes her for sleep, while he finds himself most interested and receptive when the weekend is approaching and he's able to put away his work-week worries. Or, he wants her to swallow his ejaculate when she brings him to orgasm orally, but she finds the idea repugnant.

Such items need not be reason for significant emotional or relationship distress, yet they often are just that. Occasionally, the issue is a serious case of Low Frustration Tolerance (LFT) in one or both partners; the individual simply "cannot bear" not getting his or her own way. More typically, however, I have found the problem to lie in the idiosyncratic meaning the partner places on the other's behavior. Attributions are assumed and not checked, and the individual goes on to become distressed over an incorrect presumption. For example, when she will not swallow his ejaculate, he mentally compares her lack of interest in this element to other partners he had (or, more usually, has read about!), decides that her choice means that she doesn't really love him fully (metaphorically, he is "distasteful" to her), and that the end of the relationship is near, an eventuality he would greet with great anguish. In this example, we see a good illustration of the focus of the RET/cognitive therapist: the therapeutic issue is not merely the behavior, but the cognitive/emotive underpinnings.

When such couples come for sex therapy, I am often struck by how well they are able to function as a unit in other areas of their lives; they may be communicative, flexible, and good problem solvers. In the arena of sex, however, there may be little communication, negotiation, or compromise. Why? What would block an individual or couple from taking the first step in problem solving, that of bringing the item up for discussion? Often, the block is that of fear: fear of the repercussions that might ensue if one asserts what one wants or does not want—such as fear of reprisal, rejection, or denial. If a problem area has been mentioned, the couple may have failed to proceed to negotiating a solution because of underlying beliefs that (for example) sex should be spontaneous and naturally terrific. If they had to negotiate a solution, such a couple would automatically devalue the process as well as the product unless the core irrational beliefs were successfully challenged. Finally, in the process of negotiation, both parties would do well to understand that a "perfect" solution will not be attainable, and compromise is the name of the game. Some couples block themselves from the idea of sexual compromise because, again, they may hold core concepts about "Real Sex." For example, if he is interested in a sexual encounter and she is not, a compromise might be reached in which he masturbates while lying snuggled in her arms. However, if the couple has mentally declared that Real Sex = Intercourse, any option such as the above would be unacceptable. The importance of assessing and helping the couple to modify sexually restrictive belief systems had better not be overlooked.

In some cases the differences between the partners' sex drives is more than incidental. Problems of *hyperactive sexual desire* or *inhibited sexual desire* occur, and will present a clinical problem not only for the sufferer but obviously for the partner as well. Hyperactive sexual desire in the male is known as *satyriasis,* and in the female as *nymphomania.* In our society there is a cultural expectation that men are more sexual and have a higher sex drive than women; in many instances, in fact, women have been punished or put down by a partner who was threatened by her obvious responsiveness. Symons has remarked that the "sexually insatiable woman is to be found primarily, if not exclusively, in the ideology of feminism, the hopes of boys and the fears of men" (1979, p. 92).

In either sex, excessive desire is a clinical rarity (Allgeier & Allgeier, 1984, p. 254), and usually symptomatic of other emotional distress. Kaplan (1979) suggests that the condition is reflective of an obsessive-compulsive reaction; sexual activity is used to distract from or to relieve feelings of tension or anxiety. In one recent case, a woman was sent to one of my women's sexual enhancement groups by her husband, who wanted her to find out why she was not interested in sex. It turned out that she was not disinterested, but could not keep up with her husband. Every evening, when he arrived home for dinner and she was busy with two small children and mealtime preparations, he demanded that she leave her work and have sex with him. For the husband, an orgasm was the only way he knew to turn off the pressures of the day; it was the sexual equivalent of two martinis, and in the wife's perception, not very sexy at all. A redefinition of his phenomenologic experience from "horny" to "tense" enabled the couple to brainstorm some alternative relaxation strategies.

In a similar case it was the wife who was desperate for sex. She alternated between anger episodes at his sexual passivity, and courtship routines in which she would don a black negligee and look soulfully at him while he studied the TV screen. We began by working on her anger. She learned to reinterpret his behavior; for example, she reasoned that his standoffishness was not a reflection of her ugliness or his lack of caring for her. He cared for her "in his own way" and she had other indications that he (as well as other men) found her attractive. She worked at not being so "subtle" in her sexual requests, and simultaneously worked at not awfulizing about a rejection; communication between the pair became more clear and more positive. Nonetheless, her tally of encounters registered a very low frequency of initiations by her husband and a low rate of positive acceptances by him. Within a few weeks, her irritation began to build to a sense of urgency. We went on a hunt for the relevant cognitions.

What this mid-life woman was thinking related to a sense that her life and youth were slipping away while she remained sexually unfulfilled. She had never "unleashed her sexual potential," and if her husband did not hurry up and learn to perform better she might lose her chance to replace him; she had to hurry before her "body went completely." I soon realized that what I was learning was that this "oversexed" woman did not know how to orgasm, was not sure that she owned a working clitoris, and did not view masturbation as an "OK" thing to do. She had married in order to legitimize her sexuality; her attitude was that with a man, sex was kosher, and it was up to the man to see that she was fulfilled. As we talked, the problem became reformulated; she concluded:

- No man, not even the best lover in town, was going to be able to unleash her. She had leashed herself with half-buried negative cognitions and punitive attitudes about sexuality.
- No one could change her attitudes but herself.
- Her sense of needing a great deal of sex, interpreted as horniness, was perhaps a mislabeling of her sense of urgency (Honey, hurry and get it up and turn me on before it's too late).

Similarly, in cases of hyposexuality, the individual may have an artifically lowered sex drive, one suppressed by anxieties or by hostility toward the partner. One recent study found that low sex drive was often associated with depression, a Roman Catholic upbringing, the presence of a sexual dysfunction, aversion to oral-genital contact, aversion to female genitalia, aversion to masturbation, and marital problems that were obvious to the clinician but denied by the couple (LoPiccolo, 1980).

If sex drive differences are the presenting problem, the first question is whether it is correctly labeled. If so, the couple may decide to (a) try to adjust and accommodate the other, (b) leave the difference alone but work at not upsetting themselves about it, or (c) develop a supplement for the higher-sexed partner with masturbation and/or other sexual outlets.

No Sexuality: The Ultimate Sexual Option

To review, we have thus far examined unusual sexuality, homosexuality, autosexuality, and unequal sexuality. Perhaps that leaves us at the bottom line: what of those people who wish no sexuality? Is this a legitimate option?

The question, when examined with typical RET logic, must be rephrased to be sensible, that is, not stated in overly simplistic, dichotomous terms. The absence of sexual desire may occur for many reasons, some indicative of serious emotional distress and worthy of a therapeutic examination, and others, quite normative and expectable and not requiring change. What, then, are some of the "unhealthy" and "healthy" reasons for an absence of sexuality.

Among the "unhealthy" thinking patterns that can inhibit sexuality is the oft-cited madonna/whore syndrome. Some individuals operate as if women can be divided into these two classes; the madonnas are the ones who marry and procreate (seemingly asexually), while the whores are those who have sexual appetites and passions. Husband, wife, or both may have such a dysfunctional attitude.

Other unhealthy reasons include hostility toward one's spouse, unaddressed apathy or boredom, a fear of intimacy, and guilt about outside partners or unacceptable sexual impulses. Some people relinquish their sexual behaviors with a sigh of relief. For example, not infrequently, a post-menopausal woman will declare an end to her "wifely duties," sex having been just another chore that she performed without expecting or receiving pleasure from it.

What might fall under the heading of "healthy" reasons for an absence of sexuality? Paradoxically enough, physical unhealth is a prime factor in lack of libido, and one ought not worry if one's sex drive fluctuates with one's physical condition. Similarly, extentuating life stressors may normally interfere with a lusty sexual interest. Some individuals find that an extremely engrossing project pushes their sexual cauldron to the back burner. And some individuals deliberately select a lifestyle of celibacy, based on religious vows or simply on the fact that they have not found a partner with whom they choose to build an emotive-sexual relationship.

At issue, then, is not what one does or does not do, but (a) why one behaves in a particular way, (b) the consequences of one's choice, and perhaps most important, (c) how one feels about it. A nice summary statement that could serve to illustrate the RET practitioner's philosophy was written by Reverend William Stayton in an article entitled "Lifestyle Spectrum, 1984":

> As a society we need to be more accepting and open to the various alternatives that fit people's emotional, social, and sexual needs or desires. If it involves no inherent physical or emotional harm and no infringement on the rights of others, a chosen lifestyle has the right to exist—as an individual's "typical way of life." (p. 4)

Final Thoughts

Sex therapists have developed various classificatory systems for the common sexual dysfunctions (e.g., arousal dysfunctions and orgasmic dysfunctions). These categories are often broken down still further into primary dysfunctions (occurring under all conditions) and situational dysfunctions (occurring only under specific conditions). Closer examination of these categories, however, suggests that the same dysfunctional processes are operative in virtually all cases, in males as well as females.

It appears that the core ingredients in all of the diagnostic categories are a high level of emotional distress induced by cognitive errors of evaluation, often coupled with cognitive errors of perception. The end product is an individual who approaches the job of sex (rather than the joy of sex) as a way to prove oneself (rather than to enjoy oneself) . . . certainly a very unsexy attitude.

Positive sexual experiences are a smooth amalgam of stimuli and responses, the flow between them guided by correct perceptions and positive evaluations. When this process occurs, the emotional climate of the individual will be untroubled and sex play will be pleasant or even joyful. Positive sexual experiences, therefore, are the result of more than good sex technique; no amount of "sexpertise" can overcome inhibitions, guilt, anxiety, depression, or anger. It is these blockages in the emotional final common pathways that are the prime foci of rational-emotive therapy.

References

Allgeier, E. R., & Allgeier, A. R. (1984). *Sexual interactions.* Lexington, MA: Heath.

Annon, J. S. (1973). The therapeutic use of masturbation in the treatment of sexual disorders. In J. P. Brady & J. D. Henderson (Eds.), *Advances in Behavior Therapy,* Vol. 4 (pp. 199–215). New York: Academic Press.

Beck, J. G., Barlow, D. H., & Sakheim, D. K. (1983). The effects of attentional focus and partner arousal on sexual responding in functional and dysfunctional men. *Behavior Research and Therapy, 21,* 1–8.

Bieber, I., Dain, H. J., Dince, P. R., Drellich, M. G., Grand, H. G., Grundlach, R. H., Kremer, M. W., Rifkin, A. H., Wilber, C. B., & Bieber, T. B. (1962). *Homosexuality: A psychoanalytic study.* New York: Basic Books.

Brody, J. E. (1982, May 18). Impotence: Experts urge greater attention to physical causes. *New York Times,* pp. C1, C8.

Davison, G. (1968). Elimination of a sadistic fantasy by a client-controlled counter-conditioning technique: A case study. *Journal of Abnormal Psychology, 73,* 84–90.

Dutton, A., & Aron, A. (1974). Some evidence for heightened sexual attraction under conditions of high anxiety. *Journal of Personality and Social Psychology, 30,* 510–517.

Ellis, A. (1958). *Sex without guilt.* Secaucus, NJ: Lyle Stuart.

Ellis, A. (1962). *Reason and emotion in psychotherapy.* Secaucus, NJ: Citadel Press.

Ellis, A. (1975). The rational-emotive approach to sex therapy. *The Counseling Psychologist, 5,* 14–22.

Ellis, A. (1976). *Sex and the liberated man.* Secaucus, NJ: Lyle Stuart.

Ellis, A. (1977). The basic clinical theory of rational-emotive therapy. In A. Ellis & R. Grieger (Eds.), *Handbook of rational-emotive therapy* (pp. 3–34). New York: Springer.

Ellis, A. (1984). Rational-emotive therapy. In R. J. Corsini, (Ed.), *Current psychotherapies* (pp. 196–238). (3rd ed.). Itasca, IL: Peacock.

Foster, A. L. (1978). Changes in marital-sexual relationships following treatment for sexual dysfunctioning. *Journal of Sex and Marital Therapy, 4,* 186–197.

Harbert, T. L., Barlow, D. H., Hersen, M., & Austin, J. B. (1974). Measurement and modification of incestuous behavior: A case study. *Psychological Reports, 34,* 79–86.

Heiman, J. R. (1977). A psychophysiological exploration of sexual arousal patterns in males and females. *Psychophysiology, 14,* 266.

Hoch, Z. (1983). The G spot. *Journal of Sex and Marital Therapy, 9,* 166.

Hughes, R. C. (1977). Covert sensitization treatment of exhibitionism. *Journal of Behavior Therapy and Experimental Psychiatry, 8,* 171–179.

Kahn-Ladas, A., Whipple, B., & Perry, J. D. (1982). *The G spot and other recent discoveries about human sexuality.* New York: Holt, Rinehart & Winston.

Kaplan, H. S. (1979). *Disorders of desire.* New York: Brunner/Mazel.

Kinsey, A. C., Pomeroy, W., & Martin, C. *Sexual behavior in the human male* (1948). Philadelphia: Saunders.

LoPiccolo, L. (1980). Low sex desire. In S. R. Lieblum & L. A. Pervin (Eds.), *Principles and practice of sex therapy.* New York: Guilford Press.

Marquis, J. N. (1970). Orgasmic reconditioning: Changing sexual object choice through controlling masturbation fantasies. *Journal of Behavior Therapy and Experimental Psychiatry, 1,* 263–272.

Masters, W. H., & Johnson, V. (1966). *Human sexual response.* Boston: Little, Brown.

Masters, W. H., & Johnson, V. (1970). *Human sexual inadequacy.* Boston: Little, Brown.

McAuliffe, S. (1983, March). Is sexual deviance a biological problem? Psychology Today, p. 84.

Money, J. (1970). Use of an androgen-depleting hormone in the treatment of male sex offenders. *Journal of Sex Research, 6,* 165–172.

Money, J. (1977). Paraphilias. In J. Money & H. Musaph (Eds.), *Handbook of sexology.* Amsterdam: Excerpta Medica.

Money, J. (1980). Genetic and chromosomal aspects of homosexual etiology. In J. L. Marmor (Ed.), *Homosexual behavior,* New York: Basic Books.

Money, J., & Ehrhardt, A. A. (1972). *Man and woman, boy and girl.* Baltimore: The Johns Hopkins University Press.

Nolen, W. A. (1981, November). Impotence. *Esquire,* pp. 132–141.

O'Leary, K. D., & Arias, I. (1983). The influence of marital therapy on sexual satisfaction. *Journal of Sex and Marital Therapy, 9,* 171–181.

Robinson, P. A. (1976). *The modernization of sex.* New York: Harper & Row.

Sager, C. J. (1976). *Marital contracts and couple therapy.* New York: Brunner/Mazel.

Schachter, S. (1964). The interaction of cognitive and physiological determinants of emotional state. In L. Berkowitz (Ed.), *Advances in experimental social psychology.* New York: Academic Press.

Schwartz, M. F., Money, J., & Robinson, K. (1981). Biosocial perspectives on the development of the proceptive, acceptive, and conceptive phase of eroticism. *Journal of Sex and Marital Therapy, 7,* 443–455.

Schwartz, M. F., & Masters, W. H. (1983). Conceptual factors in the treatment of paraphilias: A preliminary report. *Journal of Sex and Marital Therapy, 9,* 3–18.

Spark, R., White, R., & Connolly, P. (1980). Impotence is not always psychogenic: Newer insights into hypothalamic-pituitary-gonadal dysfunction. *Journal of American Medical Association, 243,* 750–755.

Stayton, W. R. (1984). Lifestyle spectrum 1984. *SIECUS Report, 12,* 1–5.

Storms, M. D. (1980). Theories of sexual orientation. *Journal of Personality and Social Psychology, 38,* 783–792.

Symons, D. (1980). *The evolution of human sexuality.* New York: Oxford.

Thorpe, J. G., Schmidt, E., & Castell, D. (1963). A comparison of positive and negative conditioning in the treatment of homosexuality. *Behavior Research and Therapy, 1,* 357–362.

Walen, S. R. (1980). Cognitive factors in sexual behavior. *Journal of Sex and Marital Therapy, 6,* 87–101.

Walen, S. R., & Roth, D. (in press) Cognitive theories. In J. H. Geer & William O'Donohue (Eds.), *Theories of human sexuality.* New York: Plenum Press.

Walen, S. R., & Wolfe, J. (1983). Women's sexual enhancement groups. In A. Freeman (Ed.), *Cognitive therapy in couples and groups.* New York: Plenum Press.

Wolfe, J., & Walen, S. R. (1980). Cognitive factors in sexuality. In R. Grieger & I. Z. Grieger (Eds.), *Cognition and emotional disturbance* (pp. 148–173). New York: Human Sciences Press.

Wolpe, J. (1969). *The practice of behavior therapy.* New York: Pergamon.

Zilbergeld, B., & Evans, M. (1980). The inadequacy of Masters and Johnson. *Psychology Today, 14,* 29–43.

7

The Psychology of Homosexuality

IAN M. CAMPBELL

Much has been written about homosexuality. Male homosexuality, probably more than female homosexuality, has been defined and discussed from almost every conceivable position by writers interested in human and animal behavior. Psychologists, psychiatrists, sociologists, moralists, philosophers, educationalists, and geneticists, to list some of the commentators with all manner of views, have focused on homosexuality with an attention that few other topics have received. It is of interest to follow the changing patterns and fashions that have characterized the discussion of homosexuality over the decades (Karlen, 1971, offers a fine review in that regard). Today the study of human sexuality and particularly homosexuality remains a changing field and a topic of some controversy. Homosexuality is the focus of a range of current definitions and opinions, some less than more related to data.

The psychology of the individual is a subject about which all humans can be expert given that we all have firsthand experiences of the self. Humans freely offer comment not only about behaviors with which we have direct experiences, including sexuality and sexual preference, but also about the behaviors of others that fall outside of our respective individual experiences. Our views frequently contain explicit and implicit moralisms. Many people will subscribe to an attitude relating to goodness–badness or rightness–wrongness about aspects of human sexuality. Fewer people, it seems, can be neutral about the topic. Such diversity of opinion and conviction, often in the absence of data (indeed, even in the face of data to the contrary), reflects much that is charac-

IAN M. CAMPBELL • Department of Psychology, University of Melbourne, Parkville, Victoria, 3052 Australia.

teristic of being human. Psychological theories of human behavior within the specialty literature show a range of views about sexuality not so much of actual genital activities, which presumably lie somewhere near the heart of the matter, but of hypothesized central and associated pathologies, motivations, and other features of relevance for both individual and group functioning. Various schools of personality theories look differently at the topic of sexuality; they variously focus on different environmental and/or intrapsychic and/or physiological features for their respective accounts of sexuality and homosexuality. The literature is confused.

It is not the intent of the present paper to review extant theories of homosexuality, and little heed is paid to the bulk of the research literature. This author several years ago ceased to take seriously much of both theory and research literature concerning genesis and maintenance of homosexual behaviors because of their usual underlying determinist view of human functioning, a philosophy still almost invariably subscribed to within academic psychology schools. Such a view, in a simplified sense, carries the central assumption that humans are somehow victims of their past and present environments, a model at odds with a humanist view which puts free will and self-determination (witting or unwitting) as being central to psychological functioning. A second reason for remaining skeptical about the theories and research findings about male and female homosexuality lies within the definitional problems of the term *homosexuality*. As discussed by Gonsiorek (1982a), defining who is homosexual remains highly problematic. Following Kinsey, Pomeroy, and Martin (1948), sexual preference is seen best as a continuum on which people can be located according to relative frequencies of homosexual-heterosexual fantasies, feelings, and behaviors. As those authors showed, a substantial number of people lie between the extreme points of the two exclusivities of sexual preference. Yet even to assign a Kinsey rating of sexuality to an individual may lead to great oversimplification of the concept as it tends to obscure important individual differences. By way of comparison, the term *African* denies the many obvious and fine distinctions along many dozens of dimensions among the individuals comprised by such a group. Africans, particularly in Africa, are more validly described as black, white, northern, southern, Tanzanian, Ugandan, etc., than by merely the most undescriptive and camouflaging term *African*. Yet even those subcategories remain global and hardly discriminative. Homosexuals, in the same way, can be only very grossly grouped even by a Kinsey rating. The relevant individual behaviors that are taken to define homosexuality are many, and individual humans vary markedly in terms not only of the dimensions but also of the frequencies and the intensities of the behavioral expressions. Those many dimensions relate not only to the specific, directly sexual behaviors, emotions, and feelings but also to the larger, more constellating social sex roles. Given the embedded dangers of generalized use of the term *homosexual/s,* however, that designation will be used, for linguistic convenience, through this chapter.

The issue of adequate measurement and definition of sexually related variables remains a big problem. Gonsiorek (1982a) nicely summarizes and gives samples of the major ongoing difficulties. It is relevant to mention several of his conclusions. He says, for example, that "without being iconoclastic or extreme, it can safely be said that no research endeavor to date has used a representative homosexual sample" (p. 372). Using North American research he concludes that the homosexual population in general differs not at all from the United States population in general, except that the homosexual population tends to be disproportionately unmarried and childless. He indicates, however, that every study has been biased in terms of particular, and at times unusual, demographic variables such as social, economic, educational, ethnic, racial, religious, and regional. Similarly, with the aim of attempting to show differences between homosexual and heterosexual groups, studies have used data bases of the former which are enormously biased in terms of such variables as nonsexual pathologies, legal complications, criminal variables, social and friendship networks, and subject willingness to volunteer for research. Gonsiorek states that the research on homosexuality has been characterized by poor and biased sampling procedures and vague, erroneous, or simplistic assumptions about the definition of homosexuality: "It is not possible to make noteworthy statements about homosexuality in general, given the problematic state of the literature" (p. 376). It is clear that whereas some research exists that is seen as adequate in relation to particular parameters associated with specific homosexual behaviors, to generalize beyond specific samples of individuals, always the temptation, is hazardous, to say the least. Similarly, aspects of some theories no doubt hold true but only for well-defined behaviors within well-defined groups of people.

The focus of this chapter is on the psychology of homosexuality. The discussion follows two interrelated themes. The first involves the view that whereas heterosexual individuals and homosexual individuals can and do differ quite clearly from each other in terms of a number of significant sexual and social expressions, homosexuals do not have a particular monopoly on psychological styles different from those motivating heterosexuals. It is the author's position that it is an error to view homosexuals, however defined, in any less or more simplified ways than one would view heterosexuals. That view relates to the notion of whether or not homosexuality is pathologically motivated, and this chapter shall argue that pathology is independent of the issue of sexual preference. The second theme involves the view that human sexuality, including homosexuality, can be adequately accounted for within a noncomplex theory of human psychology even though sexuality in general is interactive with many other areas of human behavior. Sexuality is highly modifiable by other aspects of human psychology and is seen to be subject to psychological variables no different from other goal-oriented human behaviors.

To those ends, this chapter presents a model of the psychology of human functioning, which, while following the views of Ellis (e.g., 1977a), clarifies several points of RET theory. The present view follows that of Campbell, Lowe, and Burgess (1983). During discussion of the model, only passing reference will be made to human sexuality and homosexuality; focus on those areas, particularly in relation to sexual preference and pathology, follows the outline of a cognitive view of normal and abnormal functioning. As an introductory caveat, the discussion of issues will be brief, and the author is aware of the usual potential criticisms from several quarters in terms of that abbreviated treatment and the somewhat narrowed focus within the psychology of homosexuality. It is understood, for example, that the psychology of the individual is closely related to social phenomena. Deliberately, those associated topics will not be pursued in this chapter.

A Model of Human Psychological Functioning

Rational-emotive theory (RET) is a theory of personality (Ellis, 1973). It encompasses a major metatheoretic assumption of humanism and allows definition and description of normal and abnormal human functioning. RET postulates the universality of two superordinate human goals of aliveness and happiness (following Darwin and Bentham respectively), which Ellis refers to as the biosocial goals of humankind (1977a). It is trite to point out that most humans, having the power and capacity to kill themselves virtually at any time, choose (usually vigorously) to remain alive, and, similarly, most humans will work, again vigorously at times, to obtain and maintain levels of personal happiness.

The notion of happiness requires clarification. It is a relative concept and a relative state; it is seen as dimensional, being present in greater or lesser degrees for the individual at one time than at another time or in relation to one set of circumstances than to another set. It is self-defined in terms of individual goal attainment. What action or situation or state of affairs for one individual will lead to a high degree of satisfaction will for another individual lead perhaps to only moderate or mild (or a degree of negative) satisfaction. Humans have what may be seen as major foci for their happiness ideals in terms of (at least usually) domestic, occupational, leisure, artistic, sportive, and sexual, to name only a few, that are not mutually exclusive. The notion of happiness, dimensionally and individually defined, is also subject to the human capacity of time projection: we can meaningfully talk in terms of happiness from short-term goals and happiness from long-term goals. Often they may be in contrast. A student's studying for a class paper, on a topic of not momentous interest, in order to obtain higher grades that will contribute to the probability of longer-term financial rewards is a standard example. As has been discussed by Ellis (e.g., 1977a) and will be a focus here, the notion of short-term hedonism at the expense of longer-term hedonism plays a significant role in neurotic thinking styles.

One may usefully view the various content foci, such as domestic, occupational, and sexual, in terms of a second system relating to themes; one may slice the same pie into different segments. Ellis (1979, 1980), Garcia and Blythe (1977), Grieger and Boyd (1980), and Hauck (1974) all agree on three major themes of human functioning. Garcia and Blythe talk of the "needs" for love, for success, and for comfort; Grieger and Boyd talk of the human anxieties related to approval, to ego (or success), and to discomfort; Hauck talks of the fears of rejection and of failure and of fear itself (the super fear). Ellis uses notions of *ego anxiety,* which combines the fears of failure and rejection, and *discomfort anxiety* (the fear of fear). Goldfried (1979) talks of two fundamental beliefs underlying emotional disturbance. They are (a) "I must be loved" and (b) "I must be successful." There is agreement (although Goldfried agrees with only two of the three) about subgoals or major themes through which the larger, more general happiness goal is translated into the daily activities of the individual. Those major themes may receive interesting speculation in terms of their universality for humans, both phylogenetically and ontogenetically. Ethologists for a long time have hypothesized about the phylogenetic significance of behaviors, a tradition more recently receiving persuasive argument in psychology (e.g., Eysenck, 1976, in terms of his model of neurotic behavior; Clarke & Jackson, 1983, in terms of the significance of different stimuli modalities for the etiology of human anxieties). We may assume that Neanderthal humans required love approval from members of their domestic community in order to attain success at hunting (presumably a group activity) and therefore eating and comfort. The achievement of all of those goals was essential for physical survival. Ontogenetically, we have a similar story. For the babe in arms, literal absence of love approval (nonnurturance) would mean nonsuccess at obtaining food, warmth, etc., and thus comfort. Those goals are the essence of success for early survival. It makes good sense to assume that historic factors are important in the lives of humans and it seems no accident that the three subgoals of success, love, and comfort are pervasive among human adults. It is generally agreed that the key concept in human development is that of psychological and physiological differentiation (Piaget & Inhelder, 1966). Human psychological growth is interactive with physical growth. The major subgoals in human development began at the same point, that being survival in a physical sense. Adults quite clearly can have psychological goals involving love, success, and comfort unrelated to physiological requirements for survival. The increase of physiological and psychological independence means the separation of the two superordinate goals of aliveness from happiness along with the differentiation of the related subclasses of happiness.

Humans have two biosocial, superordinate goals of aliveness and happiness with three subclasses of the latter in terms of love approval, success, and comfort. Those goals are in general pervasive across humans in relation to any number of behaviors, including sexual behaviors. It is true that (a) individuals may differentially hold goals with varying degrees of intensity in relation to particular content areas (e.g., making money success; spouse approval; sexual comfort), and (b) the same individual may differentially emphasize the same goals at different times (e.g., gaining approval for sexual behaviors will be more important in one situation than in another). The intensity of goals, translated as the degree of strength of belief about them along with the motivation to attain them, is central to RET and to the present discussion about sexual preference.

Within the literature on cognitive processing, the concept of *schema* is a complex and important one. Schemata in part describe which stimuli in the environment will at any one time be focused on by the individual. An aspect of an experiment by Anderson and Pichert (1978), for example, showed that individuals, given different instructional sets, attended to and processed different stimuli from the same available set. The literature from social psychology, particularly research on stereotyping and prejudice (e.g., Gonsiorek, 1982a), adequately demonstrates the very active and selective natures of information perceiving and processing. There is a tenable hypothesis that the individual's psychological goals in large part determine what activating events from the available array will be selected and receive attention (Figure 1). Directionality is somewhat simplified in Figure 1 and is not merely one way. The goals are seen as directing attention to particular stimuli, the processing of which leads to certain emotional and behavioral consequences that will be consonant with those initial goals and thus reinforce them. The relationships among all variables in Figure 1 are interactive. Processing of information that is preferential leads to nonneurotic consequences; that which is absolutistic leads to consequences that are neurotic. Definitions of preferential and absolutistic processing require elucidation, as follows.

Absolutistic processing centers on Ellis's (1977b) four irrational thoughts; they are: (a) the demand ("should be"); (b) the awfulization; (c) the low frustration tolerance; and (d) the generalized rating. The notion of sequence of those four irrational thought processes was proposed by Campbell, Lowe, and Burgess (1983) in order to show better the interrelationships among the human neuroses. Their argument was along the following lines. Philosophically it is seen that the demand (usually in the self-statement form of the "should" or the "must") is an assumption that is false. The accompanying evaluation as "awful" can be seen as quite a logical deduction from the initial although faulty assumption. If the individual believes that something absolutely must be the case, then logically it will be absolutely bad that something is not the case. It seems that the demand and the awfulization complementarily go together, and it is difficult to see the former being present without the latter; perhaps they are simply different forms of stating the same thing. It is the cognitive focus on the awfulization that leads to the

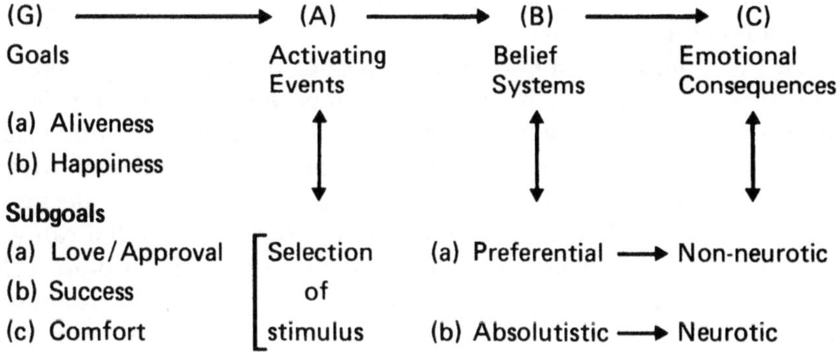

FIGURE 1. Simplified outline of relationships between goals and consequences.

emotional consequence (or a better term, concomitant) for the individual. A focus on the demand itself predisposes one to, but does not contain, an emotional concomitance. If the individual believes that a particular state of affairs is awful, then quite understandably and properly the autonomic nervous system responds with fear-anxiety to the cognitive message of utter danger-peril. In other words, the anxiety phenomenon involves a cognitive focus on the awfulization, a view in line with Ellis (1979). Similarly, to believe that "I can't stand it" (low frustration tolerance (LFT)) follows quite logically and is a reasonable evaluation of a threat that is absolutely bad. LFT, within the neurotic style, is a reaction to the self-created anxiety pain phenomenon. Acting in terms of an LFT philosophy directly leads to such various avoidance behaviors as diversions and procrastinations and such more centrally accepted neurotic states as phobias, varieties of obsessive-compulsive disorders, and hysterias. The fourth irrational belief, the globalized rating, from the specific bad act or event to the general scene or person (which may be the self), again follows quite logically. If a situation is defined as totally bad, that totality can well include a context of that situation. Such generalized rating is central to the angers and the depressions, as has been discussed by Ellis (1977b). The angers carry an additional erroneous assumption, namely that bad people should be punished, which then frequently is acted on by the angry individual. Depression less frequently carries that faulty assumption. The concomitant, if present, is guilt, although guilt is not invariably a feature of depression.

The sequencing of beliefs just outlined does not imply that all four irrational beliefs (iBs) are given focus by the individual during a neurotic episode. The proposal contains the idea that individuals create their own neurotic pain by believing the initial assumption and that the particular form of neurosis will depend on how far they proceed along the sequence of the following three iBs.

At this point, it is important to introduce the notion of preferential processing—in other words, the rational alternatives to the four iBs just referred to. A brief overview will be offered to explain the nonneurotic thinking styles and processes, and some points will be relevant to later discussion. Preferential thinking is concerned with wishes or desires or preferences that individuals hold in relation to their goals that can vary in strength along a scale but that can never attain an absolute value (theoretically they can always be stronger). RET holds that preferences for goal achievement ("I *want* you to like me") are rational; in cases where goals are not attained or realized, the concomitant emotion will be seen as appropriate. That is to say, the individual holding a preference that is not fulfilled will be, say, disappointed or sad or irritated or concerned (versus upset or disturbed), will recognize that such a state of affairs, although unpleasant or frustrating, is tolerable (versus intolerable), and will realize that, because a blockage to a goal exists, it does not mean that everything else is bad. Such emotions of frustration, even though negative, are viewed as appropriate because they are the result of, and concomitant with, reality-focused cognitions. Such emotions do not lead to self-defeating, goal-defeating behaviors. They serve as motivation to attempt to remove the particular blockage to goal attainment. The attempt may or may not be successful. A simple example is the appropriate frustration felt by the individual whose sexual advances to another are not accepted. That frustration may serve as greater motivation to try harder a second time. If that next attempt also is unsuccessful, then the individual would be disappointed, perhaps very disappointed, but would recognize that he or she can tolerate disappointment and that, although disappointed, the rest of the world remains unchanged. It is important to point out that the negative nonneurotic states are different from the negative neurotic states. For example, sadness is not a lesser version of depression; irritation is not a lesser version of anger; concern is not a lesser version of anxiety: the first mentioned feeling in each of the respective contrasts is appropriate to a particular state of affairs that goes against an individual's goals and that can vary in intensity. One may be, for example, very sad, highly annoyed, or most concerned; the differences with their respective neurotic counterparts lie not with intensity of emotion but with quality of emotion. Neurotic emotions involve very different concomitant thought foci and are therefore different emotions.

Neurotic Emotions and Behavior

To turn attention to the psychology of neurotic behaviors and their relationships to human sexuality, it is important to discuss the interrelationships among the four absolutistic beliefs and their respective neurotic emotions and behaviors (Figure 2). By way of overview, the model states that the initial disturbance is one of anxiety (usually ego anxiety) that individuals create about their success and/or approval schemata. Other neurotic disturbances are consequent on anxiety and may be seen either as avoidance (conscious or subconscious) of that pain or as a resignation to that pain. The particular reaction to anxiety, if the individual invokes an LFT philosophy, is hypothesized principally to depend on the individual's own developmental history of successful and unsuccessful action strategies.

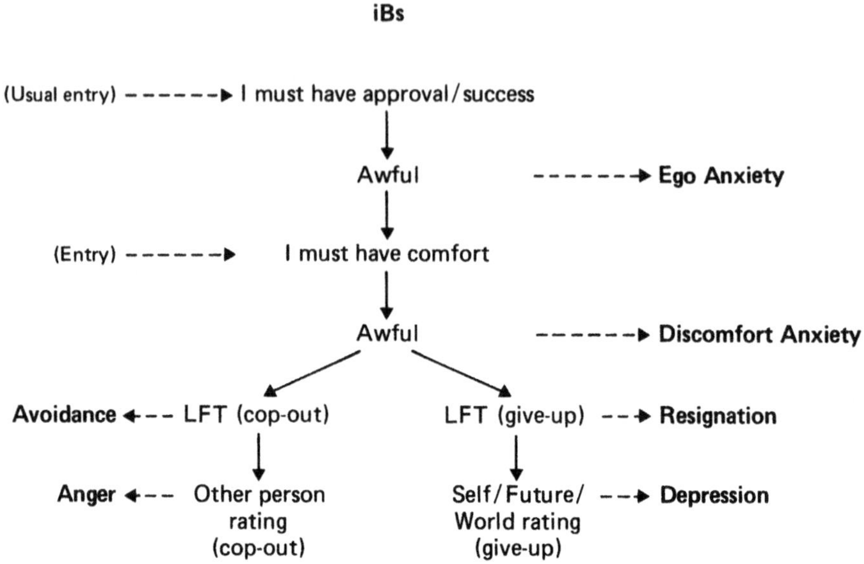

FIGURE 2. Sequence of irrational beliefs.

Ego Anxiety

The first iB involves "I must have approval and/or success" and is followed by iB number 2 "and wouldn't it be awful if I fail at obtaining those." Ellis discusses both schemta of approval and success under the heading of ego anxiety (1979). Usually it is the case that the individual links the two in a form such as "I must be successful in order to obtain approval." However, success and approval can be treated separately by the individual as will be indicated in relation to the emotions of shame and guilt. The present view, following Ellis, sees ego anxiety as primary and dramatic. Although discomfort anxiety can also be primary, also in agreement with Ellis, it appears that ego anxiety is by far the usual first step and that, again frequently, clinical anxiety presents in a client a picture of both ego and discomfort anxieties. It is noted that ego anxiety can exist without, or with minimal amounts of, discomfort anxiety, the case of the anxious performer having been documented (Gambrill & Richey, 1975).

It is well known that more than moderate degrees of anxiety are inhibitory to genital and particularly orgasmic performances. In relation to the many intimate and not so intimate behaviors involved with sexuality, the potentials for ego anxiety are practically limitless. Many will arise from and be variants of puritanical training of an individual: the individual "does wrong"; that is, an action that was unsuccessful in terms of obtaining approval from a significant other person (punishment may also be involved) even though the sex-related behavior in itself may have been pleasurable. Repetition of such puritical training of the individual may lead him or her automatically to adopt anxiety-related thinking styles about certain sex behaviors as being "wrong" and "bad." Other ego anxieties for the individual very commonly originate from perfectionistic demands (usually defined as the need to be more than merely adequate) of successful sex performance with, and thus approval from, a particular partner. For males and females, sexual performance anxieties make up a sizable proportion of problems for psychological practitioners, and the literature is replete with various therapy approaches to assist people with such anxieties. Given the noncontent, processing emphasis of RET, there is no reason to assume that performance and approval anxieties originate in any different way for homosexual and heterosexual individuals. Although no accurate data are available for frequencies of presenting anxieties in relation to sexual preferences, the mechanisms for generating the anxieties are the same regardless of the sex of one or one's partner. Homosexual individuals are no less or more immune from the human capacity to think irrationally in any area and particularly in relation to sexual functioning. An individual can overfocus on the demand for love and approval from a person of either gender and the strength of the concomitant awfulization ("in case I don't get what I need to have") will determine the degree of the anxiety emotion and behavior.

Discomfort Anxiety

As indicated, discomfort anxiety is the usual second step and involves a self-statement such as "I must have comfort and wouldn't it be awful if I am in discomfort." Given ego anxiety, the individual has a pain stimulus as a basis from which to irrationally demand comfort. The consequence (or concomitant) of ego anxiety becomes an activating event for discomfort anxiety. In certain cases, discomfort anxiety can be seen as primary. There may be an external stimulus over which the individual has no current control and which is uncomfortable in its intensity. A simple sexual example would be a harmless and mild genital rash which is irritated during intercourse. The "I must have comfort and isn't it awful that I haven't got it" may be invoked in such a circumstance which is seen not to involve the demands of either approval or success. Discomfort anxiety, as elaborated, is the emotional aspect of LFT that theoretically, but probably not practically, can be separated from the behavioral aspect (see the following section). It is useful to point out that the separate terms *ego anxiety* and *discomfort anxiety* refer only to points of origin of anxiety, namely needs for approval and success and comfort respectively. The physiological anxiety patterns that are associated with each cognitive focus are seen as the same. The intensity of emotional pain will depend on how strongly focused the individual is on the cognitions of awfulization about the states of affairs that are not the way they "should" be. The model, so far elaborated, allows for a cycle within the sequencing of iBs. That is to say, the demand for comfort, followed by the awfulization, follows the initial demand for success and approval.

As was made plain for ego anxiety, discomfort anxiety equally can apply to heterosexual and to homosexual behaviors; the same psychological processing mechanisms apply. An example is the situation in which an individual is overconcerned about sexual performance with a particular partner of either sex and who then, through invoking the discomfort-anxiety paradigm, becomes anxious about his or her own anxiety. Simple situations like this can become more complicated by the individuals' reinvoking the ego-anxiety paradigm by insisting to themselves that they "must not" let their partner see them as anxious. Again, because the RET model fundamentally stresses a psychological processing mechanism as being independent of psychological substance or content, there is no reason why a particular sexual preference group would have a monopoly on the particular psychological mechanisms leading to discomfort anxiety.

Low Frustration Tolerance

LFT is Ellis's pivotal concept in his explanation of the neurotic styles, and he gives it a good deal of focus in his discussions of the pathology of homosexuality. Cognitive theorists have emphasized the active nature of motivation, and central to that interpretation is the human capacity to recognize relationships among events and to predict the likelihood of outcomes on the basis of prior experience. Those cognitive skills have been referred to as "expectancy," and Bolles (1974) has identified Tolman's (1932) model of behavior as prototypic of subsequent models of human action. Humans value strategies that they expect will reduce pain and will invoke actions consistent with such plans. In that regard, the present model proposes two basic versions of the behavioral aspect of LFT that are consequent on the emotional aspect (discomfort anxiety). The cognitive focus of "I can't stand it" has two aspects, those of copping out (where the individual has a history of successful avoidance strategies), and (b) giving up (resignation; where there is a history for the individual concerned of failure of avoidance strategies).

Cop-Out LFT

There are numerous possible self-statements (sometimes called rationalizations) that can lead to the myriad behaviors that humans undertake in order to avoid their discomfort. Clinicians are familiar with clients' notions of, for example, "It's too hard, I'll do it later" or "I didn't want to achieve that goal anyway." The notion of cop-out LFT is a protection device for the individual against his or her own self-created anxiety pain associated with the pursuit of the longer-term, self-defined, self-benefitting goals. Those longer-term but difficult goals receive a cognitive distortion in terms of a current lessening of their importance in favor of an immediate, less difficult, diversionary action plan. The short-term pain-avoiding neurotic (longer-term, self-defeating) behaviors are legion and include excessive alcohol intake, inactivity, withdrawal and laziness, smoking, overeating, and dozens of possible other-goal-directed activities. All serve a common purpose of allowing a focus on an activity that thereby displaces (usually only temporarily) the focus on the original goals.

Ellis (1962, 1965) originally saw homosexuality within the cop-out LFT paradigm. Homosexuality was maintained basically through a heterosexual anxiety. Even when their society punishes them for doing so, homophiles follow short-term, relatively anxiety-free, soft options, which are likely to involve longer-term societal difficulties. Ellis (1976) has changed his views and now holds that exclusive homosexuals are not necessarily disturbed. An outline of Ellis's more recent views follows later in the chapter where it will be argued that pathology is independent of sexual preference. Discussion of nonpathological motivation for sexual direction is reserved for that later subsection. At this point, discussion focuses on sexual preference and neurosis.

There is no doubt that much (particularly male) homosexual behavior is motivated by LFT where the individual goes for immediate gratification, with little or no associated anxiety or effort, at the expense of longer-term heterosexual acceptance. Most clinicians are familiar with the not uncommon situation where the individual erects sometimes huge heterosexual performance anxieties that, along with cop-out LFT, maintain a homosexual orientation. There is an evident cop-out LFT philosophy centering on the view that it is too difficult (i.e., "My anxiety is too high") to pursue strategies that will increase heterosexual activities and reduce heterosexual anxieties. Other related views and attitudes are also usually, in varying degrees, clearly distorted, erroneous, and indeed delusional about specific information and more global ideas of heterosexuality. Such views are particularly noted within groups of exclusive (or fixed) homosexuals who justify their continuing homosexuality in terms of misinformation in the absence of any experience and first-hand data to the contrary. As Ellis states at length (1965), those particular homosexual individuals frequently display neurotic symptoms, again usually involving cop-out LFT, in relation to many other areas of their lives. Their neuroses frequently are strong and pervasive and are evident even to the untrained diagnostic eye. They tend to be unhappy and underachieving people. Homosexuals within the LFT paradigm are seen as addicts to their pain and effort avoidance patterns about which they may show little insight.

It is important to state the obvious in relation to the similar patterns within a heterosexual orientation. It is true that many heterosexuals continue to pursue self-defeating patterns; for example, repeatedly choosing "instant" sex from easily available partners who, in terms of longer-term socially acceptable goals, are inappropriate. Further, within a heterosexual orientation, many subtle and frank sexual deviations occur that are pathologically motivated. Not only are cop-out LFT attitudes evident in terms of the sexuality of heterosexuals but neurotic symptoms are associated with many other areas of their lives.

It appears that a number of homosexual individuals who subscribe to an LFT philosophy are aware of their neurotic styles in the same way that phobic individuals usually are aware of their (avoidant) neurotic styles. Insights into self-sabotaging behaviors of longer-term, self-defined goals may be very acute. A phobic individual would find it easier, say, to ride elevators than to walk stairs even though there would be short-term pain in pursuing such longer-term self-benefitting actions. The homosexual individual within that paradigm would conceptually prefer (the basis of all goals) heterosexual activities and associated behaviors in the longer term, for whatever reason(s), even though, because of discomfort anxiety, to pursue such activities in the short-term would be painful and effortful. Although adequate research on the question is lacking, it is agreed that some, although probably a minority of, homosexual people have a fundamental heterosexual orientation but continue with homosexual activities via a conscious cop-out LFT view of the world.

LFT may also play central roles in the homosexual orientation itself. Not uncommon are homosexual individuals who would prefer a homosexual longer-term relationship but who, in their continuing sexual activities, go for the more transient, perhaps more anonymous, sexual contacts, a style of sexual activity not conducive to their longer-term goal. That is to say, the effort of pursuing individuals more appropriate to a longer term relationship is seen as too difficult or requiring too much effort.

Overall, the author agrees with Ellis's emphasis on LFT in the neurotic styles, and, per the theme of the present paper, homosexual individuals are seen as potentially neurotic as heterosexual individuals. It is true that homosexuality in many instances is a result of pathological motivation. In relation to cop-out LFT (in varying degrees "the human condition"), individuals divert their sexual activities into the usually readily available homosexual direction away from heterosexuality with which they have associated their self-created anxieties and ideas that lead to an LFT cop-out life-style. Neurotically motivated homosexuals may or may not have insight into the motivations that underlie their behaviors.

It would be senseless to discuss any aspect of sexuality without offering full recognition to the potential and actual physical and emotional pleasures associated with sexual activities. It is pertinent (if, to some, commonplace) to point out that, just as heterosexuals have these pleasures, so too do homosexuals. Consequently, to discuss motivation even within the pathological group of homosexuals only in terms of avoidance reactions is to offer a myopic view. Clearly an attraction is present between chosen sexual partners, whatever their gender, based on physical, emotional, and cognitive aspects.

Give-Up LFT

Within the present model, give-up LFT is seen as the equivalent of passivity or learned helplessness and does not involve active behavioral concomitants. To that extent, it is different from the avoidance, cop-out variety. Give-up LFT instead focuses on the belief "I can't stand it" in the form of "I can't cope" and contains the implication that an avoidance behavior is unavailable because of an inhibition associated with it. A not uncommon example of this is the individual who creates approval anxieties about particular females and males and, as a consequence, has no interactional sexual activities. Give-up LFT, or resignation, represents behavioral inactivity and is a conduit linking the pain of discomfort anxiety (with which the individual "cannot cope") with depression, of which this anxiety is a part. Give-up LFT, in the present model, results from (a) the strength of the irrational beliefs underlying ego anxiety and discomfort anxiety, and (b) the individual's developmental history wherein it is postulated that, probably from an early age, avoidance activities have been generally unsuccessful. Resignation to pain (neither coping with nor avoiding pain) implies a failure to meet cognitive needs.

Anger

Just as avoidance LFT is a protection against pain, so too is anger. A cop-out LFT philosophy is included within the psychology of anger. The steps from the initial ego anxiety leading to anger, following Ellis's ABC notations, are as follows.

A: A non-compliant act by another person;
B: "I need your cooperative action in order to be successful and for you to show that you love-approve of me, and isn't it awful that you don't cooperate";
C (A): Ego anxiety;
B: "I shouldn't feel uncomfortable and isn't it awful that I do";
C (A): Discomfort anxiety;
B(i): "I can't stand my discomfort";
C(i): Avoidance;
B(ii): "I can't stand your noncooperation";
C(ii): Blame.

In other words, it is hypothesized that anger results from a simultaneous cognitive focus on avoiding discomfort anxiety and externalizing the cause for the discomfort anxiety onto the noncooperative individual. In effect, the individual is seen as replacing one neurotic state (anxiety) with another (anger). That view therefore sees the angry individual fundamentally as a fearful individual, who requires certainty and predictibility from others and the world and who is threatened when events go in an unpredicted way. Anger is the mechanism that protects the individual against his or her own pain (the threat), and it is hypothesized that the degree of anger will reflect the degree of initial anxiety. The steps as detailed above are probably not conscious to the individual while he or she is being angry. Frequent rehearsal of cognitive processes will lead to subconscious, automatic thinking and, as can be readily seen, the angry individual often has a good deal of fervent self-righteousness behind such a statement as, "you should not have done that action."

It is well known that varying amounts of anger and physical aggression may be motivational for both heterosexual and homosexual activities. Anger, in the sense of retaliation, is one of the many nonsexual goals to which sexual activities can be directed. The power–control (success) motive in individuals can be strong. There is large topic of varieties of aggression within sexuality. Suffice to indicate here that, for example, the various sado-masochistic elements within subgroups of heterosexuals and homosexuals are often neurotically driven by variants of the basic iBs relating to ego anxiety.

Depression

Depression centrally involves the cognitive focus on "I cannot cope and I will never be able to cope," which, with the generalization to future occurrences, contains the emotional concomitant of "doom and gloom." As Beck (1976) points out, generalized doom and gloom can have a differential focus (although usually involving a mixture of all three aspects) on the self, the world, and the future. Ellis (1979) indicates that the depressive paradox of self-deification and "self-devilication" is contained in the grandiose ego anxiety focus of "I must be successful—I must have love" and the global rating self-statement of "I am no good." Within the present model, depression is seen as following resignation LFT. The cognitive focus of depression, which is additional to that of resignation LFT, is a generalization of the type "It will never be any different"; "I will never succeed"; "It is all bad"; "I am all bad"; "It's all my fault."

Depressed individuals usually suffer from lowered sex drive and interest along with other physical behaviors; they tend to be sexually inactive even when opportunities for sexual activities are presented. It is noted, however, that some individuals will be motivated by their depression (usually mild) into heightened sexual activities, to more frequent and perhaps promiscuous episodes, in order temporarily to allow themselves diversion from their depression. Humans may have a specifically sexual basis for depression just as they may have a specifically nonsexual basis. To be not loved by a particular partner is not an uncommonly given reason for depression. Needless to say that the direction of sexual preference has no bearing on individuals' capacities to depress themselves.

Guilt

The cognitive mechanisms of guilt follow from the schema of success ("I must succeed and I didn't: I broke *my* rules!") and is consequent on the individual's refusal to accept his or her own poor performances. The general irrelevance of the approval schema in guilt can be seen in the common situation of an individual's continuance of strongly negative self-ratings in the face of exhortations from others to the contrary. Guilt is seen as additional to depression.

Human sexuality is frequently associated with guilt. Homosexuality in our Western society has more taboos than heterosexuality. These generally become internalized through indoctrination within the thinking processes of developing children and adolescents. It is indeed rare to find the homosexual individual for whom there has been parental and societal sanction for his or her sexual expression in the way that is commonplace for the heterosexual individual. As Pillard (1982) says,

> Gender identity is a personality attribute that emerges in the first years of life and is reinforced by practically every human interaction. We continually train the child in appropriate gender behavior and how to direct sexual impulses in socially approved ways. (p. 412)

To act against those learned constraints is, for many, to begin the psychological processes involving guilt. However, there are data to suggest that differences between homosexuals and heterosexuals are nonexistent in terms of measures of psychological disturbances or maladjustment (Gonsiorek, 1982b). Even among those better studies of homosexuality and adjustment (e.g., Bell & Weinberg, 1978) which did find significant differences between heterosexual and homosexual individuals, there were somewhat mixed results. Whatever the case may be, heterosexually related guilt problems are as commonplace as homosexually related ones for males and females in a clinician's client population. Given that individuals become anxious about any number of sex-related issues, they have the potential to become guilty.

Shame

Within the RET domain there has been confusion about aspects of shame and guilt (e.g., Grieger & Boyd, 1980; Wessler & Wessler, 1980). Shame, according to this view, contains a focus on the schema of love and approval held by the individual, of the kind "I must have your approval and love, and if you saw me acting this way I suspect that you might disapprove: I am breaking *your* rules." Shame, therefore, is primarily ego anxiety involving approval which, almost invariably, also contains a large secondary component of discomfort anxiety. It is usual for ashamed individuals to follow a cop-out LFT track and avoid facing the person(s) in front of whom they are ashamed. Shame, being an anxiety phenomenon, does not contain self-judgement nor self-punishment. Shame is the result of iBs in individuals who accept their own (poor) behaviors but which they want kept secret from others.

In a basically heterosexual society, it is clear that shame motivates many homosexuals to remain "in the closet," particularly those individuals for whom no real other (say, occupational or financial) disadvantage would accrue as a result of their open display of homosexual preference. To "come out," for many, is to confront a good deal of their own shame in front of their parents and friends, within their own community, and with other people whom they might meet. The courage that such an action takes for many homosexuals is the courage principally of confronting their own anxieties about that situation. Shame need not be the only reason for individuals to hide their sexual preference. There may be very real occupational disadvantages to openly declaring one's homosexual preference. Similarly, many homosexuals choose to remain covert about their activities in order to prevent, say, their parents from embarrassment (i.e., the parents' own shame).

Shame may be a secondary feature of depression and guilt as would be the case for the individual who thought irrationally within both approval and success schemata and who followed the resignation LFT path (Figure 2).

General Comments

The sequencing of the four irrational thought processes, with the concomitant emotional and behavioral disturbances of the latter three, indicates that disorders at a particular level result from disorders at earlier levels. Related to that is the question of whether or not individuals with disturbances beyond anxiety are conscious of sequentially prior disturbances. In that regard, the separation of avoidant LFT from resignation LFT is pertinent. The notion of give-up LFT may, but need not, carry with it an awareness by the individual of escape from discomfort anxiety, as was discussed earlier. It appears that any awareness of motives for the many possible behavioral and cognitive avoidances, including sexual, reflects the habit strength underlying such tactics. Anger, as generally is evident, does not contain the conscious awareness of anxiety. Anger, as defined in the present model, in fact, is a protection against personal pain and generally results from automatic processing of cognitions involved with fear. The resignation LFT track by definition does contain awareness of personal pain. For example, the clinical presentation of depression frequently contains a major subcomponent of anxiety.

The model as presented so far deals only with what may be termed *first-run* problems. Although sequencing is explicit, individuals do have emotional disturbances about their own emotional disturbances, which may be termed *second-run* problems. The point in the second sequence that receives the individual's focus, and that thereby determines the second-run problem, may not be identical to that of the first sequence. The second sequence focus will be influenced by the first-run problem, itself having become an (internal) environmental variable (an experience) for the individual, which may differentially relate to schemata other than those involved with the initial disturbance, and by such other likely factors as distance from the initial activating event (i.e., perceived strength of stimulus). In practical psychology, clients' problems are usually multitiered. Individuals become upset about having become upset; also they become upset that they might become upset. Discomfort anxiety about possibilities of reexperiencing other disturbances, including anxiety, is not uncommon (Ellis, 1979, 1980).

A further comment is required about ideas presented on avoidant LFT and resignation LFT in order to allow illustration of the depressed individual who sometimes shows anger. It is probable that such a situation may result not from anger about depression (i.e., a second-run problem) but rather a temporary alternation within the LFT framework (from resignation to avoidance). Within the present model, LFT links the two emotional states; anger includes avoidant LFT and depression includes resignation LFT. However, anger is clinically contained within depression (and is not the primary disorder in its own right) because of the individual's greater focus on resignation philosophy.

Sexual Preference and Neurosis

It is important to outline a model of human psychological functioning in order to draw attention to the differences between normal and neurotic behavior that can be understood not in terms of differences among human goals and preferences but in terms of thought mechanisms that process those goals. Humans have three broad, guiding schemata of love/approval, success, and comfort respectively. Schemata influence goals in life that are definable on a short–long term continuum. The interrelationships among the schemata and the more specific life goals, through which those schemata find expression, no doubt are complicated and span any individual's lifetime from a very early age. The RET model focuses on cognitive processes as being independent of cognitive goals, and attention is given to how individuals think about their particular goals. It is the thinking styles (rational or irrational thought processing), not the particular goals, that are concomitant with emotions and behaviors that, in turn, are diagnosed as normal or abnormal. Rational-emotive therapy, naturally enough, involves changing individuals' thought processing from irrational to rational.

A major aspect of the RET model is the level of frustration tolerance people hold in relation to their goals. To achieve most goals, interaction with one's environment is essential. Some goals, because of an uncooperative environment, will never be attained; others will require effort sometimes over many years; others are relatively easy to obtain. Individuals, because of their LFT, frequently do sabotage particularly the more difficult, longer-term goals in order for more immediate reinforcements. Thus, in therapy, emphasis is given to an individual's goals in relation to thought processing.

In terms of sexuality, a person's particular preference is not the basis for determining the question of psychological normality. Indeed, as Ellis (1962, p. 248) says, homosexual acts "in themselves are normal enough," a view consonant with that of Davison (1976, 1978) and others within the specialist psychology literature. The argument concerning abnormality is necessarily focused on psychological mechanisms involved with, rather than, sexual preference *per se*. The model presented earlier allows demonstration of the neurotic involvements with homosexuality and heterosexuality, which are seen to be the same. The model also gives focus to nonneurotic thinking styles in terms of preferences for goals.

There are conflicting ideas about gender identity (Karlen, 1971) within a determinist tradition and no single, even broad view enjoys general consensus. Gender identity clearly is the result of complicated processes and we simply do not know much about them, although there are reasonable hypotheses to describe particular instances and variables associated with homosexuality (e.g., prison homosexuality). Whatever adequately designed and executed future research will explain about the phenomenon, it is clear that humans do have preferences over many areas of their functioning, including sexuality, and they are by no means necessarily victims of their earlier psychological training. Humans need not be irrevocably fixed in terms of their sexual expression. They have choice over goals in relation to their happiness ideals, to which RET gives strong emphasis.

A number of ideas are put forth, particularly by writers of the psychoanalytic persuasion (cf. Pillard, 1982), indicating homosexuality necessarily to be pathological. It is of interest to look to some of those views.

1. A homosexual orientation is at the expense of acceptance within a heterosexual society, and therefore homophiles display LFT when they ignore those societal sanctions, however unjust those sanctions may be. The homosexual, within this view, perhaps with appropriate therapeutic guidance, is able to work at and overcome anxieties associated with the

more socially sanctioned and therefore more self-benefitting, longer-term heterosexual pursuits. In a more extreme LFT thinking style, there are individuals who, in their quest for immediate gratification, follow sexual action strategies on a promiscuous rule-breaking basis (e.g., public lavatory haunting) for which there are more immediate penalties from being caught.

Several comments may be made. As discussed earlier, many homosexuals are seriously maladjusted in terms of LFT, not only about sexuality but about other significant areas of their lives. It is reiterated that homosexuality *per se* is not the problem, although it is clear that homosexuality can lead to a problem if the individual runs risks of being apprehended by society for breaking rules. The lavatory-haunting homosexual, like the heterosexual "flasher," who overfocuses on immediate gratification, runs risks of negative consequences in most Western societies. Those who undertake such activities, particularly on a regular basis, when odds of being apprehended are increased, are functioning in terms of LFT, unless they have subnormal intelligence. Most observers would agree that such individuals are shortsighted. In this example, the definitions are clear and the likely disadvantages (being apprehended) are fairly immediate when they occur. Some professionals think that the same LFT, shortsightedness model also applies to homosexuals who do not chase instant, promiscuous sex. They may be in a satisfactory homosexual relationship but, because they are homosexually oriented in a heterosexual society, are also self-defeating in a longer-term context. In this kind of example, definitions become blurred and disadvantages more distant and hypothetical. Clearly the more moderate homosexual, although he (keeping to the male gender) may be tempted to seek more readily available sexual gratification, demonstrates high frustration tolerance in the same way, to use Ellis's (1965) example, that heterosexuals who would love to have intercourse with teenage girls "sanely" accept the fact that society would incarcerate them for doing so. The moderate homosexual resists LFT urges. He gives appropriate focus to longer-term reward. He wants to maintain his homosexuality and his nonincarcerated status. Although society may have sanctions against homosexual activities, he will reduce risks of being caught by exercising a high frustration tolerance.

The notion of frustration tolerance involves criteria for the individual that are hypothetical and probabilistic because the goals being considered are in the future. There are no guarantees that goals will be obtained, nor are there any certainties that goals will bring anticipated degrees of personal happiness; there are only probabilities. In all humans, the mental equations involving goals and preferences, required efforts, environmental blocks, and other variables have few constants; they are changing equations. The moderate homosexual who is content (i.e., undisturbed) about his sexual expression, which is considered low-risk in a forbidding society, operates in terms of a mental equation that is appropriate within his sexual preference. He does not operate in terms of those absolutist thinking styles characteristic of the obsessive cruiser, and he can delay gratification to an appropriate time and place. At issue is whether or not homophiles who are undisturbed about their homosexual orientation are wise in reducing risk by exercising high frustration tolerance in societies where there are penalties for homosexuality. The argument is not about whether LFT or neurosis in general leads people to become homosexual.

It is unwise to talk of society as a whole as being highly restrictive to homosexuals. Many societies have legalized homosexuality (e.g., Britain, some Australian states), which ensures that people cannot legally be discriminated against in terms of sexual preference. Society is not a unitary concept across Western cultures. However, the mere existence of a statute ensuring nondiscrimination does not mean that psychological and social pressures do not arise from various groups within a society. Whatever the laws, many groups will continue to discriminate in theory and practice against homosexuals. Of course, individuals do not interact with all groups in a society and, just as there are groups unfriendly to homosexuals, there are those that are friendly, even in societies where there is legal sanction against homosexuality. Like most other subcultures, homosexuals tend to function mostly in social, leisure, and occupational subgroups that are accepting and friendly, be they large or small, homosexual or not. The various support groups are reinforcing of particular aspects of the individuals' lives.

2. Some authorities hold that homosexuals are disturbed because they will not try heterosexual activity but will then prejudicially conclude that they prefer relations with members of their own sex. It is true that large numbers of homosexuals have not had heterosexual experiences, but that situation, alone, would appear to be an unusual basis on which to diagnose neurosis. The same point could be made in terms of exclusive heterosexuality, for example, or about individuals who have not sampled the game of chess or the study of philosophy in order to discover those respective pleasures. Homosexuals, for reasons not well understood, choose a partner of the same sex with whom they can have physically and emotionally enjoyable experiences. The mere existance of an alternative is not a reason for an individual to take up that alternative if he or she is satisfied with the chosen option. However, the point about prejudices is well taken. Prejudices are seen as a function of (reaction

to) basic anxieties, and they can be held by individuals about all manner of topics. When heterosexuals are prejudiced about homosexuals, or vice versa, such views are clearly indicative of pathological thought processes.

Some authorities point out that many homosexuals do have heterosexual relations (they may even get married) but remain basically homophilic because either they never give heterosexuality a full chance, or they find it to be as good as or better than homoerotic relations but find the latter more easily available or more attractive for nonsexual reasons. This author agrees that such a view no doubt is true for many homosexuals. For example, many heterosexually married males will actively pursue relatively quick and easily found homosexual relations for the thrill-seeking, immediate gratification that may not be available with their wives. To assume, however, that all heterosexually experienced homosexuals who continue with even intermittent homosexuality do so for nonsexual reasons is to believe that *all* sexual pleasures are available through heterosexuality and to deny the possibility that certain, different sexual pleasures are available through homosexual relations. Homosexual activities are seen by many who are experienced in both preferences as being pleasurably exciting in a way different from heterosexual activities. Individuals undisturbedly may desire homosexual pleasures along with heterosexual pleasures.

3. Some writers hold that homosexuals are neurotic because they commonly have many fears, such as of rejection, heterosexual impotence, intense emotional involvement, and marital responsibilities. These fears are all seen as ego anxieties related to fears of failure and lack of approval. Although surely some homosexuals have such anxieties, there is no evidence that heterosexuals do not equally have them. Gonsiorek (1982b) undertook a critical review of studies spanning several decades relating psychological test data to homosexuals and concluded that

> these testing results overwhelmingly suggest that if there are consistent, measurable differences between heterosexual and homosexual populations, they are not in the range of scores indicative of greater disturbance in the homosexual groups. (p. 387)

Gonsiorek's critique supports the thesis of this chapter:

> this is not to say that psychologically disturbed homosexuals do not exist; nor does it mean that no homosexuals are disturbed because of their sexuality. Rather the conclusion is that homosexuality in and of itself bears no necessary relationship to psychological adjustment. (p. 394)

4. Some mental health professionals hold that homosexuals have high degrees of LFT, doing things the seemingly easy way in the sexual

area and also avoiding responsibility, hard work, and long range planning in other important aspects of their lives. The author agrees that neurotically motivated homosexuals indeed have LFT cop-out philosophies that are seldom restricted in their lives only to areas of sexual functioning. But to claim that almost all fixed or obligatory homosexuals are within that category of generalized neurosis and short-range hedonism is to rely on what appears to be a biased sample of homosexuals. It is not hard to locate fixed homosexuals within our society who display very adequately a high degree of frustration tolerance in relation to their numerous goals in life.

5. It is clear that one can meaningfully talk about the notion of sex disturbance; for example, sadomasochism, pedophilia, obsessive-compulsive fixations, bizarre and exhibitionistic sexual behaviors, and other clearly disordered, neurotic and psychotic activities. To reiterate, disturbed thinking and behavior is a function of being human and not of being homosexual. Disordered sexual acts are not the domain only of homophiles. Disturbed thinking, even of serious dimensions, relates to any number of behavioral patterns, including sexuality.

Sexual Preference and Sanity

A large number (probably a majority) of homosexual individuals, including those who are politically active within and outside the many gay rights groups, would disagree that *ipso facto* they have a fundamental psychopathology, an argument that has been put forth many times in both the popular gay and non-gay press. In the briefest of terms, they respond that homosexuality is a legitimate and nonpathological direction of sexual expression and that society, if it forbids homosexuality, is wrong and that therefore public attitudes and the laws in the particular society require change. Homosexual individuals who subscribe to that view would and do, often vehemently, discount any implication of their own sexual expression with pathology. Much in the psychological literature also follows the same line (e.g., Gonsiorek, 1982a).

The argument from the elucidation of the RET model indicates that individuals may be motivated in their sexual expression by preferential cognitive processing or by absolutistic processing. Individuals may engage preferentially in homoerotic activities and in heteroerotic activities just as individuals may engage compulsively in homoerotic and heteroerotic activities.

Ellis (1958) takes the position that the great majority of people are born with strong plurisexual tendencies; that is, they are prone to become sexually aroused and to achieve orgasm by (a) masturbation, (b) heterosexual contacts, (c) homosexual involvements, (d) sex with animals, (e) sex with inanimate objects, and (f) thoughts, fantasies, and dreams. Whether men and women have strong tastes and preferences (for biological and environmental reasons) to be heterosexual or homosexual, Ellis holds that they are still innately plurisexual and that they can train themselves, albeit with some degree of difficulty, to become sexually aroused and orgasmic with members of the sex to whom they are "naturally" unattracted. Ellis hypothesizes, in other words, that virtually all fixed homosexuals can learn to enjoy heterosexual acts (though not necessarily as much as they now do in same-sex participation) and that, similarly, virtually all exclusive heterosexuals, if they want to take the trouble of trying to change, can distinctly enjoy homosexuality. The fact that both homosexuals and heterosexuals tend to deny that they have bisexual capacities and the fact that heterosexuals often become homophobic and that homosexuals become heterophobic is largely because they are turning rational preferences for one form of sex into irrational fixations and compulsions. *Preferential* homosexuality and heterosexuality are healthy; *rigid, obsessive-compulsive* sexuality in both gay and straight individuals is neurotic (Ellis, 1976).

Thus the notion of sexual deviation, which is behaviorally based, can be only statistically meaningful. To quote Ellis (1976):

> I would tend to recommend that we stop speaking about sex deviations at all, that we drop the nasty, pejorative connotations that almost invariably go with the use of such terms and that instead we merely try to distinguish between sexual (and non-sexual) behavior that occurs in an emotionally disturbed and in a non-disturbed manner. Even then, we may have difficulty defining the word *disturbance*. But not as much as we seem to have with *deviation, perversion,* and *abnormality!* (pp. 285–286)

Conclusions

The psychology of homosexuality has been a muddy topic and one injected with as much opinion as fact. Inadequately designed and poor research with subsequent "bad" data are hallmarks of the area. This chapter has taken the view that there are too many unknowns relating to the origins and development of gender identity and sexual preference for authoritative statements to be made.

RET discusses both normality and abnormality of human functioning in terms of thought processing, and this chapter gives attention to the various neurotic styles and their relationships to heterosexuality and homosexuality. Sexual preference, like any human goal, is subject to absolutistic processing, hence neurosis, and to preferential processing, hence nondisturbed functioning. Many homosexuals operate in terms of neurotic disturbance with their sexuality as a central neurotic focus; the same is true of heterosexual individuals. Similarly, many homosexuals and heterosexuals operate in a markedly nonneurotic, undisturbed manner in terms of their sexuality. Sexual preference is not in and of itself definitional of disordered thinking and is unrelated to an adjustment–maladjustment dimension.

Given the thesis of this chapter, the author has resisted offering case material from homosexual clients that would illustrate issues of rational-emotive theory and homosexual preference. To do so would (a) give focus only to individuals whose homosexuality is implicated with neurosis (adjusted individuals do not present to a clinician), and (b) give focus to an example of homosexuality and neurosis when the same explications could be made in terms of heterosexuality and neurosis. To offer adequate caveats within the case material so as not to distort the present argument would require space beyond that permitted. Suffice it to say again that just as both homosexually and hetersexually oriented expressions can be the focus of neurotic motivations in terms of the model of pathology that has been presented, so too can each be the focus of nonneurotic, preferential motivations.

Homosexuality will continue to be controversial, and no doubt inadequate research will continue to find its way into the literature. However, there is justifiable interest in factors that determine sexual preference, and adequate data on that topic will contribute to an understanding of issues involved with homosexuality. At the present time, to consider homosexuality as symptomatic of a neurotic style is not justified, and the RET model, with its emphases on self-defined preferences or goals and self-determined thought processes and behaviors in relation to those goals, nicely allows a focus on factors other than homosexuality *per se* as being implicated with normal and abnormal functioning.

References

Anderson, R. C., & Pichert, J. W. (1978). Recall of previously unrecallable information following a shift in perspective. *Journal of Verbal Learning and Behavior, 17,* 1–12.

Beck, A. T. (1976). *Cognitive therapy and the emotional disorders.* New York: International Universities Press.

Bell, A. P., & Weinberg, M. S. (1978). *Homosexuality: A study of diversity among men and women.* Melbourne: Macmillan.

Bolles, R. C. (1974). Cognition and motivation: Some historical trends. In B. Weiner (Ed.), *Cognitive views of human motivation.* (pp. 1–20). New York: Academic Press.

Campbell, I. M., Lowe, B., & Burgess, P. M. (1983). *RET anatomy of neuroses.* Unpublished manuscript. Department of Psychology, University of Melbourne.

Clarke, J. C., & Jackson, J. A. (1983). *Hypnosis and behavior therapy: Treatment of anxiety and phobias.* New York: Springer.

Davison, G. C. (1976). Homosexuality: The ethical challenge. *Journal of Clinical and Consulting Psychology, 44,* 157–162.

Davison, G. C. (1978) Not can but ought: The treatment of homosexuality. *Journal of Clinical and Consulting Psychology, 46,* 170–172.

Ellis, A. (1958). *Sex without guilt.* Secaucus, NJ: Lyle Stuart.

Ellis, A. (1962). *Reason and emotion in psychotherapy.* Secaucus, NJ: Citadel Press.

Ellis, A. (1965). *Homosexuality: Its causes and cures.* Secaucus, NJ: Lyle Stuart.

Ellis, A. (1973). Rational-emotive therapy. In R. Corsini (Ed.), *Current Psychotherapies.* (pp. 167–205). Springfield, IL: Peacock.

Ellis, A. (1976). *Sex and the liberated man.* Secaucus, NJ: Lyle Stuart.

Ellis, A. (1977a). Basic clinical theory of rational-emotive therapy. In A. Ellis & R. Grieger (Eds.), *Handbook of rational-emotive therapy.* (pp. 3–34). New York: Springer.

Ellis, A. (1977b). *How to live with—and without—anger.* Secaucus, NJ: Citadel Press.

Ellis, A. (1979). Discomfort anxiety: a new cognitive-behavioral construct, Part I. *Rational Living, 14*(2), 3–8.

Ellis, A. (1980). Discomfort anxiety: a new cognitive-behavioral construct, Part II. *Rational Living, 15*(1), 25–30.

Eysenck, H. J. (1977). *You and neurosis.* London: Temple Smith.

Gambrill, E. D., & Richey, C. A. (1975). As assertion inventory for use in assessment and research. *Behavior Therapy, 6,* 550–561.

Garcia, E. J., & Blythe, B. T. (1977). *Developing emotional muscle.* Athens, GA: Georgia Center for Continuing Education.

Goldfried, M. R. (1979). Anxiety reduction through cognitive behavioral intervention. In P. C. Kendall & S. D. Hollon (Eds.), *Cognitive behavioral interventions: Theory, research and procedures.* (pp. 117–152) New York: Academic Press.

Gonsiorek, J. C. (1982a). An introduction to mental health issues and homosexuality. *American Behavioral Scientist, 25,* 365–384.

Gonsiorek, J. C. (1982b). Results of psychological testing on homosexual populations. *American Behavioral Scientist, 25,* 385–396.

Grieger, R., & Boyd, J. (1980). *Rational-emotive therapy: A skills based approach.* New York: Van Nostrand Reinhold.

Hauck, P. A. (1974). *Overcoming frustration and anger.* Philadelphia: Westminster.

Karlen, A. (1971). *Sexuality and homosexuality: A new view.* New York: Norton.

Kinsey, A. Pomeroy, W., & Martin, C. (1948). *Sexual behavior in the human male.* Philadelphia: W. B. Saunders.

Piaget, J., & Inhelder, B. (1966). *The psychology of the child.* London: Routledge & Kegan Paul.

Pillard, R. C. (1982). Psychotherapeutic treatment of the invisible minority. *American Behavioral Scientist, 25,* 407–422.

Tolman, E. C. (1932). *Purposive behavior in animals and man.* New York: Appleton.

Wessler, R. A., & Wessler, R. L. (1980). *The principles and practice of rational-emotive therapy.* San Francisco: Jossey Bass.

8

Healthy Living

Gary Witkin

Introduction

People generally find it easier to define healthy living than to display it openly. I see healthy living as the moderation of short-term pleasures in order not to compromise the attainment of longer-term goals such as personal happiness, a longer life, and self-actualization. My definition of healthy living allows for the use of "recreational" drugs such as alcohol, cigarettes, and marijuana. For some people, moderate use of these substances may have distinct personal advantages. I see a healthy lifestyle demonstrated by the individual who values temperance in eating, work, and recreation. Many of us simply enjoy an occasional smoke or drink. However, if people are expecting a newborn or if they have an illness, they would be wise to abstain from smoking and drinking entirely. Long-term chronic use of alcohol, tobacco, marijuana, and especially powerful drugs such as narcotics rarely bring about real advantages—rather, they usually result in great avoidance of responsibility, in withdrawal, and in conflict.

Healthy living is becoming almost a national obsession of Western industrialized societies. For example, in the United States, since 1960, the number of Americans who exercise regularly has increased from 45 to 75 million people (U.S. Department of Health, Education & Welfare, 1982). From the 39 million runners to the 11 million racquetball players to the 12 million aerobic dancers, Americans everywhere are choosing to exercise.

Professional and lay interest in healthy living has seen a remarkable

Gary Witkin • Behavior Modifiers, Valley Stream, New York, 11581.

increase in the past few years. Psychologists, social workers, physicians, nurses, pharmacists, and educators as well as politicians, journalists, and businessmen are all currently involved in helping people to live healthier lives. Today it is unusual to read a psychology, public health or related periodical without encountering at least one article on some aspect of healthy living. Newsstands are filled with popular magazines featuring articles on staying slim and physically fit. Major fast food chains such as McDonalds and Burger King have shown their sensitivity to changing food preferences by including vegetarian meals on their menus.

Health programs in industry have existed from the first days of the company nurse and physician. Now more than 300 companies employ full-time fitness directors (Fielding, 1979). An article in *The New York Times* (August 24, 1981) reported that at least 300 companies also have health programs for their employees. Ride along any parkway, beach boardwalk, or park trail, and you will notice individuals, young and old, bicycling, jogging, waterskiing, boating, horseback riding, playing golf, or simply walking briskly. As the "healthy living movement" comes of age, new industries are being developed and expanded. Racquet and tennis clubs, health spas, running and marathon racing clubs, and cross-country bicycling groups are proliferating across the Western industrialized nations. They are quickly becoming the modern social clubs. Moreover, as a result of the increasing demands placed on people, coupled with the growing awareness that traditional medicine is focused on pathology and not prevention, individuals are accepting an increased responsibility to improve the quality of their lives.

With this movement towards healthy living has emerged a trend toward fads and fanaticism. Recent television and newspaper reports have brought to our attention the excesses that can take place with respect to athletic training and eating. It has now been established that some athletes, women in particular, can become so vigilant about what and how much they eat that they create an anorexic and/or bulimic disturbance. Male and female body builders and other types of athletes have been expelled from pre-Olympic games because urine samples have revealed the consumption of steroids and other dangerous drugs. Even more widely consumed and dangerous are the liquid protein, appetite suppressant, and other dietary substances that hundreds of thousands use to lose weight. With the growing emphasis on a slim athletic figure has emerged a strong desire for a tan complexion. As a result we are now being cautioned that the increased incidence of skin cancer such as melinoma carcinoma may soon reach epidemic proportions (Weisman, 1979).

Today, despite a multimillion-dollar-a-year vitamin and health food industry, many individuals in modern societies remain unhealthy. For each individual who demonstrates a healthy living charcteristic that we value (e.g., a slim athletic physique, regular exercise, temperance in food, alcohol, and smoke) there are countless thousands who exhibit these behaviors too much or too little. Current approaches to remedy this problem are primarily based upon educating the public about healthy living. No one can say just how effective these approaches have been. However, measureable and significant environmental behavior changes have occurred as a result of employee programs in industry, for example, smoking, weight reduction, and stress management (Brownell, 1982; Donoghue, 1977). As rational-emotive therapy is applied to modify unhealthy life-styles in employee assistance programs now being offered to corporations, we will see how it improves the physical and mental well-being of employees at the worksite.

In this chapter I will discuss healthy living from an RET–humanist perspective (Ellis, 1962, 1973; Ellis & Becker, 1982; Ellis & Harper, 1975). I will present the cognitive distortions that many individuals have concerning healthy living. The RET program for helping modify weight, exercise patterns, and smoking will then be outlined. A discussion of problems involved in helping people to maintain newly acquired healthy living habits as well as the self-defeating nature of fanatical and excessive adherence to principles of healthy living will conclude the chapter.

RET Humanism and Healthy Living

Rational-emotive therapy has made a major contribution in helping people to initiate and maintain a healthy living style of life. In working with individuals who smoke or eat too much and exercise too little, RET professionals have at their disposal a variety of behavioral, cognitive, and affective change techniques. RET aims not only to help people to understand how they got themselves to overeat, underexercise, or smoke—although, this is certainly important. But more importantly, RET methods teach people how to (1) lose their weight, stop smoking, and initiate exercise, (2) identify and change ideas and thoughts that prevent them from both changing unhealthy behavior and from maintaining changes over time, (3) anticipate high-risk situations that are tempting and are likely to lead to "slips," lack of adherence, and recidivism, (4) accept themselves if they have either a lapse or a full-blown relapse, and (5) tolerate discomfort in these and other areas of their lives. Different healthy living techniques, such as self-monitoring, stimulus control, contractual agreements, and other cognitive-behavioral strategies are highly effective but only when they are initiated and then adhered to during and following treatment. In my experience, this is an important area where rational-emotive strategies are quite effective.

One need only review the literature on smoking, obesity, and exercise to see how extraordinarily high the dropout and recidivism rates are in these areas. In a recent article Schacter (1982) has demonstrated that most people who enter professionally administered treatments to lose weight and stop smoking have not been successful in their first or second attempt in modifying their own behavior. They will, however, try several times and many (66%) will eventually succeed. In other words, those individuals who choose professional treatments to lose weight and to stop smoking have probably repeatedly failed on their own. This means that they may be more difficult to treat and they are probably seeking help because they believe that their chances of being successful on their own are slight.

What are the implications of Schacter's findings for the rational-emotive practitioner? First, his data suggest that we best consider the reasons that the treated individual did not previously succeed, either with or without guidance. Unless we elicit these facts I think that we may repeat history, or if we do succeed, our success will only be temporary. Second, the initial expectations and intensions generated when individuals again consider entering programs for their weight, smoking, or exercise are as much the domain of the rational-emotive practitioner as the upset created when individuals fail during treatment or fail to maintain changes over time. No therapy is, in my opinion, as well suited to treat emotional upset, before, during, and after healthy living habits are formed, as is RET.

The third reason for utilizing the rational-emotive philosophy is far more important. In teaching principles of healthy living we are creating a strong bond between healthy attitudes and healthy behaviors. Each is mutually interacting with and directing the other. A rational-emotive humanistic approach to healthy living is not the same as an improvement in self-esteem based on a habit change (such as better nutrition, exercise, smoking cessation or weight loss). Improved habits do not make an individual a "good person," only a person who is behaving healthfully. In rational-emotive therapy we aim to achieve a profound and lasting philosophical change in people's attitudes about themselves, other individuals, and the world. We strongly and persuasively advocate long-term over short-term hedonism and encourage present discomfort (if it is necessary to achieve a desirable goal) for future pleasure. We try to teach self-acceptance, irrespective of one's behavior, as well as tolerance for the fallibilities of other humans. This is the RET–humanist philosophy. Why inculcate this philosophy? Because we hypothesize that in the long run people are happier if they are healthy and live longer, and more harmoniously with themselves and others around them.

Let me use an example to emphasize the value of teaching the rational-emotive humanistic philosophy within an environment where healthy living is promoted. Picture yourself as a member of an exercise program where you are learning to give up smoking cigarettes. For the last 21 days you have been able to taste food the way that it was originally intended to taste. You are no longer coughing up brown phlegm in the morning and you are able to walk up a flight of stairs without huffing and puffing. At the same time, while you are accomplishing these desirable healthy habits your attitudes about yourself and others are changing by learning the RET principles of self- and other-acceptance and the taking on nonblaming attitudes. You find that you are more able to tolerate your own and others' imperfections. You are more able to cope with stress and discomfort because you now know how to change the way you feel and behave. Your new attitudes are reinforcing your ability to maintain your new healthy habits; and your new habits are contributing to the attitude change as well. By vigorously using RET, you are creating a strong bond between healthy behaviors on the one hand and rational thinking on the other. Although you may have little influence over events in Lebanon, unemployment, interest rates, urban crime, or the threat of nuclear war, you can strongly grasp the reins that control your health.

Let me give an example of a facility where RET is being combined with healthy living promotion. In the smoking cessation, cardiovascular exercise, and weight reduction programs at Behavior Modifiers our participants listen to RET tape recordings, they watch RET videotapes, and they read RET books and pamphlets. Our cardiac rehabilitation participants view RET stress management videotapes while they are connected by holter monitors to the electrocardiogram machine and while they exercise on the stationary bicycles and rowing machines. At the same time that they are creating collateral blood vessels in their hearts through the supervised exercise, they are creating an association between rational behavior change and rational attitude change. To accomplish attitude changes we are attempting to first reinforce healthy behaviors directly. In the course of this bonding process principles of learning are used to facilitate attitude and behavior change.

It is not, in my opinion, sufficient for us to simply present rational-emotive pamphlets, books, and videotapes to individuals with unhealthy patterns of behavior and expect them to result in lasting alterations in attitudes and behaviors. We are educators, and part of being an educator is to be a role model. I have found that the individuals we work with are most enthusiastic about learning RET when it is presented by healthy, athletic-minded individuals with charismatic personalities. If they are not themselves athletic-minded, they are at least action oriented. They use songs, experiential exercises, music, self-disclosure, posters, cartoons, and *in vivo* activities (such as exercising and doing shame-attacking exercises with their "students").

I have presented the basic philosophical values that, I believe, define RET and that largely support its practice of helping people to live healthier lives as well as to avoid falling back into old habits. In the next section I will discuss several categories of irrational thinking that pertain to healthy living.

Cognitive Distortions in Healthy Living

Like the term *self-motivation,* the RET term *low frustration tolerance* is often a label. I have occasionally seen people use the term to put themselves down. Others may use the shorthand acronymn LFT as an excuse and then make no attempt to change the way they are behaving (e.g., "What's the use. I've got LFT"). By itself, the label may reinforce hopelessness. When used to describe rather than to label, the term LFT is a useful shorthand way to describe the irrational, self-defeating cognitions that cause people to seek longer and even more rewarding pleasures. Individuals who fail to attend exercise, smoking cessation, and weight reduction sessions pollute themselves with a host of excuses, rationalizations, and distortions. In a way, they want their taffy when they want it: yesterday, not tomorrow! Low frustration tolerance thinking is private self-talk that is repeated over and over with high volume (Ellis 1979, 1980).

Below I have listed several of the self-defeating thoughts that I have heard verbalized by individuals trying to achieve weight loss, to stop smoking, and to achieve physical conditioning. What is promising is the fact that none of these thoughts are inborn. Because they are learned or invented, it is possible to unlearn them. The first step is to become aware of these thoughts; the second, to actively dispute them; the third, to actively push to behave in a more adaptive and personally rewarding fashion, even though it does not feel right at first; and the fourth, to continue to practice thinking and behaving rationally. When I have observed people following through on these four steps, I have seen people stay in exercise, smoking, and weight programs long enough to see permanent changes in their style of life.

SELF-DEFEATING THOUGHTS IN WEIGHT REDUCTION

1. I need what I want when I want it!
2. I deserve something to eat after the awful day that I've had; life shouldn't be so hard.
3. It's impossible for me not to taste the food that I'm preparing for my family.
4. I'll only eat a handful and make up for it tomorrow.
5. I'll have one less mouthful tomorrow. Screw it! I blew it. I might as well finish the whole box.
6. Why can't I be like a normal person and eat like them? I can't stand this. I need something to chew.

SMOKING CESSATION

1. It's too hard. I'm addicted.
2. One cigarette won't hurt . . . as long as no one sees me.
3. My father lived until he was 85 and he smoked a pack each day since he was 16 years old.
4. Everyone's got to die of something.
5. At least I smoke a brand that is low in nicotine.
6. It's my only bad habit.

PHYSICAL FITNESS

1. I get enough exercise at work. I'm on my feet all day.
2. I can't stand being seen in leotards. My legs are too fat.
3. I need to be in the right mood to go to the gym.
4. Those people who work out are all stuck up.
5. I'm not the athletic type.
6. What would happen if I run into someone who knows me and they see what terrible condition I am in?

I have listed several common irrational thoughts or beliefs about exercise. I have found that these thoughts are largely present in sedentary individuals who, although not at risk medically, could particularly benefit from some form of activity. Next to each self-defeating thought is the core irrational philosophy or concept that is central to it. Once the basic self-defeating thought is elicited and acknowledged it is then possible to actively and persuasively dispute the core concept. Changing and reinforcing the core irrational belief is what distinguishes clinicians who aid people to remove their symptoms from those who help them effect a deep and profound philosophical change. In my experience, to do the former will result in either superficial change, relapses, or recurrent disturbances. To abet and then reinforce the latter will result in a durable change, with reduced probability of relapse and with lasting prophylactic effects.

Common Irrational Thoughts or Beliefs about Exercise	*Core Irrational Concept*
It is absolutely necessary to have an exercise facility nearby to where I live or work before I can even consider exercising.	The world should make things easy for me.
With so many different exercise programs available, it is totally necessary to be sure that I choose the proper one.	There is invariably one right precise and perfect solution and it would be terrible if this perfect solution is not found.
I must first lose weight before I can even consider doing any exercise. OR I'm not coordinated, I'd just make a fool of myself, OR I must have the right clothes to wear in order to exercise	I should be thoroughly prepared, competent, adequate, and achieving in all possible respects
I can't begin today, I think that I'm coming down with something OR I'm getting my period OR By the end of the day, I don't have enough energy left to get home, much less to work out.	Discomfort is horrible. One should remain sedentary and at rest when faced with even mild discomfort.

Helping People Develop Healthy Living Habits

To successfully lose weight, stop smoking, or adhere to an exercise program, people will more likely achieve their goals if they possess a heavy dose of frustration tolerance, realistic expectations, and self-acceptance. More than ever before we now have effective techniques to help people to eat better and lose weight, to stop smoking, and to exercise. But whereas we have good techniques to alter maladaptive habits, some say we are sorely lacking a technology of compliance. I disagree. I believe that we have the "technology" to improve compliance, but few of us are willing to use it for a sufficient period of time.

Poor eating, smoking, and exercise habits are learned over a lifetime. To expect that many years of developing maladaptive behavior can be undone during a 12-week program is just unrealistic. In rational-emotive therapy we teach people how to develop tolerance for frustration so they can reach and maintain their goals. We inquire as to what degree people's expectations are realistic before they embark on a program of healthy living. And we instruct them not to rate and measure their self-worth or humanness by success or failure. Unless they develop this RET philosphy and reinforce and refine it over a prolonged period of time I believe that most individuals will fall back into their old unhealthy habits.

How can we help change people's core irrational beliefs? And, most importantly, what can we do to encourage lasting changes in their behavior?

Exercise

Let us take as an example a woman who believes that she is not coordinated and therefore will make a fool of herself exercising. The RET therapist does not first question what she means by "coordinated." She may very well not be coordinated or the therapist may not agree with her definition of coordinated behavior. To argue this point is inefficient and focuses on a secondary issue.

A comprehensive and efficient plan of action with regard to this and other self-defeating beliefs is to get this woman (1) to assume the worst (e.g., "I am uncoordinated at this particular activity."); (2) to see her inadequate behavior as part of her human fallibility (e.g., "I am not a foolish or *worthless* person even though I behave foolishly and though I am worth *less* in the eyes of some people."); and (3) to *push* herself to take the risks of making errors and getting rejected (e.g., "it's a pain in the ass to make errors and bear rejection, but it's only hard, not *too* hard!"). This program will likely result in a durable change in her core irrational belief that she must be thoroughly competent, adequate, and achieving in all possible respects.

Another technique that can be employed with this same self-downing woman is to have her conduct a survey of other people. For example, she may ask 30 people about their opinions on individuals who lack coordination; she may inquire whether they believe that uncoordinated people are fools who should be rejected. This may, however, prove to be a palliative solution at best. At worst, this type of assignment may even backfire and produce an effect opposite to that originally intended. Thus, she may interview a small biased sample; or she may not believe the respondents of her survey; or she may report that she gets the point of the assignment "intellectually" but doesn't feel it "emotionally"—and she certainly may not behave any differently! On more than one occasion I have seen Albert Ellis skillfully translate this back to a client as follows:

> You understand *lightly* and *occasionally* that you are not a worm for being completely competent, but "emotionally"—meaning *strongly* and *often*—you still believe, "It is all right for others not to behave totally competently, adequately, and achievingly, but it is terrible for *noble* me!"

Here again the difference is marked between superficial and deep rational-emotive therapy.

Disabusing people of their self-defeating inertia-producing thoughts is not sufficient. The litmus test is their *behavior,* getting them to "turn up the volume" of their health-enhancing thought (e.g., "I am a fallible human being who will not achieve or perform well all of the time") and translating this into action. For example, "getting to the gym is only hard—not too hard!" Let us get our clients to change their behavior in the desired direction even though it feels phoney or unnatural at first. Sensible philosophies and healthy living habits get stabilized mainly by steady practice and not mere repetition.

The thoughts listed above are not exhaustive of the list of self-defeating thoughts that lead to and maintain disturbances in healthy living. Indeed, for many individuals even the word "exercise" results in knee-jerk negative associations such as "work," "discipline," "sweating," "denial," "pain," and "competition." I have found these connotations to be most often present for activities such as rope jumping, rowing, basketball, jogging, weight lifting, squash, tennis, and swimming, whereas bicycling, brisk walking, dancing, and other similar activities are less likely to meet with resistance due to these negative associations.

Rather than dispute these adjectives and the meanings behind them, I have found it most efficient first to get the individual inspired rather than perspired. Heated in-session debate, disputation, and confrontation are likely to be met with considerable resistance and inertia. I prefer to educate. You can bring to people's attention several good reasons why they personally would find it desirable, but not necessary or obligatory, to engage in more activity. There are fringe benefits to regularly exercising beyond the rewards of increasing high density lipoproteins and decreasing one's blood pressure. Individualize the discussion of the benefits of exercise to meet the personal motives of the person (e.g., more contact with members of a particular group, age group, social class, gender). Health spas, country clubs, tennis and racquetball facilities, boating, golf, horseback riding centers, and other locations are only the tip of the iceberg regarding places to enjoy activity. The information that helps to encourage us to change our minds about exercise is vast. What are the benefits of exercise?

1. If you exercise regularly, you will probably burn calories overtime and you will not be as hungry (Katch & McArdle, 1977). Not only does your body burn calories faster while you exercise, but it continues to do so for four or more hours afterwards, as well.
2. Conscientious exercise not only provides an outlet for energy, but it actually decreases the muscles' electrical charges in the same way that many of the leading tranquilizers do (Greist, Klein, Eischens, Gurman, & Morgan, 1979). Preliminary studies (Margolies, Sperduto, & Witkin, 1982) have attempted to demonstrate the benefits of exercise in conjunction with group cognitive therapy in treating depression. Exercise appears to improve sleep (Folkins, Lynch, & Gardner, 1972) and problem-solving (Folkins & Sime, 1981) in some individuals.
3. It has been associated with improved cognitive and intellectual functioning in children, adults and geriatric individuals (Gruber, 1975; O'Connor, 1969; Powell, 1974).
4. Regular exercise may help us to stay warmer in the winter. Research (McArdle, Katch, & Katch, 1981) has shown that the metabolism of active people speeds up more in cold weather than that of sedentary types, providing them with a highly effective internal furnace even when they are not engaged in strenuous exercise.
5. Physical activity may bring some relief from headaches (Atkinson, 1977) and asthma (Marley, 1977). Only 15 years ago an individual who had experienced a heart attack could be required to rest in bed for six or more weeks. Now, physical training is considered a standard prescription for individuals recovering from a heart attack (American Heart Association, 1980).

Overcoming Problems in Noncompliance

Assuming that it is possible to get people to initiate some form of physical activity, to what extent can we predict which ones are likely to maintain their participation? Nonadherence is an often overlooked problem. This is unfortunate because any treatment and the treatment's homework assignments are useful only to the extent that they are followed. Moreover, the amount of money that is spent on unused memberships to health clubs is probably equivalent to the gross national product of some third world nations.

In attempting to predict who is likely to drop out of a cardiovascular exercise facility versus those who are likely to regularly attend and renew their membership, research that I have conducted at the Hofstra University Health Dome (Witkin, 1983) focused mainly on demographic, biographical, physiological, and psychological trait variables. The investigation was able to account for 85% of the variance in discriminating those who dropped out from those who regularly attended and renewed their membership. Other researchers have correlated nonadherence to exercise with lack of spouse support (Andrew & Parker, 1979), smoking (Nye & Poulsen, 1974), blue collar status (Oldbridge, 1979), a poor credit rating (Taylor, 1969), and self-motivation (Dishman & Iches, 1981). It is hoped that in the near future we will be able to predict noncompliance on the basis of contemporary cognitions that precede and immediately follow enrollment in an exercise program.

Most studies attempting to explain relapse rates have noted that treatment of major addictions (such as overeating, smoking, alcoholism, and heroin dependence) all follow curves that are similar to those representing adherence to exercise programs (Morgan, 1977). These curves are characterized by a rapid and substantial decrease in the percentage of participants staying in treatment during the initial three to six months, an asymptote at this point, and a fairly stable plateau across the next 12 to 15 months. This similarity is provocative in suggesting the possible operation of a common mechanism. Dishman and Iches (1981) who have developed a paper and pencil test to predict nonadherence to exercise (Self-Motivation Index) have been able to account for most of the variance regarding dropping out.

Attrition from exercise programs averages at least 50% after six months (Brownell, 1982). Adherence is poor even among individuals who would be expected to be highly motivated such as men and women in cardiac rehabilitation programs (Carmody, Senner, Malinow, & Matarazzo, 1980). Among the techniques that we can use to help people maintain their participation in exercise programs are contingency contracting (Wysocki, Hall, Iwata, & Riordan, 1979), lotteries (Epstein, Thompson, & Wing, 1980), stimulus control for structuring the antecedents of exercise, for example, time and setting (Keefe & Blumenthal, 1980), individualized positive reinforcement such as praise, graphs of progress, and personalized temporal or distance-based goals (Martin,

Kattell, Webster, & Zegman, 1980), a buddy system, and telephone prompts. Recent research (King & Frederickson, 1980) has established the efficacy of cognitive procedures such as training individuals to better prepare for and to cope with specific relapse situations (Marlatt & Gordon, 1980), in this case, related to exercise.

Behavioral programs for obesity often prescribe lifestyle activity (Wilson & Brownell, 1980). These activities include parking some distance from the entrance to stores, disembarking from a bus before one's destination and using stairs rather than elevators or escalators. Originally, these activities were encouraged because few clinicans expected obese persons to be capable of strenuous activities. They have now found favor outside of the obesity area because of their potential for increased adherence and confidence in one's ability to discipline oneself. In particular, regular stair climbing has been associated with a reduced risk of heart disease (Paffembarger, Wing, & Hyde, 1978). As people can accomplish this, they may be able to increase their activity to more strenuous levels.

To summarize, in helping people to begin and (more importantly) to maintain a recreational exercise program it is best to: (1) get them to express the self-defeating cognitions and negative associations they have about exercise, (2) use either the socratic or hypothesis-testing approach to get them to see how their negative beliefs are false, unproven, unproveable, and especially interfering with their personal happiness, (3) have them express the advantages of defining exercise in broader terms and include many different types of recreational activity where they are using their bodies (as well as their minds), (4) get them to totally accept themselves as fallible humans who can tolerate imperfect solutions, discomfort, and the unfairness of the world, (5) educate them about why it would be personally desirable for them to participate in recreational activity, (6) illustrate the physiological rewards that they will obtain, and (7) anticipate and change the cognitions that in the past have resulted in relapses back to a sedentary life-style.

EATING

As noted above, very few individuals who enter programs to reduce their weight actually achieve their goals. Weight reduction programs are a revolving door whereby people pay large sums of money, attend a few sessions, and soon drop out.

A major departure from this norm is now taking place at facilities like Mt. Sinai Hospital in Cleveland, Ohio, Kaiser-Permanente Hospital in San Diego, California, and Behavior Modifiers in Valley Stream, New

York. Each of these facilities uses rational-emotive therapy (Ellis, 1962, 1973; Ellis & Bernard, 1983; Ellis & Grieger, 1977; Ellis & Whiteley, 1979) to help overweight individuals to abstain from eating regular foods, and instead to drink a nutritional supplement five times each day. The average male loses four to five pounds each week and women lose an average of three to four pounds each week.

Because of the clinically significant weight losses that keep occuring each week, the tape recorded RET sessions, telephone support, and strict medical supervision, protein-sparing supplemented fasting will, in my opinion, become in the next decade the treatment of choice to treat obesity.

Over several years we have gained considerable experience in predicting the thoughts that people tell themselves to begin nibbling on extra food, to go on a binge, and to miss sessions. In our RET groups we openly discuss these thoughts. By "innoculating" and preparing our overweight members to anticipate high risk situations we have been remarkably successful in helping people to sustain fasting long enough to acquire durable changes in their weight, blood pressure, sugar, and fats. Most people enter our program with little or no prior training in totally abstaining from food. They have repeatedly failed what Michael Mahoney has called the "rhythm method of girth control"—fasting on Monday to atone for Saturday and Sunday's indiscretions. Nevertheless, due to the bonding of rational behavior change with rational attitude change many of these individuals remain in our type of program much longer than anyone would have originally predicted. Many more will also probably keep their weight off longer than they would if they entered a more conventional treatment plan for their obesity.

More than three fourths of the individuals who enter supplemented fasting programs to reduce weight are women. Sally K., the individual I discuss in the next section, is an example of a woman who entered our weight reduction program with a medical diagnosis of hypertension and diabetes exacerbated by her chronic obesity. Sally is quite illustrative of the emotional upset that some women have encountered before they begin our program and how RET can address their problems.

Case Study of a Treatment Success

Sally K., a 40-year-old woman, was self-referred to the Behavior Modifiers Weight Control Program. During the initial interview she reported that, although she weighed 360 pounds, most of here excess weight had occured immediately after her marriage. She and her husband differed on how to raise their three children as well as on many other family matters.

Rather than leave the children with a man who cared very little about them, Sally decided that she had better do something about her life-threatening obesity. She was saying, in effect, "I'm staying alive for the sake of the children."

Typical of many members of our program, Sally had been prescribed diuretics as well as antihypertensive and diabetic medication by her personal physician to control her blood pressure and blood sugar. Like many, she avoided going to her physician mainly because of the embarrassment of being examined. The last time she had seen her physician he "yelled" at her to lose weight. To motivate her to lose weight he actually told her to buy a $100,000 life insurance policy and to name him as the beneficiary. The physician's paradoxical sarcastic remark, which was meant to motivate her, backfired. She responded to his comments and the barbs of her family by eating even more food and gaining more weight. While this was her typical response to perceived criticism, she also responded by eating when she felt even the mildest of any negative emotion—anger, jealousy, boredom, anxiety, and so on. Sally was fat not due to any deep-seated unconscious personal conflict, family conflict, or endocrine disturbance. She was fat because she ate too much and too frequently.

Protein-sparing supplemented fasting (Vertes, 1978) under weekly medical and psychological supervision was prescribed for Sally due to the severity of her obesity. She agreed to see our physicians and psychologists and to undergo a very extensive set of medical and psychological tests to determine if she was a candidate for the program. Several factors suggested a good prognosis: (1) Sally was self-referred, and although her husband was not supportive, she obtained a bank loan on her own to subsidize the program; (2) she was diagnosed as hypertensive and diabetic—Sally recognized that these symptoms would cause her early death and thus leave her children with a father who was "unloving" and "uncaring"; and (3) her scores on the Millon Behavioral Health Inventory (Millon, Green, & Meagher, 1982) suggested that she would adhere to a treatment program that was structured, well-explained, and included an initially high level of professional follow-up and reinforcement. Her self-efficacy expectation responses (Bandura, 1977) on our battery of tests indicated a realistic (60%) degree of confidence that she would lose 150 pounds.

Sally was shown that in order to remain in the program she would have to (1) lose weight each week, (2) self-monitor her responses to "high risk situations" and consumption of the supplement, (3) attend a rational-emotive therapy group each week, (4) make up missed sessions, and (5) tape-record each session. A red diagonal line was drawn on a weight graph representing a projected minimal weekly weight loss of two pounds per week. Two pounds is the absolute minimum we would expect an individual to lose each week on 420 calories per day. If she failed to lose weight for two consecutive weeks, or crossed the red line, she would have to be seen by the therapist, individually, for an additional expense, until she continued to lose weight. If she regularly missed sessions (psychological or medical), failed to make them up, did not self-monitor, (or self-monitored poorly), or consistently did not tape-record her sessions she would also not be permitted to remain in the group. If this occurred she would be seen on an individual rather than on a group basis.

Sally's psychologist and physician were instructed to reinforce her strongly, literally by shaking her hand, each week she showed a weight loss. The first week on the supplement she lost 12 pounds of water. Her blood pressure and blood sugar completely normalized within two weeks. Each week the weight graph and graphs of her reduced blood pressure, triglycerides, and cholesterol levels were shown to her. Reinforcement for abstinence from food and compliance to the program was immediate and very powerful. Sally lost 50 pounds in eight weeks at which time she was given her first parchment Certificate of Accomplishment. She was consistently "stroked" by the group and told that although she had little support at home she succeeded on her own and thus owed full responsibility for her success to herself.

Each week Sally was required to read a chapter of Ellis and Harper's (1975) *New Guide to Rational Living* and Penelope Russianoff's (1983) *Why Do I Think I Am Nothing Without A Man.* In addition to bibliotherapy, the ABC concept of emotional disturbance, RET posters, tapes by Albert Ellis such as *I'd Like to Stop, But . . .* (Ellis, 1976), rational-emotive imagery (Maultsby & Ellis, 1974), the rational barb technique (Kimmel, 1976), rational role reversal (Kassinove & DiGiuseppe, 1975), and a variety of other RET educational techniques were presented to Sally and her group colleagues.

During the initial telephone follow-up calls to her at home (at least once each week) Sally reported how little support her husband and children provided her. However, she took advantage of several additional individual consultations with her therapist, sat in on other groups, and played the tape recordings of these sessions on a Sony Walkman machine in her car and at home. As the weeks passed, Sally was using RET vocabulary to describe difficult situations. By talking other group members out of their disturbance she was at the same time convincing herself that the rational-emotive philosophy also applied to herself. She was beginning to acquire the long-range hedonism philosophy that her therapist and physician employed with her in other areas of her life as well.

With weight reduction, self-acceptance, and confidence, Sally has obtained part-time employment outside of her home. At the present time she is discussing whether a separation from her husband would be in her own best interests and improve the welfare of her children. Sally is a vivid example of the bonding of rational attitude change with rational behavior change. She has reduced her weight by 165 pounds, stabilized her blood pressure and blood glucose, and regularly participated in our aerobic dance program. Although she is now at her ideal weight she plans to stay in the weight reduction program for another six months in order to prevent relapses.

In the next section I present Donna. Unlike Sally, who accomplished a profound shift in attitudes and behavior, Donna represents the vast majority of individuals who in many programs lose weight, regain it, and then procede to berate themselves.

Case Study of A Treatment Failure

Often we find our clients with severe self-downing while we are helping them to lose weight, stop smoking, or begin exercising. In these cases I strongly recommend their using the ABCs of rational-emotive therapy and especially focus on disputing their self-defeating beliefs that involve self-ratings. This was successfully done with a woman named Donna who considered herself a worthless human being for having successfully lost a great deal of weight only to regain it. Donna believed that she had let down the other members of her group, particularly after all the assistance they had given her. Most of them had graduated to the next phase of the program where they were reintroduced to regular foods. Not only did she castigate herself as a failure as a weight loser, but also as a total human being. To "prove" how hopeless her situation was she produced as "evidence" the recently published book *The Dieter's Dilemma* (Bennett & Gurin, 1982) as "proof" that she was hopeless. She had already received ten 90 minute sessions of rational-emotive therapy in her group and reminded me that "even RET can't help me!"

Rather than "walk on eggs" and patch her up with palliative empirical disputes (e.g., "How likely is it that you were the only one in the group that regained some weight?") Donna was shown that she did indeed fail to lose weight and keep it off. But, what did this mean about her as a human being? We could correctly argue that she is worthless as a weight loser and that some in the group may have devalued her on this dimension; but where is the evidence that she is therefore worthless as a total human? If she lost all of her excess weight and kept it off for the remainder of her life, would that make her a worthwhile human?

These vigorous and persistent challenges to her self-defeating assumptions did not have an immediate enhancing impact on Donna. Only through using a variety of socratic questions was she able to see that she was definitely not equal to her traits, deeds, acts, or performances, although they were certainly important aspects of her identity. Even though she did manifest exceptionally bad characteristics, such as her obesity, smoking, and lack of exercise, these were only a few of her major aspects. To say, therefore, that she, a total human, was bad or worthless because some characteristics (her lack of self-control and bad habits) were bad was a vast overgeneralization and could not be logically or empirically validated.

Through the useful "fruit bowl" analogy, Donna was also shown that her totality as a human was so complex that she could not legitimately give herself a global rating. She, like everyone else, was an ongoing, everchanging process, with a past, present, and future. Although she disappointed others and herself, in the past, and might occasionally continue to be "worth*less*" to these people in the future, she agreed that she never need rate herself as a whole as worthless. If she rated herself as worthless when fat and worthwhile when thin, her emotional life would be as fragile as a "fiddler on a roof."

Donna was also shown that it was not set-point theory or any theory of obesity that caused her relapses. Rather, it was her failure to utilize the skills that were taught in the RET sessions, as well lack of her later reference of this theory, that caused her needless anxiety, depression, feelings of hopelessness, and additional overeating. If she wanted, she could either wisely choose to work harder to lose the weight and keep it off (as set-point theory suggests and as some people do) or she could choose to accept herself as obese, just as most people accept themselves as tall, short, or thin.

Occasionally it was beneficial for me to speak quite authoritatively and emphatically, using strong language, to help Donna comply with the program, and to avoid later dropping out of therapy. At the Institute for Rational-Emotive Therapy in New York City, I have often seen Albert Ellis vigorously employ irony, humor, and various kinds of witticisms to get his clients not to cop out. On more than one occasion I have seen Ellis ask a client something like, "What do you keep telling yourself immediately before you cram that food down your gullet and into your craw? 'I hate food'? 'I just eat to keep up my strength'?, 'I'll fix my dead mother by showing her that I can eat all I want without getting fat'? Or do you mean to tell me that the food automatically jumps out of the refrigerator, onto your plate, into your mouth, and forces you to swallow it?" I had better mention that before using humor and paradoxical intention, it is beneficial for a therapist to have a good relationship with the client.

In addition to humor and paradoxical intention, the RET practitioner can also use him or herself as an example of healthy living. For example, Ellis is a diabetic who during a group therapy session will bite into a sandwich of measured quantity and quality at the same time each week because he had been prescribed a strict diet. Witnessing his persistent, disciplined behavior has a lasting effect on many clients.

Smoking

It has been estimated that 360,000 persons die each year because of cigarette use and that one's life is shortened 14 minutes for every cigarette smoked (Julien, 1978). In addition to being responsible for the most common cancer among American men, cancer of the lungs, cigarette smoking mothers increase the rates of spontaneous abortion, stillbirths, and early postpartum deaths of their infants.

Reviews of the smoking cessation literature have consistently concluded that despite immediate treatment success, clients frequently fall back when followed up three to six months later. Thirty percent to 50% of smokers who develop chronic cardiac and pulmonary disease quit smoking after the disease is diagnosed. This has been empirically demonstrated in studies conducted by Russell, Wilson, Taylor, & Baker (1979) and Pederson (1981). However, smokers who do not quit soon after such diagnoses are made often continue to smoke indefinitely and experience considerable difficulty in quitting if they attempt it at all (Daughton, Fix, Kass, & Patil, 1980).

The following is a brief case history of Paul, a chronic smoker who failed to remain abstinent from cigarette smoking despite a serious heart attack. Although he is only one individual, and the results of his treatment are dramatic, his treatment is illustrative of how a rational-emotive therapist may work with a "hard-core" smoker.

PAUL: Case Study of a "Hard-Core" Smoker

Paul is a 57-year-old man who was referred by his physician to our smoking clinic to stop cigarette smoking. He began at the age of 17 when he entered college and smoked one and one-half to two packs each day until his first severe heart attack in April 1982. Despite his physician's injunctions to remain abstinent, Paul resumed smoking by June, after leaving the hospital.

An initial assessment was made of Paul's cognitions, emotions, and behaviors, before, during and after each cigarette. In addition to self-monitoring each cigarette that he smoked, an instrument called the Smoking Motives Questionnaire (Horn & Waingrow, 1966) was administered to assess Paul's motives for smoking. Of the six factors representing six smoking motives—addiction, habit, reduction of negative affect, pleasure, stimulation, and sensory motor stimulation—Paul scored highest on the pleasure and reduction of negative affect scales. In going over the items of these scales Paul answered "always" for the following items:(1) When I feel ashamed or embarrassed about something, I light up a cigarette. (2) Smoking cigarettes is pleasant and relaxing. (3) Few things help better than cigarettes when I am feeling upset.

Paul and I agreed to a two-week, seven-session smoking cessation program, following which he would come for biweekly booster sessions for six months. A two-pronged approach was used during the first seven sessions. The first half-hour of each session after the first week's baseline was devoted to practicing a new procedure known as smoke holding (Kopel, Suckerman, & Baksht, 1979). The second half of each session centered on reviewing the previous week's homework assignment.

Smoke holding is one of several new alternative smoking cessation procedures which I regularly use with smokers. The procedure uses a highly aversive smoking component while eliminating the health risks of rapid smoking, such as acute nicotine and carbon monoxide intoxication (e.g., Hauser, 1974; Dawley, Ellithorpe, & Tretola, 1976). Smoke holding rather than rapid smoking was decided as the better approach to work for Paul due to his heart condition.

During each session Paul was required to bring in his regular brand of cigarettes and a lighter or matches. I supplied several clear plastic cups with a half inch of water to serve as an ashtray, glasses filled with water, a data recording form, and a stop watch.

The smoke holding technique that I used during each session with Paul included nine steps:

Step 1: He was required to puff on a lit cigarette, holding the smoke in his mouth (not inhaling) for a maximum of 30 seconds. Paul was instructed to "push" himself to maximize the amount of smoke that he held for the full duration.

Step 2: While the smoke was held in his mouth, Paul was to focus his attention on the negative sensations of cigarette smoking.

Step 3: Once he blew the smoke out of his mouth, Paul rated his subjective feelings of unpleasantness on a seven-point scale.

Step 4: Thirty to 45 seconds were allowed between trials.

Step 5: Three sets of ten smoke-holding trials were conducted at each session.

Step 6: Following each set, Paul focused his attention on the negative sensations of cigarette smoke and he wrote a short narrative description.

Step 7: Paul was then allowed a three-minute rest where he and I openly discussed the experience and he was permitted to drink water.

Step 8: Paul repeated steps 1 through 7 for two additional sets of trials each.

Step 9: Between sessions Paul was told to not smoke; however, if he did smoke he was to use the smoke holding procedure.

Utilizing Marlatt and Gordon's (1980) relapse prevention techniques, Paul and I openly discussed high-risk situations that in the past led to his smoking one cigarette after another. He identified a list of the situations that triggered high levels of agitation that usually led to smoking. Putting these situations on paper heightened Paul's awareness of the cues which in the past set him off to reach into his pocket, pull out a cigarette, place it in his mouth, and light it up. Each situation triggered a set of cognitions suggestive of low frustration tolerance (e.g., "if I don't have one I think I'll go out of my mind!") and self-downing (e.g., "There must be something terribly wrong with me if I had a heart attack and still don't stop smoking.")

During the first relapse prevention session, Paul received a "what to do if a slip occurs" card tailored to his smoking habit. He was shown how to dispute mistaken personal attribution (e.g., "I had one cigarette, therefore, I must be a smoker") and to contradict the idea that one lapse has to lead to a full-blown return to smoking.

Paul was quick to see that it was not the high risk situations that caused him to light up cigarettes; rather, in each situation it was what he was telling himself that encouraged him to do so. During the first month after his heart attack he was shown that he frequently and strongly told himself that cigarettes would kill him. As a result, he did not smoke and he felt reasonably in control. However, when he went back to work, sat at his desk again, and feverishly answered the telephone he told himself occasionally and lightly that "cigarettes will kill me." He also was saying to himself, forcefully and persuasively, "I *need* a cigarette." In a sense, Paul was using negative self-suggestion to tolerate less and less discomfort once he resumed his work activities.

Before applying to our smoking clinic Paul vehemently downed himself. At times, he would very forcefully try to convince me that he really was a terrible person when he "slipped" and smoked. He endorsed the Alcoholics Anonymous philosophy that once you are addicted to a substance you are always addicted. He went beyond this premise and concluded that addictive behavior made him a weak-willed human being. In order to generalize disputing his self-defeating thinking from discussions during our sessions to high risk situations outside of our sessions I had Paul listen to several tapes (e.g., *"I'd Like to Stop, But . . . ,"* Ellis, 1976; *"Conquering Low Frustration Tolerance,"* Ellis, 1975) and to do this listening at his desk at work for 10 minutes, once each day. By wearing headphones, Paul managed to feel only mildly concerned that others would notice what he was doing. And even when they did (which, as it turned out, one coworker did) Paul would tell them the truth in order to face possible feelings of shame or embarrassment (emotions that he answered "always" on the Smoking Motives Questionnaire) and stubbornly refused to smoke while he worked through these negative feelings.

During the booster session Paul and I imaginally rehearsed "emotional fire drills." For example, during one scene Paul imagined himself reaching for an idle package of cigarettes on someone's desk, taking out a butt, placing it in his mouth, and strongly telling himself thoughts that would keep him from smoking. Paul listened to tape recordings of these imaginally rehearsed situations and then I gave him a situational competency test. He was to actually carry out, *in vivo,* what he had imaginally rehearsed—and still stop himself from smoking. With considerable prodding and larger and stronger doses of disputing, Paul managed to successfully do the *in vivo* exercise.

One year after his treatment to stop smoking, Paul's wife suddenly died from a stroke. He remains in therapy to work on adjusting to his wife's unexpected death, but he has not smoked in ten months.

Fanaticism

Exercise and a proper diet are things that improve the quality of our lives. But too much of a good thing can be harmful. I once recall someone saying that fanaticism consists of redoubling your efforts when you have forgotten your aim. Because dieting improves health there will always be individuals who will diet to extremes. The same applies for exercise. How do we know if what we are doing is too much or too little? In rational-emotive therapy we diagnose fanaticism by looking at the long- and short-term consequences for the individual and for his or her close associates. Are disciplined behaviors in our own best interest? Are they likely to get us what we want? Will they let us feel the way we want to feel? What are the facts and the realistic probabilities of these actions leading to happiness?

Toxic levels of vitamins, minerals, and trace elements exist that provide reasonable, accurate guidelines for foods. Similar guidelines also exist for exercise. But some individuals do not think rationally or are misinformed. When people enter treatment with symptoms such as migraines, panic attacks, depression, and so on, they often do so with a constellation of rigid rules and assumptions about how to treat their ailments. If they have read that migraine or vascular headaches are exacerbated by eating sharp cheeses, chocolate, or red wines, they will sometimes alter their diet and alleviate their distress. If they learn that vaginal candida is aggravated by consuming alcohol, sugar, and fruit peels, they will often zealously convert not only themselves but all their female friends to a diet free of these foods. But by fanatically "curing" themselves and proselytizing their friends they often exaggerate a response whose original intent was realistic. When we suspect that our family or friends are frantically medicating themselves we had better inquire who diagnosed their condition. Did they read about these panaceas from a magazine or get them from radio or television? What exactly are they taking and how much? If they are age 35 or above and they are exercising on their own, have they had an exercise tolerance test on a motor-driven treadmill with a cardiologist and exercise physiologist in attendance? These are the kind of questions to which we had better get answers.

> Bob was a 39-year-old client who entered therapy because he could not decide on a more profitable career. Further interviewing indicated that he was having trouble getting out of bed in the morning. He no longer found pleasure in jogging or sculpting, and he would become seriously depressed when passing an individual on the street who looked "as though they were just about ready to snap." Bob earned a graduate degree in sculpting and taught on a college level, but his work could not provide him with a sufficient income, nor was he making ends meet by painting residential homes.

Rather than demonstrate how RET operates by discussing his vocational choices, I decided to address Bob's beliefs about how he defined a person's self-worth. To prove to himself that he was not a total shit Bob would force himself to jog seven miles each day. Although he enjoyed pizza, frankfurters, french fries and other "bad" foods, he avoided eating these at all costs. He also defined watching the television as "bad." He not only defined these acts as "bad" but also equated these "bad" acts with his being a worthless person.

When Bob had visited the Veteran's Administration hospital several years before for a hemorrhoid condition, something interesting happened. He encountered veterans, many who were near his own age, dressed poorly, unshaven, pale looking, and unemployed. His hemorrhoids were instantly "cured." Bob immediately left the hospital. He avoided seeing the physicians, felt quick temporary relief, and confirmed his belief that the worst thing that could happen would be to end up in a V.A. hospital. The veterans he saw did not exercise, eat properly, or work. They also watched television. Therefore, they were worthless, and anyone, including Bob, who behaved at all like them, would also be worthless.

The short-term consequences of Bob's holding these beliefs was to "prove" that he was worthwhile as long as he adhered to his strict rules of self-rating. However, the long-term consequences were seriously disturbing. Because his thinking was so rigid and dogmatic, Bob was losing the love and affection of his girlfriend, was spending an inordinate amount of time preparing proper foods, was giving large sums of money to health food stores, and was exercising nearly three hours each day.

Bob and I collaborated in a series of experiments to test his assumptions. He agreed to exercise 90 minutes each day for one week and then to eat several items from his "unhealthy foods, hall of shame list." The following week he exercised for 60 minutes each day and watched one hour of television every other day. The rationale for these assignments was to test Bob's belief that he would get lazy and flabby if he loosened up on his usual routine. His weight did not change; in fact, he slept better and he found it easier to get out of bed in the morning. His records indicated that he derived greater pleasure from his painting and sculpting, and his relationship with his girlfrend vastly improved.

The important lesson that Bob learned was that his beliefs were not facts. By testing his assumptions he was able to make a deep philosophical change. He replaced his superstitious thinking and self-downing with self-acceptance and moderation in healthy living. Before therapy, Bob was not aware of his private discussions with himself. But with the help of a rational-emotive therapist he was able to look at his self-talk, discuss its effect on himself and others, and to profoundly change it. I believe that this philosophic change, when reinforced again and again with compatible behaviors, enables people to make stable alterations in the quality of their lives.

Summary

The linking of RET attitude change with RET behavior change is central to rational-emotive theory and therapy. The bonding of attitude change and behavior change significantly helps people to initiate and maintain a healthy lifestyle.

Protein-sparing supplemented fasting is only one medical procedure to insure weight loss, but in the next decade I predict that combining it with RET will become increasingly popular. Similarly, smoke holding is only one of a variety of techniques that reliably eliminate smoking. Combining RET with stimulus control techniques, hypnosis, nicotine fading, and rapid smoking also is effective. Rational-emotive therapy emphasizes moderation in many aspects of living—eating, drinking, recreational use of chemical substances, and so forth. With the increased interest in programs that promote a healthy style of life, we can expect to see RET incorporated in worksite fitness programs, professional sports, the leisure industry, and sports medicine.

References

American Heart Association. (1980). *The American heart association heartbook: A guide to prevention and treatment of cardiovascular diseases.* New York: Dutton.

Andrew, G. M., & Parker, J. O. (1979). Factors related to dropout of post myocardial infarction patients from exercise programs. *Medicine and Science in Sports, 11,* 376–378.

Atkinson, R. (1977). Physical fitness and headache. *Headache, 17,* 189–191.

Bandura, A. (1977). Self-efficacy: Toward a unifying theory of behavior change. *Psychological Review, 84,* 191–215.

Bennett, W., & Gurin, J. (1982). *The dieter's dilemma: Eating less and weighing more.* New York: Basic Books.

Brownell, K. D. (1982). Behavioral medicine. In C. M. Franks, G. T. Wilson, P. C. Kendall, & K. D. Brownell (Eds.), *Annual review of behavior therapy; Theory and practice* (pp. 144–181). (Vol. 8). New York: Brunner/Mazel.

Carmody, T. P., Senner, J. W., Malinow, M. R., & Matarazzo, J. D. (1980). Physical exercise rehabilitation: Long-term dropout rate in cardiac patients. *Journal of Behavioral Medicine, 3,* 163–168.

Daughton, D. M., Fix, A. J., Dass, J., & Patil, K. (1980). Smoking cessation among patients with chronic obstructive pulmonary disease. *Addictive behaviors, 5,* 367–374.

Dawley, H., Ellithorpe, D. B., & Tretola, R. (1976). Aversive smoking: Carboxyhemoglobin levels before and after rapid smoking. *Journal of Behavior Therapy and Experimental Psychiatry, 7,* 13–15.

Dishman, R. K., & Ickes, W. (1981). Self-motivation and adherence to therapeutic exercise. *Journal of Behavioral Medicine, 4,* 421–438.

Donoghue, S. (1977). The correlation between physical fitness, absenteeism and work performance. *Canadian Journal of Public Health, 68,* 201–203.

Ellis, A. (1962). *Reason and emotion in psychotherapy.* Secaucus, NJ: Citadel Press.

Ellis, A. (1973). *Humanistic psychotherapy: The rational-emotive approach.* New York: McGraw-Hill.

Ellis, A. (Speaker). (1975). *Conquering low frustration tolerance.* (Cassette Recording). New York: Institute for Rational-Emotive Therapy.

Ellis, A. (Speaker). (1976). *I'd like to stop but . . . Overcoming addictions.* (Cassette Recording). New York: Institute for Rational-Emotive Therapy.

Ellis, A. (1979). Discomfort anxiety: A new cognitive behavioral construct. Part 1. *Rational Living, 14*(2), 3–8.

Ellis, A. (1980). Discomfort anxiety: A new cognitive behavioral construct. Part 2. *Rational Living, 15*(1), 25–30.

Ellis, A., & Becker, I. (1982). *A guide to personal happiness.* North Hollywood, CA: Welshire Books.

Ellis, A., & Bernard, M. E. (Eds.). (1983). *Rational-emotive approaches to the problems of childhood.* New York: Plenum Press.

Ellis, A., & Grieger, R. (Eds.). (1977). *Handbook of rational-emotive therapy.* New York: Springer.

Ellis, A., & Harper, R. A. (1975). *A new guide to rational living.* North Hollywood, CA: Wilshire Books.

Ellis, A., & Whiteley, J. M. (Eds). (1979). *Theoretical and empirical foundations of rational-emotive therapy.* Monterey, CA: Brooks/Cole.

Epstein, L. H., Thompson, J. K., & Wing, R. R. (1980). The effects of contract and lottery procedures on attendance and fitness in aerobic exercise. *Behavior Modification, 4,* 465–479.

Fielding, J. E. (1979). Preventive medicine and the bottom line. *Journal of Occupational Medicine, 21,* 79–88.

Folkins, C. H., Lynch, S., & Gardner, M. M. (1972). Psychological fitness as a function of physical fitness. *Archives of Physical Medicine and Rehabilitation, 53,* 503–508.

Folkins, C. H., & Sima, W. E. (1981). Physical fitness training and mental health. *American Psychologist, 36,* 373–389.

Griest, J. H., Klein, M. H., Eischans, J. F., Gurman, A. .A. , & Morgan, W. P. (1979). Running as treatment for depression. *Comprehensive Psychiatry, 20,* 41–54.

Gruber, J. J. (1975). Exercise and mental performance. *International Journal of Sport Psychology, 6,* 28–40.

Hauser, R. (1974). Rapid smoking as a technique of behavior modification: Caution in selection of subject. *Journal of Consulting and Clinical Psychology, 42,* 625–626.

Horn, D., & Waingrow, S. (1966). Behavior and attitudes questionnaire. Bethesda, MD: National Clearinghouse for Smoking and Health.

Julien, R. M. (1978). *A primer at drug action,* (2nd ed.). San Francisco: Freeman & Company.

Kassinove, H., & DiGiuseppe, R. (1975). Rational role reversal, *Rational Living, 10,* 44–45.

Katch, F. I., & McArdle, W. D. (1977). *Nutrition, weight control, and exercise.* New York: Houghton-Mifflin.

Keefe, F. J., & Blumenthal, J. A. (1980). The life fitness program: A behavioral approach to making exercise a habit. *Journal of Behavioral Therapy and Experimental Psychiatry, 11,* 31–34.

Kimmel, J. (1976). The rational barb in the treatment of social rejection. *Rational Living, 11,* 23–25.

King, A. C., & Fredericksen, L. W. (1980, December). Increasing exercise compliance through social and cognitive procedures. In: J. E. Martin, (Chair) *Exercise: Promoting adherence and physical fitness.* Symposium presented at the Association for the Advancement of Behavior Therapy, New York.

Kopel, S. A. , Suckerman, K. R., & Baksht, A. (1979, December). Smoke holding: An evaluation of physiological effects and treatment efficacy of a new non hazardous aversive smoking procedure. Paper presented at the 13th annual meeting of the Association for Advancement of Behavior Therapy, San Francisco.

Margolis, M. F., Sperduto, W. A., & Witkin, G. (1982, December). The use of exercise in conjunction with group cognitive therapy in treating depression: A preliminary analysis. Paper presented to the Association for the Advancement of Behavior Therapy, Los Angeles.

Marlatt, G. A., & Gordon, J. R. (1980). Determinants of relapse: Implications for the maintenance of behavior change. In P. O. Davidson & S. M. Davidson (Eds.) *Behavioral Medicines Changing Health Lifestyles,* (pp. 248–285). New York: Brunner/Mazel.

Maultsby, M. C. Jr., & Ellis, Albert. (1974). *Techniques for using rational-emotive imagery.* New York: Institute for Rational-Emotive Therapy.

Marley, W. P. Asthma and exercise: A review. (1977). *American Corrective Therapy Journal, 31,* 95–102.

Martin, J. E., Katell, A. D., Webster, J. S., & Zegman, M. (1980). Enhancing exercise adherence and skill level. Paper presented at the second annual meeting of the Society of Behavioral Medicine, New York.

McArdle, W. D., Katch, F. I., & Katch, V. L. (1981). *Exercise physiology: Energy, nutrition and human performance.* Philadelphia: Lea & Febiger.

Millon, T., Green, C., & Meagher, R. (1982). *Millon Behavioral Health Inventory Manual.* Minneapolis: National Computer Systems.

Morgan, W. P. (1977). Involvement in vigorous physical activity with special reference to adherence. In: L. I. Gedvilas & M. E. Kneer (Eds.) *National college of Physical Education Proceedings.* (pp. 235–246). Chicago: University of Illinois at Chicago.

Nye, G. R., & Poulsen, W. T. (1974). An activity program for coronary patients: A review of morbidity, mortality and adherence after five years. *New Zealand Medical Journal, 79,* 1010–1013.

O'Connor, C. (1969). Effects of selected physical activities on motor performance and academic achievement of first graders. *Perceptual and Motor Skills, 29,* 703–709.

Oldridge, N. B. (1979). Compliance in exercise rehabilitation. *Physician and Sports Medicine, 7,* 94–103.

Paffenbarger, R. D., Wing, A. L., & Hyde, R. T. (1978). Physical activity as an index of heart attack risk in college alumni, *American Journal of Epidemiology, 108,* 161–175.

Pederson, L. L. (1981). Compliance with physician advice to quit smoking: A review of the literature. *Preventive Medicine, 1,* 269–273.

Powell, R. R. (1974). Psychological effects of exercise therapy upon institutionalized geriatric mental patients. *Journal of Gerontology, 29,* 157–161.

Russell, M. A. H., Wilson, C., Taylor, C., & Baker, C. D. (1979). Effect of general practitioner's advice against smoking. *British Medical Journal, 2,* 231–235.

Russianoff, P. (1983). *Why do I think I am nothing without a man?* New York: Bantam.

Schacter, S. (1982). Recidivism and self-cure of smoking and obesity. *American Psychologist, 37,* 436–444.

Taylor, H. L. (1969). Prospective investigation of exercise therapy in patients with a high risk of coronary heart disease. Unpublished report to the U.S. Public Health Service, University of Rochester.

U.S. Department of Health, Education, and Welfare. (1978, March 15). *U.S. Vital Statistics Advance Report,* No. 19.

Vertes, V. (1978). Supplemented fasting: A perspective. *Drug Therapy,* 73–80.

Weisman, A. *Coping with cancer.* (1979). New York: McGraw-Hill.

Wilson, G. T., & Brownell, K. D. (1980). Behavior therapy for obesity: An evaluation of treatment outcome. *Advances in Behavior Research and Therapy, 3*, 49–86.
Witkin, G. (1983, August). Psychological, biographical, demographic, and physiological predictors of attendance at a cardiovascular exercise facility. Paper presented to the American Psychiological Association, Los Angeles.
Wysocki, T., Hall, G., Iwata, B., & Riordan, M. (1979). Behavioral management of exercise: Contracting for aerobic points. *Journal of applied Behavior Analysis, 12*, 55–64.

9

RET and Substance Abuse

VINCENT GREENWOOD

INTRODUCTION

The nation's number one public health problem? Substance abuse. It maims and destroys lives. Our legal, educational, and health care systems have been unable to solve it. We try to educate about it and legislate against it. However, our health, our families, and our spirit continue to be compromised by substance abuse. The costs? Staggering. Failing prevention, we face the consequences. And those medical, rehabilitative, and law enforcement efforts consume a significant piece of our national budget. The need for effective treatment strategies cannot be overestimated.

This chapter provides a model of the psychological factors involved in substance abuse. The model produces clearcut treatment implications in the framework of the rational-emotive therapy system. We believe there are common psychological triggers and predisposing beliefs that create and perpetuate substance abuse. These psychological notions are found whenever abuse, of any sort of substance, occurs. Indeed, they seem relevant to other dysfunctional habits, such as overeating and compulsive gambling. Rational-emotive therapy provides a particularly good "fit" for the effective treatment of substance abuse.

VINCENT GREENWOOD • Washington Center for Cognitive Therapy, 5225 Connecticut Avenue, N.W., Washington, D.C. 20015.

Scope of the Problem

For individuals and the society they compromise, the consequences of substance abuse are immense. We define substance abuse herein as: excessive use of legal drugs (e.g., alcohol, tobacco); improper use of restricted but easily obtainable drugs (e.g., barbituates, amphetamines); and any use of illegal drugs (e.g., heroin, cocaine). The ways substance abuse can devastate people and society are many—too numerous to catalogue. However, it may be enlightening simply to cite the kinds of undesirable consequences associated with substance abuse.

First, there are effects we can measure, such as the health consequences and the financial drain on the individual and society because of illegal drug traffic. Other effects—distressingly apparent—are harder to measure. These include the abuser's loss of self-control and concomitant psychological deterioration; disruption of the family unit when one of its members is addicted; the endemic spiral of crime generated to support hard drug habits; and the insidious way in which substance abuse can tear at the social fabric of a community.

Unfortunately, we face here a problem not to be confined to a small element of society. The prevalence of substance abuse is great. In America, estimates point to 10 million alcoholics and problem drinkers, over a half million hard drug addicts, and approximately 47 million smokers who have tried but failed to quit.

To cite only one problem—smoking—gives a feel for the enormous costs of substance abuse. It is estimated that 37 million Americans will die early because of smoking; each year, 300,000 lives are cut short. Smoking has been clearly implicated in the development of cardiovascular disease, chronic broncho-pulmonary diseases, and various cancers. If smoking were eliminated, there would be one-third fewer middle-aged (35–39) male deaths, 85% fewer broncho-pulmonary disease deaths, 33% fewer cardiovascular disease deaths, and 90% fewer deaths from cancer of the lungs. The health care costs of smoking are crippling. It is estimated that smoking accounts for a loss of about 30 billion dollars per year or about 11.3% of the costs of all diseases (Pechacek & Danaher, 1979).

Similarly grim statistics accompany the abuse of other drugs, particularly alcohol and heroin. Furthermore, every year we discover more undesirable consequences of drugs (e.g., the fetal alcohol syndrome in children, the damaging effects of long-term marijuana use to the brain and reproductive functions). And the grim, final note: there is a trend toward increased abuse of harmful substances.

Virtues of the RET Model in Combatting Substance Abuse

Substance abuse is a complex phenomenon. A wide range of factors clearly contributes to the development of substance abuse. These factors include a genetic predisposition for some substances, the abuser's family background and socioeconomic status, "subculture" pressures, and the personality dynamics of the abuser. Nor can we underestimate the availability of harmful substances. With substance abuse, there is a true mix of biological, sociological, economic, and psychological factors. For this reason, numerous approaches to counteracting the problem have been considered.

This chapter focuses on the psychological factors involved in substance abuse. Although substance abuse is a complex problem resulting from a range of factors, psychotherapy can serve as a strong countermeasure. This is so because the complex and particular forces converge into a central problem: how clients think about themselves and the world and the meaning that the substance abuse has acquired in their life.

Unfortunately, psychological approaches to substance abuse so far have been long on theory and short on effective clinical application. Neither psychoanalytic nor strictly behavioral therapies have been able to provide effective treatments for the main categories of abuse. From this we infer crucial flaws in the psychoanalytic and strict behavioral models, making them ineffective in counteracting drug abuse. These models' basic assumptions are simply not responsive to the inner world, and the rigorous change efforts required, of the substance abuser (Beck & Emery, 1977; Ellis, 1982).

Here we will delineate the dynamics of substance abuse from the perspective of rational-emotive therapy. Of all the current psychotherapeutic systems, the RET system "matches" the psychopathology of substance abuse particularly well. The RET model includes theoretical elements that directly address the key philosophical assumptions of substance abusers, and are also sensitive to their inner turmoil (Ellis, 1962, 1974, 1976, 1982; Ellis & Becker, 1982; Grau, 1977; Higbee, 1977; Maultsby, 1978; Wolfe, 1979).

1. A primary RET tenet focuses on the difficulty of basic change, particularly that of overcoming a substance abuse habit. For the substance abuser to overcome his habit much hard work will be required. Why is this an important tenet in working with substance abusers? First, it realistically prepares the therapist and client for a major struggle to achieve change. Second, it avoids the pitfall, so common in the treatment of substance abusers, of interpreting the client's failure to achieve quick

change as "resistance." Interpreting the client's failure to achieve quick change as a need to suffer, or to get even with others (or whatever), will often drive the client out of treament and is probably off base (Ellis, in press).

2. Likewise, RET deals explicitly with the philosophical issues that block change. After recognizing the dynamics of and desirability for changing, many clients refuse to work at changing their disturbance. The philosophical premise thwarting change, entitled Low Frustration Tolerance (LFT), is a belief that, in making the effort to change, one should not have to endure discomfort. Unlike other schools of psychotherapy, RET shows clients why they are not carrying through efforts to change, and how to counteract the sabotage caused by their low frustration tolerance (Ellis, 1979, 1980).

3. RET explicitly addresses the issue of short-range versus long-range hedonism. Most substance abusers appear to be short-range hedonists, that is, they appear to choose immediate and easy gratifications at the expense of long-range satisfactions. Most of these individuals, however, profess a desire to achieve more enduring long-range satisfactions (e.g., an interesting career, good health). In RET, this contradiction is quickly brought out in the open. Clients are encouraged to define clearly their short- and long-range goals and to realize what will be required to meet them. Most substance abusers believe they can have it both ways, that seeking maximum gratification in the moment will not jeopardize long-range goals. We ask clients to look at their goals, critically, at what is required to meet these goals and how they may conflict. We thereby hope to reduce contradictions in clients' lifestyles and help to provide a more realistic blueprint for maximizing their happiness (Ellis, in press).

4. RET also emphasizes how important it is to counteract clients' secondary symptoms. Clients frequently upset themselves about being disturbed. With substance abusers this is a pervasive problem and unless specifically targeted for change, it can become a stumbling block to effective treatment. RET is one of the very few psychotherapy systems that specifically looks for and aggressively challenges this secondary level of symptoms (Bard, 1980; Ellis & Grieger, 1977; Ellis & Harper, 1975; Ellis & Whiteley, 1979).

5. RET emphasizes the importance of making changes directly and quickly in clients' self-defeating behavior. As Ellis (1979; Ellis & Whiteley, 1979) notes, RET practitioners often use more behavioral strategies than do classical behaviorists. This compatibility with behavioral strategies is especially useful with this patient population. Some substance abuse problems seem intractable and behavioral techniques often can provide a desirable catalyst.

Treatment of Substance Abuse

Overview

When people who suffer from some kind of substance abuse problem seek treatment, two goals present themselves: (1) to help clients *stop* or significantly reduce the substance abuse, and (2) to help them *maintain* this desirable change. To help clients counteract the substance abuse habit, we highlight the cognitive dynamics underlying their decision to indulge and their resistance to stop. Then, various cognitive, emotional, and behavioral techniques are employed to reduce the substance abuse habit itself. To help clients maintain the elimination or significant reduction of substance abuse, we identify the cognitive dynamics underlying their desire to indulge and, then, choose appropriate techniques to counteract this desire. Finally, long-term control over substance abuse requires us to understand the cognitive dynamics involved in periodic relapse, and to develop strategies to minimize the frequency, duration, and severity of the relapse periods. There are subtle but important differences among the cognitive dynamics involved in each of these components of the problem. RET practitioners had better be aware of these subtle differences in order to assess the correct pivotal philosophical assumptions that will in turn lead to the most effective therapeutic strategies.

As the RET practitioner helps substance abusers gain control over their habits, a more fundamental and elegant goal is being pursued: namely, to help clients alter some of their most basic philosophical assumptions about themselves and the world. Then we can encourage enduring changes in their levels of emotional distress and weak discipline—the cornerstones of the substance abuse habit.

Before detailing the cognitive underpinnings and recommended treatment strategies, we will highlight some of the important assessment issues of the substance abuse problem.

Assessment of Substance Abusers from a RET Perspective

Whereas RET practitioners typically adopt a very critical stance toward traditional psychodiagnostic procedures (see especially Ellis, "Toward a New Theory of Personality," Ellis & Whiteley, 1979, and Grieger & Boyd, 1980, "Rational-Emotive Psychodiagnosis"), more attention has recently been paid to the RET assessment process. Recent books and articles (e.g., Walen, DiGuiseppe, & Wessler, 1980; Grieger & Boyd, 1980; Wessler & Wessler, 1980; Grieger & Grieger, 1982) illuminate some of the basic principles of how we assess irrational beliefs. Creative assessment techniques to identify key problem areas have been described. These encourage client and therapist to formulate problems so that they are more amenable to treatment. The clinical payoffs are a quicker restoration of hope for clients—by seeing clearly the essential role their beliefs play in the development of self-defeating behavior—and increased efficiency and flexibility on the part of the therapist.

What are the relevant principles underlying RET assessment?

1. Regardless of the assessment strategies or therapeutic techniques employed, the RET practitioner's main focus and goal is to identify and change clients' faulty inferences and irrational evaluations.

2. The RET practitioner seeks an in-depth and comprehensive understanding and appreciation of the beliefs resulting in the self-defeating behavior. RET practitioners need to be skilled at teasing out and showing clients the interplay of their various irrational beliefs with their self-defeating behavior and feelings.

3. The ABC format continues to serve as an effective cornerstone of the RET assessment process. Whereas the clients' beliefs (B) are the primary focus of change, RET theorists (Wessler & Wessler, 1980; Dryden, 1984) have noted the importance of fully exploring the A (situational forces) and C (consequences i.e., undesirable feelings and behavior) components of the diagnostic equation. By clearly tying the clients' beliefs to events in their life, and vividly showing how these beliefs lead to undesirable consequences, the practitioner will accomplish the greatest therapeutic change.

The above-noted principles apply to the assessment and treatment from a RET perspective of all disorders. Listed below are the major assessment concerns of particular relevance in the treatment of substance abusers.

1. The great majority of substance abusers exhibit discomfort anxiety and low frustration tolerance beliefs. These closely related beliefs involve clients' intolerance of painful feelings and the implicit demand that they not suffer such feelings. As Albert Ellis (1979, 1980) pointed out in his original articles on discomfort anxiety, the therapist needs a clear conceptual understanding of discomfort anxiety and low frustration tolerance for at least two compelling reasons.

First, clients are usually unaware of the philosophical assumptions behind these feelings. Such assumptions are rather subtle and typically lie beneath other concerns. Therefore, it is incumbent on the RET practitioner (usually, in a forceful fashion) to show substance abusers the instrumental role these assumptions play in their dysfunctional behavior.

Second, it is usually necessary to deal with discomfort anxiety and low frustration tolerance as separate issues from what Ellis calls ego anxiety. This dictum is particularly true in the treatment of substance abuse. For although the predisposition or desire to drink is frequently a product of the painful feelings caused by ego anxiety ("I *must* achieve well, be loved by a significant other, etc."), the *decision* to drink is almost always a product of discomfort anxiety ("I *can't stand* these painful feelings . . . and I deserve/need to get high"). The different philosophical issues inherent in discomfort anxiety and ego anxiety require different therapeutic maneuvers.

2. Most substance abusers suffer from what has been called "symptom stress" (Walen, DiGiuseppe, & Wessler, 1980). Symptom stress refers to clients' upsetting themselves about their undesirable behavior. In the RET diagnostic scheme, clients' original problems and symptoms become a new activating event (A). We then subject this to a separate RET analysis. Symptom stress, as it frequently occurs in substance abusers, is illustrated in the following:

A. Original symptom, that is, patient observes self-indulging.
B. "There I go again . . . I'm a real loser. I screwed up again—I'll never be able to control this."
C. Guilt and helplessness; further indulgence.

Typically, it is advisable to counteract this secondary level of symptoms at the outset of treatment. Until clients minimize self-condemnation about their undesirable behavior, it is going to be very difficult to constructively focus on and change the substance abuse itself. Illuminating and dealing with this secondary level of symptoms, a unique contribution of RET, provide a frontal assault on substance abusers' self-blame and helplessness attributions.

3. More so than with other presenting problems, the RET therapist fully explores the situational factors (A's) involved in clients' substance abuse. Two factors justify this emphasis. First, research underscores the powerful role of situational factors in the abuse of a wide range of harmful substances (e.g., Marlatt, 1978; Eisinger, 1971). Secondly, one of the main barriers to successful treatment is the patients' beliefs that they are helpless to control their substance abuse habit. At the beginning of the treatment this belief is often more susceptible to change through behavioral techniques. A therapist, thoroughly assessing situational factors, can propose behavioral interventions to provide patients with an experiential foundation for overcoming their sense of helplessness.

The therapist can undertake a complete functional analysis of the patient's problematic behavior—see Kanfer and Saslow (1969), and Sobell and Sobell (1976) for detailed descriptions of this assessment strategy. Together, the therapist and patient employ a keen awareness of the places where the substance abuse occurs; the time; the pressures the patient experiences in these situations; and the precise consequences of indulging.

4. The RET practitioner will assess the patient's substance abuse problem by looking for emotional triggers—see Walen, DiGiuseppe, and Wessler (1980) for an excellent description of how to evoke a vivid and thorough assessment of the patient's distressing feelings. The substance abuser typically suffers two kinds of Cs (undesirable Consequences) in high-risk situations (A's): the substance abuse itself and a painful feeling that triggers the substance abuse. For example:

A. Sitting home alone after an argument with my girlfriend.
B. "She's going to break things off with me—I couldn't stand the loneliness."
C_1. Depression; hopelessness.
C_2. Heavy drinking.

The RET therapist tries to uncover these pivotal triggers by asking the client, "What feelings or things inside you trigger the desire to indulge at that moment?" While the substance abuse habit frequently needs to be treated in its own right, the client remains at high risk for relapse unless these precipitating feelings are ameliorated.

With this overview of key assessment issues to which the RET practitioner is alert, we would now like to propose three kinds of questions that the therapist can pose and answer at the outset of treatment. The course of therapy will be determined largely by the answers to these questions.

1. What are clients' cognitive psychopathologies? What are their major irrational beliefs to be altered? What are the information processing distortions that maintain and reinforce their irrational beliefs and premises? Most fundamentally, what are the distortions of evaluation that predispose patients to maintain their substance abuse?

2. What are the most effective therapeutic strategies to affect cognitive change? It would be useful at this point to reiterate and highlight the distinction made by Glass and Arnkoff (1981) and others between therapy *process* and therapy *procedure*. Therapy process refers to the model of change that underlies a course of therapy, whereas therapy procedure refers to specific techniques used to bring about change. The RET practitioner will find this distinction particularly useful with substance abusers as some of their irrational beliefs and faulty attributions appear more amenable to change via behavioral, as opposed to cognitive, techniques. RET practitioners "think cognitive" and yet operate in a

multimodal fashion, perhaps more so than with other disorders, in order to exploit opportunities for constructive change.

3. Should treatment efforts focus on the substance abuse itself or on the predisposing cognitive and emotional vulnerabilities that have led to the substance abuse? Although substance abuse is typically considered to be a consequence (i.e., symptom) of predisposing beliefs, for a number of reasons it is frequently counteracted in its own right. First, depending on the nature of the harmful substance, substance abuse can be a powerful habit that may persist even if some of the predisposing factors are eliminated. Secondly, because of the serious health and legal consequences frequently associated with substance abuse, it is usually desirable to counteract the habit itself as quickly and as efficiently as possible. Finally, as noted above, substance abusers often generate strong, upsetting reactions to their indulgent tendencies. These self-blaming reactions had better be minimized before the predisposing factors are tackled.

Consequently, the following discussion of the treatment of substance abusers takes two stages: (a) helping clients stop or minimize the abuse and (b) helping them maintain the desirable change. The second stage involves exploring and changing their predisposing cognitive/emotional dysfunction that originally prompted the substance abuse and coping with the possibility of relapse. For each stage the essential cognitive psychopathology will be discussed and treatment strategies suggested.

Stopping Substance Abuse

Cognitive Dynamics

Three basic beliefs comprise the abuser's inability to refrain from using harmful substances. Unless these beliefs are brought out in the open and forcefully challenged, the substance abuser will probably have little success overcoming this habit.

Belief #1: Discomfort Anxiety and Intolerance. This belief usually takes the following form: "I cannot stand the frustrations of life—particularly my own painful feelings—and therefore I need and/or deserve something to make me feel better."

This belief has two parts. First, clients exaggerate the discomfort and frustrations they are experiencing. By doing so, they actually exacerbate such feelings. Second, clients then feel driven and/or entitled to a life free of discomfort ("I must have what I desire"). Implicit in this belief is their choosing short-range hedonism (i.e., blotting out discomfort) over long-range hedonism (facing and working through their frustrations to achieve a more profitable adjustment).

This belief often takes shape in specific thoughts:

- Things have really been going against me—I deserve to get high.
- I feel so lousy, I really need a drink.
- The arguing, financial problems, etc. won't bother me and will go away after a few drinks.

Belief #2: Helplessness. After trying to control their habit by will power, most abusers conclude that they are utterly incapable of overcoming their habit. They, therefore, suffer from what Albert Bandura (1977) has termed low self-efficacy, that is, the belief that there is little they can do to produce a desired outcome; in this case, it would be stopping a dysfunctional habit. Clients' perceived self-efficacy directly influences whether they try new treatment strategies and how much effort they will expend to counteract their habit. If their conclusion that they are incapable of change is not altered, treatment efforts will not get off the ground and chronic abuse may be unaffected.

Some of the specific thoughts reflective of this belief include:

- An alcoholic is an alcoholic is an alcoholic.
- I'm too weak to control this.
- Others make me take drugs.

Belief #3: Self-Condemnation. Most people with dysfunctional habits believe they are "rotten people" because of their habit. For although most substance abusers feel entitled to indulge, they will then turn on and condemn themselves for indulging. They take their self-defeating behavior as evidence of their worthlessness (e.g., "I'm a born loser"). This self-condemning tendency is to be dealt with at the outset of treatment as it frequently triggers further substance abuse. RET practitioners break this vicious circle of self-reproach and self-destructive behavior. Typical thoughts, reflective of self-blame include:

- What the hell is wrong with me? Why can't I change?
- I'm a real jerk for not being able to control drugs—I've let everyone down.

Recommended Treatment Strategies: Disputing Substance Abusers' Irrational Beliefs

As Albert Ellis (1979) pointed out, disputation remains the most popular and elegant technique of rational-emotive therapy. Here are disputational strategies to zero in on the substance abuser's core assumptions.

Disputing Discomfort Anxiety. To counteract discomfort anxiety the initial task is to help patients change their evaluations of discomfort from something "awful" that they "can't stand" to something "unpleasant" that they surely "can stand." Asking for evidence that they "can't stand" the discomfort often helps patients realize how they exaggerate their discomfort and define an unpleasant situation as an intolerable one.

T: Where is the evidence that you *can't stand* going without a daily dose of cocaine, that it is *unbearable?*

C: Well, in a literal sense, I guess I could stand it. But, when I go without cocaine, it really is unbearable.

T: Wrong! Try to be more precise; when you go without it, the only consequence is unpleasantness and discomfort—which you detest, but you can bear.

The goals in confronting the clients' awfulizing and "I can't stand it" tendencies are: (1) to actually reduce the level of discomfort by being semantically precise, and (2) to help clients realize they are *choosing* to continue indulging. To choose not to indulge would be uncomfortable, not unbearable.

Another disputational foray requires exposure of the underlying assumption that clients should not have to tolerate discomfort, that is, that life really must be comfortable and without pain. Clients' "gain without pain" philosophy keeps them mired in the dysfunctional habit. An open discussion about the validity and consequences of such a premise is desirable. The therapist can offer the following didactic disputation:

> Paradoxically, by insisting on a life without pain, you actually bring on more pain. Your life is quite painful right now. You worry about when you're going to get your next fix and about the consequences drug taking has on your personal life and health. By demanding immediate comfort and gratification you literally create a wide range of other hassles and anxieties.

Perhaps the most persuasive line of inquiry for substance abusers involves helping them develop a meaningful hedonic calculus. Hedonic calculus refers to the process whereby people rationally analyze the trade-offs between short-range gratification and long-range hedonism, and commit themselves to a course of action that maximizes their enjoyment. The first step: ask clients to list the advantages and disadvantages of continuing, and of stopping, the substance abuse. This exercise enables them to expand their thinking and become aware of the full range of consequences of their indulgence. If they agree it is advantageous to change their dysfunctional habit, ask them, "Are you willing to work hard and tolerate the discomfort to secure these advantages?" This helps solidify their commitment to therapy and underscores the significant point: learning to face and tolerate discomfort is a prerequisite to meeting difficult, long-range goals.

One caveat: an RET therapist can introduce the concept of hedonic calculus, but clients are to think through, on their own, the pros and cons of substance abuse. Many clients rebel and display antagonism toward authority figures. Should a therapist try to impose his or her notion of the advantages to overcoming substance abuse, clients' rebelliousness may easily be triggered, thereby heightening their resistance. More importantly, clients require considerable motivation to overcome their substance abuse. This motivation comes primarily from the clients seeing clearly that it is in their best interest to overcome their habit. *They* had better value this goal.

Disputing Helplessness. The clients' conviction that they are helpless to change (e.g., "Once an addict, always an addict") is to be addressed immediately in RET, so that clients can quickly acquire a sense of hope. The cognitive shift desired is from "I have no control" to "I can/might achieve control." Cognitive strategies are useful to create hope. Once clients have some hope of controlling their habit, behavioral strategies often enhance their sense of self-efficacy ("I do have control").

Clients' conclusions that they are helpless is a distorted perception of their behavior. To this they may also add distorted evaluation (e.g., "It's awful to be helpless"). To elicit hope at the outset of treatment, the RET therapist usually focuses on clients' distortion of their behavior. A major cognitive strategy, therefore, is to heighten clients' awareness of their cognitive distortions and to correct such distortions.

Some of the major cognitive distortions that contribute to the patient's hopelessness include:

Overgeneralization	• Since I've failed to overcome my habit, I'm a failure. • Since I've failed in the past, I'll always fail.
All-or-none thinking	• If I don't have total control over the habit, I have no control. • I'm just one drink away from a drunk.
Selective abstraction	• I sometimes cope well but because I often don't I'm really no good at coping.

The therapist's main tasks are to ask questions that encourage more logical, objective thinking. Questions that ask for evidence, logical consistency, and semantic clarity include (Walen, DeGiuseppe, & Wessler, 1980):

- Where's the evidence for your belief?
- Is that true? Why not?
- Why is that an overgeneralization?
- Can you prove you'll fail in the future?
- Are you using ultimatum words that aren't accurate?
- Are you taking examples out of context?
- Are you overlooking your strengths?
- Can you cite examples where you have handled tough situations without turning to drugs?
- Are you jumping to conclusions about your future behavior?
- How do you know you'll fail?

The hoped-for outcome of this questioning and challenging process is to have clients gain a realistic basis for overcoming their habit. Whereas they recognize that it will take a great deal of work to change their behavior, they no longer define their situation as abysmally helpless and hopeless and thereby stall treatment efforts at the starting gate.

If clients maintain a helpless stance toward substance abuse, RET counselors illustrate both the power and illogic of their self-fulfilling prophecy. They show clients that their continued indulgence results from their *conviction* that they are helpless—and not because of some inalterable characterological or biological necessity. Continued abuse is largely evidence of the power of clients' irrational belief system. If they come to understand the role that self-fulfilling prophecy plays in their failure to change, they are more likely to collaborate with treatment efforts.

Disputing Self-Condemnation. Rational-emotive therapy, perhaps more so than any other school of therapy, focuses on clients' secondary level of symptoms, that is, when they give themselves hell for being disturbed. The RET practitioner often takes the following steps upon detecting "symptom stress" in the substance abuser:

1. Explains the concept of symptom stress to clients. Symptom stress is often a subtle and pernicious habit which had better be understood before it is counteracted. Since clients rarely "target" symptom stress as their presenting problem, the therapist explains the importance of dealing with it as a problem in its own right. The likely consequences of symptom stress is pointed out. Specifi-

cally, symptom stress typically results in painful self-downing and increased substance abuse to blot out such painful feelings.

2. Shows clients precisely how they are putting themselves down for abusing harmful substances—and the specific emotional and behavioral consequences of their put-downs.
3. Explores clients' reasons for condemning themselves. Many substance abusers believe it is "honorable" to condemn themselves for indulging; or that it "makes it okay" to indulge as long as they condemn themselves; or that condemning themselves will motivate them to stop indulging. The therapist brings these real or imagined "payoffs" for self-condemnation out in the open and examines them for their accuracy and utility.
4. Disputes clients' self-condemning philosophies and assumptions. There are two general disputational strategies to help the patient give up his self-condemning tendency: The most elegant and fundamental strategy, of course, is to help clients stop equating their admittedly lousy behavior pattern with (what Albert Ellis has eloquently called) their "shithood," that is, their beliefs that they are worthless people. There have been many discussions and teaching strategies suggested—see especially Ellis (1962, 1971); Ellis & Becker (1982); Ellis & Harper (1975); Lazarus (1977)—to convey the fundamental point: engaging in substance abuse (or any other self-defeating behavior) makes one a fallible human being, not a rotten person). The second disputational strategy to mitigate symptom stress is to help clients to realize the negative consequences of their self-damnation, for example, "What good will calling yourself a shit do?" "What happens after you condemn yourself for indulging?" If clients realize that their self-criticism is not only harsh but also counter-productive, they will often then be willing to work at counteracting it.

Other Cognitive Techniques

Over the past decade a wide range of cognitive techniques have proliferated to counteract self-defeating behavior. Virtually any cognitive technique can be creatively applied to the treatment of substance abuse. I would like to describe two cognitive techniques that are of particular value with this problem.

Referenting. Referenting is a cognitive technique developed by Danysh (1974) and designed specifically to help clients alter dysfunctional habits, particularly indulgent behavior. The technique aims to help people expand and be more objective in the associations they have to the harmful substances.

When people crave a harmful substance (e.g., cocaine) they are almost exclusively aware of positive associations (e.g., the pleasure of it; the feeling of control it will give them). Contrarily, when thinking of abstaining, the individual develops negative associations (e.g., the pain and discomfort of quitting). In referenting, clients are asked to write down *all* associations to both indulging and abstaining from a harmful substance. By bringing into mind negative associations regarding indulging and positive associations regarding abstaining, they shift their hedonic calculus. For example, when people think of cocaine, they are shown how to referent the negative aspects of indulging (e.g., health risks, risks of psychological addiction, possible prosecution) and to referent positive aspects of stopping (e.g., saving money, improving health). Referenting increases their power to abstain by bringing into awareness a more thorough and responsible accounting of the consequences of indulging and abstaining.

Coping Statements. Coping statements can serve as "cognitive brakes" to counteract the craving for a harmful substance. Coping statements are simply brief messages designed to help people act and feel the way they want. They are particularly appropriate for those substance abusers who are psychologically naive or otherwise unwilling to engage in a thoroughgoing disputation of their irrational beliefs. Coping statements are also useful for all substance abusers in high-risk situations. A high-risk situation is any clearly defined situation (e.g., a party where drugs are available, being home alone after a grueling day) where people's urge to indulge is particularly strong. Clients and therapists can construct coping statements tailored to counteract the thoughts that trigger indulgence. Clients then repeat and absorb these statements in order to reduce their emotional vulnerability and promote their discipline. Table 1 presents a sample of coping statements designed to counteract some primary cognitive triggers of indulgence.

Behavioral Techniques

Any discussion of the treatment of substance abuse would be remiss if it failed to underscore the important role of behavioral techniques. There are two basic reasons why RET practitioners include behavioral strategies in the treatment of substance abuse: (1) Because behavioral techniques quickly promote mastery behavior, they are probably the most efficient strategies to counteract people's sense of helplessness. (2) The power of high-risk situations to help trigger substance abuse makes

TABLE 1. Sample of Coping Statements to Counteract Substance Abuse

Statements to counteract discomfort anxiety:

- I can stand this discomfort.
- I'll focus on getting better, not just feeling better.
- The world won't end if I abstain.
- The more I abstain, the more emotional muscle I'll build up.
- There's no reason why I shouldn't have to endure discomfort.

Statements to counteract helplessness:

- It's only very difficult, not impossible to change this habit.
- I've changed in other areas, I can do it here.
- Just because I have had difficulty changing in the past, doesn't mean the future is hopeless—that's a cop-out.
- I would like ____, but I don't need ____.

Statements to counteract self-blame:

- I'm not perfect.
- It's tough enough changing this habit. Condemning myself won't help.
- Taking drugs is only one aspect of my behavior.
- Remember: It takes time and a great deal of effort to change.
- I'm not a shit for indulging, only a fallible human being.

behavioral strategies designed to alter specific behaviors very useful in such specific situations.

The goal of the RET practitioner in using behavioral strategies remains firm: to help clients change some of the basic philosophical assumptions that predispose them to, and precipitate, their substance abuse behavior. As they utilize behavioral techniques, the therapist keeps assessing, evoking, and reinforcing any constructive cognitive changes.

After the therapist conducts a thorough functional analysis and asks clients to closely monitor the objective and subjective determinants of their substance abuse behavior, the following behavioral techniques can be considered.

Stimulus Control. As noted previously, much substance abuse occurs in high-risk situations. A quick way for people to gain some control over substance abuse behavior is to avoid such problematic situations. After identifying high-risk situations, clients and their therapist can discuss ways of avoiding such situations. It is important to note that high-risk situations include particular kinds of events (e.g., parties where drugs are available), specific people (e.g., acquaintances who provide drugs and who reinforce drug-taking behavior), or specific places (e.g., a favorite bar or street corner). Stimulus control aims first to heighten clients' awareness of these high-risk situations and then devise concrete strategies to minimize exposure to them.

Behavioral Chains and Preplanning. Substance abuse can be viewed as the last link of a chain of fairly predictable events. Once the client and therapist have a detailed awareness of the sequence of events leading to substance abuse, they can more easily "break up" this behavioral pattern. For example, a male client was able to identify a sequence of events that always resulted in drug abuse: (1) a hard day at work that left him fatigued and irritable; (2) an argument with his wife shortly after getting home from work; (3) leaving the house and seeking out friends in a neighborhood bar; (4) leaving the bar with these friends and going to another friend's house to take drugs. Noting this sequence, this man can preplan, at each link in this chain, alternative activities that would break up the pattern. Thus, he can take a nap or undergo a 20-minute deep relaxation session when he gets home to reduce feelings of fatigue and irritability. He can plan an enjoyable activity with his wife (e.g., going out to dinner) after a difficult day. He can contract with himself not to go to a bar nor leave it to go to a drug-taking friend's home. Obviously, it is best to break up such chains at the earliest links.

Operant Conditioning. Clients can be shown how to reward themselves for achieving some discipline over their substance abuse tendencies. Thus, a woman can contract with herself that, should she avoid high-risk situations for a specified period of time, she will reward herself (e.g., buy herself a gift or go on a special vacation). Since most substance abusers often feel deprived of life's pleasures and enjoyments, operant conditioning provides two benefits. It not only reinforces their discipline in counteracting substance abuse, but also promotes the habit of engaging in nondestructive forms of indulgence.

Maintaining Control over Substance Abuse

Should clients stop or significantly reduce their substance abuse, they have realized an important goal. Furthermore, they have probably begun to confront and change some of their basic self-defeating philosophical premises. In carrying through the decision to stop indulging, they have begun rethinking how much discomfort they can tolerate; how capable they are of controlling their own behavior; and how they accept themselves when unable to live up to their ideals.

The therapeutic task is not yet complete, however. The RET practitioner now tries to build on the achieved cognitive changes by addressing those predisposing emotional and cognitive vulnerabilities that prompted the substance abuse. Maintaining control over substance abuse will probably depend upon working through such vulnerabilities.

Assessment Strategy

Once the focus of therapy turns toward changing predisposing factors, clients have already been taught the RET perspective and methods. They have learned to quickly identify the key activating events (As) and distressing feelings (Cs) that typically trigger indulgent behavior. The RET practitioner continues to explore the crucial irrational beliefs that specifically determine their distressing feelings. Again the reader is referred to excellent discussions by Grieger and Boyd (1980) and Walen, DeGuiseppe, and Wessler (1980), on how to explore underlying beliefs.

Substance abusers usually have little insight into the factors motivating their abuse. Many exhibit denial and avoidance of their emotional problems. Also, the habit itself may have dulled or impaired their perceptual and analytical abilities. To uncover the important predisposing cognitive and emotional vulnerabilities: (1) explore in detail the specific emotional triggers that precipitate incidents of substance abuse; (2) explore in detail the real or imagined payoffs of clients' substance abuse.

To see how a therapist can help bring into sharp focus the motivating factors behind a client's desire to indulge, consider this exchange:

C: I did it again last night—went on a real drinking binge.
T: Do you know what triggered it?
C: Nothing . . . I just started drinking.
T: Let me ask you to try something. Close your eyes. Go back to last night and picture, as clearly as you can, what you were doing, thinking, and feeling about a half an hour before you started drinking. Can you picture this?
C: Yeah . . . I had brought some work home from the office and I was trying to get through it. It was hard to understand—and I was getting uptight.
T: Uptight about what?
C: Falling behind in work . . . and what my colleagues would say if they knew I couldn't grasp this stuff. I mean, it's pretty technical—but I should get it.
T: And your colleagues would think . . .
C: You know . . . that I'm incapable . . . a moron.
T: And if they did?
C: Well, obviously, that would be terrible.
T: And when did you start drinking?
C: Right then. I just said, "The hell with the work!"
T: And how did you feel at that moment?
C: Anxious and . . . I don't know . . . sort of critical of myself.
T: What happened when you started drinking?
C: Well, I felt better. I always do. I just forgot about work.
T: What did you think about when you were drinking?
C: I'm not sure. Oh yeah, it's coming back. I started thinking about college—you know, the good old days.

T: Yeah, in college you felt on top of things.
C: You bet.
T: Now, let me ask you to try something else. Go back to the point just before you started drinking—when you were feeling anxious about your work. Okay . . . now, play the scene out—this time without drinking. What happens?
C: This is hard. I just feel myself getting very frustrated. I'm too upset to work. I don't know what to do . . . the whole night is ruined.
T: And how do you feel about this scene?
C: Awful . . . sort of helpless and angry, too. I mean, I have to work and worry all day. I shouldn't have my nights spoiled also.

By carefully pinpointing the emotional triggers and the real or imagined payoffs of indulgence, the therapist can quickly determine the critical irrational beliefs motivating the client's substance abuse. The dialogue above illustrates how both ego anxiety ("It would be awful if others thought poorly of me") and discomfort anxiety ("I shouldn't have to experience painful feelings") are often behind the client's indulgence.

Cognitive Dynamics

The desire—not the decision—to drink appears to emanate from a wide range of dysfunctional beliefs. There are numerous emotional triggers to substance abuse (e.g., depression, boredom, anxiety, anger). Likewise, there are many real or imagined payoffs to indulging. Thus, it is important to carefully assess the salient irrational beliefs for each client, rather than assume a particular set of beliefs that predisposes one to substance abuse.

However, recent research (Marlatt, 1979) suggests some fairly common situational and emotional "risk factors" that threaten continuing control over a particular substance abuse habit. It is noteworthy that these risk factors appear to operate across the range of harmful substances. This may point to common factors in the maintenance phase of conquering dysfunctional habits.

Three of the risk factors found in the study accounted for over 75% of the relapses in which the client, after achieving abstinence for a significant period of time, returns to substance abuse patterns. It behooves the RET practitioner to look for these factors, as they suggest specific irrational beliefs.

Inability to Cope with Intrapersonal Negative Emotional States. Thirty-seven percent of those who returned to their habit had failed to cope with their own negative states. The relapse scenario followed a predictable course. First, the abusers were alone and feeling distressed. The distress might have been depression, anxiety, frustration, etc. They would then indulge in a harmful substance to alleviate or block out their emotional pain. The irrational belief implicit in this pattern is: "I can't stand and shouldn't have to bear this pain."

Inability to Cope with Interpersonal Conflict Involving Significant Others. Eighteen percent of those who relapsed did so after experiencing conflict in a close relationship. In the typical pattern, indulging followed an argument in which clients felt put down by a loved one. The predisposing cognitive vulnerability appears to be what Burns (1980) called "love addiction," that is, the belief that one must be loved by significant others, and that life is intolerable without such love.

Inability to Cope with Social Pressure to Indulge in Harmful Substances. Twenty-four percent of those who relapsed yielded to social pressure to start indulging again. The basic cognitive dynamic underlying this lack of assertive behavior appears to be approval seeking. That is: "If I don't go along with others' wishes or requests, I'll be rejected. That would be awful! I *must* have their approval!"

Treatment Strategies to Prevent Relapse

The wide range of cognitive and emotional vulnerabilities predisposing someone to subtance abuse indicates a wide range of interventions. Here we will specify interventions suggested by the major risk factors associated with relapse.

Dealing with Painful Feelings When One Is Alone. A major risk factor for recovered abusers occurs under the following circumstances: (1) the abusers are alone; (2) they are emotionally distressed, and (3) they judge their distress as "unbearable." The therapist can underscore the risk in such situations. It is also helpful to "reframe" the difficult situation as an opportunity. Clients can be told:

> When you're alone, upset, and tempted to indulge, try to view this as a learning opportunity to deal with painful feelings, to really strengthen yourself. When you're alone and upset, you can say to yourself, "I'm strong enough to stand this" and "I'll just observe the pain, not tell myself I can't stand it." As you practice this, you will notice you can increase your tolerance of painful feelings. There are a number of benefits to this. First, you will develop the confidence that you are not increasing painful feelings. Second, you will gain a greater sense of control and personal mastery as you learn to live with pain without resorting to harmful substances to alleviate it.

Encourage clients to plan alternative coping responses when alone and tempted to indulge. They might, for example, make a list of friends they can call for support and succor; or engage in a pleasurable, non-destructive activity (e.g., going to a movie, taking a long, hot bath).

Dealing with Social Pressure to Indulge. Frequently, substance abuse behavior is tied to well-established social rituals with friends and loved ones. Thus, when abusers stop indulging, they're often subject to a good deal of pressure to return to the destructive rituals. The strategy to handle such pressure is twofold: to challenge the thinking that leads clients to yield to such pressure and to develop the assertive skills to enable them to persistently refuse requests to indulge. Clients' fears of displeasing others leave them vulnerable to such social pressure. They fear that if they refuse offers (to indulge) from friends, they will be rejected—a prospect they dread.

A number of cognitive strategies can be used to help dispel this fear of rejection. The therapist can dispute it by asking:

1. What are the chances of permanent rejection if you refuse offers to indulge?
2. Would it be *awful* to be rejected by someone who insists you conform to their expectations?
3. Would such a rejection prove that you're worthless, destined always to be without friends?

Clients can be asked to make a list of the consequences of yielding to requests to indulge. For example, David, a recovered heroin addict, came up with the following arguments to assist him in refusing offers to take drugs.

1. Taking heroin is not in my best interest. It hurts me physically, emotionally, and financially.
2. If I yield to a friend's request to take drugs, I'll never know whether the friendship is based solely on taking drugs together.
3. To feel intimidated by others getting upset with me for not taking drugs gives them control over me.
4. By always "going along" some people may dislike me for being so weak.
5. Always worrying if others are going to be upset with my refusing drugs is draining and a waste of time.

Once clients begin counteracting their fear of being rejected because of not "going along," they can learn and practice assertive skills. Specifically, they can practice refusing offers of drugs, particularly because such offers are often made in a persistent and guilt-inducing fashion.

Clients and therapists can role play various ways to refuse requests for harmful substances. Clients can anticipate situations in which there will likely be social pressure to indulge. The client and the therapist can then practice how to handle such situations. In the following interchange, the therapist models assertive behavior while the client attempts to pressure him into taking drugs.

C: How about some stuff?
T: No thanks.
C: Oh, come on.
T: No, I really don't want to get high now.
C: What's up—you going straight on me?
T: Actually, I have decided to give up drugs—for a number of reasons.
C: (*sarcastically*) Jesus, you're a lot of fun!
T: (*laughing*) Well, I don't plan to be miserable.
C: So, come on. Just a few hits. You'll make me feel weird if I have to do this alone.
T: I don't think you're weird. And I hope you can feel comfortable with me, whether or not I'm taking drugs. I value our friendship.

Persistently refusing others' requests to go along with their wishes is both a decision and a skill. The assertive skills involved in resisting social pressure include disengaging from others' aggressive or guilt-inducing comments; making disarming comments; coping with upsetting feelings before and during the encounter; clearly stating one's own preferences; and asking other people to forego their pressuring tactics.

Coping with Relapse

Give the difficulty in overcoming a substance abuse habit, as well as the ease with which such habits can be reestablished, relapse is always a distinct possibility. Therefore, the therapist had better acknowledge this possibility to clients and propose strategies to minimize the severity and duration of the relapse period. Indeed, long-range success in counteracting substance abuse is dependent on clients' ability to bounce back quickly and effectively from relapse.

Cognitive Dynamics.

G. Alan Marlatt (Marlatt & Gordon, 1979), a research psychologist at the University of Washington, has studied closely the cognitive and emotional determinants of the relapse process. His findings illustrate the central role that clients' thought processes, particularly their self-evaluations, play in determining whether they cope constructively or destructively with relapse. Marlatt has pinpointed a common destructive response to relapse, which he has termed the "abstinence violation effect" (AVE). There are two cognitive components of the AVE. First, clients attribute their relapse solely to personal character flaws (e.g., "I'm weak . . . I have no willpower"). Second, clients then harshly condemn themselves for having violated their self-imposed limits on substance abuse (e.g., "I'm a worthless person for having no willpower").

The AVE not only directly leads to intense feelings of guilt and helplessness, but also practically insures an extended period of relapse. Feeling helpless and guilty, clients easily slide back into a pattern of chronic abuse.

Treatment Strategies to Cope with Relapse

The fundamental strategy in counteracting the AVE is to prepare clients to view their relapse in a more dispassionate and constructive fashion. A particularly useful cognitive technique to accomplish this is de-attribution. De-attribution helps to counter gratuitous self-blame by showing clients how to discover the main factors associated with relapse (e.g., being in an emotionally charged situation, the availability of drugs, feeling fatigued). De-attribution not only helps clients correct their exaggerated sense of self-blame, but also suggests ways in which they may avoid or cope with high-risk relapse situations in the future.

The following rationale, developed by Marlatt and Gordon (1979), can show clients how to cognitively reframe a relapse episode so as to reduce feelings of guilt and helplessness and thereby reduce the risk of an extended relapse period:

> A slip is not all that unusual. It does not mean that you have failed or that you have lost control over your behavior. You will probably feel guilty about what you have done, and will blame yourself for having slipped. This feeling is to be expected; it is part of what we call the Abstinence Violation Effect. There is no reason why you have to give in to this feeling and continue to drink. The feeling will pass in time. Look on the slip as a learning experience. What were the elements of the high-risk situation that led to the slip? What coping response could you have used to get around the situation? Remember the old saying: One swallow doesn't make a summer? Well, one slip doesn't have to make a relapse, either. Just because you slipped once does not mean that you are a failure, that you have no will power, or that you are a hopeless addict. Look on the slip as a single, independent event, something which can be avoided in the future with an alternative coping response.

Rational-emotive imagery, a technique originally developed by Maultsby (1974; Maultsby & Ellis, 1974), is an excellent tool to promote a constructive coping response to a relapse episode. The following vignette illustrates how the technique can be applied to this problem.

T: Close your eyes . . . take a few deep, slow breaths . . . and get as comfortable as you can. . . . Now, picture yourself in a situation in which you would feel very tempted to drink. Picture yourself as clearly and vividly as you can. . . . Can you imagine that?

C: Yes . . . there are a number of situations in which I'd love a drink.

T: Fine . . . focus on me. . . . Now I want you to imagine going ahead and taking a drink—a clear violation of the commitment you made to yourself to abstain. Can you picture that?

C: Yes.

T: Keep focusing on it. Now, how do you feel right now?

C: Terrible. How could I slip up? What's wrong with me?

T: Describe your feelings.

C: At first I felt agitated. . . . Now I feel down . . . in despair.

T: Yes. . . . Now I'd like you to change your feeling of intense agitation and despair to only concern and regret. Keep the image of yourself drinking, but only feel concern and regret. Can you do it?

C: It's hard.

T: Yes . . . keep pushing yourself to feel only concern and regret. You can do it.

C: Okay. I've got it. I just feel resentful.

T: Good. How did you change the feeling?

C: I thought it's not helpless. I stopped drinking once, I can do it again.

T: Anything else?

C: Something we've been talking about. No one is perfect . . . and it's unrealistic to think I'll never screw up.

T: Excellent. Do you see what you did to change? You gave yourself some rational and realistic thoughts. That's what changed your feelings.

C: Yeah, when I realized I could bounce back from this slipup, I felt more in control.

T: Yes . . . and I'm sure there are additional realistic thoughts you can come up with to help you cope with the possibility.

C: Yes.

T: Now, the more you practice this, the more you will prepare yourself for handling a relapse constructively. How about practicing this five minutes a day?

C: Fine. I'd like to feel I can take a relapse in stride.

In many treatment programs, relapse is considered as a treatment failure, or worse, a sin. The view advocated here is that relapse is unfortunate but not catastrophic. When relapse occurs, clients are shown how to "accept and cope" rather than "condemn and mope." Rational-emotive imagery promotes this view by encouraging them to imagine "the worst" and then work out an appropriate and sensible response instead of a horrifying, self-immolating feeling.

In some cases it may even be desirable to actually program a relapse. The therapist accompanies the client in order to provide supervision. If clients have very little confidence they could bounce back from a slip, a programmed relapse might be useful. It would provide them with an opportunity, with the therapist's support and coaching, to learn and practice the critical cognitive and behavioral coping respones. The hoped-for outcome: the client is innoculated against the all-or-none response to a slip that can lead to a lengthy relapse period.

Summary

Combatting a substance abuse habit requires persistent effort applied in a precise and knowledgeable manner. Enduring change will be difficult unless clients change some of the basic premises and beliefs that drove them to substance abuse in the first place and make it ever so easy to return to their habit. In this presentation, we have pinpointed the key beliefs that RET explores and shows clients how to change so that they can overcome substance abuse. The rational-emotive therapy system, as a theory and a set of procedures, is particularly well suited to the treatment of substance abuse. The basic tenets of RET sensitively capture the inner world of substance abusers and realistically present them with behavioral treatment tasks to counteract this difficult and pernicious addiction.

References

Bandura, A. (1977). Self-efficacy: Toward a unifying theory of behavior change. *Psychological Review, 94,* 191–215.

Bard, J. (1980). *Rational-emotive therapy in practice.* Champaign, IL: Research Press.

Beck, A. T., & Emery, G. D. (1977). *Individual treatment manual for cognitive behavioral psychotherapy of drug abuse.* Philadelphia: Center for Cognitive Therapy.

Burns, D. D. (1980). *Feeling good.* New York: Morrow.

Danysh, J. (1974). *Stop without quitting.* San Francisco: International Society for General Semantics.

Dryden, W. (1984). *Rational-emotive therapy: Fundamentals and innovations.* London: Croom Helm.

Eisenger, R. A. (1971). Psychological predictors of smoking recidivism. *Journal of Health and Social Behavior, 12,* 355–362.

Ellis, A. (1962). *Reason and emotion in psychotherapy*. Secaucus, NJ: Lyle Stuart.

Ellis, A. (1971). Twenty-two ways to stop putting yourself down. *Rational Living, 6*(1), 9–16.

Ellis, A. (Speaker). (1974). *I'd like to stop but . . . Overcoming addiction*. (Cassette recording). New York: Institute for Rational-Emotive Therapy.

Ellis, A. (Speaker). (1976). *Conquering low frustration tolerance*. New York: Institute for Rational-Emotive Therapy.

Ellis, A. (1979). Discomfort anxiety: A new cognitive behavioral construct. Part 1. *Rational Living, 14*(2), 3–8.

Ellis, A. (1980). Discomfort anxiety: A new cognitive behavioral construct. Part 2. *Rational Living, 15*(1), 25–30.

Ellis, A. (1982). The treatment of alcohol and drug abuse: A rational-emotive approach. *Rational Living, 17*(2), 14–24.

Ellis, A., & Becker, I. (1982). *A guide to personal happiness*. North Hollywood, CA: Wilshire Books.

Ellis, A., & Grieger, R. (Eds.). *Handbook of rational-emotive therapy*. New York: Springer.

Ellis, A., & Harper, R. A. (1975). *A new guide to rational living*. North Hollywood, CA: Wilshire Books.

Ellis, A., & Whiteley, J. M. (Eds.). (1979). *Theoretical and empirical foundations of rational-emotive therapy*. Monterey, CA: Brooks/Cole.

Glass, C. R., & Arnkoff, D. B. (1981). Thinking it through: Selected issues in cognitive assessment and therapy. In P. C. Kendall (Ed.), *Advances in cognitive-behavioral research and therapy. Vol. 1*. New York: Academic Press.

Grau, A. F. (1977). Dealing with the irrationality of alcoholic drinking. In J. L. Wolfe & E. Brand (Eds.), *Twenty years of rational therapy* (pp. 225–230). New York: Institute for Rational-Emotive Therapy.

Grieger, R., & Boyd, J. (1980). *Rational-emotive therapy: A skills-based approach*. New York: Van Nostrand Reinhold.

Grieger, R., & Grieger, I. (1982). *Cognition and emotional disturbance*. New York: Human Sciences Press.

Higbee, J. (1977). RET in dealing with alcohol-dependent persons. In J. L. Wolfe & E. Brand (Eds.), *Twenty years of rational therapy*. New York: Institute for Rational-Emotive Therapy.

Kanfer, F., & Saslow, G. (1969). Behavioral diagnosis. In C. M. Franks (Ed.), *Behavior therapy: Appraisal and status*. New York: McGraw-Hill.

Lazarus, A. A. (1977). Toward an egoless state of being. In A. Ellis & R. Grieger (Eds.), *Handbook of rational-emotive therapy* (pp. 113–118). New York: Springer.

Marlatt, G. A. (1979). Alcohol use and problem drinking: A cognitive-behavioral analysis. In P. C. Kendall & S. D. Hollon (Eds.), *Cognitive-behavioral interventions: Theory, research and practice* (pp. 319–356). New York: Academic Press.

Marlatt, G. A. & Gordon, J. R. (1979). Determinants of relapse: Implications for the maintenance of behavior change. In P. Davidson (Ed.), *Behavioral medicine: Changing health lifestyles*. New York: Brunner/Mazel.

Maultsby, M. C. (1974). *Help yourself to happiness*. New York: Institute for Rational-Emotive Therapy.

Maultsby, M. C. (1978). *A million dollars for your hangover*. Lexington, KY: Rational Self-Help Books.

Maultsby, M. C. & Ellis, A. (1974). *Technique for using rational-emotive imagery*. New York: Institute for Rational-Emotive Therapy.

Pechacek, T. F., & Donaher, B. F. (1979). How and why people quit smoking: A cognitive-behavioral analysis. In P. C. Kendall & S. D. Hollon (Eds.), *Cognitive-behavioral interventions: Theory, research and practice.* New York: Academic Press.

Sobell, M. B., & Sobell, L. C. (1976). Assessment of addictive behavior. In M. Hersen & A. S. Bellak (Eds.), *Behavioral assessment: A practical handbook* (pp. 305–337). Oxford: Pergamon.

Walen, S. D., DiGiuseppe, R., & Wessler, R. L. (1980). *A practitioner's guide to rational-emotive therapy.* New York: Oxford.

Wessler, R. A., & Wessler, R. L. (1980). *The principles and practice of rational-emotive therapy.* San Francisco: Jossey-Bass.

Wolfe, J. L. (1979). A cognitive-behavioral approach to working with women alcoholics. In V. Burtle (Ed.), *Women who drink* (pp. 197–216). Springfield, IL: Charles C Thomas.

10

Religion and RET

Friends or Foes?

PAUL A. HAUCK

The very fact that I have been asked to contribute a chapter on religion for a book on the applications of RET raises a question: Is there sufficient compatibility between these secular and spiritual endeavours so that adherents to either persuasion can benefit from the other? Such a question is not as likely to be asked of other therapeutic systems for the simple reason that it would largely be irrelevant. As Lawrence and Huber have pointed out (1982), and as previously observed by Miller (1977), other schools of therapy have a different philosophical and anthropological base than that of the pastoral counselor. Whether it be gestalt therapy, transactional analysis, nondirective therapy, or psychoanalysis, these approaches to the understanding and assistance of humankind are not particularly concerned with values, ethical positions, or moral issues—precisely the subject matter so important for the spiritual counselor (Ellis, 1973; Grau, 1977; Hailparn, 1973).

Rational-emotive therapy, on the other hand, has a great deal to say on the matter of ethical behavior and moral values (Ard, 1967; Beaman, 1978; Ellis, 1962, 1972a,b, 1981; Hauck, 1967, 1972; Hauck & Grau, 1968; Holland, 1968; Primavera, Tantillo, & DeLisio, 1980). Many RET authors have written on the subjects of sin, contrition, dogmatism, guilt, human worth, punishment, and faith. Although other schools of psychotherapy have shown interest in religious matters, they have largely been tangential and brief rather than substantial and in depth.

PAUL A. HAUCK • Clinical psychologist in private practice, Rock Island, Illinois 61201.

Rational-emotive therapy differs from other schools of therapy in that it deals not only with how human behaviors can be understood by uncovering forgotten memories; not only with when and how to make interpretations; not only with how to listen with unconditional positive acceptance; not only with how to interpret dreams; not only with why transferences are likely to develop and what can be done about them. RET often concerns itself with all these matters. But, being a cognitive therapy, it does not lengthily pursue some techniques on which psychoanalysts would spend many sessions; and it does not reflect feelings as long-windedly as do Rogerians. RET not only discloses and disputes irrational philosophies but also may use the best of other methods that have proved useful. To this end, the rational-emotive counselor is not infrequently grateful for the work done by Freud (1938) on dream analysis, for Berne's (1964) work on scripts, for the newer developments on hypnosis (Erickson, 1948), and for the latest findings on stress reduction (Selye, 1956; Gray, 1971; Benson, 1975).

What is RET's uniqueness that sets it apart from other modalities? And how does this uniqueness make it especially appropriate for the pastoral counselor and the client wanting a spiritual emphasis?

Having practiced psychotherapy for thirty years, and having for years sought with some sense of desperation for a therapeutic system that achieved the kinds of results I always felt were acceptable, I feel confident in stating that RET is the preeminent modality which addresses clinical *and* ethical issues in all the depth that the spiritual counselor could possibly want from a secular approach.

Cognitive therapies focus on the statements subjects make over issues. Such statements can be of several kinds: relaxation statements, such as "I feel serene, calm down, breathe deeply"; self-encouraging statements: "I *can* do this, I'm *not* going to let this get me down, I'm a survivor"; distracting statements: "I'm not going to think about this, I'd better get busy with something so I won't focus on my worries"; and rational statements: "I don't need to be perfect, it isn't going to upset me unless I let it."

Of these types of cognitions, only RET focuses primarily on the rational statements. In so doing, it goes to the very core of an emotional problem—the philosophical underpinnings that feed the disturbance. This emphasis on the profound beliefs and values held by clients makes it a comfortable and friendly medium for the pastoral counselor and religious client.

The major compatibilities and incompatibilities between RET and religious thought, will, when compared, indicate convincingly how applicable rational-emotive therapy can be with religion.

Compatibilities and Incompatibilities between Religion and RET

The welfare of each person, indeed, the good of society, are the goals of both religion and RET. Neither accepts total resignation as an acceptable solution to mankind's problems. Rather, both staunchly believe that human intervention makes a difference in the affairs of people. Though there is disagreement between the two approaches over how that effort is to be made, both pursue human and societal betterment.

Religion attempts to guide the faithful through education via the scriptures. Rational-emotive therapy relies on the gradual accumulation of knowledge through empiricism, logical processes, and the scientific method. The former relies on faith, the latter on cognitive restructuring through disputation and homework assignments. Religion views ethical and moral principles as fixed and unchangeable. RET, along with all scientific pursuits, views current values and knowledge as always in a state of flux if further knowledge requires revising prior assumptions.

The minister influences his flock through sermons, prayer, emotive appeal, and adherence to a body of principles enunciated in a written body of knowledge: the Bible, the Koran, the Torah, and similar recorded collections that usually refer to a divinity. (Confucianism is an exception.)

The RET therapist uses logical disputation, education, humor, emotive appeal, and reliance on a system of principles enunciated in cognitive-behavior literature, not divinely inspired, but collected from any source that can withstand the test of scientific inquiry (Ellis, 1952, 1962, 1972a, 1973, 1981, 1983, 1984).

Among the more obvious differences between spiritual and secular counselors is their view of fallibility versus infallibility. Religion has the comfort of relying on teachings that are divinely inspired, not the conclusions of mortals. Scriptural teachings are incontestable for the pastoral counselor. Most of his religious principles follow naturally from the fundamental teachings of his particular religion.

The scientifically oriented counselor never views any principle as being infallible, including the scientific method itself and principles of therapy. Though therapists may fear and may agonize over giving up one therapeutic orientation for another, they do change nevertheless when reality urges them vigorously to examine their assumptions.

I see no major compromise between those who base their philosophies on faith versus those who honor experience. But we need not conclude that a personal customizing of therapeutic techniques to religious uses it not possible (Wessler, 1984). I have for years served pastoral counselors as a psychological consultant and have never felt frustrated by the pick-and-choose process that those counselors always went through in adapting RET teachings to their own.

What precisely are those accommodations the spiritual counselor will make if he or she takes interest in becoming more rational-emotively oriented? Let us examine several key religious issues to see if successful rapprochement can be made between the pastoral and the secular therapist. Some of the relevant subjects which require closer scrutiny are forgiveness, sin, guilt, atonement, and excessive passivity.

Forgiveness

People who have committed a wrong have been taught to view such an act in two ways: first, to disapprove of the errant act, and second, to disapprove of themselves because of those unacceptable acts. Most of us have been taught to regard our behaviors and ourselves as inseparable entities. It is for this reason that self-hate, guilt, inferiority complexes, and a crushing sense of being sinful have been generated in millions of people over the centuries. It also accounts for the sorry history of the church and society at large regarding the manner in which mistake-makers were treated. The burning of thousands of wretched women at the stake because they were accused of witchcraft, and the incredible tortures of other thousands for "morally reprehensible" acts, support this thesis.

From our ancestors' point of view there was logical consistency in such practices. If person and behavior are indistinguishable, then it is obviously impossible to deal with them separately. In other words, if behavior is unacceptable and must be punished, then so is the individual unacceptable and must be punished.

It is highly ironic that, in view of religion's claim that we are sinners and can never behave perfectly and that we are permitted forgiveness for our sins by an all-forgiving God, that the devout are often the cruelest victims of an unforgiving mentality. I have counseled hundreds of staunch churchgoers who were capable of reciting biblical writings verbatim by chapter and verse and I have counseled numerous clergymen from the major denominations, and have been stunned by the severity of self-blame they all practiced against themselves despite the fact that they unequivocally espoused total forgiveness for others, based on religious teachings and divine edict.

It goes without saying that if a minister suffers from unforgiveness, his parishioners are likely to suffer also. And why does self-damnation exist amongst a group of people who make forgiveness a core belief in their lives? Because they do not know *how* to forgive in any other way but through faith. The faithful are spared the agonies of self-castigation suffered by those weak in faith. But being told to have faith does not work for all of us. Many of us require a rationale and a precise technique to do what the believer supposedly does effortlessly.

Rational-emotive therapy provides such a technique. It is the only therapeutic school that deals with moral and ethical issues as part of its technique and content. It is therefore eminently suitable to the pastoral counselor and his following. The fact that the founder of RET is an atheist, or that some practitioners of RET are religiously unenthusiastic, does not detract a whit from its applicability to religion. The positions it espouses via some of the rational beliefs that make up psychological health are as noble, decent, and compassionate as the profoundest teachings from Christianity (Ellis, 1981, 1983, 1984; Hauck, 1972; Wessler, 1984). Indeed, a close study of scripture and RET's rational positions indicates a remarkable similarity of viewpoint, a fact which has been observed by Lawrence and Huber (1982), among others. They point out that RET is "most compatible with biblical teachings of all current major psychotherapeutic systems." These writers then list a number of scriptural statements and their compatible counterparts from RET literature. For example, irrational idea No. 1 states that unless people are approved of, they have no intrinsic value. Biblical thoughts on a similar theme come from Psalm 118:6, "With the Lord on my side I do not fear. What can man do to me?"

Is there any real difference between these sentiments except for the reference to a divinity? Precisely the same attitude is expressed in Psalm 118:18, "It is better to take refuge in the Lord than to put confidence in man."

The secular therapist would disagree on two points with the pastoral counselor by advising clients to accept themselves unconditionally instead of relying on God for self-acceptance. Aside from this distinction, religious counseling and RET both make the critical point that it is nonsense to believe that we are unworthy people if and when others whom we value dislike us.

The second technical point of disagreement between the psychological and the religious view is the matter of conditionality. The minister must of necessity profess that mankind has value aside from the attitudes of the whole world, as long as God still gives His divine blessing. But would this still hold if God disapproved of us?

The RET position makes no such condition. It states unequivocally that the opinions others have of us, though they can influence us for good or bad, can never make us unworthy of remaining alive and happy if we choose not to accept negative judgments about ourselves.

With reference to the matter of forgiveness specificially, religion and RET both take a firm stand and are in close harmony. RET postulates, in disputing irrational idea No. 3, that there are no bad people in the world, only bad behavior and that people who commit sins, or crimes, or who behave unacceptably in any other manner, should not be treated harshly, or regarded as evil (Ellis, 1962). No matter what their behavior, they, as persons, are always entitled to total forgiveness.

The pastoral counselor will no doubt quickly recall two scriptural messages which reflect this sentiment: from Romans 13:9, "You shall love your neighbour as yourself," and from Matthew 7:1, "Judge not, that you be not judged."

In my experience I have found forgiveness, whether of self or others, an extremely difficult task for the human being to carry out. It appears to be such an easy mental leap for the human brain to conclude that unacceptable behaviors must originate in unacceptable people that the illogical reasoning underlying this process is not easily detected. This is why, I believe, all of us, even those who are urged each Sunday to be forgiving for all sins, find ourselves blaming ourselves and others, if not over every rude act, then certainly over those acts we regard as singularly reprehensible. The atheist, the believer, and the minister are alike seduced into this false logic. When we all learn to accept ourselves truly as imperfect beings, then we will be unconditionally forgiving. But this will not happen until we learn to deal with the issue in an enlightened manner.

Sin

A sin is not merely a sample of faulty behavior. Even if it has huge consequences that cause great pain, the act, to be declared a sin, has two characteristics: it is viewed as being distinctly undesirable, *and* it regards the doer of that act as correspondingly evil.

It is with the second judgment that RET takes exception (Ellis, 1962, 1972b). If rating of behavior and rating of people are separated, then it is wrong to judge people by their actions and total forgiveness is logically allowed; one need never damn others or oneself, and it is wrong to feel guilty at any time over any act.

Before I give the reasons why we have a moral obligation never to blame or feel guilt, let me explain the use of these two terms as practiced by RET therapists.

Blame is the act of ascribing responsibility for an act to someone, and if that act is thought to be unacceptable, to conclude that the person is evil. RET has no difficulty with the first task but tries always to avoid the second. People are responsible for their faulty actions, to be sure. If they performed the objectionable act, they are responsible and will be dealt with by society or their own sense of ethics to bring about a change in those actions in the future. If penalties, fines, or even imprisonment are needed to control misbehavior or immoral actions, then so be it. The secular therapist is not normally inclined to excuse crime for any reason simply because he or she is not inclined to blame the wrongdoer. If a change in behavior can be achieved by gentle means, such as a scolding, then it is hoped a castigation of only the act is all that would be recommended.

But, if stronger measures are clearly called for, then these will also and unhesitatingly be recommended, such as noncooperation, termination of a relationship, or even a jail sentence. RET is not soft on wrongdoing even though it never views the person as evil.

To understand RET's stand on guilt it is again necessary to make a distinction between *being* guilty and *feeling* guilty.

To identify a person as being guilty signifies that you believe that person has committed a wrong. To believe, however, that the person must also feel hideous about himself or herself means we want that person to commit an act of self-violence. We would suggest that it is much more moral and humane to focus always on the wrong and how to correct it than on the definitional evil of the person committing the wrong. We contend no one is bad, only human, and therefore inescapably error prone. However, if rating behavior is kept separate from rating people, then no one is good either, but is only accomplished, talented, or skilled in one or more human pursuits.

On what grounds, aside from the sweeping realization that mistakes of all magnitudes are an integral part of what it means to be human, can RET therapists hold that no person should ever be blamed or made to feel guilty over misdeeds?

There are three causes of all misbehavior, and for which we have a right to self-forgiveness. These are: deficiency, ignorance, and disturbance.

We are deficient in numerous ways. No one is so endowed that he or she can master every task in such a fashion as to be beyond criticism. In short, no matter how talented or brilliant we are in some pursuits, we are equally inept in scores of others. Neither desire, dedication, or labor will ever make us capable in those ways our genes and our social history ordained we will probably forever be deficient.

Therefore, some of us will never carry a melody, draw a decent picture, become a sports idol, or be an acceptable parent. All require a minimum of personal assets that make these accomplishments possible. Without them we fail in these pursuits all our lives.

If these inherited and acquired shortcomings lead us to violence, impatience, or poor judgment, we can regret them, to be sure. That is a rational conclusion. But to consider ourselves inferior and unworthy as a human being because we were born of small stature, with a large nose, or deprived of normal intelligence, is to confuse our traits with our totality.

The second reason we often behave badly is due to our ignorance. If you have not had the opportunity to learn a skill, how can you rationally hate yourself for what you have not learned? Though that ignorance may result in enormous destruction, as in the case of an accidental explosion, we can still hold that the person responsible for the mistake is guilty of the accident, but never is worthless, evil, bad, wicked, or blameworthy as a human because of the unfortunate event.

The protest that ignorance is no defense makes sense perhaps from a legal perspective, but never from a moral one. To suggest that we must feel guilty for acts that we have never learned to avoid is to ignore the obvious. Would you insist that everyone is unacceptable and damnable who does not know how to fly an airplane? No? Then you cannot make the same conclusion for parents who abuse their children if they have been taught that beatings are sensible child-rearing practices.

The third reason we have a perfect right to forgive a person for his or her undesirable behavior is when that behavior resulted from emotional disturbance. Once again the individual is largely powerless to behave otherwise. In this instance, we cannot base our forgiveness on that person's inability to learn (deficiency), or because the necessary learning did not yet occur (ignorance). We hold, instead, that a human is forgivable and unreprehensible if emotional control is absent. The victim of a tragic mishap can normally not report important details of the accident. The shock and the fear on such occasions normally disrupt one's powers of observation and concentration. That is the way we behave under powerful emotive forces. We expect it, we understand it, and we forgive ourselves for our disturbed behavior *because* we are disturbed. Could we rationally ask upset people to behave as though they were not upset? Can we sensibly ask an inebriate to behave soberly while he or she is drunk? In the same vein, we would not demand that an epileptic not have seizures, or that paranoids not be suspicious. Though we deplore the behaviors that eventuate from emotional disorders, we insist that the disturbed person is disturbed, has a right to be wrong and imperfect, and is entitled to our acceptance as a worthy person even while we are planning that person's correction.

The Catholic church has long held a similar view regarding the degree of guilt a sinner has a right to assume for errant behavior. It has taught its followers that there are five modifiers of behavior: passion, ignorance, force, fear, and habit. This breakdown is more detailed than the one offered by RET, but otherwise, the similarity is surprisingly close. The church does not have a category that is similar to deficiency. Ignorance as a modifier is shared with RET, while passion, force, fear, and habit can all be seen as reasonably related to RET's third category: disturbance.

Bearing these arguments in mind, it perhaps seems more reasonable that (a) the rating of people and their actions can be differentiated from each other, (b) the concept of sin requires rethinking, and (c) forgiveness can be unconditional. The pastor can readily accommodate these views into his God-centered counseling if he will but be receptive. Although they are accustomed to their theological principles, I find that spiritual clients are not offended when a large dose of rationality is interspersed along with religious views. There is a scriptural counterpart for most of the rational ideas on which RET bases its philosophical stance. Some of these comparisons, which can easily be made by the informed, show remarkable similarity.

The rational idea that we are imperfect and can forgive ourselves for our shortcomings is also reflected in Romans 3:23, "For all have sinned and come short of the glory of God." RET urges us not to hate or love ourselves (since these evaluations are dependent on our performances) but to accept ourselves until we can change or even if we never change. One well-known religious commandment, from Romans, 13:96, says: "Thou shalt love thy neighbor as thyself." We would object to the word "love" and suggest the word "accept" instead since it does not involve positive affection. RET states we become upset when we believe we must focus on dangerous possibilities rather than to dispute the wisdom of worry. From John 14:17 we have a similar thought, "Let not your heart be troubled, neither let it be afraid." And from Matthew 6:25-26, "Take no thought for your life, what ye shall eat . . ." or from Proverbs, 3:25, "Be not afraid of sudden fear, neither of the desolation of the wicked, when it cometh."

One of the strongest irrational ideas RET asks us to challenge is the idea that we must become upset if we do not get what we want or deserve. From Phillipians 4:11, we read "Not that I speak in respect of want: for I have learned, in whatsoever state I am, therewith to be content." Here again is some agreement between psychotherapy and religion. And this similarity could be demonstrated with countless other examples.

Unwelcomed Thoughts

A very common source of emotional disturbance is the guilt people experience at the mere perception of thoughts normally alien to their finer sensibilities. The actual fact that there is not the slightest possibility of acting out such a thought does not often relieve the sufferer of guilt. Such an outcome is the result of believing always that there is no distinction between a thought and a deed. Proverbs 23:7 says, "As a man thinketh in his heart, so is he." It is this principle that troubles the pastoral counselor so very much when dealing with clients who have thoughts of greed, hate, violence, or infidelity. And why should they not be concerned over such behavior when, after all, behavior is often preceded by thoughts that analyze, plan, evaluate, and organize one's actions?

Taken unconditionally, without qualifications, the unfortunate victim of an evil thought has the moral obligation to conclude that an immoral act has been committed because it was contemplated.

It cannot be emphasized enough what an inhuman burden this places on us. It means that we must literally do the impossible: be aware of our thoughts before we have them, and then, so informed, stop them. This is comparable to screening a series of TV shows for our children without actually seeing them. Yet the church does not hesitate for a moment to declare us sinful for having unflattering thoughts which fleetingly pass through our awareness and, once judged unacceptable, are often ignored and rejected.

What else is one to do? What else can one do? It is not possible to reject a thought until one has it. But this is precisely what the minister has insisted we do, as though we can correct our actions retroactively. Am I belaboring the point unduly if I remind the reader that we cannot undo the past, only influence the future? What is done is done. We do not have precognition (at least most of us do not), with which we can be aware of feelings and thoughts before they enter our awareness. But even here, even if we possessed precognition, we would be no better off since we would actually be aware of unacceptable impulses in the form of intuitions, sensations, or hunches, or whatever form precognitions take.

The less made of such events the fewer unwelcomed thoughts one tends to have. To magnify a passing violent or lustful thought elevates it to a prominence it does not deserve. Only by seeing it calmly as a freakish event, or one that is absurd, humorous, or fanciful, is one likely to get control over it. The less fuss the better. The more fuss, the worse it gets.

The pastoral counselor is, therefore, strongly advised to be reassuring to his client who hastily arrives in his office after having a murderous thought toward his mother. And if that unwelcomed thought is judged to be of the spontaneous and random variety of thoughts we all have, the matter had better be dealt with as though it were an incidental occurrence governed by the laws of generalization and transposition (Kimble & Garmezy, 1963), according to which two events that occur closely together in time or location, or both, are more likely to be connected into a whole perception. It is in this way that one of my clients made the frightening connection to bury his hammer into his child's head as he was nailing down a floor while his infant son played by the window a few yards away.

Such persons are never helped when told to feel guilty over such cognitions. Only by minimizing the seriousness of such an absurd notion, and others like it, can the sufferer gain the relief he or she fully deserves.

But suppose the client does not entertain frivolous, capricious, and unflattering thoughts that are clearly not the product of generalization and transposition? Suppose the client harbors deliberate and well-thought-out intentions of greed, lust, or violence? Are we to cajole that person, as though there were no substance to such covert sentiments? That too would be absurd.

In such instances it is important that such dangerous or improper thoughts be accepted at face value but without personal condemnation. Rejecting the bearer of bad thoughts either (a) causes such thoughts to be repressed, not abolished; (b) encourages silence rather than confession; or (c) condemns rather than instructs. The minister will be perfectly at home in teaching the principles of his religion in this instance. Should he or she want to add psychological techniques to the teaching of scriptural principles, nothing need prevent this. The minister can explain on moral grounds why greed, violence, or lust are wrong and then use our knowledge of the causes and correction of procrastination and anger to excellent advantage.

In my haste to reassure spiritual leaders that unwelcome thoughts do not justify self-persecution, I hope you have not missed the point that the scriptural quotation "As a man thinketh in his heart, so is he," refers to the second category of obsessive thinking, not the first. The words "in his heart" mean that the subject wants to perform the thoughts he or she entertains. If they are immoral thoughts they constitute wrongdoing that had better be disputed vigorously. The spontaneous, unwelcome thoughts, however, do not come from the heart; they are ideas that flash through our minds, are immediately rejected as abhorent, and are best dealt with through distraction, self-forgiveness, relaxation exercises, pleasant imagery, or cognitive restructuring (Ellis, 1962, 1973; Lazarus, 1981).

The modification of behavior according to RET principles calls for the following steps: (1) the detection of those irrational ideas underlying the objectionable behaviors or symptoms; (2) the active disputation of those faulty philosophies until they are dismissed thoroughly; and (3) the displacement of new and more acceptable behaviors and symptoms for the old.

When these objectives have been accomplished, we are content that we have done all we can and all that had better be done. The atonement is inherent in the corrective process itself (Hauck, 1972). It matters not whether those changes are made through great struggle and suffering, or if with relative ease and an absence of anguish. Long and drawn-out remorse or crushing guilt are likely to perpetuate the same problems or even create new ones.

To make a change in behavior last, we want to help the client be as self-confident and as self-respecting as possible. Life is hard enough, even at its best. When we are out of sorts, however, and when we have grave doubts about ourselves, we can be fairly sure that the hard knocks of life are going to make sensible coping more difficult, not less. It behooves us, therefore, to penalize or punish only to the extent required to bring about the desired changes, and not a whit more. To urge clients to do otherwise generates resentment, further convinces them of our deep disgust, reduces their self-respect and self-confidence, and sets a deplorable example of unforgivingness.

The methods traditionally used to achieve atonement have been (1) physical punishment or confinement, and (2) psychological or spiritual damnation. The first can easily be carried to extremes by police, judges, employers, or parents who neurotically believe that there are such things in the world as bad people and that we can transform bad people into good people if we are severely harsh with them.

The second set of techniques (psychological or scriptural damnation) achieve questionable results even if torture is omitted.

So damaging can be the psychological-spiritual atonement path, that at times we create disturbance worse than the symptoms we sought to cure. The hellfire and brimstone approach to corrective behavior not only is likely to scare the sinner out of sinning again, but it can make him too fearful to be spontaneous again. Expecting people to become victors in the eternal conflict with Satan after we insist that they grovel in the dust of repentance is not reasonable.

Redemption, strength, and growth are more likely to follow from our corrective measures if we leave our charges with stronger, not weaker, feelings of self-acceptance. That individual who feels deserving of recovery and a better life will *allow* improvement to endure. Not to allow deservingness in the course of corrective process is to put in the heart of the troubled victim doubt that he is worthy of the good fortune we steer him toward. A favourable outcome is more likely to occur when we see the good in humans, endorse their potential for change and improvement: when we regard their wayward period as a path they did not entirely choose to take but one which they were partly trained and programmed to take. In the final analysis, behavior is learned through modeling, trial and error, and the reinforcement principle. When training has gone awry, it is not always a result of free will, but more often because of faulty education. What one can learn, one can unlearn. Therefore, why not let the matter rest there? Why burden the sufferer with further shame and guilt while he or she is in the very process of gaining rational self-control?

Excessive Passivity

Healthy-minded people tend to have this characteristic in common: they are able to wrestle enough satisfaction and benefits from life to make their existence at least reasonably content (Hauck, 1984). When, for reasons of fear, charity, or guilt, they choose to love their neighbors more than they love themselves, they may lose self-respect and develop a host of symptoms that eventually affect those whom they are supposedly pleasing.

This image of the saintly person has been depicted in art and sermons as the truly religious ideal. The good person is the self-sacrificing person. He puts himself last, always in the service of others. To show his deep love, he sacrifices endlessly and returns bad behavior with good.

In my experience I have learned that there are healthier options to this rule. If the pastoral counselor and the devoted churchgoer want to be of greatest help to this silent and long-suffering majority, it is time to reconsider the position they have held for generations: that passivity is unequivocally better than noncooperation, that good should always be returned for evil.

If you would desire to teach your flock how to obtain reasonable satisfaction in this life, it is imperative that you teach self-interest. Make a distinction between self-interest and selfishness because it is the fulcrum about which this issue pivots.

Let us consider the definitions of each: first, selfishness. Selfish people are takers. They demand more and more, unmindful of any deep sense of reciprocity. They are greedy for what you can do for them and may use guilt, emotional blackmail, and aggression to gain their ends.

Self-interested people are not unmindful of obligations to others and do not ignore the obligations others have to them. They want favors for themselves to be sure, but are perfectly willing to reciprocate in kind. They create a two-way street, a give-and-take. Such people do not feel guilty asking others for a personal service because they understand the interrelatedness in all human exchanges. Theirs is not a slave mentality. They do not encourage manipulation and abuse. Instead, they rightfully make the recipient of their favors responsible by expecting payment in return.

For too long has this attitude been regarded as self-centeredness. The very healthy and religiously sound benefits to be gained by treating people with reciprocal expectations can no longer be overlooked. Those benefits are: cooperation, respect, and love, conditions that the human doormat seldom enjoys.

Interpersonal harmony depends to a large extent on the degree to which cooperation, respect, and love have been met *reciprocally*. Please observe the order of their presentation; it represents the normal course of development in mature interactions. The more we feel fulfilled by those about us, the deeper our feelings for them grow (Hauck, 1977). A modest amount of mutual fulfillment of each other's deep desires and needs generates the condition of cooperation. A more intense degree of satisfaction promotes respect, and the most complete satisfaction of deep desires and needs generally leads to love.

This view would seem to coincide with religion's historical emphasis on being a loving person in order to bring forth love from others. This attitude has led to the habit of assuming a passive stance vis-à-vis others. And from this there developed the image of the saint who uses self-denial as a cloak of holiness. Passivity, humbleness, charity, and selflessness have become the standards by which the Christian measures humankind.

As noble as it is to be giving, to turn the other cheek, and to put the welfare of others before our own, we can no longer escape the simple fact that when this model is emulated to a degree that brings us below the point of reasonable personal contentment, we have behaved unwisely, unhealthily, and (most interestingly of all), immorally.

To make this last point more clearly understood I will have to take the spiritual-minded reader into the psychological laboratory and reveal some extremely important research findings about the acquisition of behavior patterns.

The work by Skinner (1938) on operant conditioning tells us that behavior which is rewarded is strengthened. A corollary of this principle would suggest another phrasing of this finding: if complex behavior exists, it is being rewarded. With respect to excessive passivity these principles are vital if we are to understand the strange penchant people have for flogging themselves with unseen whips.

Is this the destiny God ordained for His children, to become self-loathing neurotics who relinquish their right to belong to the most amazing species on this earth? Absurd! We were meant to live with dignity and pride in our awesome talents. To espouse a program that robs human giants of their stature is foolish. What is needed is a view of humankind that is uplifting and reassuring. There is no better way to do this than by teaching people how to give and to receive cooperation, respect, and love.

Madsen and Madsen (1970) have expressed several principles of learning in unique language. Their first rule repeats the essence of operant conditioning: if people behave nicely toward us, we had better behave nicely toward them. Do you notice the similarity with the golden rule? Their second rule is startling: if people behave badly to you, behave badly toward them.

The religiously oriented client will surely be discontented with this program because it leaves out the element of patience and forgiveness. For this reason I have used one of the rules rejected by the Madsens and offer it as an intermediate step between the two offered above: if someone does something bad to you, do something good to them anyway, *but only for a reasonable period of time.*

It is on this issue (specificially the matter of limiting one's largesse within a time frame), that disagreement is most likely to arise.

A number of religious groups espouse not only total forgiveness for errant behavior (which is perfectly consistent with rational psychology and with most religions) but they also espouse unending tolerance for unacceptable actions. Remember, being forgiving does not preclude being assertive or stern. These religious groups are consistently forgiving *and* passive. They do nothing of substance to train sinners to be less wrong.

They only advise, lecture, and pray for them. Doing something about people's unacceptable behavior by, for example, arresting them, firing them, grounding them, annoying them, or being decidedly uncooperative strikes these people as unchristian. The motto of these extreme religionists is to "show your love with unconditional tolerance."

The rational psychologist objects to excessive passivity because it is one of the main causes of human misery. Being an endlessly tolerant person is not healthy or satisfying behavior. It is neurosis-producing of the worst sort. Let me show you why.

When behavior is rewarded it is strengthened. Remember? Therefore, when someone does you a bad turn and you tolerate it, your tolerance or silence condones the behavior. The eternally tolerant person becomes the instrument of his or her own abuse. In short, people who are too good are not good to others in the long run.

The time has come that we teach people to be more self-respecting and less tolerant of petty, mean, and inconsiderate behavior. Instead of supporting such actions and believing that good returned for bad will work, let us realize that turning the other cheek generally accomplishes its end only with mature and untroubled individuals (Hauck, 1984). They are not inclined to take heedless advantage of people's generosity. But the immature and the troubled people do frequently. To be generous beyond reason trains them to be leeches, takers, and manipulators. For them, generosity is a wolf in sheep's clothing.

How much more sensible when we discourage nasty behavior by following Madsen and Madsen's next principle, which asks us to return one frustration for another, but to do it *without anger*. This has the effect of not rewarding people for wrongdoing. Instead, it penalizes bad behavior and thereby sets limits to their refusal to treat others with cooperation, respect, or love. It forces them to grow.

Does this sound unchristian? Then consider for a moment how uncompromising Christ, his disciples, and the heroic figures of the Bible were toward injustice. It was not they who were endlessly tolerant. They turned the other cheek, went the extra mile, and loved those who trespassed against them. And when that proved to be of no avail, they acted with firmness—not hatred, just firmness—as Ellis (1957) had advocated when RET was in its infancy.

When dealing with objectionable behavior we have four main options: (1) toleration without resentment, (2) protest, (3) separation or divorce, and (4) toleration with resentment. If we do not want to break up a relationship (Option #3), and we do not want to suffer neurotic disorders (Option #4), then we are left with accepting behavior (Option #1) or resisting behavior (Option #2).

Manipulated people feel great guilt when even in their own self-defense they contemplate making others uncomfortable. Sad to say, much of this reluctance to put oneself first stems from religious teachings that advise us (or do we merely make this interpretation?) to be humble, meek, and self-sacrificing. To a point, those are civilized sentiments. Carried to an extreme, however, they have helped raise generations of passive and fearful persons.

If my recommendation of returning firmness for nefarious conduct seems offensive because it conjures up visions of petty revenge (An eye for an eye . . .), be not concerned. I mean no such thing. Merely making someone uncomfortable in response to immature or disturbed behavior is not vengeance if carried out without malice and if meant truly to reeducate the offender through instruction (Hauck, 1984). Without these two ingredients, we would lower ourselves to the neurotic level of our aggressors. But, if we return penalizing actions, without anger and damnation, and with a genuine desire to educate (a program I heartily recommend), we invalidate the accusation that we are being immoral.

Practical Applications

Just as one picture is worth a thousand words, so one example is worth a page of theorizing. Let me show you, therefore, how we can all be simultaneously forgiving and intolerant.

> A young lady complains bitterly about the thoughtless tardiness of her lover, who makes appointments and is almost invariably late. Remonstrations are ignored. Pointing to the injustice and rudeness of his behavior only has a temporarily ameliorative effect. Her attempt to compromise by having him phone when he knows he will be late also works only briefly. The result is that she feels angered and hurt and slowly loses affection for him.
>
> A review of the four options open to her indicates that she initially tolerated his thoughtlessness but had to forsake this approach when his offense continued (Option #1). Then she felt forced to tolerate it with resentment (Option #4). This produced the symptoms of anger and depression (self-pity). When this was unrelieved, she entertained Option #3 (separation). At this juncture she sought counseling and I urged her to protest (Option #2) and to return his tardiness with penalties of her own choosing and to do so without malice.
>
> She immediately began making appointments that she did not keep, or she arrived impressively late. Naturally there were unpleasant repercussions but he started treating her respectfully in about two months time.

> As his considerateness increased, her love did also. He learned to be more thoughtful because (1) she made the initial change of not tolerating his nonsense, (2) she thought enough of him and the potentials in their relationship to risk losing him, and (3) she was able to see the normal rightness of her plan, which prevented guilt from weakening her resolve.

In similar fashion, rude children may be grounded to the home or to their rooms; profane children may be ignored until their language becomes more acceptable; and mean or selfish heirs may be left out of wills. Husbands who habitually come home late to dinner may have their food served cold. In-laws who find repeated fault with their daughter's husband may not be invited back. Workers who repeatedly take on new assignments while neglecting their other work and who then desperately ask their co-workers to bail them out may one day be refused. Family members who borrow tools and lose them, dirty them, or lend them to others, may be denied access to them again. Adults who abuse their spouses or children may find themselves separated, divorced, or jailed.

Such penalizing behaviors can be interpreted as mean, nasty, or petty. They need not be. Often they are merely corrective, rating not the person but only the performance, and calling for decisive action to alter the person's performance.

Summary

Are religion and RET friends or foes? Aside from the understandable disagreements that are inherent between theology and science, I view these two enterprises as being largely compatible. If that can be interpreted by the reader as also meaning friendly, all the better.

References

Ard, B. N. (1967). Nothing's uglier than sin. *Rational Living*, *2*(1), 4–6.

Beaman, A. (1978). Rational-emotive therapy and Christian contrition. *Rational Living*, *13*(1), 16–18.

Benson, H. (1975). *The relaxation response*. New York: William Morrow.

Berne, E. (1964). *Games people play: The psychology of human relationships*. New York: Grove Press.

Ellis, A. (1952, October). The case against religion: A psychotherapist's view. *Independent*, Issue 126, 4–5.

Ellis, A. (1957). *How to live with a "neurotic."* (Rev. Ed.) 1975. North Hollywood, CA: Wilshire Books.

Ellis, A. (1962). *Reason and emotion in psychotherapy*. Secaucus, NJ: Citadel Press.

Ellis, A. (1972a). Philosophy and rational-emotive therapy. *Counseling & Values, 16*, 158–161.

Ellis, A. (1972b). *Psychotherapy and the value of a human being*. New York: Institute for Rational-Emotive Therapy.

Ellis, A. (1973). *Humanistic psychotherapy: The rational-emotive approach*. New York: Crown & The Julian Press.

Ellis, A. (1981). Science, religiosity and rational-emotive psychology. *Psychotherapy, 18*, 155–158.

Ellis, A. (1983). *The case against religiosity*. New York: Institute for Rational-Emotive Therapy.

Ellis, A. (1984). Rational-emotive therapy (RET) and pastoral counseling: A reply to Richard Wessler. *Personnel and Guidance Journal, 62*, 266–267.

Erickson, M. (1948). Hypnotic psychotherapy. *The medical clinics of North America*, 571–583.

Freud, S. (1938). *Basic writings*. New York: Modern Library.

Grau, A. F. (1977). Religion is rational. In J. L. Wolfe & E. Brand (Eds.), *Twenty years of rational therapy*. New York: Institute for Rational-Emotive Therapy.

Gray, J. (1971). *The psychology of fear and stress*. New York: World University Library.

Grossack, M. (1974). The revolutionary social philosophy of Albert Ellis. *Rational Living, 9*(2), 17–21.

Hailparn, M. (1973). Rational thinking and religion. *Rational Living, 8*(1), 37–38.

Hauck, P. A. (1972). *Reason in pastoral counseling*. Philadelphia: Westminster.

Hauck, P. A. (1977). *Marriage is a loving business*. Philadelphia: Westminster.

Hauck, P. A. (1984). *The three faces of love*. Philadelphia: Westminster.

Hauck, P. A., & Grau, A. F. (1968). Comparisons: Christianity and rationality. *Rational Living, 3*(2), 36–37.

Holland, G. A. (1968). Deliverance from sin: Ellis vs. Mowrer. *Rational Living, 3*(1), 20–23.

Kimble, G. A., & Garmezy, N. (1983). *Principles of general psychology*. (2nd ed.), New York: Ronald.

Lawrence, C., & Huber, C. H. (1982). "Strange bedfellows?" Rational-emotive therapy and pastoral counseling. *Personnel and Guidance Journal, 61*, 210–212.

Lazarus, A. (1981). *Multi-modal therapy*. New York: McGraw-Hill.

Madsen C. K., & Madsen, C. H. (1970). *Teaching/discipline: Behavioral principles toward a positive approach*. Boston: Allyn & Bacon.

Miller, J. S. (1977). Therapies ministers use. *The Christian Century, 94*, 504–507.

Primavera, L., Tantillo, J., & DeLisio, T. (1982). Religious orientation, religions behavior, and dogmatism as correlates of irrational beliefs. *Rational Living, 15*(2), 35–37.

Selye, H. (1956). *The stress of life*. New York: McGraw-Hill.

Skinner, B. (1938). *The behavior of organisms: An experimental analysis*. New York: Appleton-Century-Crofts.

Wessler, R. (1984). A bridge too far: Incompatibilities of rational-emotive therapy and pastoral counseling. *Personnel and Guidance Journal, 62*, 264–266.

11

Student Burnout

A Rational-Emotive Education Treatment Approach

WILLIAM J. KNAUS

INTRODUCTION

Since I developed rational-emotive education (REE) and first presented the system in 1974, it has become clinically and empirically clear that this positive mental-health approach has significant practical value for counselors and teachers who deal daily with a broad spectrum of child and adolescent adjustment problems. Moreover, the system gains potency through its dual application: as a preventive mental health system and as a counseling intervention system.

In this chapter, I will suggest how educators and counselors can apply the rational-emotive education system to a condition I call student burnout—a most common, underrated, potentially serious, and pernicious symptom I have observed in school-age children. For organizational purposes, I have divided this chapter into three sections.

In the first section I begin by describing burnout—what it is, how it appears, who are the youngsters most likely to be affected. Then I compare student and teacher burnout. In the second section I discuss rational-emotive education, provide a description of the dynamics of the system, and discuss how the REE method can be applied to what may be an epidemic student burnout problem in many school districts. Next I tell how the REE psycho-educational system can be used to help chil-

---

WILLIAM J. KNAUS • Psychologist in private practice, Longmeadow, Massachusetts 01106.

dren deal effectively with school stress, reduce the risks of burnout, develop self-confidence, improve frustration tolerance, and develop academic competencies. I discuss why schoolchildren procrastinate and highlight the reciprocal relationship between this dysfunctional habit and burnout. Finally I describe how the REE system helps children overcome procrastination and avoid burnout. In section three I present a case example that describes how I used a rational-emotive educational approach to counsel a ten-year-old boy with a mild learning disability. This child had symptoms of the school stress syndrome and was at risk of burning out.

When Adults Burn Out

Much of the early work on burnout was done with adults. So let us first look at adult burnout.

Burnout is not just a modern day problem. Writers from different eras have described the process in different terms. For example, Elton Mayo (1933) described "work fatigue," which is related to burnout. Clark Hull (1952) described "work inhibition," a condition which may precede burnout. He uses Eysenck's term, *cortical inhibition,* to describe an inhibition of the brain that results from continuous practice. This condition can result from repeating rote tasks.

Traditionally, *burnout* is a term that has been used to describe an occupational stress condition. This condition most frequently occurs in people-intensive work settings: police work (Lester & Mink, 1979; Maslach & Jackson, 1979) house parenting (Behrman, 1978), nursing, (Storlie, 1979), and psychotherapy (Farber, 1978). While burnout normally occurs in people-intensive work settings, it can happen to anyone working in any setting, including children who work in the school setting.

The burned out person routinely feels "fatigued," believes he has no control over his job, and feels insecure, anxious, depressed, and irritable (Mackay & Cox, 1979). This emotionally charged state frequently generalizes to previously satisfying aspects of this person's life. For example, the recreational golfer no longer enjoys playing the game.

Student Burnout

The feelings of fatigue and reluctance to repeat unrewarding work activities that are part of a syndrome of stress, frustration, and burnout are all too familiar to contemporary men and women. But schoolchildren experience these same feelings too. Depending on the school setting,

10% to 25% of students burn out. They suffer from the effects of school stress just as adults suffer from the effects of occupational stress.

We have traditionally viewed burnout as a negative by-product of the work place, a condition that only affects adults. However, schoolchildren work under similar conditions. For example, they have work assignments that the teacher expects them to do on schedule, they follow an administratively established routine, they respond to the wishes of authority, they receive "pay" in the form of grades. Furthermore, many youngsters are exposed to schoolwork conditions they view as repetitive, frustrating, and unrewarding.

Williams (1981), in a discussion of the school curriculum, saw parallels between the school and the factory. She reported that the attitudes and behaviors needed to maintain compulsory attendance and large-group instruction in the schools were parallel to factory work where spontaneity and personal interactions were shaped by the demands of the work process. Indeed, conventional school curricula may powerfully restrict individuality in order that school personnel can conduct and manage large classes—desks lined up in rows, no-talking rules, work alone rules, little allowance for variations in assignments, lockstep system, compliance rules (line up for lunch, line up for assembly). This demand to conform contributes to some children believing they have no control over the school environment, a belief that can cause frustration, apathy, and distress.

Obviously, differences do exist between work for pay and work for grades. Differences also exist in terms of the amount of freedom a schoolchild has compared to an adult worker. For example, the worker can quit his job but a sixth-grader generally cannot quit school. Indeed, few individuals have less freedom of choice than do schoolchildren.

Clearly some degree of order is required for schools to fulfill their educational mission. It is hoped this new order will be a balance that will allow for creative self-expression within an orderly learning environment. When the school atmosphere, however, becomes too institutionalized, then the structure weighs too heavily on the side of regimentation. When the classroom atmosphere is characterized by passive indifference, then the structure is too loose.

School burnout may occur because of the child's inability or unwillingness to adjust to what Woody (1969) describes as socially acceptable norms for behavior. Consequently the child disrupts his or her own academic progress, possibly disrupting the learning efforts of fellow classmates, and most probably the quality of interpersonal relations.

Finally, in this age of the "information revolution," children may be more prone to suffer from *information overload*, where they become saturated with too much information and feel a sense of loss of control. Realistically, there is just so much information children can absorb and integrate at any one time. Repeatedly overtaxing children's information-processing abilities can lead to great frustration and distress, which interferes with effective information processing. Viscerally sensitive and learning-disabled children (especially those with attentional deficits) are the most probable victims of information overload.

Symptoms of School Burnout

Most children adapt to the school environment, exercise adequate control over their behavior, and progress in their academic subjects. However, the child who views the school environment as stressful, perceives no real self-control, and must "endlessly" repeat tasks that hold no real value to him or her, is likely to burn out.

Because of the high emotional and education costs associated with burnout, it is important that we examine the parameters of the burnout process and identify key symptoms for diagnostic and reeducation purposes.

Common symptoms of the school stress syndrome include alienation and a sense of isolation; a consequence of responding to an environment over which one believes one lacks control and is powerless to alter. In some cases, perceptions of lack of control, alienation, and isolation interact with a developing self-concept disturbance and result in behavior disturbances: delinquency, school phobias, conduct disorders, underachievement, and school failure. In some instances, depression enters into this dynamic pattern. Correspondingly, the risk of suicide increases among the burnout group. Indeed, suicide appears on the increase, especially among young adults 15–24 years of age. Suicide is now the third-leading cause of death for that population. Among youngsters 5–14 years of age, suicide is now the eighth-leading cause of death. So we would be wise to be aware that those youngsters who are at risk of burning out are likely to be at higher suicidal risk than their non-burned-out peers.

B. F. Skinner (1965) implied the existence of student burnout when he discussed how adversive educational conditions can negatively affect student performance. He noted that the conditions of learning too often evoke student responses to avoid and escape learning activities. Some of these escape and avoidance activities include vandalism, violence, disruption, refusal to learn, daydreaming, etc. McGuire (1979) has described these same behaviors as *causes* of "teacher burnout," a condition I will describe later in this section.

WHO IS MOST LIKELY TO BURN OUT?

Who are prime student burnout candidates? Prime candidates for burnout include the "disinterested" child, children who display poor study and organization skills, children with attentional deficits, behavior disordered children, and children who suffer from performance anxieties. Disinterested children (and youth) view schoolwork as unattractive, unrewarding, and unpleasant. They expend minimal effort on their studies, perform marginally, and psychologically drop out. Children with poor study and organization skills require more time to learn, and more frequently experience frustration compared to their more efficient peers. Those with attentional deficits have difficulty focusing on what is relevant and are more likely to forget what they learn because they do not normally verbally rehearse what they are taught; they simply get too distracted by internal and external stimuli. Children with behavior problems find reinforcement in antisocial, nonacademic, and rule-breaking pursuits. Children who routinely experience performance anxieties in school-learning and test situations will perform less adequately due to the interfering effects of anxiety on attention, concentration, and memory. In addition, youngsters who perfectionistically struggle, strain, and fret over school achievement also underachieve and burnout because they become distracted by painful emotions and almost invariably view school learning as adversive.

VARIATIONS IN THE SCHOOL STRESS SYNDROME

Children can be classified into four general burnout categories. Each category describes a different form of the school stress syndrome: type one, *aggressive;* type two, *apathetic;* type three, *avoidant;* and type four, *overconscientious.* (Excluded from these categories are seriously disturbed children and children with serious neurological impairments, as they constitute a population outside of the normal school stress syndrome population.)

1. The child with the type one pattern generally has poor impulse control, which is evidenced in: misconduct, truancy, cheating, vandalism, disruptiveness, and so forth.
2. Type two, apathetic children, characteristically withdraw, appear blocked, seem unresponsive, and exude "surface unemotionality" (do not appear to exhibit any emotion although they may hurt inside).
3. Type three, avoidant children, characteristically clown, daydream, or engage in other avoidance actions such as procrastination.

4. Type four, overconscientious youngsters, fret about their school performance. They tend to hold to perfectionistic performance standards and down themselves if their performance does not match their standards. They comply with the system and may achieve academic success but at a high personal cost.

Burnout-prone children, with the exception of some overly conscientious types, will tend to procrastinate on homework assignments or spoil their assignments by rushing them. Also, whereas some youngsters may display ineffective coping styles throughout the school year, many others follow a pattern in which they start September on a positive note. About midyear, they show signs of steadily deteriorating performance and may fail near the end of the school year. Others are classified as underachievers. They seem to underperform routinely, if we use their intellectual potential as a barometer.

Depending on circumstances, a child can fit into one burnout category at one time and a second at another time: such as the overconscientious student who acts out aggressively at home. However, each pattern contains the common elements of weak problem solving skills, poor self-concept, and low frustration tolerance. These same elements are common to adult burnout, including teacher burnout.

Teacher Burnout

Burnout represents a serious occupational hazard for the teaching profession. McGuire (1979) describes burnout as reaching epidemic proportions among teachers. He notes that problems such as school violence, vandalism, disruptive students, involuntary transfers, interfering paper work, and oversized classes correlate with burnout. Symptoms of insecurity, anxiety, and despair dominate the thoughts and feelings of a significant number of teachers employed in such educational environments.

Not all teachers "drop out" and most do not burn out, so some know better than others how to manage their classrooms and themselves. According to Fulcher (1979), a person who learns to exercise control over his or her environment can reduce the effects of prolonged vocational stress. I might add that such control involves effectively managing the inevitable job frustrations and expanding upon opportunities to achieve job satisfaction. I will say more on this topic of managing frustrations to promote satisfaction when I discuss rational-emotive education methods.

Teacher and Student Burnout: A Reciprocal Process?

Do some teachers and students develop adversary relationships that contribute to the burnout condition?

Teachers and students can mutually contribute to conditions conducive to burning each other out. For example, a teacher may act out of control and blame his or her response on student indifference to learning, on parents and administrators failing to appreciate the teacher's efforts, and so forth. Teacher-out-of-control behavior, such as rigidity, helplessness, yelling, blaming, often disrupts the learning environment and heightens the likelihood that students will worry or feel hostile. Such highly charged emotional responses interfere with learning and retaining academic material, thus further frustrating the teacher's educational efforts.

Children whose learning is frustrated due to a subtle learning disability, perfectionistic outlook, fear of failure, interpersonal worries, fatigue, illness, or family problems, may act out by procrastinating, rebelling, becoming apathetic, and so forth. The teacher may take such behaviors personally and eventually teach with an overly generalized attitude that educating resistant students is an act of futility, and that most students are resistant. Some of these teachers will physically drop out and seek other careers, others will put themselves on "automatic pilot" and try to glide until they retire. Still others will compulsively stick to the curriculum and rules, so that their own lack of flexibility proves self-injurious and their students feel coerced by the rigid system they try to instill.

The Dynamics of Student Burnout

Student burnout has at least two major interlocking and interacting psychological dynamics: self-doubt and low frustration tolerance. Both dynamics divert the child from developing effective problem-solving and organizing skills. The following describes these processes.

Self-doubting children will often be their own worst critics, second-guessing what they should do and, as a consequence, they will hesitate and procrastinate. Not uncommonly, this self-doubting will lead to self-downing and to self-blaming or blaming of others for one's own unsatisfactory behavior. Negative and nonproductive self-talk disrupts attention and concentration and contributes to poor school performance. The self-doubting belief system which is prominent in the burnout pattern leads afflicted children to convince themselves that they are powerless to improve on the situation or powerless to achieve up to their expectations or up to the expectations of peers or adults.

The second self-defeating belief system leads to low frustration tolerance. Children (and adults) resist the hard work necessary for improving their problem-solving skills when they predict that the effort required to solve problems will prove too unpleasant or uncomfortable. Their frustration tolerance is lowered further when they believe that inconveniences and having to work hard should not be applicable to them and that what they want they should have immediately. This outlook (and corresponding feelings of frustration-distress) has a disrupting effect on children's ability to organize their thoughts and actions, thus limiting their ability to cope effectively, study, and learn. Thus, many children suffering from low frustration tolerance periodically have a psychological hornet's nest in their heads: a discord of clashing and jarring thoughts blending with hostile feelings and oppositional acts.

On average, coping skills become less accessible for use (or they lag in development) in proportion to children's intolerance to tension. The lower the children's frustration tolerance, the more likely they will burn out because of poor problem-solving and organization skills.

Low-frustration-tolerance-prone children (and adults) frequently interpret the tension sensations as signals to avoid or to remove expediently what they perceive as the source of the stress. Such impulsive responses not only detract from effective problem solving but reinforce avoidance behaviors (Knaus, 1982a, 1983a).

Managing Student Burnout: A Rational-Emotive Education Approach

In this section I will describe three psychoeducational methods. One was based on *The New England Primer* and was a major component of the curriculum during colonial days. The second system was developed by two ministers and based upon their *Little Golden Book of Rules Concepts*. It is a rather sophisticated system that presumably allows children to come to their own conclusions concerning what is right and wrong. However, its stated intent is illusionary. The real intent appears directed toward fostering compliance. These two systems are examples of formalized educational approaches designed and employed to get school children to unflinchingly conform to the rules of the groups that created them. *These methods include all the necessary ingredients to promote conflict, stress, and overcompliance.* They stand in contrast to the third approach, rational-emotive education (REE), a system designed to help children develop frustration management skills, problem-solving skills, perspective-taking skills (seeing more than one side to a situation and envisioning alternative actions that can be taken), self-acceptance and other cognitive states that limit the risk of their burning out.

I will begin by describing the two sectarian systems that were used to manipulate and restrict children's behavior through guilt and coercion. Both systems limit autonomous exploratory behavior and curiosity, conditions important to the development of self-confidence and mastery. In a rather extreme way, they illustrate how to set the stage for burnout and are therefore worth talking about. Next, I will briefly discuss some of the teachings of Dewey, Piaget, and Kohlberg, who taught fresh and valid ideas concerning how children learn and develop values and moral principles. Then I will discuss REE as a primary method of helping children to develop a sense of inner control, confidence, and emotional freedom.

Psychological Education in Colonial Times

Since colonial times, schools in the United States have taught not only reading, writing, and arithmetic, but also the prevailing moral principles. For example, the primary reader of the seventeenth and eighteenth century, *The New England Primer,* included many puritanical ideas that children were required to read and rote memorize, such as:

- "In Adam's fall, we sinned all."
- "He who n'er learn his ABCs forever will a blockhead be."
- "Whoso curseth father and mother, let him die the death." (Ford, 1897)

The Puritans sought to psychologically educate children through drilling "moral" ideas into their heads. The rationale was that if you repeat an idea often enough it will be believed and put to practice. However, as research clearly demonstrates, preaching moral principles does not guarantee "moral" actions, especially when the principles run counter to human nature and desires.

Records indicate that during that puritanical period many students suffered from the school stress syndrome and burned out. They played hookey, played tricks in class, and acted out.

Psychological Education in the Early Twentieth Century

In the early part of the twentieth century, Sneath and Hodges (1913) developed a story-telling approach to psychologically educate children in "proper behavior." In their program, students listened to stories from the *Little Golden Book of Rules* on the virtues of accuracy, the evils of error, the necessity of perfect cleanliness, the necessity of guarding against dangerous air-based microbes, and the evils of sex. The stories were structured, according to Sneath and Hodges, to allow children to come to their own conclusions as to how to behave after considering their meanings and implications. Although some of the ideas had merit (such as preventing disease through cleanliness), the moralistic manner in which the concepts were presented easily evoked highly self-critical and self-damning thoughts, leading to feelings of guilt and needless inhibitions among the students. Under such coercive learning conditions, many of the student participants were at burnout risk as they were subjected to repetitive, unrewarding, and self-defaming moralistic thinking.

Contemporary Thinking on Psychological Education

John Dewey (Bernstein, 1960) kindled a new era of student self-determination. His approach was dramatically different from that of the puritanical principles behind *The New England Primer* and the moralistic principles behind the *Little Golden Book of Rules*. Dewey emphasized using the classroom to provide opportunities for children to choose and develop their own mores, attitudes, and values. His approach was based upon helping children develop an experimental approach to learning. Dewey's methods are often included in the REE system.

The work of Piaget and Inhelder (1970) on stages of learning and development, and Kohlberg's (1975) research on the stages of moral development suggest that young children have cognitive limitations that confine their rate of moral development and level of problem-solving skills to age-expectant parameters. Piaget's and Kohlberg's data marked an important advance in our understanding of child development and imply that psychological education programs had better accommodate to children's developmental levels. Moreover, as MacFarlane, Allen, and Honzik (1962) have noted, normal behavior problems tend to follow a predictable developmental sequence. If we can roughly predict the sequence we can better deal with developmentally linked problems as they emerge.

REE in the Classroom

The REE system uses as its cornerstone rational-emotive therapy concepts as described by Ellis (1962), Ellis and Whiteley (1979), and Ellis and Bernard (1983). Although intended as both an educational and counseling delivery system for children, it can be employed as a method to aid teachers develop self-management skills that can be used to reduce their burnout risk and increase their psychoeducational skills.

Teachers and counselors who use the REE system teach children problem-solving strategies through a flexible series of lessons that I describe in my manual (Knaus, 1974). The lessons include topics such as: What are feelings and where do they come from? Why is it that different people may feel differently about the same event? What is the difference between assumptions, opinions, and facts? Challenging feelings of inferiority; managing frustration; developing perspective; understanding the concept of responsibility; and understanding and dealing with name-calling and school bullies. A variety of experiential games are included, such as the Expression Guessing Game where children learn that one cannot always tell how people feel just by looking at their expressions. Each concept is discussed in the manual in order to give the teacher or counselor background material and a foundation for the lesson. The lessons are designed so that children can apply them to a wide spectrum of problems throughout their lives.

To help burnout-prone children deal effectively with themselves in the school environment, teachers and counselors can employ teaching and modeling strategies designed to help children gain self-control skills, build self-confidence, increase tolerance for frustration, and improve their ability to attend to and concentrate on learning. Real change, however, can best occur when the helper acts as a catalyst for these children to engage in problem-solving *activities* where they can practice their new learning.

Originally presented as a preventive mental health program for "normal" children (Bingham, 1982; Knaus, 1974; 1977a; 1977b; Knaus & Eyman, 1974; Gerald & Eyman, 1980), REE evolved for use in classes for the learning disabled (Knaus & McKeever, 1977), for children with impulse control problems (Knaus, 1977), and for misconduct-prone adolescents (Block, 1978). In addition, it has undergone encouraging preliminary research evaluations by: Albert, (1972); Brody, (1974); Casper, (1981); DiGiuseppe, (1975); DiGiuseppe & Kassinove, (1976); Katz, (1974); Knaus & Bokor, (1975); Krenitsky, (1978); Leopold, (1984); and Miller, (1977). The REE system has five basic assumptions:

1. Children who learn and use REE problem-solving strategies will more effectively alleviate their emotional and behavior problems compared with youngsters from the same population who have not learned these principles.
2. Children cannot apply what they do not know, so they first need to know the basic principles prior to applying them.

3. Most normal and troubled children can best profit from learning how to cope with a wide range of different problems.
4. Multiple interventions typically prove more effective than single interventions in disrupting a dysfunctional psychological burnout process.
5. The REE system approximates an organic process that undergoes modification and change based upon experience and experiment.

Rational-emotive education strategies, applied to the two burnout dynamics of self-doubt and low frustration tolerance, can prevent or disrupt the burnout process. For example, the REE self-concept pinwheel strategy (Knaus, 1974), enables the child to look at his more constructive competencies and attributes. This helps reduce self-doubts. REE lessons on how to accept human imperfection can also help initiate positive changes in the child's self-view. A child taught how to recognize and deal with faulty predictions about discomfort will act with higher frustration tolerance. Furthermore, the child who realistically understands the meaning and inevitability of frustration will less likely fall victim to low frustration tolerance thinking and feelings. In all cases, the child can improve both self-concept and frustration tolerance if given the opportunity to replace burnout patterns with productive problem-solving behavior patterns.

Rational-emotive educational strategies are directed toward cognitive restructuring and behavior change. Through formally and informally using the well-known rational-emotive ABC change/growth model, the REE practitioner provides opportunities for youngsters to master a highly effective problem solving model, one that often is positively reinforced because of the validity of the learnings that result from its applications.

Clearly, the REE system aims to provide children with alternative ways of obtaining inner self-control. Once they have learned rational concepts and practiced actions that can cause constructive things to happen, they tend to experience a reduction in tension, greater self-confidence, increased willingness to face up to problems, and improved ability to attend, concentrate, and learn. These competencies replace the negative dynamics inherent in the school stress and burnout syndrome.

The School Stress Syndrome and Procrastination

A prime symptom of the school stress syndrome is procrastination. Although this symptom may differ among burnout types—the overly conscientious children may promptly hand in assignments but put off developing social relationships—it almost always is a correlate. This self-defeating habit can have a dramatically disruptive effect on the development of children's academic competencies, self-confidence, frustration tolerance, and problem-solving skills. A procrastination pattern is a key element in the school stress syndrome, as this habit of needlessly postponing or delaying timely and relevant high priority actions ultimately results in distress and limits opportunities (Knaus, 1979, 1982b).

Procrastination, as an act of avoidance, often results in temporary relief but long-term stress. This long-term stress exacerbates the burnout condition, rendering its disruption and change difficult—especially when children and adults who chronically procrastinate suffer from depression, anxiety, and other disturbances.

Common reasons for childhood procrastination include inadequate problem-solving skills, weak organization skills, self-doubts (leading to a self-concept disturbance), and weak frustration management skills. Rational-emotive education provides strategies to counter procrastination by helping children build effective problem-solving skills, develop a realistic and healthy self-concept, and effectively manage the inevitable tensions and frustrations that are part of daily living. This process, however, requires taking at least the following five steps: consciousness raising, self-awareness training, problem-solving training, self-confidence development, and frustration tolerance training, which I describe in detail in another publication (Knaus, 1983a).

1. *Consciousness Raising*. This includes helping children understand what procrastination is, why people procrastinate, and what can be done to change. The consciousness raising phase is a generic approach to the problem. The following steps are used to provide specific and personal approaches to help children overcome procrastination and alleviate burnout.

2. *Self-Awareness Training*. This helps children recognize when they procrastinate and why. It includes helping children see the relationship between procrastination and stress, and between how they interpret their perceptions and how such interpretations can, if erroneous, lead to mistaken actions (procrastination) and distressed feelings.

3. *Problem-Solving Training*. This training includes helping children to develop problem-solving skills and to apply experimentally to their task behavior the skills they are learning. The ABC theory is an integral part of this phase as children learn to monitor their thoughts and discriminate between those beliefs and perceptions that are sensible and those that produce poor results.

4. *Self-Confidence Development*. This training includes helping children recognize and develop their positive and constructive attributes. Often this is accomplished through feedback and through experimentation.

5. *Frustration Tolerance Training.* This training includes helping children use frustration as a signal to employ problem-solving skills and thereby resolve the frustrating problem or condition. It involves helping children experientially see the benefits of delaying gratification as well as learn how impulsive actions lead to poor results.

Of course, some time-management principles can improve organizing skills, such as goal setting, establishing priorities, breaking the task into subtasks. However, in cases where the child's academic and personal problems are due to serious self-doubts and low frustration tolerance, the youngster may not profit from such procedures. Indeed, the procedures may result in some children feeling guilty because they procrastinate putting the principles to practice. Consequently, it is important to monitor carefully the manner and spirit in which a child employs time-management principles. Better yet, one should work to help the child develop frustration management skills and self-acceptance. I have found that time-management skills are more easily taught and applied when we simultaneously help children to challenge irrational ideas behind frustration and self-concept disturbances, develop frustration-management skills, and acquire a firm sense of self-acceptance.

Children can also be aided to reduce procrastination behaviors by counselors and educators who:

1. Actively model problem solving behaviors.
2. Diagnose and build upon student strengths.
3. Systematically use positive reinforcement to counter procrastination behaviors.
4. Listen carefully for misconceptions that students periodically develop and take time to show the students how to "perception check."
5. Use humor appropriately to help reduce stress and tension the procrastinating student may be sitting upon.

In helping children overcome procrastination, I have found that youngsters respond to characters that represent the procrastination process; they try hard not to be fooled by these characters. The Wheedler and the Time Thief are two such characters that I have used successfully in working with groups of burned-out and procrastinating youngsters to help them have fun learning.

The Wheedler is a furry creature with a big smile and down-turned eyes; thus he looks both inviting and sinister. The Wheedler plays tricks on children. He tries to convince the child that it is better to avoid what is uncomfortable than to master uncomfortable problems. For example, our mythological creature, the Wheedler, may tell the child: "Go out and play now, you can do your homework after supper." Then after supper, the Wheedler might say: "You don't want to miss your favorite TV show. Pretend you got your homework done and then your mother [or father] will let you watch the show."

After the children learn about the Wheedler and his many tricks, I introduce the Time Thief and show how this character rips off time and what happens when he succeeds. After the Time Thief has been exposed, then the children learn how the "Wheedler sets you up and the Time Thief rips you off." Next, the children decide how to *beat the Wheedler*. This *beat the Wheedler* phase involves providing opportunities for the youngsters to learn and invent problem-solving strategies, then to test them and find out if they work. Such strategies often include helping children to learn about personal strengths and how they can apply their talents to master the inevitable frustrations that occur in any new learning situation, use those strengths to stop procrastinating, and thus limit their chances of burning out.

While the conceptual framework for counseling children who procrastinate and who are at risk of burning out is not complicated, implementation normally takes time and lots of work. And while procrastination and burnout are often change resistive processes, children can learn to alleviate these conditions.

In this therapeutic process of change and growth, it is important to adopt a realistic "can do" tolerant attitude in dealing with youngsters. Equally important, we try to have fun as we work with them. Most youngsters are quick to pick up on "Dr. Gloom" therapist attitudes and easily become discouraged. After all, if a therapist acts as though it was hopeless to change procrastination or burnout patterns, yet perfunctorily goes through the paces of trying without conviction, why should not children fulfill the pessimistic prophecy?

In this educational and therapeutic process of change, we had better keep focused on the child's developmental level. Developmental Psychologist, Lawrence Kohlberg's six stages of moral development can provide valuable guideposts for decisions on the form and level of positive mental health program lessons and interventions.

Most children have to mature considerably before they can use abstract principles such as the reasons for justice being selectively administered. We can set the stage for such learning that may occur at a later date. However, some youngsters have limited ability to think and act at higher levels of moral development and to pursue opportunities for self-actualization and growth. Perhaps it is only at the final stage of moral development that the person begins to autonomously seek opportunities to self-actualize and willingly face frustrations. Nevertheless, educators and counselors can make significant psychoeducational contributions that can enable children to reduce procrastinating temptations and function effectively. The aforementioned materials set the broad parameters. The following case provides a practical example for translating the REE principles into action.

REE with a Ten-Year-Old Learning-Disabled Boy

I applied Rational Emotive Education methods with Peter, a bright, procrastinating ten-year-old boy with a mild attentional deficit. The process I followed included: diagnosis of major problem areas, rapport building, expressive vocabulary development, application of rational-emotive lessons, and cognitive-restructuring through experiential learning. Collectively, these steps comprise a self-concept development and frustration tolerance training program.

Peter's learning problem went undetected until behavioral symptoms of procrastination and poor academic performance were well established. By that time he pretended to go through the daily school routine like other youngsters in his class. In actuality, he mainly attended to internal stimuli, such as daydreams. He seemed well on the road to burnout.

His school learning problems were recognized when he entered fourth grade and his teacher saw that his excuses for postponing homework assignments and his high absenteeism rate were symptomatic. Up until that point, he was classified as a nice kid who was a little slow in getting his work done.

In conference with his parents and teacher, I learned that Peter was rarely ill during holiday and vacation periods. In contrast, during his third grade year, he was absent fourteen times. Most of the absences were due to "headaches" and "stomachaches," which seemed to occur mainly on days tests were scheduled.

Setting the Stage for Change

When Peter first entered therapy, he did not articulate what was wrong except to say he wasn't "doing good in school".

The first step in the therapeutic process was to diagnose Peter's problem and establish a therapeutic relationship. This was accomplished by using diagnostic tests as games to gather data about his learning problems and help him feel at ease. Properly used, diagnostic tests provide opportunities for children to receive positive reinforcement for their efforts, as well as provide the examiner with data concerning their problems. In Peter's case, the evaluation provided data that was valuable in the diagnosis of his attentional deficit.

The second step was to help Peter build an expressive vocabulary so that he could more accurately talk about his feelings, thoughts, and the events that occurred in his life. I accomplished this second phase by employing a series of rational-emotive education lessons targeted toward aiding Peter identify and discriminate between various human emotions (Knaus, 1974). I then showed him how to use this knowledge to express his feelings and desires. This was followed by experiential lessons designed to teach him about where feelings come from and lessons designed to teach him about his positive qualities and capabilities. With these foundation skills, he was able and willing to express how and why he felt as he did.

Once Peter became comfortable with me and learned to clearly articulate his thoughts about himself, he admitted that he thought he was a real dummy. He thought no one at school liked him and that his parents wished they had a different kid.

Peter felt inferior to other youngsters whom he saw as better able to handle daily academic routines. He felt frustrated because he did not absorb material as well as most of his peers. In addition, his older sister was a quick learner and earned honors for her achievements. Peter continuously matched his performance against her's and felt inferior by comparison. He did not want to feel as he did, but he had not thought there was much that could be done to change his feelings because, as he put it, "if you're stupid, you can't do anything right."

The Turnaround

The diagnostic test series and basic REE lessons helped Peter see that he was far more capable than he thought and that he could exercise considerable control over what and how he learned. Once these concepts were established, I followed-up with an experiment that allowed him to recognize his attentional problem, understand the effects of the problem, and know what he could do to improve. In REE counseling, I often improvise techniques so that the child can experience the meaning of an important concept, such as "we are more effective thinkers when we don't distract ourselves."

I believe that a cognitive restructuring approach, such as rational-emotive education, has greater potency when the concepts are tied to direct experiences. So I staged a series of experiments that showed Peter that he had a problem attending to verbal stimuli and that if he did not attend, he could not expect to retain much from his lessons. As part of the experiment, I told him I would recite a series of numbers and I wanted him to say them after me. Under these demanding test conditions he recalled only up to four numbers because he distracted himself by thinking about how hard it was to remember the numbers. Then I asked him to choose how many numbers he wanted me to recite. He began with two numbers. But under the relaxed "choice" experiment, he worked up to, and recalled, seven numbers. From this experiment, he learned that when he chose to concentrate and was relaxed, he performed better. As a by-product of this lesson, he saw that concentration requires relaxed effort.

The number experiment offered Peter hope that he could change and improve his school performance. So we worked out a method that he could use in school and that would help him attend for increasingly long time periods. The steps consisted primarily of basic strategies, such as note taking, self-instruction, verbal rehearsal, and reflection methods.

Through his REE experiences, Peter started to see himself in a different light, as he proved to himself that he could improve his school performance. The number experiment allowed him to experience a very important concept: he thought more clearly and worked better when he found ways to concentrate on what he was doing and not on worrying about how much he was learning. The most important result of this program, however, was that the REE lessons helped Peter see that something such as a "listening" problem does not make you a stupid person. Only *you* can make you feel that way! His great discovery was that he made himself feel stupid and that he had the ability to change that outlook.

Problems do not disappear overnight and Peter's case was no exception. He had to learn how to work at reducing schooltime daydreams and at recognizing and combating his negative self-view. As Peter put it: "When I'm thinking bad about myself I don't listen too well; when I don't listen, I don't learn. Then I think I'm stupid all over again."

Over the past three years, Peter has made slow but steady progress. With steadily improving school performance, he was absent only five times in the fourth grade and twice in the fifth. His "headaches" and "stomachaches" completely disappeared. He now no longer refers to himself as stupid. His self-regard, frustration tolerance, social skills, standardized test results, and academic achievement continue to show significant improvement.

Acknowledgments

Thanks go to Nancy Haberstroh, Frank Eldridge, Paula Eldridge, and Sarah Verasco for their helpful thoughts and comments.

References

Albert, S., (1972). *A study to determine the effectiveness of affective education with fifth grade students,* Unpublished master's thesis, Queens College.

Behrman, J. K., (1978). *The ecology of group home parenting: Role stresses and personal adjustments.* Unpublished doctoral dissertation, University of Nebraska.

Bernstein, R. J., (1960). *Dewey on experience, nature, and freedom.* New York: Liberal Arts Press.

Bingham, T. (1982). *Program for effective learning*. Blanding, VT: Metra.
Block, J. (1978). Effects of a rational emotive mental health program on poorly achieving, disruptive, high school students. *Journal of Counseling Psychology, 25*(1), 61–65.
Brody, M., (1974). *The effect of rational-emotive affective approach in anxiety, frustration tolerance, and self-esteem with fifth grade students*. Unpublished doctoral dissertation, Temple University.
Casper, E., (1981). *A study to determine the effectiveness of rational-emotive education upon the academic achievement of sixth-grade children*. Unpublished doctoral dissertation. University of Virginia.
DiGiuseppi, R., (1975). The use of behavior modification to establish rational self-statements in children. *Rational Living, 10*(2), 18–20.
DiGiuseppi, R., & Kassinove, H., (1976). Effects of rational emotive school mental health program on children's emotional adjustment. *Journal of Community Psychology, 4*(4), 382–387.
Ellis, A. (1962). *Reason and emotion in psychotherapy*. Secaucus, NJ; Lyle Stuart.
Ellis, A. & Bernard, M. E. (Eds.). (1983). *Rational-emotive approaches to the problems of childhood*, New York: Plenum Press.
Ellis, A. & Whiteley (Eds.). (1979). *Theoretical and empirical foundations of rational-emotive psychotherapy*, Monterey CA: Brooks/Cole.
Farber, B. A., (1978). *The effects of psychotherapeutic practice upon the psychotherapist: A phenomenological investigation*. Unpublished doctoral dissertation, Yale University.
Ford, R. (Ed.). (1897). *The New England primer*, New York: Dodd, Mead.
Fulcher, L. C., (1979). Keeping staff sane to accomplish treatment. *Residential and community child care administration, 1*,(1), 69–85.
Gerald, M., & Eyman, W. (1980). *Thinking straight and talking sense: An emotional education program*. New York: Institute for Rational Emotive Therapy.
Hull, C., (1952). *A behavior system: An introduction to behavior theory concerning the individual organism*. New Haven: Yale University Press.
Katz, S., (1974). *The effects of emotional education on locus of control and self-concept*. Doctoral dissertation, Hofstra University.
Knaus, W. J. (1970, January). Innovative use of parents and teachers as behavior modifiers. Paper presented at the Seventh annual school psychologists conference, Queens College, New York.
Knaus, W. J., (1974). *Rational emotive education: A manual for elementary school teachers*. New York: Institute for Rational-Emotive Psychotherapy.
Knaus, W. J., (1977a). Rational emotive education. In A. Ellis, & R. Greiger (Eds.), *Handbook of rational emotive therapy* (pp. 398–408). New York: Springer.
Knaus, W. J., (1977b). Rational emotive education. *Theory into Practice, 14*(4), 251–255.
Knaus, W. J., (1979). *Do it now: How to stop procrastinating*. Englewood Cliffs, NJ: Prentice-Hall.
Knaus, W. J. (1982a). *How to get out of a rut*. Englewood Cliffs, NJ: Prentice-Hall.
Knaus, W. J. (1982b). The parameters of procrastination. In Greiger R. & Greiger, I. (Eds.). *Cognition and emotional disturbance*. New York: Human Science Press.
Knaus, W. J. (1983a). *How to conquer your frustrations*. Englewood Cliffs, NJ: Prentice-Hall.
Knaus, W. J. (1983b). Children and low frustration tolerance. In A. Ellis, & M. E. Bernard, (Eds.), *Rational-emotive approaches to the problems of childhood*, New York: Plenum Press.
Knaus, W. J., & Bokor, S. (1975). The effects of rational emotive education lessons on anxiety and self-concept in sixth-grade students, *Rational Living, 11*(2), 25–28.
Knaus, W. J., & Eyman, W. (1974). Progress in rational emotive education. *Rational Living*, 2, 27–29.

Knaus, W. J., & McKeever, C. Rational emotive education with learning disabled children. *Journal of learning disabilities, 10*(1), 10–14.

Kohlberg, L. (1975). The cognitive developmental approach to moral development. *Phi Delta Kappa, 56*(10), 671.

Krenitsky, D. L. (1978). The relationship of age and verbal intelligence to the efficacy of rational-emotive education with older adults, Doctoral dissertation, Hofstra University.

Leopold, H. (1984). *Cognitive training with seriously disturbed children: Effects of cognitive level, cognitive strategy, and additional time in training.* Unpublished doctoral dissertation, Hofstra University.

Lester, D., & Mink, S. B. (1979). Is stress higher in police officers? An exploratory study. *Psychological Reports, 45*(2), 554.

MacFarlane, J. W., Allen, L., & Honzik, M. P. (1962). *A developmental study of the behavior problems of normal children between 21 months and 14 years.* Berkely, CA: University of California Press.

Mackay, C. J., & Cox, T. (1979). *Response to stress: Occupational aspects.* England: Guilford Press.

Maslach, C., & Jackson, E. (1979). Burned out cops and their families. *Psychology Today, 12*(12), 58–62.

Mayo, E. (1933). *Human problems of industrial civilization.* New York: Macmillan.

McGuire, W. H. (1979). Teacher Burnout. *Today's Education, 68*(4), 5.

Miller, N. J. (1977). Effects of behavior rehearsal, written homework assignments, and level of intelligence on the efficacy of rational-emotive education in elementary school children. Doctoral dissertation, Hofstra University.

Piaget, J., & Inhelder, B. (1970). *The psychology of the child.* New York: Basic Books.

Skinner, B. F., (1965, October). Why teachers fail. *Saturday Review,* pp. 80–82, 90–103.

Sneath, H. E., & Hodges, G. (1913). *Moral training in the school and home: A manual for teachers and parents.* New York: Macmillan.

Storlie, F. J. (1979). Burnout: An elaboration of a concept. *American Journal of Nursing, 79*(12), 2018–2111.

Williams, J. M. (1981). *An exploratory look at alienation in elementary school children.* New York: Springer.

Woody, R. (1969). *Behavior problem children in the schools.* New York: Appleton-Century-Crofts.

12

A Rational-Emotive Mental Training Program for Professional Athletes

MICHAEL E. BERNARD

There are several important factors that determine the extent to which a professional or an amateur elite athlete achieves sporting excellence. Most important among these are physical skills (coordination, agility, speed), the degree of physical fitness (strength, endurance), and technical skills related to the sport in which the athlete participates (kicking, catching, foul-shooting). In team sports, an athlete's performance also depends largely on team cooperation skills (blocking, being given the ball when a good opportunity arises, unselfish play). One factor that is now becoming increasingly recognized as critical to individual and team performance is the athlete's mental approach (attitudes, skills). Coaches and athletes alike in all sports are learning that talented athletes and winning teams who finish first have a mental approach that is different from athletes who never quite make it, teams that finish second.

It is interesting to note that whereas the "mental side" of sporting performance has been a major focus of training programs in certain parts of the world (e.g., Eastern Europe, Scandinavia), it has only recently begun to be taken seriously by coaches of Olympic and professional teams in North America and Australia. That is to say that whereas, for example, in Sweden over 5,000 athletes have participated in mental training programs (Unestahl, 1982), a sampling of coaches of professional teams in the United States conducted by this author revealed only a limited amount of interest and concern for the mental training side of

MICHAEL E. BERNARD • Department of Education, University of Melbourne, Parkville, Victoria, 3052 Australia.

the game. Indeed, there still prevail broad-scale irrationalities and myths held by professional coaches and sportsmen (as well as sporting administrators, who control the purse strings necessary to purchase the services of sport psychologists). These include: (1) "Good athletes should be mentally tough enough to make it to the top without outside help, and if they have to rely on someone else psyching them up, they will never succeed." (2) "Since some successful athletes and teams of the past and present have not emphasized mental preparation in their training programs, a mental training program cannot and, therefore, should not be included in today's preparation of elite athletes." (3) "Because I succeeded as an athlete without mental training assistance, it is an unnecessary frill." (4) "Sport psyching is up to the coach, and, anyway, all that mental 'mumbo jumbo' is a lot of bull that doesn't really work anyway."

The 1980s have shown a growing interest in the mental side of the game in countries and in sports which hitherto remained ignorant of its potential role, importance, and effectiveness. One of the main catalysts for this increasing awareness has been the personal testimonies of successful, top athletes who have attested to the importance of their mental attitude and preparation towards competition. Additionally, there have appeared commercially available mental training materials (books, cassette tapes, videotapes) that have helped to educate coaches, sports administrators, athletes, and the sporting public to the potentialities of mental training programs.

This chapter presents a mental training program that has been employed with a professional football team in Australia. The program incorporates basic principles and practices of rational-emotive therapy (RET) (Ellis, 1962, 1973, 1979; Ellis & Abrahms, 1978; Ellis & Becker, 1982; Ellis & Grieger, 1977; Ellis & Harper, 1975) that themselves prove to be eminently suitable as basic building blocks for a mental training program for athletes. In designing this program, it became obvious to this author that currently available mental training programs incorporate basic RET ideas, sometimes crediting the work of Albert Ellis and sometimes not. Additionally, basic mental training skills that have not been directly derived from Ellis's writing (e.g., relaxation, goal setting) are readily subsumable within the parameters of RET and are used in this program.

What follows, then, is the actual rational-emotive mental training program that was used with 40 top performing professional footballers during their 1984 preseason training program. Readers familiar with RET will readily see the tie between the program's content and Ellis's theory. At a general level, the program is both psychoeducational and psychotherapeutic. It provides the athlete with cognitive (e.g., positive attitudes, disputation of negative-irrational beliefs, positive thinking), emotive (e.g., relaxation, rational-emotive imagery), and behavioral (e.g., goal setting) skills that if employed appropriately will help the athlete overcome the stresses of football as well as become more positive, goal oriented, and happier.

In preparing this program, the following books provided not only concrete illustrations of the principles of rational-emotive mental training, but also helped in the writing of specific material which was presented in the program: Keith F. Bell's *Championship Thinking* (1983), Timothy Gallwey and Bob Kriegal's *Inner Skiing* (1977), David R. Kauss's *Peak Performance* (1980), Denise McCluggage's *The Centered Skier* (1977), Robert M. Nideffer's *The Inner Athlete: Mind Plus Muscle for Winning* (1976), Brent S. Rushall's *Psyching in Sport* (1979), Thomas Tutko and Umberto Tosi's *Sport Psyching* (1976), and Lars-Eric Unestahl's *Better Sport by IMT-Inner Mental Training* (1982).

Rational-emotive ideas and skills reported in recently published literature that applies the principles of rational-emotive therapy and cognitive-behavior therapy (CBT) to the field of sports have also been incorporated within this program (Bell, 1980; Desiderato & Miller, 1979; Ellis, 1982; Gologor, 1979; Gravel, Lemieux, & Ladouceur, 1980; Klinger, Barta, & Glas, 1981; Meyers, Schleser, Cooke, & Cuviller, 1979; Orlick, 1980, 1982; Shelton & Mahoney, 1978; Simek & O'Brien, 1981; Weinberg, Gould, & Jackson, 1980; Wessler, 1980). Although other forms of psychotherapy have made a few significant contributions in the sports area, RET and CBT seem to be making real research and clinical advances in this area; and the rational-emotive mental training program outlined in this chapter is an outcome of these efforts.

The Rational-Emotive Mental Training Program

A five-week program was developed by the author specifically for Australian Rules Football. The general objectives of the program were to help individual players improve their mental approach to the game in these five areas.

1. Confidence
2. Consistency
3. Commitment
4. Calmness under pressure
5. Concentration

The focus of the program's context was twofold. First, the sessions included specific mental skills and attitudes that were presented by the team's psychologist (present author). Second, players identified stressful situations that have the potential for unsettling themselves and the team, and they provided suggestions (along with team's psychologist) for handling stressful situations that occur both before and during a game.

Expectations of what players would get from the program were realistic. The following explanation was presented to players during the introductory session:

> What can you expect to get from the program? Because you are a team of individuals, your mental strengths and weaknesses in the mental area differ quite a bit. I expect each of you will get something different from the program—ideas, skills. Also, because of the size of the group, it may be difficult to individualize how the material to be discussed applies to you. This mental training program will sensitize you to various aspects of mental preparation and different mental skills so that after the session and during the session we can work on those specific areas you would like to see improved.

The 40 players who were seen as definite starters for the season were selected to participate. To ensure maximum participation, the coach agreed to make attendance mandatory and fines were administered to players who failed to attend the initial session. The 40 players were assigned to one of four groups and each group was composed of players of equal experience. Groups met once a week for one hour. Dinner in the form of a cold buffet was served before each session and helped to maintain motivation.

The organization and content of sessions is presented in Table 1. It will be seen that one skill was introduced each week over the five weeks. During each session, provision was made for specific player contributions as well as for group practice of the specific skill being introduced. Players were assigned homework each week in the form of practice of a specific skill. In addition, the author designed four 30-minute cassette tapes on the following topics: relaxation, mental practice, eliminating negative thinking, and positive mental attitudes. These tapes were distributed to all players during the mental training program.

What follows is a presentation of the major activities and important material contained in each mental training session. A description of the ABCs of the mind-body relationship (as taught in RET) will be followed by a discussion of stress and how it affects playing performance. These background concepts and principles were presented to players during the lecture part of the first two sessions of the program. Verbatim tran-

TABLE 1. Outline of Mental Training Program

Lecture topic	Skill	Homework review	Player contribution	Group practice	Homework for players
Untapping the power of your mind and body	Relaxation	Introduction of program, expectations, and responsibilities	General discussion of stressors outside of football which drain mental and physical reserves on Saturday; which stressors most intense	Group relaxation experience	At least 4 relaxation sessions using tape
Programming your mind to take control of your body	Mental practice	Brief review of stress and relaxation; discussion of stress; questions; discussion of solutions	Individual players who use it with success describe when; what they practice. Players write down outside stresses.	Mental practice with individual players	At least 4 sessions of mental practice
Overcoming your fears and worries through winning attitudes and positive thinking	Winning attitudes; positive thinking	Discussion of any player problems in learning to use mental practice; role playing of good illustrations	Players fill out stress inventory; group discussion of how players handle *trouble spots*—before, during, after game	Role play of handling outside stresses	At least 4 sessions of mental practice: listen to positive-negative thinking tape
Setting goals; your road to success	Goal setting	Review of winning attitudes and positive thinking; discussion of "trouble spot" data	Goal-setting form; discussion of players' short-term and long-term individual team goals	Role play of handling stresses before and during a game; rational-emotive imagery	List of personal individual and team goals; 4 sessions of mental practice
Improving your concentration	Concentration	Review of goal-setting data	Players discuss how they maintain concentration when tired, worried; identify "dead" spots.	Concentration activities; handling stresses	Putting it all together

scripts of the cassette tape mental training program and brief summaries of ideas related to goal-setting and concentration will also be presented. A summary of this author's impressions of program effectiveness as well as problems in program implementation will round out the chapter.

The ABCs of RET Applied to the Mind and Body

Players were given the following example of how, according to RET, their mind influences their body and, hence, their playing performance. A play was diagrammed on the blackboard of a situation in Australian football where a player in the center of the field receives the ball from another player in the defense, runs three steps, and kicks the ball short to another of his players (half-forward flank) further downfield. In one of two possible scenarios, Wingman 1 who plays near the center, sees the play developing. Wingman 1 pauses as the center kicks the ball to his teammate (the half-forward flank) and waits to see what happens. As the half-forward flank catches the ball, Wingman 1 starts running (cautiously) at three-quarter pace toward the half-forward flank (hoping to help out but not wanting to do the wrong thing and make a mistake). He never really gets into the play and the half-forward flank, not having anyone to throw the ball or kick to, gets tackled by an opposing player and loses possession of the ball. In the other scenario, Wingman 2 sees the play developing and as the center kicks to the half-forward flank, Wingman 2 starts to run forward, hoping to be in position should he be needed. As the half-forward flank catches the ball, Wingman 2 runs past, yells for the ball to be passed to him, yells again, receives the ball and kicks a goal. (In other words, for readers unfamiliar with Australian Rules Football, Wingman 1 was playing halfheartedly, not confidently, afraid; whereas Wingman 2 confidently performed what was expected of him).

Players were asked to consider the question as to why Wingman 2 ran past and Wingman 1 did not, given that both wingmen were of the same build, age, speed, strength, experience, and kicking ability. After some general discussion, the following explanations were given. Wingman 1 had different mental attitudes from Wingman 2. Wingman 1 held the attitudes of "I don't really believe in myself, I don't really know if I'm a good kick or mark. I may not succeed. I must never make a mistake because that would show others I'm not only a poor footballer, but a hopeless person." Wingman 1 had a self-defeating initial interpretation of the play. He thought "I might fall, make a mistake, miss catching the ball or kicking for goal." Subconsciously he thought "I couldn't stand making a mistake and be criticized by my teammates, coach, or fans.

I'd really be a hopeless no-good failure if that should happen." To make matters worse, in his mind was the image of him missing the kick. He felt anxious, worried, and fearful, his body tense and mind distracted inwardly by the thoughts and images of failure.

Wingman 2 had different thoughts running through his mind. He interpreted the situation positively as an opportunity to make a good play, to succeed. In the back of his mind he saw himself receiving the ball (not dropping it), and kicking a goal. His deep down attitudes were "I will succeed; I believe in myself; I'm a good kick; if I miss, at least I tried; if I keep trying I'll be a winner in the end." The body of Wingman 2 felt loose, strong, fluid, and quick; his mind focused on the play; his emotions were of anticipation, exhilaration, and confidence.

Further discussion with the players identified the following aspects of mind and body which were relevant to their playing performance.

Mind	*Body*
attitudes	muscle tension
images	muscle strength
self-talk	air supply
emotions	heart rate
concentration	blood supply

Stress in Football

During sessions, a great deal of time was spent discussing how a player's state of mind both during the week and before a game will influence how his body feels and performs during a game. The "inverted U hypothesis" was presented to demonstrate how too much or too little stress and arousal can negatively influence performance.

It was explained that too much emotional stress (anger, anxiety, depression) can set off the body's general adaptation syndrome, leading to the excessive production of hormones and biochemicals as the body readies itself for fight or flight (The Diagram Group, 1982). Some of the concomitants of too much emotional stress and related bodily changes include excessive muscle tension, which causes uncoordination and muscle fatigue, shortness of breath ("choking"), rapid heart beat, pupil dilation, and injury proneness. The effects of stress on the body of a player can also upset a player's head by focusing attention away from play onto the body. Additionally, increased autonomic symptom detection by the brain serves as a message from the body that something is wrong: emotions become edgy and irritability is increased. Thus players were encouraged to think about stress factors in their own lives as a prerequisite to learning stress control skills presented in the program.

During the first two weeks of the mental training program, players answered open-ended, and then multiple-choice questions concerning stressful events ("trouble spots") that they found could negatively affect how they felt and played in a game. The results of these inquiries led to the development of Tables 2 to 5, which indicate the percentage of players who found the event to be stressful when it occurred.

Players were encouraged to use the mental skills presented in the program to overcome specific trouble spots before and during a game. It was pointed out that sometimes a player who is tired on the day of

TABLE 2. Stress during Week Which Affects Football Performance[a]

Rank	Stressful event	Percentage of players who find event stressful
1	Thinking about how I played last week	57
2	Thinking about how I'll do next week	48
3	Having my game criticized by others (fans, press, friends, coach)	43
4	People around me talking too much about football	40
5	What I eat and drink	40
6	Too much mentally demanding work	34
7	Not enough time in my life	34
8	Waiting to hear where I'll play (team, position)	31
9	Not happy with my work	28
10	Hassles with girlfriend or wife	28
11	Active social life	23
12	Training schedule (hard work, effort)	23
13	Thinking about how some players get treated better or fairer than myself (more privileges, salary, position)	23
14	Hassles at work with other employees or boss	20
15	Having a disagreement or being ignored by the coach	20
16	Money worries	20
17	Worries about other members of my family	17
18	Too much physically demanding work	11
19	Not getting on with teammates (being teased, excluded)	8
20	Just knowing there is another game to play on Saturaday	3

[a] Listing of stressful events that players find negatively influence their mental and physical energy either right before or during a game

TABLE 3. Stresses of Football on the Day of the Game[a]

Rank	Stressful event	Percentage of players who find event stressful
1	Thinking about good opponent I'm playing against	61
2	Thinking about my bad form	54
3	Thinking about letting the team down	48
4	Being too tense and lacking confidence	45
5	Warned about being dropped if I don't play well	39
6	Thinking negatively (about opponent, playing badly)	36
7	Playing in a big game	33
8	Insincere people in locker room having access to players	30
9	Being overlooked by coach before a game	30
10	If I'm not on the team or in the position I want	27
11	Too much quiet before a game	27
12	Not concentrating on game	24
13	Not having mentally prepared myself	21
14	Too many distractions (noise outside, players laughing)	21
15	Bad weather conditions	18
16	Physical revving up and body contact before a game	18
17	Other people (coaches, trainers) putting pressure on me	15
18	Pregame yelling and psyching up	15
19	Not enough time to prepare myself physically	12
20	Coach giving too many instructions	9

[a] Listing of stressful events that happen before a game and which players find can negatively affect how they feel and play in a game

a game may be so because of mental hassles and unfinished business during the week, rather than as a consequence of too hard training sessions during the week. Basic mental skills that players were directed to use before and during a game to stay in control were relaxation, mental practice, and positive thinking.

SKILLS TAUGHT IN PROGRAM

Relaxation (verbatim transcript)

Relax. Play relaxed. It's important to kick and mark relaxed. These are words that I'm sure you have heard from coaches, other players, from the press, and even from your own voice inside your head that tells you how to play. Is relaxation as important as people make it out to be? I believe it is. First, as you know in yourself, when your body is tense and uptight, it is almost impossible to play well. The man who has scored the most points in the history of American football, George Blanda, says "When I am faced with kicking a field goal the main thing is to try to relax, to stay loose. If I start tensing up or try to muscle the ball, I'll be off." Relaxation is important. Why? Briefly, your body has muscles designed to move you around and to enable you to do all the different physical movements required of you in football. To move you around, your muscles do two types of things: contract and expand. When you have a lot of tension in your body, some of your muscles are expanded or contracted beyond their normal resting point. So when you start to make a precise movement in football, such as running for the ball, you must first overcome some initial resistance just to get to your muscles' normal resting position. Another even greater problem is that when you are tense your muscles contract and tighten. This directly conflicts with any movement that involves expanding muscles, like running, stretching, and reaching. This explains why some players at times have a jerky motion when they go for the ball; these players are playing with body tension they cannot get rid of. Dr. David Kauss, a well-known sport psychologist and author of "Peak Performance," has found that footballers have much greater control over their muscles when they are relaxed. Oh yes, something else about playing with tense muscles. Over the past several years of working with and observing football players, I have found that players who play with too much tension and can't relax are the ones who get injured most frequently.

TABLE 4. Stress in Football Arising during Game from Individual Play[a]

Rank	Trouble spot	Percentage of players who find event stressful
1	My opponent playing well	73
2	Making mistakes and feeling I let down the team	67
3	Feeling I'm out of position and not getting the ball	67
4	Not being in play	64
5	Playing poorly when trying hard (fumbling, making mistakes)	64
6	When I don't play well early in the game	51
7	Thinking constantly about whether I've done enough	51
8	Thinking about how well I've done against opponent	48
9	Being shifted out of position	43
10	When I don't go in	39
11	Bad umpiring	36
12	When I go for marks from behind	33
13	Getting started after halftime	33
14	Opposition tagging me too closely (niggling me, harrassing)	33
15	Thinking about the score	15

[a] Listing of "trouble spots" (different aspects of an individual player's game) which can negatively affect how he feels and plays during a game

TABLE 5. Stress in Football during Game Arising from Team Play[a]

Rank	Trouble spot	Percentage of players who find event stressful
1	Not being given the ball by my teammates when in best position	70
2	Teammates not backing up, chasing, or picking up opposition	67
3	Teammates who are selfish	61
4	When my teammates stop trying and give up	57
5	Teammates not talking	55
6	Criticism by teammates	51
7	When teammate doesn't use ball constructively (overdoes handpass, kicks blindly)	51
8	When going for the ball and no one talks	45
9	Making a good lead and being ignored	45
10	Teammates not doing hard stuff (tackling, blocking)	45
11	Not being acknowledged (teammates, coach) when I've done something well	33
12	When teammate "shits" himself	33
13	Lack of encouragement from teammates	33
14	Being criticized at quartertime or halftime	24
15	Not being talked to about my game during halftime	15

[a] Listing of trouble spots that refer to aspects of team play and on-the-field behavior that can negatively affect how players feel and play

Being able to relax is also a way of handling big game pressures. Many players who play well against some teams, seem to come unstuck against big teams or in finals, because of the anxiety and tenseness that occupies their minds and bodies.

Edmund Jacobson (1942) an American physician, who developed relaxation methods to combat tension and stress, showed that one cannot experience anxiety when muscle tension is reduced. He also found that when one's muscles are relaxed, it was almost impossible to experience an emotion at the opposite end of the emotional spectrum such as edginess or fear. So relaxation can help you combat the many pressures, demands, and stresses of football, such as anxiety and fear as well as prevent physical injury.

Another benefit of knowing how to relax is that it helps reduce the overall stresses of everyday living. Now there are few more stressful activities I know of than playing Australian rules football. Outside of football you do no doubt have a large number of demands and stresses, including another job or school, as well as a personal life, each of which saps into your mental and physical energies. Inside football, there are the expectations and criticisms of the fans, press, teammates, and friends which you have to deal with before, during, and after a game. People are always talking about your game, about the team, win, lose, or draw; why you played well, why you didn't. The demands on you are greater than ever and your reactions to these stresses can and often do influence how you feel during the week, and how you perform on Saturday. It works the other way too. The demands of football will often make it more dificult to function in other areas of your life at work and at home. One large benefit of relaxation is that it provides you with *time out* from these stresses. Relaxation is extremely *restorative*. Specifically, it helps you rest and makes it easier for you to sleep. Surprisingly, in some ways relaxation is even better than sleep in that you take control of the outside world and your inside world while awake. It leaves you with a greater sense of personal mastery and self-confidence.

Now, if relaxing was as simple as saying to yourself *relax* whenever you felt uptight and anxious either on or off the football field, then no player would ever be uptight. But as you know, when you get the heebie-jeebies it's damn hard to shake them. You can, fortunately, teach yourself to relax tense muscles, and as a consequence, gain your own emotional control in order for you to deal with your world both inside and outside of football. Now learning to relax when you're emotional and your muscles are tense takes time. Don't expect it to come right away, and be prepared to do enough practice so that you can see the beneficial effects of relaxation. There are two methods of relaxation that you will be learning. The muscle relaxation method teaches you how to become more aware of varying amounts of tension in your muscles. In this way you will learn to control the proper amount of muscle tension you need to play at your peak. This procedure consists of tensing and relaxing various muscle groups of the body one at a time. By contrasting what it's like to be tense with what it feels like to release that tension and relax, you will learn how to intentionally relax your muscles completely and to achieve a deep state of relaxation.

Another method of breaking up your tension is through good deep breathing. When you are nervous, the muscles in your diaphragm, chest, and throat tighten and constrict. Your breathing becomes shallower and more rapid in order to compensate for less air going in and out. To play intensively in a game you need lots and lots of air. If at the same time your breathing is being inhibited by emotional tension, you literally choke yourself by having your air supply cut off. The shortness of breath you may occasionally feel is brought about by emotional pressure. This in turn adds to your feelings of anxiety and panic. The fastest way to panic is having your air cut off. The golfing great, Sam Snead's advice for dealing with pressure is "Get loose as a goose." This looseness doesn't mean falling asleep but rather getting rid of excess muscle tension. Fortunately, you can learn to gain control of your breathing by becoming aware of how you can release tension through deep breathing. The breathing easy method teaches you to slow and deepen your breathing for a short period, especially when you find yourself uptight and out of breath on the field. By saying to yourself the word *relax* each time you breathe out slowly after you have taken a deep breath, you will learn how to take command over a most important part of you—your breathing. By so doing you will gain a sense of confidence, your attention will focus itself away from your anxiety and onto your breathing. The program which follows will teach you both the muscle tension and breathing easy methods of relaxation.

(Details of these methods can be obtained from Dr. Michael E. Bernard, Department of Education, University of Melbourne, Parkville, Vic., 3052, Australia.)

Mental Practice (verbatim transcript)

Mental practice (or as it is sometimes called, mental rehearsal) is used by many athletes in many different sports. Jack Nicklaus takes an imaginary practice shot before he hits the ball. In his book *Golf My Way* (1974), he writes:

> I never hit a shot . . . without having a very sharp, in-focus picture of it in my head. It's like a color movie. First I "see" the ball where I want it to finish, nice and white and sitting high up on the bright green grass. Then the scene quickly changes and I "see" the ball going there: its path, trajectory, and shape, even its behavior on landing. Then there is a sort of fade-out and the next scene shows me making the kind of swing that will turn the previous images into reality. (p. 65)

Bruce Jenner, the United States decathalon champion, used mental rehearsal at home each evening to practice the different decathalon events in preparation for the 1976 Olympics. I have also heard of stories of athletes who were able to maintain their physical skills through mental practice even though they did not have the opportunity to train. The story of Robert Foster, a former national rifle champion, illustrates the power of mental practice. Foster mentally practised target shooting 10 minutes a day for a year while on noncombat duty in Vietnam. After he returned to the United States and with almost no actual practice with the rifle he used in competition, he broke his own world record in the first national meet he entered.

Mental practice is not a new technique. The Zen Buddhists in the 1920s in China taught their students who were learning archery to form pictures of the targets in their heads. Today, thousands of professional and Olympic athletes are finding that consistent, hard physical training combined with regular mental practice produce the smooth and fluid skills and motion that bring about peak performance.

What exactly is mental practice and why does it work? First, it is not to be confused with positive thinking. Positive thinking is concerned with giving yourself confidence so that you can accomplish your goals in football. Mental practice focuses on how you go about achieving your goals; imagining what you are going to do. It is similar to you running a film through your mind—of you playing football—and being successful in each aspect of your play. Here is how Dr. Thomas Tutko and Umberto Tosi in their book *Sports Psyching* explain the idea behind mental practice.

> Say you want to get your tennis racquet or bowling ball out of the closet. Ordinarily, you wouldn't tell yourself verbally, "Go to the closet, open the door, locate it, grasp it, pull it out, close the door," and so on. Instead, you simply decide to do it. The computer that is your nervous system has already been programmed, and it throws the right switches to take appropriate action. But with mental rehearsal you are doing this programming in a more deliberate way. You are saying to your nervous system: "Here's what I'll be wanting you to do." (p. 146)

Mental practice works because when you imagine that you perform an action, impulses are produced which travel the nervous pattern which is directly associated with that action [Rushall, 1979]. This is known as the Carpenter Effect. What mental practice does, then, is program your nervous system so that during a game it automatically performs the action you want. The more you mentally practice, the more likely it is that you will successfully perform the skill without thinking about it. Does this mean that if you mentally practice different football skills four to six times a week that your game will significantly improve? Yes!

Mental practice will also help you maintain and extend your concentration as it gives you practice staying in the here and now, focused on the play, nowhere else. This helps you to keep your anxieties out of your consciousness and to stay in emotional control. The picture of yourself succeeding over and over again will come to direct your actions on the field, rather than thoughts about the last play, or whether you will succeed or fail on the next.

One major way you can help program your mental computer so that your body knows what to do on the field is to make sure that the instructions you feed into your computer are presented as pictures or images. The more detailed the image, the better your body will understand what to do. If you practice your game enough mentally, imaginally, playing exactly how you want to play, your muscles will subtly respond to your thoughts during a game and even though you won't be aware of it, your mind will be in perfect control of your body. You will achieve higher and higher levels of playing excellence.

Before we begin, there are a few things to know about how mental practice works best. First, it is easier for your mind to program your body when you are relaxed, so get relaxed before starting your mental practice. Second, while you are imagining yourself performing, your perspective is to be from the inside looking out. Rather than observing yourself playing as if you were watching a film of yourself, you will want to be a participant and practice what you see, feel, and smell as you are playing. More on this later. Third, when practicing imaginally it is important that your images of yourself and the different sensations you experience are as real and vivid as possible. Try to see as clearly as possible the field you will be playing on, the colors of the opposing team's uniforms, have the smell of the day greet your nostrils, and hear the sounds of the football being kicked and other players running. Of real importance is concentrating on imagining the feel of your body, your movements and your actions. For example, if you were practising mentally kicking for goal, you would, as you begin to walk a few steps forward to kick the ball, feel your legs moving toward the ball. As you begin to step forward and your foot meets the ball try to have your leg actually feel as if it is moving back, meeting the ball, and following through. Any nerve impulses in your muscles you can get to respond to your mental images will help greatly to program your nervous system. Fourth, do not imagine yourself making errors, but imagine yourself performing successfully. Fifth, perform the skill you are imagining in its entirety: from the time you are entering a play or are beginning to kick, mark, handball, tackle, smother, or block to its successful completion, including the positive feelings that accompany success. And sixth, the skills you rehearse during mental practice usually are to be only slightly higher than those you have actually performed. If you have never flown through the air over a pack to take a mark, and feel you are still a fair way away from doing so, then do not attempt imagining yourself doing so. Set the difficulty of the performance you want to practice as a realistic goal which slightly improves on your current performance. In the above example, you might wish to practice timing the flight of the ball, getting in front, and not dropping your head. Oh yes, one more thing. Mental practice is not as easy as it sounds. All of us are so used to thinking in words that we find it difficult to shift to pictures and images. Also, some people are good mental imagers, while others take time to learn how to do it. So don't be discouraged if it takes a while for you to get your images in focus and to learn mental practice. If it does take time, don't worry, it will be worth it in the end. The remainder of this tape will present a shorter relaxation program followed by mental practice.

(For a transcript of the rest of this tape write to Dr. Michael E. Bernard, Department of Education, University of Melbourne, Parkville, Vic., 3052, Australia.)

Eliminating Negative Thinking (verbatim transcript)

Since the earliest of times, the great thinkers of the day have recognized that your personal happiness as well as your personal miseries come from how we perceive and think about your world, rather than directly from events outside yourselves. Epictetus, a well known stoic philosopher who lived almost two thousand years ago, wrote that "People are not affected by events, but by the view they take of events." More recently, William Shakespeare noted that "Things are neither good nor bad but thinking makes it so." What other philosophers, as well, have noted is that your thoughts have a tremendous bearing on how you feel and how you behave. This is because it is in your thoughts that reality is represented. These same writers have also observed that our greatest power which distinctly separates us from other animals is our ability to take control of our minds, our thoughts, and our attitudes and in so doing to take responsibility for our feelings and, ultimately, our own destiny. Let me give you an example to show how important your mind is in affecting your football performance.

Several years ago I worked with a player, Ian, who was down in the dumps because he had played a few games and was not playing anywhere near the level he would like. When I asked him to tell me what he was thinking, out poured "I keep telling myself I have to do well and if I keep at it, it will come. Things really seem too hard and I'm not enjoying playing. Everything I do seems wrong. Everything seems hopeless. My timing is off. Maybe, I've lost it. My confidence is down and my nerves are shot." I said, "It's no wonder that you're off with your game. Your whole frame of mind prevents you from playing well. You are saying a number of things to yourself that are making you feel not only very down and angry with yourself about how you're playing, but also overly worried about how you're going to play tomorrow. These thoughts destroy your concentration and make it almost impossible for you to regain your confidence."

"Well," Ian said, "I know that I'm thinking pretty negatively, but how is that going to help me play better?"

I explained, "Your mind is like a double-edged sword. It can hurt you by allowing in ideas that cut away your confidence, or it can implant thoughts that cut away your anxiety and free you to more fully develop your football skills. Right now," I said, "your mind is working against you. What you can do is rid yourself of your negative mental habits that are causing you to drop your bundle and replace them with ideas that will help you regain your confidence and control. A negative mind attracts trouble as does a positive mind attract pleasant results."

With a look on his face and expression in his voice that suggested he was talking to Carnak the Magician, he asked, "You mean, all my problems are in my head and that if you could magically change them to more positive ones, my problems will disappear?"

"You are partly right," I said, as I pulled a few rabbits out of my hat. "You are mostly responsible for what goes on in your mind, and it is those thoughts and images of failing and your doubts about whether you'll succeed and how sensitive you are to people's criticism that are the main factors which prevent your body from playing like it already knows how to play. You are also right in believing that by changing your thoughts and the attitudes behind your thoughts you can change how you are playing. However, you are quite wrong in thinking that the only way you can change your self-defeating thoughts is through magic."

By this time, our forlorn player was wondering whatever possessed him to talk to me. If it wasn't magic or hypnosis—which he didn't believe in anyway—then what? He began to see pictures in his mind of acupuncture needles sticking in his head or, worse yet, his head being clamped down and electrical shocks being pumped into him to make his mind a blank. I went on, "over the past few years, I have helped many sportsmen change their thinking. Your mind has tremendous untapped potential, and one thing you can train it to do is to decide what attitude you will take and what thoughts you will allow in, positive or negative. More simply stated, your mind can decide whether your thoughts will control you or whether you will take control of your thoughts. You can learn to change your attitudes and thoughts."

Fortunately for me, Ian was not one of those players who believes that you can't teach an old dog new tricks. That is, he was prepared to accept the possibility that he could change his frame of mind to his play and in so doing improve his game.

"You mean to say that a person, myself, can learn new ways of thinking about myself, about my game, as well as how to handle pressure?"

"That's precisely what I mean. From what you told me a minute ago, you have several losing attitudes that are causing you problems. First, you said to me that you absolutely *have* to do well. Not just that you very much *want* to do well, but that you *should* do well 100% of the time. This thought often reveals the belief, 'For me to be a worthwhile person and a successful football player, I must be perfect and never make a mistake in a game.' This attitude leads to fear of failure, the fear of making mistakes. When your mind observes you making a mistake it puts you down because of your losing attitude that anything less than a perfect performance means you are a hopeless player and, worse yet, a hopeless person."

Reflecting upon my wisdom, Ian asked, "Do you mean that because I demand perfection to show myself and others how terrific I am, I somehow fall apart when I start to do badly in a game?"

"Precisely the point," I said. "You magnify each error you make if deep down you think it shows you to be less of a football player. Therefore, you had better work hard at positively accepting *yourself* while still hating your *mistakes.* How? By clearly seeing and then forcefully changing your self-downing attitudes towards making mistakes. You also seem to hold another losing attitude which leads to uptightness each time you make a mistake and which therefore saps your confidence. Like many players I've talked to, you seem to have a strong fear of failure, of making mistakes, because they are afraid that others will disapprove of them and put you down if you fail."

"Let's get this straight," Ian said, "you mean that after I've missed a couple of kicks and I find my confidence going down and feel like crawling under a rock, what I fear most is not that I might miss the shot but what others like the coach or fans might think of my game?"

"That's it in a nutshell. If you can imagine yourself being not too bothered by whatever happens after you miss a kick, then even after missing a few kicks you wouldn't be worried about missing another one and you would never be panicked. You know, the goal posts aren't going to crack you on the head, are they, if you miss a kick?"

"I guess not."

"Okay, if you see now how your confidence plummets by your attitudes about making mistakes, you have the power to rid yourself of these attitudes and replace them with more helpful ones that will create less upsetness when you fail. Are you with me?"

"I'll try anything if it'll get me on the right track."

"Great. Now, one way to start changing your attitude is to discipline your mind not to *awfulize* every time you make a mistake, like missing a mark or like being beaten several times."

"*Awfulize*, what does *awfulize* mean, what is it?"

"Awfulize is what your mind does when it exaggerates the unpleasantness of something. Like in your case, you make your mistakes much worse by blowing them out of proportion. When you awfulize about having played badly, you are really saying to yourself, playing poorly is not only unfortunate and irritating because it prevents me from accomplishing my goals of playing well, but making errors is 1000% awful, the worst thing that could ever happen to me! And because it is so awful, I can't stand it! By making the *hassles* of playing poorly into *horrors*, you literally drive yourself into such a state of emotional turmoil that your confidence and concentration go down the drain, your body becomes overly tense, and because of your frame of mind and state of body, you make it quite difficult to set yourself right."

Ian carried this idea even further by asking "Is the reason I awfulize—you might even call it *awfulitis*—because I'm overly concerned about what others think of me when I make a mistake?"

"You got it," I cried excitedly, as I could see Ian was having some real insights into the inner workings of his mind. My next step was to help him to stop awfulizing when he played less well than he wanted.

"One way," I said, "to counter your awfulizing, is to look at mistakes you make and ask yourself 'Does making several mistakes really make me a hopeless footballer?' The answer to that question is a big fat NO!, since many great footballers go through periods when they do poorly. Now, Ian, does making mistakes really make you a hopeless person?"

He thought for a while and said "I realize they don't, but I've been feeling as if they do. If I stop to think, I see that I lose confidence, because when I start to go real bad, I really get down on myself for playing so poorly. I sometimes feel I'm hopeless because I've been going so badly the past few games. And even in my last game, I remember telling myself what a hopeless dill I was for playing so poorly."

"That's right," I chimed in, "and the way to rid yourself of that losing attitude and gain confidence is to accept you are playing poorly, but not to put yourself down. Now the second attitude to get rid of is 'I must have the approval of my teammates, the coach, and my friends.' Not "I *prefer* to have it," but "I *must* have it all the time!" You can start by reminding yourself that while you would *like* others to approve of your game and of you, you don't *need* their approval. You won't fall dead if you don't get it, will you?"

"I really hate to be criticized."

"Of course you dislike it; no one likes it. But you had better learn to live with criticism without overly upsetting yourself. If you see that you can cope with others' criticism, then you won't worry quite as much about making mistakes. You'll stay more in control, you'll stay physically relaxed, and you'll ride through the bad patches until you improve. So I suggest that you practice thinking that mistakes mean only that you still have room to improve, and not in any way that you're a hopeless footballer. Second, while approval of your playing is important, you can stand not having it. If you do get criticized, it's not the end of the world. Do you understand what I'm saying?"

"I think it's sinking in. But while I can think about this during the week, I can't exactly do it during a game. What can I do if during a game I start to awfulize and get down?"

"Good question. The best way is to mentally prepare yourself in advance. You know that little voice inside your head that talks to you and really gets you down?"

"You mean it tells me how horrible I've been playing?"

"That's correct. You can learn to use that voice—let's call it your self-talk—to stop awfulizing. And this is how you do it. During this week, I want you to imagine situations during a game about which get you down—call them your *trouble spots*. Imagine situations in which you are likely to awfulize. In fact, let's start now. Give me a trouble spot in a game about which you tend to awfulize and get down."

"How about missing a goal which has come from a good kick from the back line?"

"That's a good one. Okay, now I want you to imagine this happening to you: your kick is important, as your team is down by several goals. Imagine the ball has been brought down the wing, then kicked to you. Now imagine kicking the ball—an easy kick—and the ball going through for a behind. I want you first to imagine feeling really bad, and down on yourself—as bad as you can possibly feel. See if you can imagine that and nod your head when you can imagine yourself being really down." Ian closed his eyes and within a few seconds nodded his head.

"Okay, Ian. Now imagine the same trouble spot, but this time change your feeling from being really angry with yourself and feeling down, to a feeling of being only irritated and disappointed, but still being in control."

"I don't know if I can do that."

"Sure you can. Just try it." Ian remained with his eyes closed for a longer period. I could see he was battling to get things under control. After about 30 seconds, he opened his eyes and said "Yes, it was hard, but I did it."

"How did you manage to change your feeling?" I asked.

"Well, the first time I really did awfulize about missing such an easy shot and letting my team down. I could have killed myself. But the second time, I said to myself that it was just one of those things. I wasn't going to worry about it, I said to myself 'Just relax. You can handle this. It's not the worst thing that could happen.' I also remembered something good I had done early in the game. Oh yeah, I also reminded myself what you said about how getting down on myself only hurts my game, makes me tense, and that I could still keep my cool even though I hated making the mistake."

"Now do you see" I said, "how your mind can stop awfulizing and how you can discipline it to stay in control during a game. By talking sense to yourself and thinking straight, you can combat your tendency to awfulize and to lose confidence. The imagery technique you just used, which is called Negative Rational-Emotive Imagery, can be used during the week to prepare yourself for handling trouble spots during a game. It involves the use of negative imagery, because you use it to change intense negative feelings, like anxiety, to appropriate negative feelings, like concern and displeasure. Negative appropriate feelings, like regret and displeasure, can actually motivate you to do better while playing. But inappropriate, self-defeating negative feelings, like panic and depression, will sap your confidence and help you do worse."

"Now let's try one other imagery procedure, called Positive Rational-Emotive Imagery that can help you overcome trouble spots during a game. Ian, you've been telling me that your confidence has been very low during the past few games especially when it comes to your marking. Is that right?"

"Yes, it's because of doubts I have because of my wrist injury, and I'm worried about hurting myself again."

"Okay, what I want you to do now is close your eyes and picture yourself getting ready to, and then taking, a mark. Picture yourself in a pressure situation, perhaps, with a few opposing players around you. But I want you to picture yourself feeling relatively calm and confident while you're doing it. You have your eye on the ball, your head is up, and you time the flight of the ball. You're not too worried, but feeling pretty good. You see yourself in front, grabbing the mark, hand over your head. Tell me when you get that picture clear in your head." I waited until Ian nodded his head. "Now what are you saying to yourself in order to do what you have pictured?"

"Well, I know I'm a good mark. If I just relax and concentrate, my body knows what to do. If I miss it, I'll get the next one."

"Great! Again, if you listen to your self-talk, when you feel relaxed and confident, you will see it is different from when you are uptight and worried. You have replaced negative self-talk with self-talk that helps control your worry. You know worry can kill a player's confidence. And most worry starts off with players saying to themselves 'What if I miss! What if I have a bad game! What if. . .?' I now can hear you starting to answer that 'what if' with a sensible answer such as 'Nothing that awful.' By doing that in your imagination you actually are preparing your mind to handle the stresses of competition and of staying in control.

"You know, it's amazing that I can, by using my imagination, actually get rid of some worries, and feel more confident. I feel better than I have in weeks."

"Feeling good now is important, Ian, but I want you to leave today knowing what you can do this week and during the game on Saturday to stay calm and confident in yourself. First, prepare yourself for a game by using the imagery methods we've just gone over. Write down the different trouble spots you have during a game that can unsettle your confidence. Then, in your imagination, first see yourself in those situations feeling nervous, uptight, and actually hear yourself awfulizing about having made mistakes and thinking, 'What if I screw up again?' Then imagine yourself replacing your negative self-talk with more helpful statements, such as 'Stay calm, things aren't as terrible as I think they are . . . I can handle myself.' Finally, imagine yourself feeling less upset and more in control and confident."

"You know this self-talk you're speaking about—can I also use it in a game? You know, to sort of steady myself when I start to doubt myself."

"Indeed you can! The more you practice self-talk in your imagination, the more you will be likely to automatically use it in a game to steady yourself. When you play, if you notice your confidence going or yourself getting upset, start to use positive self-talk to stay in control. You can also do this as you feel the pressure coming on. You can stay in control by saying things to yourself like:

- Concentrate on what I'm supposed to do next.
- I can handle this. I'm in control.
- No negative statements about myself.
- No worry! No 'what if' statements!
- I believe in myself. I'm a good kick and mark.
- I can psyche myself up to meet this challenge.
- I want to succeed. I expect to succeed.
- Relax. I'm in control. Take a slow, deep breath.
- No awfulizing about the past or what's happening to me today.
- Stay in the present. Pay attention out there.

"What you can do is to practice saying these things to yourself aloud during the week so they sink in and become a natural part of you. There are also specific words you can say to yourself during a game. I call them *mood* words, that can help you remain confident, strong, and tough. Here are some examples of words that can help you perform the way you want to. For example, if you want to play more forcefully and powerfully at times when you are losing concentration and are not playing as strongly and toughly as you would like, say these words to yourself—loudly and forcefully, and see how they make you feel: *boom, bang, explode, blast, rip, snap, smash, crush, squash, muscle, force, powerful, violent, strength.* Words that can help you persist include: *press, pressure, breathe, push, smother, drive, trouble, momentum, effort.*"

"It might help you, Ian, if you also write down your own mood words that occur to you and that you can employ during a game to maintain your commitment and drive."

At this point Ian looked up at me and quietly said "You know I really could play better, more so now with these new ideas you've given me. But sometimes I think that all this mental and physical training is just too damn hard. It seems so unfair that I have to put in all this effort and endure all this pain and frustration to play well. I seem to have to make so many sacrifices—strict eating, little drinking, no social life. Sometimes, I can't stand having to work so hard. Football shouldn't be so hard."

Ian was right there giving me evidence of one of the most powerful of all losing mental attitudes a person can hold. His low frustration tolerance was typical of the self-defeating attitudes to which almost all humans are prone. If we believe that we should always be comfortable and free from pain, that we cannot stand feeling unpleasantness and distress (especially when they accompany hard work) and that our life is *too* painful and that it *shouldn't be* that hard, we are likely to give up much more readily when the going gets tough.

So I said, "Ian, your particular attitude will do you little good. You seem to be saying that playing football is not only hard, but *too* hard, and that it *shouldn't be* so hard. Let me ask you a question: If your mind is convinced that something—like training or being criticized for mistakes—is unbearable and that football *shouldn't be* so hard and unpleasant, what effect will this kind of thinking have on your game?"

"Well, frankly, sometimes I think that what I'm doing really isn't worth it."

"Right. But can you pinpoint how this attitude influences how you play the game?"

"It probably makes me give up easier, not try as hard, and settle for second best."

"How do you mean?"

"Well, when I say to myself that something is *too* hard or terrible, I get pretty upset—sort of like if I am awfulizing about doing badly in a game. When I feel that way, I seem to lose interest and stop trying—sort of feel pissed off that things are going so badly and why should I have to put up with it."

"Right you are again. When you say things are *too* hard and they *shouldn't be,* you tend to become overly tense, impatient, or sometimes really scared. Such feelings encourage you to take an easy way out. You become less enthusiastic about your football. During a game, the more you feel things aren't going as well as they *should* go, the more likely you are to stop trying. You justify your giving up by saying, 'Playing football is too hard. That's unfair. It *should be* easier. So I'm entitled to give up."

"I can see what you're saying. I guess I've always been that way. What do you suggest I do to handle all the hard work and pain, without throwing it in?"

"Well, Ian, you had damned well better change your attitude that life is *too* difficult and it *shouldn't be*. Where is it written that life *has to be comfortable* and without pain?"

"What do you mean?"

"Well, you act as if someone up there ordained that your life should be easy. But it is clear that everyone's life is difficult much of the time and that most people suffer their way to success. Now, while it's too bad that you find many things in football difficult, why *must* it be easy? When things are hard, expect them to be. And when you find that football isn't easy, say to yourself, 'I *can* stand this—although it's pretty unpleasant.' Do you see?"

"I guess I have been a little soft and expecting things to be easier than they are and are not willing to try hard enough."

"Yes, when you do find the going rough and are pissed off with yourself for playing poorly, or angry at the coach for training you too hard, or upset with other players or fans for criticizing your game, remind yourself of an expression we often use in RET—*gain through pain*. The more you can hack the hard work and pain of football, the more you'll gain. Don't demand that everything you do must come easy. Football is often difficult but it is rarely *too* difficult."

Ian went away that day with his head filled with more than he could ever absorb in one sitting. During the rest of the season we kept talking over some of the things we discussed that day. Ian's game has considerably improved with our conversations. He has become recognized as a consistent, committed, and confident player, calm under pressure, and with a capacity to concentrate at playing at his best.

Positive Thinking and Winning Mental Attitudes (verbatim transcript)

Sections of this material are paraphrased and redirected to football from Denis Waitley's (1979) book *The Psychology of Winning*, and Gallwey and Kriegal's (1977) *Inner Skiing*.

What makes a top performing football player? Can we identify the qualities that distinguish winning footballers from those who do not make it to the top? As a psychologist who has worked with many football players, I see more clearly than ever before that the mind is one of the most important ingredients to success, as your mind is the best fortune teller for forecasting the actions of your body. People who work with top athletes have identified a set of mental attitudes and skills that go along with top performance. Fortunately, you can learn these winning mental habits if you wish to improve your game. And more and more athletes are now recognizing that they have the power to take control of their minds and thereby take responsibility for how their body performs. You, like other top footballers, can see how the right kind of mental preparation can lead to improvements in your football performance.

A most important quality of top performing football players is their winning attitude of *positive self-expectancy:* of their being confident of their ability to be successful. Denis Waitley, in *The Psychology of Winning,* defines positive self-expectancy as optimism, enthusiasm for everything you do, and expecting the most favorable result from your actions. Winners in life and winning footballers expect to win in advance and generally fulfill their expectations. Low achievers in life, and in football, tend to be pessimistic and negative thinkers, have little power of self-expectancy. Poor achievers expect negative outcomes—they expect to fail at school or on a test, to lose a job, to have no money, to spend another boring evening at home, to have ill health, to play poorly, to be dropped from the team. Deep down, these people do not believe in themselves. They doubt that they can ever succeed. They worry about the future.

In football, the players' sense of optimism, of positive self-expectation, of winning and succeeding seems to play a major role in determining whether they are winners or losers; whether they are on the interchange bench on the seconds or playing their tenth consecutive game on the firsts. The attitude of self-confidence paves the way to success. Not too long ago I spoke to two young players both of near equal ability in most every respect. Both quick, good marks and kicks and both with good football sense. The only difference I could detect between them was that one had an all-abiding faith in himself to succeed, to conquer all obstacles, to play on the first football Saturday of the year. He could only see himself playing well; he expected to be there and he was. The other lacked that inner core of self-confidence, expected difficulties, injury, and being beaten by someone else. He expected too little of himself, did not really believe he could make it, and in his mind doomed himself to failure—which is what's happened.

You become what you fear. If you worry about injury, you'll likely end up injured. If you preoccupy yourself in your mind with failure, you'll often end up failing. When I talk to great players about their football I sense an incurable optimism that every Saturday in every quarter, every time the ball is bounced, they believe they are going to win.

A second mental quality of top football players is that of *positive self-motivation.* Winning footballers are driven by desire; they have internalized a burning desire to win. Let me remind you what psychologists have known for many years. You become what you think about most. You move in the direction of that which you steadily dwell on and desire.

Top footballers I have worked with have developed positive self-motivation as a result of their overall attitude of self-confidence and optimism. They have developed the ability to move in the direction of goals they have set in football. They rarely distract themselves from moving towards these goals in the face of all discouragement, mistakes, and setbacks. Inner drive and desire keep top footballers moving towards attaining their goals. This desire says "I can," "I want to," "I see the opportunity," and "I will." Many of you motivate yourself negatively, out of fear. You fear the penalties of failure, of dropping marks, of miskicking, of being criticized, of pain, of disappointment, of injury, of losing. And so you try to avoid fear by trying hard and not being caught out. Yet fear is always in the back of your mind—"What if I should fail?" Fear is a constant reminder that failure and pain are likely to be repeated.

Winning footballers see mistakes as temporary setbacks, as inevitable consequences of their desire for success, and as challenges for the future. They recognize that success comes from how much mental and physical training they are prepared to do, and not from luck. All footballers have setbacks, but winners have a deep down abiding faith that through their own hard work, effort, and persistence they will achieve their goals.

One mental skill which is characteristic of most football players who make it to the top and play consistently well is tolerating discomfort, pain, and hard work they encounter. Footballers who don't make it say, "Things should come easy to me. I know if I pushed myself I could play better, but it's too damn hard and I'm not going to do it!" These players are overly sensitive to the pains and emotional stress of the up and down world of football. They refuse to believe that hard work, criticism, embarrassment, and failing are a fact of life and say to themselves, "It's too bad that things are difficult, but why must everything be easy?" Instead, they go around whining to themselves about how unfair and hard it all is and that they deserve something better. Top footballers accept reality as it comes: they learn to tolerate the inevitable frustrations and disappointments without giving up and saying it's impossible. I think that the capacity to mentally endure discomfort and frustration is what is meant by mental toughness and is the key to winning football.

Another important aspect of an athlete's mental makeup over which you have a large amount of control is the continuous stream of thoughts that flow through your mind while you are playing (some people refer to this stream of thoughts as your self-talk). You can learn two main things about your self-talk. First, that certain things you say to yourself during a game hurt rather than help you because of their influence on your feelings of confidence, on your focus of attention, and on the amount of tension that you carry around in your muscles. Second, *too* much thinking about and analysis of your game while you are playing can also make it more difficult for your body to realize its full potential.

Let's look at those thoughts that go on in your head that actually upset and interfere with your play. A part of your mind is always telling you how to play, evaluating and judging your progress, criticizing your mistakes, doubting your ability and comparing it with others, warning and worrying about failure and getting hurt. Timothy Gallwey, the well-known author of several books of the psychology of sporting performance, has described how your mind is composed of many different roles: The Instructor constantly tells you everything you should be doing, how you had better do it, and when. Afraid that nothing will go right if he is not talking, The Instructor repeats and repeats himself over and over. Not only is he convinced that you can't learn to play football without him, but he assumes you have a very short memory. Flashy Frank is not as concerned with how well you play football, or enjoy playing football as he is with how well you look to the crowd. Continually worried about what others think of you, he cripples you through self-consciousness and urges you to impress the fans with making the big play. The Competitor steadily compares your football with someone else's, insisting that you always be seen as the best on the ground even if your team loses. The Competitor is only happy if he is the star. Fearful Fred is obsessed with getting hurt and failing and is always afraid of bruising both your body and your ego. His favorite phrase is "Uh-oh, I might get hurt." His second favorite is "I won't make this." His fears and worries create tension as he searches for signs of impending disaster, and this tension is contagious, spreading throughout your body. Another voice or role you might recognize is The Critic, who has something negative to say about everything you do. Even if you are playing well, he'll focus on the one or two errors you might make. He sets impossible standards of perfection and criticizes and blames you when you don't achieve them (remember how much you hate others who criticize you? Well, think how much you hate your constant critic). Then there is Ego Tripper who is a bit like The Competitor. Ego Tripper plans everything he does in terms of how much he'll get from it. The more he gets, the bigger his ego. Deep down, Ego Tripper is so insecure in himself that he unconsciously plays selfishly. He drives himself to prove to everyone, including himself, how great he is. He is the worst team member on the field because whenever he sees a chance to show others how great he is he'll try to do it on his own rather than doing the team thing, like blocking or shepherding, which never receive the recognition he so desperately needs.

Perhaps you've recognized parts of yourself in some of these roles. When you are in one of these roles you'll find your constant chatter interfering with your football. This brings us to the second negative aspect of your self-talk. Remember how quiet and thoughtfree your mind is when you are performing at your best? When you are firing, your mind is not directing, criticizing, judging, analyzing, or being fearful; instead it is relaxed and quietly focused in the present.

To illustrate how harmful too much crooked thinking can be on your football performance, let's look at one of the greatest inner mental obstacles that blocks your realizing your football potential: the fear of failing. In our culture we have grown up to be greatly concerned about whether or not we are performing well enough to meet our own and others' expectations.

I asked a group of footballers what it was they most worried about and most agreed that even ahead of getting hurt was the fear of making a mistake, of doing the wrong thing. When I asked them why that would be so bad many seemed to feel that too many mistakes would show that they would be a failure as a footballer and that they'd lose self-esteem if they didn't succeed.

As Albert Ellis has observed, so many of us have been brought up to measure our value as people according to how well we perform—especially at sports—and to believe that poor performance means *we* are rotten individuals. If we play well, we feel that we are good, deserving of recognition, love, and respect. If we play poorly, we fear that we will lose the love and respect we absolutely need.

This belief that our self-worth is defined by success is sometimes hard to recognize in someone else, let alone yourself. But believe me, it is implicit in the minds of most people I know.

The reason that this attitude is a losing one is that at those times during a game when you are under a lot of pressure—as when you play against an imposing opponent, or you have not been playing well—your mind interprets your performances in terms of whether you have succeeded or failed as a person in your own eyes and in the eyes of others. You see difficult situations in which you may fail on the field as being of the same kind of threat as physical danger. Your body undergoes the same negative changes in muscle tension and breathing as it does when you feel that you are going to be hurt. Said another way, your body panics when your mind perceives a threat to your ego. So whether you realize or not, if you are overly afraid of making mistakes, it is because you do not think your ego can stand it.

RET shows you how to overcome this attitude by teaching you to stop measuring your worth in terms of how much you achieve in football. Your value as a person simply cannot be measured by your talent, position, role, because the value of human life is beyond measure. Moreover, you are too complex a person to be rated as a whole—you have too many strengths and weaknesses, both inside and outside of football. I suggest you use RET to accept yourself (and others) as having a basic core that is not measurable and that is unaffected by how well you achieve. By refusing to attach your accomplishments to your ego, to your value as a person, you will start to overcome your fear of failure. Remember, overconcern with achievement causes tightness and restrictions of our bodies. The greatest competitors want to win and hate to lose, but they aren't afraid to lose.

Goal Setting (handout presented to players)

Goal setting is now recognized as an important aspect of the mental preparation of athletes. The setting of goals can increase sporting performance substantially—in some cases up to 50% or more—than performance when no goals are set. In football, goals are defined as the *end result* towards which your physical and mental effort is directed. Goals can help keep you committed, motivated, and enjoying football. You can make the achievement of your longer-term goals easier by specifying short-term goals. Setting other performance goals besides just winning will help you to play better, consistently, improve more, and get more from your game.

Goals need to be specified in a certain way. Some goals can help you, others can hurt you. Use these rules in setting your goals:

1. *Place your goals under your control*
   bad example: Goal of winning a game
   good example: Increasing kicking accuracy
2. *Make your goals positive*
   bad example: Drop marks less often
   good example: Increase number of marks I take
3. *Clearly define your goals and specify exactly what you are going to do*
   bad example: Be more aggressive
   good example: Tackle, smother, shepherd more
   bad example: Be more confident
   good example: Increase frequency with which you predict and see yourself playing well (thought confidently). Feel confident by relaxing before a big game
4. *Make your goals measurable. Set how much you want to increase or improve a particular skill*
   bad example: Improve smothering
   good example: Smother at least once during a game
5. *Make your goals realistic; not too high, and reflecting readily attainable, and progressively more difficult steps*
   (for a player who last year averaged 2 goals and 5 marks a game)
   bad example: Goal of kicking 5 goals and taking 12 marks a game
   good example: Goal of kicking at least 3 goals a game and taking 8 marks

Several additional points about goal setting:

- Don't let your goals limit yourself. Set your goals to achieve *at least* some standard. Be pleased with small improvements, but strive for huge gains. Also, some players make the mistake of, once they reach their goals, not being ready for the next step. (For example: once you get to the finals prepare yourself for a winning effort in the Grand Final.)
- Give 100% on the training track—especially in those areas and for those skills you have targeted for goals. If you haven't done it on the training track, it's harder to do it in a game.

- Praise yourself intensively when you achieve a goal, no matter how small.
- If you don't achieve your goals in a game do not *overly* worry. Find out what additional physical, technical, and mental skills may be needed to reach your goal and then practice, practice, practice. Also, take the risks involved in reaching your goals and avoid the fear of failure.
- To make sure you get something positive from a game, it is a good idea to set a number of different goals. That way you do not depend on any one aspect of your football as a measure of how you are doing.
- Your efforts in training will be best when your goals for training and competition are made public.
- Goals you set are more likely to be achieved if you perform them using mental imagery during the week.
- Revise and update your goals each week.
- If you regularly monitor your progress towards your goals, you will be more motivated to continue making progress. A chart or graph is a good way of keeping track of your progress.

Concentration Training

Concentration training teaches one's mind to rid itself of distracting, evaluating, analyzing, worrisome, and irrelevant thoughts that interfere with the full expression of physical potential. Getting negative thoughts out of athletes' heads is a key to allowing their bodies to take over. Methods to establish good concentration involve decreasing interference from their conscious minds, helping athletes become more aware of the body, and helping them apply the correct attentional mode they require.

The methods of stress reduction through relaxation, positive imagery, and positive thinking that we previously discussed effectively help athletes to reduce mental and physical distractions that reduce concentration during a game.

In discussing the characteristics of concentration with players during week 5, I introduced Nideffer's (1977) model of attention to players. Nideffer describes two dimensions of attention that are relevant to athletic performance. The *internal-external* dimension describes the extent to which the athlete's attention is focused internally (inner awareness: thoughts about past and future, feelings, memories, body signals) or externally (outer awareness; what the athlete is confronted with; the present). The *broad-narrow* dimension ranges from the player's being able to take into account the entire range of awareness (which includes coordinating disparate information into an overall plan) to a more selected focus on a few things or a specific task. Nideffer describes four basic attentional modes which are available to any athlete (see Figure 1). Each attentional mode is deemed appropriate for certain tasks and situations and inappropriate for others.

The key to good concentration is being able to switch attentional modes to match the changing demands of football. As the examples in Table 6 demonstrate, the ideal football player is able to switch attentional modes as the situation changes.

Stressful conditions can reduce attentional flexibility and can lead a player into being locked into his preferred mode whether appropriate or not (attentional disturbance). *Choking* occurs during a pressure situation when a player is overloaded and attention becomes narrowed. Nideffer's (1977) Test of Attentional and Interpersonal Style was ad-

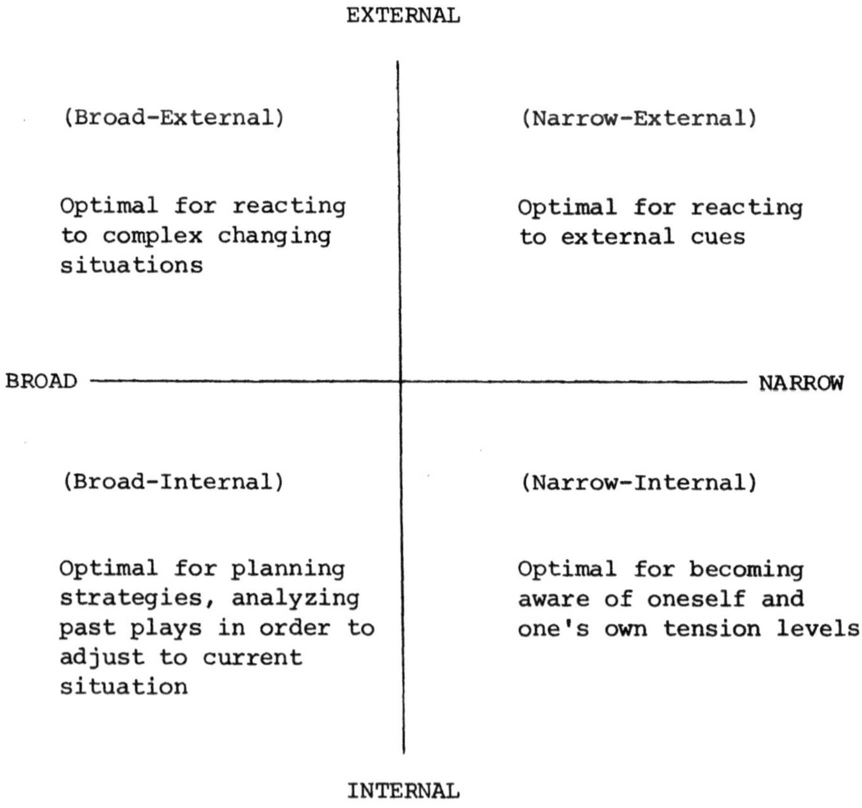

FIGURE 1. Attentional Modes in Football (adapted from Nideffer, 1977).

TABLE 6. Attentional Mode Strategies for Changing Demands of Football

Attentional mode	Adaptive measure
Broad external mode	Reads the entire field with a glance so he knows where everyone *is* at the moment.
Broad internal mode	Senses where everyone will be in the next moment and plans his actions accordingly.
Narrow internal mode	Attends to internal cues of his body and shuts out extraneous stimuli.
Narrow external mode	Focuses on field, play, goals, and shuts out all other features.

ministered during the last session and in the weeks following the program players were given feedback concerning their own attentional strengths and weaknesses.

Players were also presented with an *attention clearing method* (Kauss, 1980). This technique is useful for athletes who have trouble concentrating before and during a game and is designed to increase focused attention. The method involves improving an athlete's control of concentration by clearing away from his mind as many distractions as possible. Distractions can be external (weather, crowd, bad calls) and internal (doubts, fears). The method is to be used at home early in the week before a game. Although the method can last for up to an hour when a player first uses it, it generally occupies between 5 and 20 minutes. The method consists of the following:

1. Players identify "trouble spots" (stressful events) that distract them during a game (e.g., thinking about their opponent playing well or about not being in play). (Players in the mental training program had already identified their own trouble spots when they filled out the stress questionnaires reported in Tables 2 to 5.)
2. Players imagine scene as vividly and fully as possible. As players become aware of tension that disrupts their concentration they use methods of minimizing their tension (e.g., relaxation, positive thinking).
3. Finally, players in imagination consciously narrow their field of vision to the ball itself just as they would see it in a game, seeing its texture, seams, shape, color, size. Players stay with this image for three minutes.

Conclusion

The goals for the RET-oriented mental training program were designed to be realistic, with the objective of increasing players sensitivity to and awareness and understanding of the importance of their own mental preparation program, and approach to the game. As a result of their training, all players now seem to recognize that they can exercise some control over aspects of their mind that directly influence the quality of their play.

Through discussions with players, it appears that between 50% and 75% of them have actually employed rational-emotive ideas and skills presented in the program to improve their confidence, consistency, commitment, concentration, and self-control. Certain of the players profited most from group discussions whereas others appeared to have achieved important insights into their game through listening to the cassette tapes.

The extent to which the insights and short-term benefits are maintained during the season depends on individual follow-up by the team's psychologist. It is a long season (26 weeks) and we realistically assume that maintenance with at least occasional injections of individual booster sessions is required.

A decided (though unplanned) benefit of the RET mental training program for Australian football players was the development of rapport between the team's psychologist and players. Usually, a psychologist is viewed with mistrust and suspicion by some professional athletes and coaches. Without going into the complex reasons for this attitude, it is enough to say that psychologists often have to overcome, especially in the early stages of working with athletes, heavy resistance from players and coaches. The RET Mental Training Program significantly helped the footballers to modify the attitudes underlying their resistance and to view the potential contributions of a psychologist as well as the psychologist himself in a favorable light. So far, the program has nicely demonstrated that RET can be quite helpful in the training of football players—and presumably, as well, in improving the mental health and the performances of other types of athletes.

References

Bell, K. F. (1980). *The nuts and bolts of psychology for swimmers.* Austin, TX: Keith Bell.
Bell, K. F. (1983). *Championship thinking.* Englewood Cliffs, NJ: Prentice-Hall.
Desiderato, O., & Miller, I. B. (1979). Improving tennis performance by cognitive behavior modification techniques. *Behavior Therapist, 2,* 9.
Ellis, A. (1962). *Reason and emotion in psychotherapy.* Secaucus, NJ: Lyle Stuart.

Ellis, A. (1973). *Humanistic psychotherapy: The rational-emotive approach.* New York: McGraw-Hill.

Ellis, A. (1979). The theory of rational-emotive therapy. In A. Ellis & J. M. Whitely (Eds.), *Theoretical and empirical foundations of rational-emotive therapy.* (pp. 33–60). Monterey, CA: Brooks/Cole.

Ellis, A. (1982). Self direction in sport and life. *Rational Living, 17,* 26–23.

Ellis, A., & Abrahms, E. (1978). *Brief psychotherapy in medical and health practice.* New York: Springer.

Ellis, A., & Becker, I. (1982). *A guide to personal happiness.* North Hollywood, CA: Wilshire Books.

Ellis, A., & Grieger, R. (Eds.). (1977). *Handbook of rational-emotive therapy.* New York: Springer.

Ellis, A., & Harper, R. A. (1975). *A new guide to rational living.* North Hollywood, CA: Wilshire Books.

Gallwey, T., & Kriegal, B. (1977). *Inner skiing.* New York: Bantam.

Gologor, E. (1979). *Psychodynamic tennis.* New York: Morrow.

Gravel, R., Lemieux, G., & Ladouceur, R. (1980). Effectiveness of a cognitive behavioral treatment package for cross country ski racers. *Cognitive Therapy and Research, 4,* 83–89.

Jacobson, E. (1942). *You must relax.* New York: McGraw-Hill.

Kauss, D. R. (1980). *Peak performance: Mental game plans for maximizing your athletic potential.* Englewood Cliffs, NJ: Prentice-Hall.

Klinger, E., Barta, S. G., & Glas, R. A. (1981). Thought content and gap time in basketball. *Cognitive Therapy and Research, 5,* 109–114.

McCluggage, D. (1977). *The centered skier.* New York: Bantam.

Meyers, A., Schleser, R., Cooke, C., & Cuviller, C. (1979). Cognitive contributions to the development of gymnastic skills. *Cognitive Therapy and Research, 3,* 75–85.

Nicklaus, J., & Bowden, K. (1974). *Golf my way.* New York: Simon & Schuster.

Nideffer, R. M. (1976). *The inner athlete: Mind plus muscle for winning.* New York: Crowell.

Nideffer, R. M. (1977). *Test of attentional and interpersonal style.* San Diego, CA: Enhanced Performance Associates.

Orlick, T. (1980). *In pursuit of excellence.* Ottowa: Coaching Associates of Canada.

Orlick, T. Beyond excellence. (1982). In T. Orlick, J. T. Partington, & J. H. Salmela (Eds.). *Mental training for coaches and athletes.* Ottowa: Coaching Association of Canada.

Rushall, B. S. (1979). *Psyching in sport.* London: Pelham.

Shelton, T., & Mahoney, M. (1978). The content and effect of "psyching up": Strategies in weight lifters. *Cognitive Therapy and Research, 2,* 275–284.

Simek, T. C., & O'Brien, R. M. (1951). *Total golf.* Garden City, NY: Doubleday.

The Diagram Group. (1982). *The brain: A user's manual.* New York: Berkley.

Tutko, T., & Tosi, U. (1976). *Sports psyching.* Los Angeles: Tarcher.

Unestahl, L. E. (1982). *Better sport by IMT: Inner mental training.* Orebro, Sweden: Veje.

Waitley, D. (1979). *The psychology of winning.* Chicago: Conant, 1979.

Weinberg, R., Gould, D., & Jackson, A. (1980). Cognition and motor performance. Effect of psyching up strategies on three motor tasks. *Cognitive Therapy and Research, 4,* 239–245.

Wessler, R. (1980). How to play golf under pressure. *Rational Living, 15,* 21–24.

13

RET and Some Mid-Life Problems

ROSE OLIVER

INTRODUCTION

One of the most significant changes taking place today is the increase in life expectancy. People are living longer, healthier lives than ever before in human history. Average life expectancy has increased from 47 years in 1900, to 74 years in 1980 (National Center for Health Statistics). At the turn of the century, 3% of the population was 65 and over. Now, 11% of the population lives past the period officially designated as old age. This demographic shift presents one of the great challenges of our era. And it presents a special challenge to psychotherapists to whom more and more of an increasing middle-aged population is turning for help in improving their life situations.

Defining and delimiting the middle years presents some difficulties. Chronological age is a poor indicator of physiological, intellectual, or psychological age (Neugarten, 1973a). However, in the interest of an orderliness that does not exist in society or in nature, I will arbitrarily set the boundaries of the middle years as the period between 40 and 64, recognizing that these boundaries are permeable, and that they do not describe a homogeneous population in terms of life span development. Any definition, or any arbitrary parameters, will include a broad range of individuals, disparate in age, in age-related self-concept, in social class, in health, in ethnicity, in educational background, in occupational status, and in interpersonal relationships. And, most importantly, we must take cognizance not only of the commonality between men and

---

ROSE OLIVER • Clinical psychologist in private practice, New York, New York. Staff Psychotherapist, Institute for Rational-Emotive Therapy, New York, NY, 10021.

women, but of the differences, and the demands that these differences place on the individual.

The period between 40 and 64 is not a plateau, nor is it a holding pattern between youth and old age. It is a time when both men and women confront the finiteness of life; when the ratio between live lived and time left to live acquires new significance; when new adaptations are to be mastered, and new opportunities are to be explored. It is a time of stability and change; a time encompassing new dilemmas, and new opportunities for growth. RET addresses these opportunities within a realistic recognition of the limitations.

Some life span theorists, such as Erikson (1950), Levinson (1978), and Gould (1978), postulate development as a succession of discrete stages, each with its own agenda of life tasks to be mastered, and each with specific desired outcomes. Stage theories are age-bound, and presuppose an experiential lockstep. These theories do not take into account either the cohort effect of development within a specific historic and social context, or of the multiplicity of today's life styles, and the fluidity of today's time tables. Nor do they take cognizance of differences in men's and women's experiential histories. Each of these life span investigators, whether frankly studying only men, as does Levenson (1978), or both men and women, as does Gould (1978), conceptualize development in terms of white, middle- to upper-middle-class men. Erikson, for example, whose model of life span development has been the stimulus for much theoretical investigation, and whose major contribution to developmental theory has been the recognition of the importance of the resolution of the adolescent identity crisis, defines women's identity (Erikson, 1964) as "her kind of attractiveness, and the selectivity of her search for the man (or men) by whom she wishes to be sought." Women's identity, by this criterion, is both passive and male-defined. Nonetheless, in spite of this significant difference, which Erikson attributes to the male and female paths to adulthood, the subsequent stages that he describes, make no distinction between men and women.

Neugarten (1973b) views the life course, not as a series of discrete stages, but as a process whose salient milestones are personal and social events, such as marriage, work, birth of children, departure of children, retirement, death of parents. Neugarten's conceptualization offers a framework within which variables such as social class, ethnicity, and sex can be examined and their effect on the life course differentiated.

Research has shown that social class (Neugarten & Peterson, 1957), and ethnicity (Bengtson, Kasschau, & Ragan, 1977) are but two variables that have an impact on age-related life experiences, and age-related self-perceptions. Upper-middle-class individuals viewed age 40 as the prime of life and 50 as the onset of middle age, whereas those of a lower social class perceived both prime and middle age to be ten years earlier. Mexican Americans saw aging in more accelerated terms than did whites, whereas blacks' perception of the rapidity of aging was intermediate between the two. However, it is my belief that sex differences transcend all other differences as determinants of the developmental pattern and of age-related problems presented for therapeutic intervention.

Women's distinct developmental pattern has only recently been accorded the interest and attention required to understand women's unique developmental history (Barnett & Baruch, 1978; Giele, 1982a; Gilligan, 1982; Notman, 1980). Given men's and women's distinctive biological attributes, and their different histories of socialization, roles, work, and family relationships, it is inevitable that men and women in the middle years present problems that are unique to each, or that find different expression for each.

Although it is not possible, in this brief chapter, to examine, or even to enumerate, all of the mid-life difficulties presented in therapy, I will select some that I have encountered with greater frequency, in workshops and in individual as well as in group therapy. Comprehensive recent reviews of mid-life problems and mid-life concerns can be found in Howells (1981), and in Norman and Scaramella (1980).

Development, at all ages, is accompanied by, guided by, and shaped by cognitions, rational and irrational. An internal dialogue evaluates events, coloring one's perception of events, and influencing affect and behavior. This evaluation forms what Ellis (1962) calls the belief system, rational and irrational. Irrational beliefs motivate and sustain maladaptive emotional and behavioral responses; rational beliefs motivate adaptive feelings and behaviors.

In this presentation, I will examine the irrational belief systems that underlie maladaptive emotional responses to some common events of middle age. I will demonstrate the application of principles of RET to helping clients replace the irrational beliefs with rational ones, to enable them to pursue a more enjoyable and fruitful life.

Work

The centrality of men's lives has been achievement and mastery; for women, the major focus has been relationships. Whether this difference is innate, or is an artifact of the socialization process that has programmed women primarily for nurturing, and men for achieving, and whether this dichotomy will be blurred under the impact of the social changes now taking place need not concern us here. It is a difference which has been consistently observed (Giele, 1982a; Gilligan, 1982; Notman, 1980), and which consistently manifests itself in therapy. However, as Giele (1982a) points out, "difference" carries no implication of superiority or inferiority of either modality. Difference from the male model, which has heretofore been perceived as the norm, is not to be confused with deviance.

Men and Work

Work and achievement have been the dominant molders of men's self-perception. It is therefore in relation to work or mastery that male psychological well-being sometimes flounders.

Wealth and power are primarily controlled by middle-aged men. Captains of industry, legislators, outstanding lawyers, doctors, and tenured professors, are predominantly men in the prime of life (Neugarten, 1968). While the movers and shakers of society are predominantly men in the middle years, not all men in the middle years are movers and shakers. Most are not. However, the "successful man" is still the American ideal.

Success, defined by the individual's own or his community's standards, is frequently the criterion by which a man is measured, and by which he measures himself. When the internalized image of the "successful man," the ideal of what a man "should" be, and the image of what he perceives himself to be, are out of synch, a conflict arises that results in emotional disturbance. The ideal image, and the perceived self-image are too disparate (Horney, 1950). As long as the man clings to both images, he is beset by "musts," "shoulds," self put-downs, and a sense of hopelessness that generate emotional distress.

The following clinical example illustrates this dilemma:

> Andrew J., 43-years-old, an engineer and president of his own electronics firm, complained of anxiety attacks, particularly in the morning, extreme dislike of his work, reluctance to attend to business, profound sense of failure, and of his own inadequacy and a desire to "chuck it all."
>
> He had been shifting more and more of the work to his junior partner whom he had trained. This increased his feelings of unworthiness and guilt. He was clinically depressed.
>
> Initial exploration established that his relationships with his wife and three sons were good. His current problem focused on an aversion to his profession, an aversion which had been growing for several years. His justification was that "engineering is a mechanical profession" and that "engineers are producing hardware that confounds the world's ills."

Much as he would have liked to leave the profession, he saw no alternatives. Although Shangri-la beckoned, he was not willing to abdicate his responsibilities to his family. At the same time, he foreclosed the possibilities of retraining because there was no other field of work that appealed to him. He felt trapped.

In spite of the fact that he provided a comfortable life-style for his family, he was convinced that he was a "failure" and that he would always be a failure, both as regards professional performance and financial rewards. The following brief, and necessarily condensed, excerpts from his therapy sessions demonstrate the course of therapy:

T: What do you mean by failure?

C: Well, I certainly haven't done as well as I should. (*Note:* At this point I chose to ignore the "should," in the interest of pursuing the meaning of failure and success. "Shoulds" are generally considered red lights in RET. I prefer to think of them as red blinkers that give the therapist the option of stopping, or proceeding with caution.)

T: By whose standards?

C: Everyone's standards.

T: Please elaborate.

C: Other people I know. My friends.

T: Do you mean that your friends earn more money than you do?

C: Yes. That's one way of looking at it. I don't care that much for money, but that is a mark of success.

There followed a discussion of the relative meaning of the term *success*. We examined the fact that the friends, whose success he envied, would be considered failures in terms of income in some much more affluent circles, whereas his own financial standing and life-style would be the envy of over two-thirds of the country. What standards were acceptable to him? How many dollars add up to a worthwhile man?

C: I can't say in terms of dollars. Still, you will admit that we are taught to compete, and that people who come out ahead are the ones who are admired.

T: Yes, that's true. It is true that people are taught to measure themselves on a rating scale on some criterion, be it money, material possessions, prestige. Then they damn themselves as you are doing now, if they find themselves wanting. Do you value your worth as a person in terms of your income? The size of your car? Your home? Would your value as a person double if your income doubled?

He was asked to consider the question "What is the value of a human being?" After reading "Psychotherapy and the Value of a Human Being" (Ellis, 1977), and after much further discussion on the subject, Andrew J. finally concluded that human beings, himself included, were intrinsically not rateable. This was followed by a discussion of the difference between wanting to succeed, and insisting that he "must" succeed. In the former case he can bend his energies constructively to going after what he wants, be it financial or any other kind of rewards. In the second case, he places an absolute demand on himself, which, if not realized, places his value as a person in jeopardy, in his own eyes.

While these exchanges were taking place, the client was directed to examining his belief system as a total constellation:

1. I must succeed.
2. If I don't succeed, I am worthless.
3. I can't succeed. Therefore I am worthless.
4. Success is measured by my friends' financial success.
5. I must have other people's admiration to feel worthwhile.
6. I can have other people's admiration only if I succeed.
7. I can't succeed in this profession, because it's not a worthwhile profession.
8. Therefore I am worthless.

When the circularity of this set of beliefs was demonstrated, he realized that he was trapped, not by his life situation, but by his irrationality.

Therapy was directed to challenging the self-rating; to accepting the fact that his worth as a person was independent of his financial success; to realizing that his success as an engineer was independent of his friends' financial success in their chosen fields; to realizing that whereas it is very enjoyable to be admired by some people, it is hardly possible to be admired by everyone.

As a homework assignment, he was asked to keep a log of those daily events, however small, which, in the course of his work, gave him pleasure. He was greatly surprised to find that there was much in the profession of engineering that was socially useful, that he was very good at, and that he enjoyed doing. It soon became apparent that it was not his work that he hated, but his own feeling of inadequacy, his feeling that he could not "measure up."

When his expectations of his own performance were brought into line with realistic possibilities inherent in his work, he began to get positive reinforcement from it, and his performance increased. At the same time he gave up the global demand that engineers produce only that which he, himself, deemed socially useful. He also accepted the fact that he could not control the universe, but he could, if he chose, work with other like-minded people to change some of the negative results of what he called "engineering destructiveness." (His own firm was never involved in anything even remotely destructive.)

As the positive cognitive changes replaced the former negative evaluations of himself, his profession, and his achievements, the depression lifted, and the client entered a new period of personal vigor and professional creativity.

Andrew J. exemplified two rather frequently encountered concerns of men in the middle years: (1) the sense of failure at not having achieved what he thought he "should have," and (2) the desire to "chuck it all."

The first is based on unrealistic expectations, and self-castigation for what he perceived as lost opportunities. The second is not a wish to enter a new occupation—which could be realistic—but a dire need to escape from mundane responsibilities—which usually is not.

At mid-life, the accumulated frustrations that the man has learned neither to tolerate nor to cope with, at times find expression in the fantasy that somewhere there is a magical solution to all of his problems. Because magical solutions are elusive as magic normally is, the man becomes angry with the world for having "failed" him, and with himself for not having found the key to the easy solution that is always just outside his reach.

Cognitive restructuring guides the client, as in the case of Andrew J., to a recognition of his realistic alternatives, at the same time that it helps him to develop the coping skills to pursue those alternatives that are in his best interest.

Women and Work

Women's work histories have been, and will probably continue to be, more diverse than men's (Giele, 1982b), presenting many different patterns: continuous full-time work, part-time work, reentry into the job market with old skills, reentry in new occupations, entry into the job market for the first time in the middle years. These patterns are combined with various permutations: married, with children; married, without children; single parent; divorced, with or without dependent children; never married. For men, the continuous history of work bears no relation to marriage or family history, whereas for women, family relationships have been critical (Rubin, 1979).

For the cohorts now in mid-life, energies have been invested primarily in nurturing husbands, rearing children, and establishing relationships. Those who have worked outside the home have generally done so with divided loyalties, with families usually given priority. Investment in the nurturing role, as well as inferior status vis-à-vis her husband, have fostered a so-called "feminine" nonassertiveness (Notman, 1980), which is the antithesis of the risk taking needed to make major changes.

Today's mid-life women are at the crossroads of complex and rapid social changes. Greater social acceptance of education and achievement for women, decreasing discrimination against women in jobs, stand in contrast to many middle-aged women's socialized dependence, their internalized acceptance of inferior ability, and their lack of preparation for any but the lowest status, and lowest paying, jobs.

Margaret J., 55-years-old, was convinced that, much as she wanted to work outside the home, she would never get a job because she could never learn skills, and she would always fail, as she failed in the one typing job she held for two weeks.

She related, "I was always told that if I'm pretty, and nice, I'll marry the right man, and he'll provide for me. So I was pretty and nice, and married the right man, and life was one big struggle. My husband has had two heart attacks and now I'm afraid that I'll be left alone with no money and no skills and no way of taking care of myself. I never worked, and I won't be able to learn useful skills. I feel that I'll always fail. I fail at everything I try.

The following brief exchange illustrates one aspect of her therapy:

T: You say you never worked. Did someone else keep house for you, and raise your three children?
C: Oh no! Of course not.
T: What kind of housekeeper were—and are—you?
C: I must say, I'm excellent. I cook, I bake, I even sew very well.
T: And did you have difficulty raising your children?
C: Not at all. My children have been simply wonderful. I enjoyed raising them.
T: Then why do you say that you have never worked, and that you fail at everything you try? It seems to me that what you did was indeed work, and skilled work at that.

There are two misconceptions in Margaret J.'s presentation that I find important to address: (1) that the tasks of full-time mother, wife, and housekeeper are not "work" and (2) that competence at these tasks is not worthy of any positive consideration. The client was surprised that I stressed these accomplishments as positive achievements. I did so, not to detract from her desire to strike out on her own in the job market, but to dispel any notion that she "did nothing" with her life. Recognition of the fact that she, as had most of her generation, led her life according to the values of her own times, and did so successfully, often forms the constructive basis for the realistic evaluation of her own abilities.

An increasing number of women in the middle years, like Margaret J., are seeking to enter a job market for the first time, or to reenter after an interruption of many years. Many are impelled by economic necessity, whereas others seek fulfillment in a broader world.

The following presentation of Elizabeth N. demonstrates some of the fears and anxieties that some women face when contemplating entering the work force.

Elizabeth N., 52-years-old, was recently divorced. A settlement left her with enough money, if she lived frugally, for about two years, after which she would have to be self-supporting. She was a high school graduate and had worked for a few years as a clerk-typist. She married at twenty and lived a sheltered suburban life. Her two children were married and gone. She enrolled in an ongoing workshop for reentry women. The focus of the workshop was to explore some of the cognitive and emotional obstacles to retraining, and the application of RET to overcoming these obstacles. The following brief excerpts demonstrate the therapeutic direction:

T: What would you like to do?
C: I would like to get a job in the business world. But . . . I don't qualify for anything.
T: What aspect of the business world appeals to you?
C: I don't want a job as a typist. I want something more demanding. Something with more challenge. But I don't know where to start.
T: What would you have to do to qualify?
C: What I really want to do is to get a degree in business administration. But . . . I'm afraid it's too late.
T: Too late for what?

"It's too late" may be realistic when applied to careers like ballet dancing or professional tennis, but when expressed in relation to careers that are within the realm of possibility, like business administration, it is an expression of low frustration tolerance that frequently becomes a deterrent to further effort. It reflects the belief that "if I had done it sooner, it would have been easy" and "It should be easy." Because the past is the depository of unperformed acts and lost opportunities, Elizabeth was asked to relinquish the "should haves" and focus on the reality of the present, and the possibilities for the future.

Elizabeth's fears for her own future employment possibilities, on the level of her aspirations, were not altogether unrealistic. As she expressed the dilemma: "If I take a two-year course at the community college, I'll be 54 when I get my associate's degree. Who will hire a 54-year-old beginner?"

It is true that many employers prefer a women of 24 with no experience to one of 54 with 30 years of experience, even though the older woman, despite her years of homemaking, may have a degree in business administration. A women still faces double-edged discrimination in the business world if she is seeking employment above the typist level, because she is a woman, and because she is middle-aged. The realities of Elizabeth N.'s situation were acknowledged. However, the prediction that "Because I will probably have difficulties getting a job, I will inevitably not get one," was challenged.

T: It's true that you will face keen competition. But do you really believe that all doors will be closed to you?
C: Not all, but most.

T: Most, or many?
C: Probably many.
T: What level of assurance of a job do you feel you must have before you commit yourself to study?
C: Well, I suppose no one really has any assurance of a job.
T: Precisely. Then what level of risk are you willing to take?

A discussion of creative risk taking as opposed to the need for certainty helped the client to counter the irrational demand that one must be absolutely certain of the outcome before embarking on a new course. The requirement of creative risk taking came into head-on collision with Elizabeth's learned dependency, reinforced by years of a relationship in an unequal marriage, in a world that had approved of her subservient role.

To counter her expressed misgivings about her ability to compete with younger people, Elizabeth was asked to make a list of all of the positive attributes that her maturity would bring both to her college training and to a future job. She realized that there were, in fact, many. At the same time, assertiveness training, through group role playing and role modeling, helped her to overcome her life-long repression of the more dominant and self-enhancing aspects of her personality.

Elizabeth N. applied for admission to the community college.

Divorce, widowhood, and economic pressures are the realities that impel many unprepared women in the middle years to seek paid work for the first time or after a long hiatus. On the other hand, large numbers of women have entered the work force, not only for economic reasons, but for personal fulfillment. Frequently they face, in addition to their own adjustment, the problem of the adjustment of their families: of husbands who resent the added pressures on themselves for sharing the burden of housework (burdens that they rarely share in equal measure); of growing or grown children who may not accept the change in family functions. Usually, the woman continues to assume the major responsibilities of the household, on the assumption that this is her responsibility and that she must not "rock the boat," even if her earnings are essential to the family welfare.

Rapid social change today is affecting the status of women at all levels of employment. Such change, although liberating women to seek new goals in life, also creates conflicts that the therapist would be wise to address: conflicts between the drive toward independence and the socialized dependency of many of today's mid-life women; the conflict between personal and family needs; and between self-assertion and the "feminine" model.

When Parenting Ends

Just as the arrival of children into the family creates a new situation, requiring new adjustments in the family organization, so does their departure, at adulthood, constitute an important transition in the life of parents. Middle age, for parents, is a time of loosening of emotional and structural bonds to the emerging adult, in accordance with the developmental timetables of the parents and their offspring.

Women and Post-Parenting Conflict

In a searching analysis, Gilligan (1983) has shown that the primary motive of women's lives has been affiliation and relationships.

The mother–child relationship, one of the most fundamental of all human relationships, has never, to my knowledge, been explored as a developmental process, from the moment of birth until death. Interest has been directed toward the welfare of the child and toward advice concerning appropriate child-rearing practices. But the dyadic interaction, particularly from the point of view of the woman, and the effect of child bearing and child rearing on the woman's development, is, at present, a psychological void. It is a relationship that changes with the child's development, and with the woman's progression from young adulthood to old age.

It is in this relationship, with its biological, emotional, and social concomitants, that some women are most vulnerable.

Many women accept the change in family structure attendant upon the departure of their grown children, and many welcome the freedom it affords them to pursue their own interests (Glenn, 1975; Harkins, 1978; Lowenthal & Chiriboga, 1972; Rubin, 1979). For others, the transition is fraught with tension and conflicts. Problems generated by this transition are twofold: (1) role loss (Bart, 1971; Oliver, 1977); and (2) difficulties of restructuring the relationship with grown children (Oliver, 1982).

Role Loss

Immersion in the mothering role has been socially encouraged to the point of making it the primary focus of many women's lives. For many women, particularly those now in their middle years, regardless of their other interests, relationships, talents, or accomplishments, mothering is the function that is central to their perception of self. It is the function by which, frequently, they have been defined, and by which they have defined themselves.

A woman who equates her self-worth with the mothering role has difficulty adjusting to its termination. She senses a loss of power in the one area of her life in which, with society's full approval, she exercised power, the power inherent in the child-rearing process. She has fulfilled her socially approved role, and when deprived of this role, she experiences anger, guilt, self-blame, and self-pity. She irrationally demands, "This shouldn't change."

Rita L., a successful saleswoman, 49-years-old, suffered from insomnia, loss of appetite, withdrawal from social life, and growing reluctance to go to work. These symptoms developed after her second son married and moved to another city. She described herself as "devastated" by the "emptiness" she was feeling.

Although she did not ascribe these feelings to the departure of her son, or to the loss of her mothering role, it soon became apparent that this role loss was the precipitating and maintaining event in her depressive affect.

The cognitive components of her emotional distress clustered around irrational beliefs and demands that reflected:

1) Anger and condemnation. ("They have no right to leave me. They're selfish.")
2) Low frustration tolerance. ("It's not fair. I can't stand it.")
3) Self put-down. ("I have failed. I'm no good.")
4) Perfectionism. ("What did I do wrong? If I had been the right kind of mother, this wouldn't have happened.")
5) Need for control. ("They should stay here. I know it's better for them, here.")
6) Self pity. ("Poor me.")

Therapy was directed toward specifying and challenging her major dysfunctional cognitions, and toward behavioral exercises designed to reorient the client away from her intense focus on her children, and toward her own life. The irrational beliefs were vigorously challenged and replaced by adaptive ones, in accordance with the principles of RET (Ellis, 1962; Ellis & Grieger, 1977). Rita L. was helped to understand that her negative perception of her children's departure created her emotional disturbance, and that both her perception of the situation and her response to it stemmed from her intense overinvolvement in the mothering role.

As a homework assignment, the client was asked to refrain from calling either of her sons for one week. Her response, at first, was almost comparable to asking a drug abuser to give up a favorite drug. However, with much encouragement, she eventually complied. At the same time, she was encouraged to focus on herself, and to set goals for her own personal enrichment.

She gradually found pleasure in new activities as her affect began to change from one of anger toward her children, and pity for herself, to one of hope. She began to experience herself as a separate and distinct person, entitled to her own interests.

Entitlement to seek personal satisfaction apart from the needs of others, becomes a critical issue for some middle-aged women. It is an issue that often finds its most critical expression in relation to children.

Although all human beings internalize a set of irrational beliefs because they are imperfect and the world is imperfect, women have been taught, from earliest childhood, to equate irrational beliefs with their most cherished aims and goals in life, and with their essential "femininity." These cognitions are the desiderata of the "good girl"; the model of the perfect wife and mother; the person always available for the needs of other people; the person who always seeks to please other people and win their approval.

While this model has served some women well (Livson, 1976), for others, it is a catalyst for depression. When the traditional role of wife and mother no longer provide reinforcement for a satisfying existence for the 25 or 30 years of post-parenthood, the "good girl" often becomes a depressed woman.

Restructuring the Relationship with Grown Children

A major transition in the lives of women who have raised children to adulthood is the transition between active mothering and continuing motherhood (Oliver, 1982). Mothering is a role. Motherhood is a relationship. Mothering ends when the last child reaches adulthood. Motherhood is forever. This distinction is often blurred, causing considerable difficulty for many women. This is particularly true when the role ends, and its ending signals a new phase in the relationship.

The child that was is now an adult. But this adult is still her child. This semantic confusion sometimes translates into interpersonal confusion.

The relationship undergoes profound metamorphoses at various phases of the life cycle, necessitating new adjustments on the part of both the mother and the offspring. Just as the developmental task of the young adult is the achievement of autonomy, and the establishment of new primary relationships, so too, the developmental task of the mother is separation and the restructuring of the relationship with the newly emerged adult. And, just as the young person often experiences conflict in the transition from dependence to autonomy, so too does the mother often experience conflict in the transition from nurturer to autonomous parent in an undefined relationship with adults who will always be her children.

Society has not charted the boundaries of the altered relationship nor defined its course. But the strong emotions and the sense of responsibility generated by years of control, authority, guidance, and direction, within the confines of the nuclear family, are not automatically dissipated when the other adults, her children, become independent individuals.

Although most women accept the changed relationship with little or no conflict, and others resolve the conflict with little or no stress, some women become bewildered, angry, and self-pitying. The problem is not the so-called "empty nest." Few, if any, of these women mourn the passing of the mothering role; few wish to return to the role of primary caretaker. The problem is the ambiguity of the new relationship and the tension created by that ambiguity. If they are aware that the rules have changed, they do not know what the new rules are.

Some women would like to continue to play an active, if not necessarily central, role in their children's lives, and in the lives of their grandchildren; and they upset themselves when they feel excluded. Many are resentful of what they perceive to be their children's callousness and neglect. Some torment themselves over the paths that their children's lives have taken. Others have difficulty defining and delimiting "What do I owe them?" and "What do they owe me?"

Therapy is directed to challenging the "shoulds": "They *should* call me more often." "They *should* spend holidays with me." "That's no way to bring up grandchildren." "They *shouldn't* make messes of their lives." RET helps clients to substitute rational preferences for irrational demands. At the same time, mothers of grown children are helped to understand and accept the fact that their mothering days are over and that their children are adults who are responsible for their own lives.

We explore ways for the client to maintain a relationship without infringing on their children's independence. Fewer phone calls, fewer visits, fewer recriminations, fewer intrusive questions about personal matters are frequently helpful in initiating change. At the same time, assertiveness training teaches women to resist inordinate baby-sitting, household, and, at times, financial demands from their children. Women frequently believe that they must meet these demands or else "They won't like me and that would be terrible!" and "Isn't that what mothers are for?" They feel obliged to meet these demands even when they are contrary to their own wishes and interests.

The objective, in RET, is to help women to accept their children as autonomous people, and, at the same time, to assert themselves in such a way that their own autonomy is respected by their offspring. The adult–child relationship is replaced by an adult–adult relationship. This adult–adult relationship is unique among interpersonal relationships by virtue of the biological ties, the developmental history, and the intergenerational differences between the mother and offspring. Recognition of the changed nature of the relationship becomes a springboard for personal growth.

Men and Post-Parenting Conflict

Contrary to popular belief, some fathers also experience distress when children leave home. Roberts & Lewis (1982) found that nearly one-fourth of fathers of 118 couples chosen randomly in Georgia, reported distress when their first child left. They explained these findings in terms of the "principle of most stress"; that is, that fathers who reported more distress were those who had the most to lose with the departure of their last child. They included those whose marriages and friendships had become empty shells; those who no longer felt needed in terms of financial support; and those who were becoming more nurturant at a time when their wives and children were becoming more independent.

That men's level of distress equals that of women who have given themselves entirely to the child rearing process, is doubtful, but that this is a significant transition in the lives of men, is a fact deserving of more attention and research than this has heretofore received (Rubin, 1979).

Under the impact of the women's movement, men are becoming more involved in child rearing. Therefore, it is entirely likely that more men will experience role loss at mid-life, as their children become independent of them. And this role loss will come at a time when they are facing retirement from the work force, creating a double loss. (This double loss will also affect women, as more of them become committed to careers.)

Just as some women have difficulty redefining and restructuring their relationships with grown children, so do some men. In workshops, "Relating to Your Grown Children," which I have conducted for people in the post-parental years, as many men as women have attended. Where women tended more to express their dissatisfactions with sons and daughters in terms of hurt feelings at personal slights and injustices, as well as by self-denigration ("What did I do wrong?"), men tended more to be angry with their sons for failure of achievement, and with their daughters because of disapproval of their sex lives or their marital choices: "I worked seven days a week building my business, and now that I turned it over to him, he goes fishing on weekends." "I didn't have the opportunities he has, and what does he do but. . . .:" "My daughter married that ____and where will it get her?" "She has no right to have an affair with a married man." The loss here is the loss of paternal authority, an authority that some men have difficulty relinquishing.

The key to continuing good relations in the post-parental period is acceptance of each other's differences and each other's autonomy. The RET practitioner can help clients achieve this by challenging the "shoulds" by which parents, men and women, upset themselves over behaviors that they cannot control. Joint sessions, involving both parent and offspring, are sometimes helpful in bringing about improvement in the relationship.

Body Image

Body image is an important referent for self-perception and self-esteem. Bodily changes of the middle years evoke fears of decline and raise omens of old age. Declining body image impacts on men and women at mid-life, requiring reevaluation of the standards imposed on them by our youth-oriented society. The standard for women is beauty; for men, physical activity.

The Trauma of the First Wrinkle

Women are supposed to be beautiful. Men are supposed to be virile. Women are supposed to look young forever. Men are supposed to look mature. Beauty for a woman means youth; attractiveness for a man means ruggedness, achievement. Little lines around the eyes spell the end of the woman's dream of eternal attractiveness. Little lines around a man's eyes add charm to strength.

The double standard, slowly being eroded with respect to sexuality and sexual expression, to career goals, to sex roles, holds fast and firm with respect to social attitudes towards beauty (Rindskopf & Gratch, 1982). Movies, TV, and advertisements still proclaim the ideal woman: young, exquisitely groomed, and flawless of face and figure. The middle-aged woman is still largely nonexistent, except in ads for denture adhesive and laxatives. The double standard of aging, which, according to Sontag (1972), "denounces women with special severity," is alive and well.

At the same time that girls are taught to equate themselves with their looks, they are also taught to deny their importance. "Don't judge a book by its cover," "Outward appearances are deceitful," "Beauty is only skin deep," women are told, while they are bombarded by advice and products to preserve and enhance that fragile layer. Beauty, they say, is in the eye of the beholder. But the eyes of the beholder are well trained. And when the beholder is the woman herself, she sometimes becomes frightened at the first wrinkle, which, to her, is the harbinger of decline, not only of her looks, but of herself, her personhood.

From earliest childhood, women have received double messages: (1) The most important attribute you possess is your looks; (2) It is not "nice" to admit this. Both of these messages coalesce at mid-life, when the woman sees the decline of youthful appearance, and, at the same time pretends, to others, that it is of no importance. She carries out the pretense with little jokes about expanding waistlines and sagging chins. But pretense is rarely a healthy response to a problem. Neither is nonacceptance.

Some women accept, with equanimity, the wrinkles, the changing chin line, and the expanding waist. Some do not.

In the many workshops I have conducted for women in the middle years, women have raised issues relating to divorce, husbands, lovers, children, jobs, widowhood, and loneliness. None has ever raised any issue concerning changed appearance. One could easily have assumed that this is not a matter of concern. But, at some time during the course of a workshop, I ask, "How do you feel about your looks?" The closet doors open, and the women's fears and anxieties pour out. Fears that they no longer "measure up"; that there is something shameful about not being youthful looking; that the wrinkles are a mark of failure. Some want to stop the clock; others want to stop the clock from showing.

Some women make the irrational demand that "It must not happen to me"; that they, of all people, *must* remain eternally young and youthfully attractive. Aging may be a natural process for other people, but for themselves it is a personal insult.

Evelyn G. wanted to break all mirrors. When she looked in the mirror, she felt "shattered." She said, "That's what the world sees. That's not me. I can't relate to that image. I hate mirrors."

T: Is it the mirrors you hate?
C: I hate the "me" that I see in the mirror. I don't see the rest of me. Only the wrinkles.
T: What do the wrinkles represent to you?
C: Old age. I hate myself for looking old.
T: How can you stop hating the "you" that you see in the mirror? The image you see in the mirror is an integral part of you. Is it all of you?

Evelyn was given a homework assignment: Rather than destroying her mirror, she was to look in it for ten minutes every morning and ten minutes every evening; and to focus on the wrinkles, saying to herself, as she did so, "That image in the mirror is an image of me. That is what I look like. Those wrinkles are part of me."

Not long afterward, Evelyn reported to her RET group: "I now focus differently. I look in the mirror and see the wrinkles and I say, 'That's part of me. That's not all of me.' I feel better when I do that. There are things about me that I like. There are even things about my appearance that I like. I feel better about myself."

Obviously I could have directed Evelyn to a realistic assessment of her situation, namely, to point out that she had many positive attributes, including mature attractiveness; that sexuality and sexual attractiveness are not the exclusive province of unlined faces and firm bodies; that there is much one can do to enhance one's looks. This, as an initial approach, would have been as futile as it would have been inelegant. Instead, I focused therapy on the questions: "Why is it terrible and awful not to be beautiful?" "Why can I not stand not being youthfully attractive?" "Where is it written that I must always look young?" "Am I less a person if I do indeed look older, as I grow older?" She learned to substitute "I don't like it" for "It mustn't be." She used the rational self-statements, "I can survive, even if I don't get what I want" and "Nature is unfair, and I can stand that, too."

As a homework assignment, I frequently ask women to consider the following, and report on it to the group: "Ten years from now: How will I look? What will I be doing? What will my major interests be?" This helps women recognize that they can continue to grow emotionally even as they grow further away from the youthful ideal.

Creams, cosmetics, and calisthenics are valuable in enhancing appearance and health. It is certainly adaptive to enhance both, to the extent that cosmetology and medicine make it possible. However, a realistic acceptance of aging, and the separation of appearance from self-worth are the preconditions for the successful transition from youth to old age. This may fly in the face of the established order of things—but where is it written that the established order should not be disestablished?

Men and Bodily Change

Just before mid-life, in the normal course of events, a man's physical vigor has peaked, and some slowing down has become apparent. The athlete of 38 can no longer compete with the 20-year-old superstar. In the public arena, this is anticipated and accepted. In men's private world, this sometimes comes as a shock: "My son beat me at tennis. I didn't know whether to be proud of him, or to feel sorry for myself. I suddenly felt I was the older generation."

Decrements in physical performance come into collision with societal stereotypes that demand that a man always express his masculinity in vigorous and competitive ways. Some diminution of sexual drive, occasional erectile difficulties, diminished energy levels, or poor sports performance often arouse anxieties about physical decline and fears of aging.

The mortality rate among men 45 to 65 is 6 times that of men twenty years younger (Neugarten & Datun, 1974). This fact, coupled with the perception of physical changes, tend to focus men on their own mortality: "Last year my best friend died. It's scary. Who will be next?"

Where women respond with more distress to evidence of decline in physical attractiveness, men's self-esteem is more heavily invested in physical performance, and physical well-being.

The rational solution is the separation of the sense of self from all criteria, be they sexual performance, athletic skills, or physical well-being. Using the methods of RET (Ellis, 1962; Ellis & Harper, 1975) clients can be taught to substitute unconditional self-acceptance for self-esteem based on unrealistic stereotypes of masculinity.

As Peter J., age 43, so aptly put it: "All of a sudden I feel old. I can't play basketball the way I used to. I don't look the same. But I'm still me. The same me I used to be. But different. If I accept that, I can make the rest of my life work for me. It'll be different. But good."

Countertransference and the Practitioner's Fear of Aging

Countertransference plays a role, impeding therapeutic progress, when the therapist views the client through the prism of his or her own biases, stereotypes, fears, personal conflicts, and irrational beliefs.

Recently, I was asked to review a tape recording of a clinical session. The client, an attractive woman of 26, was obsessed with a morbid fear of losing her attractiveness as she became old. The following exchange took place between the client and her 32-year-old male therapist:

C: I get absolutely devastated when I think about losing my looks. I dread the day when I will look like an old woman.

T: You're only 26. Why worry about that now? You have so many years ahead of you.

The therapist, in this segment, demonstrated his agreement that it was awful to "look like an old woman." He focused on her "off-time" fear, rather than on the irrationality of the fear itself. The appropriate intervention would have been: "Yes, you will, if you are fortunate, become an old woman some day. Why will that be terrible? And why will it be terrible to look old when you are old? Will you be less of a person?"

In order for the therapist to help the client challenge the irrational beliefs that underlay her obsessive fear, the therapist would, himself, have to be convinced that (1) it's not terrible to grow old; (2) it's not terrible to look old; (3) it's not terrible for (1) and (2) to occur, even if the subject is a woman!

Many therapists are young. And, like most people in our society, have fears of aging, or would rather not think about it. Many are on the verge of middle age, or in middle age, and are, themselves, beginning to examine their own lives. Some are castigating themselves for lost opportunities and unfulfilled dreams. Some have parents from whom they have not fully separated, or from whom separation has been especially painful. Some are experiencing the trauma of the first wrinkle. Many struggle with fears of physical decline. All have been exposed to the negative images of the older person. And, although the therapist can view the severely disturbed, and psychotic, or the depressed, as the "other," he or she often views the aging person as "myself," if not now, then later, or "sooner than I'm prepared to admit."

To what extent do therapists' own feelings about aging bias their perception of older people? According to Blum and Tallmer (1977), the introjected social stigma associated with the aged, that is, people over 65, and therapists' negative responses to these stigma, have prevented the development of adequate models of therapy for the aged. Countertransference is a powerful shaper of therapists' response to the aged (Goodstein, 1982), engaging their own fantasies and fears that are projected onto the client.

Countertransference toward the middle aged may play a much more subtle role than toward the aged. Unless one makes a commitment to gerontology, it is generally possible to avoid dealing with the aged. However, in a clinic or general practice, the middle aged constitute a large and evergrowing population. In this case, avoidance may take the form of denying any special attributes or of special psychological differences of the middle-aged person, as distinct from the young. It may take the form of nonrecognition, not only of the specificity of the age-related problems, but of the potentiality for growth, as well as the realistic limitations that the middle years bring to men and women.

Conclusion

A number of studies have demonstrated empirically the efficacy of cognitive therapy as applied to the problems of the aged (Keller & Croake, 1975; Emery, 1981; Harris & Ivory, 1976; Meichenbaum, 1974), as well as specifying and challenging some myths and stereotypes regarding old age (Peth, 1974).

In this paper, I have selected a few of the many transitional problems of people in the middle years, in order to demonstrate the application of RET to their resolution. The problems I selected are in the areas of work, separation, and body image. These broad categories may involve different tasks for different people. For example: the work area may involve preparation for retirement, the emotional, situational, and financial adjustments which can be critical in paving the way to a more adaptive old age. The major concern of separation may not be separating from grown children, but divorce, widowhood, widowerhood, parental deaths. Body image, for women, arouses fears of loss of attractiveness, and with it, loss of selfhood; for men, bodily changes arouse the forebodings of mortality. For both men and women, the optimal transition into mid-life and later involves a reassessment of the extrinsic criteria by which personhood has been defined.

I selected these problems on the basis of the frequency with which they presented themselves in workshops I have conducted at The Institute for Rational-Emotive Therapy and in my own practice. I make no claim regarding the frequency with which they occur in the general population. The richness and diversity of life in the middle years is no doubt reflected in a broad range of problems that therapists encounter.

A great deal of research into the years from 40 to 64 is required in order to clarify the limitations and the potential for growth of this important, and growing, segment of the population.

References

Barnett, R. C., & Baruch, G. K. (1978). Women in the middle years: A critique of research and theory. *Psychology of Women Quarterly, 3*(2), 187–97.

Bart, P. B. (1971). Depression in middle aged women. In V. Gornick & B. K. Moran, (Eds.), *Women in sexist society* (pp. 163–186). New York: Basic Books.

Bengston, V. L., Kasschau, P. L., & Ragan, P. K. (1981). Cited in J. G. Howells (Ed.), *Modern perspectives in the psychiatry of middle age* (p. 4). New York: Bruner/Mazel.
Blum, J. E., & Tallmer, M. (1977). The therapist vis-à-vis the older patient. *Psychotherapy: Theory, Research and Practice, 14*(4), 361–367.
Ellis, A. (1962). *Reason and emotion in psychotherapy.* Secaucus, NJ: Citadel Press.
Ellis, A. (1977). Psychotherapy and the value of a human being. In A. Ellis & R. Greiger, (Eds.), *Handbook of rational emotive therapy* (pp. 99–112). New York: Springer.
Ellis, A., & Grieger, R. (Eds.) (1977). *Handbook of rational-emotive therapy.* New York: Springer.
Ellis, A. & Harper, R. A. (1975). *A new guide to rational living.* North Hollywood, CA: Wilshire Books.
Emery, G. (1981). Cognitive therapy with the elderly. In G. Emery, S. D. Hollon, & R. C. Bedrosian, (Eds.), *New directions in cognitive therapy* (pp. 84–98). New York: Guilford Press.
Erikson, E. H. (1950). *Childhood and society.* New York: Norton.
Erikson, E. H. (1964). Inner and outer space: Reflections on womanhood. *Daedalus, 93,* 582–606.
Giele, J. Z. (1982a). Women in adulthood: Unanswered questions. In J. Z. Giele, (Ed.), *Women in the middle years* (pp. 1–35). New York: Wiley.
Giele, J. Z. (1982b). Women's work and family roles. In J. Z. Giele, (Ed.), *Women in the middle years* (pp. 115–150). New York: Wiley.
Gilligan, C. (1982). Adult development and women's development: Arrangements for a marriage. In J. Z. Giele, (Ed.), *Women in the middle years* (pp. 89–114). New York: Wiley.
Gilligan, C. (1983). *In a different voice.* Cambridge: Harvard University Press.
Glenn, N. (1975). Psychological well-being in the post-parental state: Some evidence from national surveys. *Journal of Marriage and the Family, 37*(1), 105–110.
Goodstein, R. K. (1982). Individual psychotherapy and the elderly. *Psychotherapy: Theory, Research and Practice, 19*(4), 412–418.
Gould, R. L. (1978). *Transformations: Growth and change in adult life.* New York: Simon & Schuster.
Harkins, E. B. (1978, August). Effects of empty nest transition on self-report of psychological and physical well-being. *Journal of Marriage and the Family,* 549–556.
Harris, C. S., & Ivory, P. B. (1976). An outcome evaluation of reality orientation therapy with geriatric patients in a state mental hospital. *Gerontologist, 16,* 496–503.
Horney, K. (1950). *Neurosis and human growth.* New York: Norton.
Howells, J. G. (Ed.) (1981). *Modern perspectives in the psychiatry of middle age.* New York: Brunner/Mazel.
Keller, J., & Croake, J. (1975). Effects of a program in rational thinking on anxieties in older persons. *Journal of Counseling Psychology, 22,* No. 1, 54–57.
Levenson, D. L. (1978). *The seasons of a man's life.* New York: Knopf.
Livson, F. B. (1976). Patterns of personality development in middle aged women: A longitudinal study. *International Journal of Aging and Human Development, 7*(2), 107–115.
Lowenthal, M. F., & Chiriboga, D. (1972). Transitions to the empty nest: Crisis, challenge or relief? *Archives of General Psychiatry, 26,* 8–14.
Meichenbaum, D. (1974). Self instructional training: A cognitive protheses for the aged. *Human Development, 17,* 273–280.
National Center for Health Statistics, U.S. Dep't. of Health and Human Services (1983). In: *World Almanac,* New York: Daily News, p. 958.
Neugarten, B. L. (1968). The awareness of middle age. In B. L. Neugarten, (Ed.), *Middle age and aging* (pp. 93–98). Chicago: University of Chicago Press.

Neugarten, B. L. (1973a). Personality change in late life: A developmental perspective. In C. Eisdorfer & M. P. Lawton, (Eds.), *The psychology of adult development and aging* (pp. 311–335). Washington, DC, American Psychological Association.

Neugarten, B. L. (1973b). Continuities and discontinuities of psychological issues into adult life. In D. C. Charles, and W. R. Looft, (Eds.), *Readings in psychological development through life*. New York: Holt, Rinehart & Winston.

Neugarten, B. L., & Datan, N. (1982). Cited in L. M. Tamir, *Men in their forties* (p. 8). New York: Springer.

Neugarten, B. L. & Peterson, W. A. (1957). A study of the age–grade system. *Proceedings of the Fourth Congress of the International Association of Gerontology, 3*, 497.

Norman, W. H. & Scaramella, T. J. (1980). (Eds.), *Mid-Life: Developmental and clinical issues*, New York: Brunner/Mazel.

Notman, M. T. (1980). Changing roles for women at mid-life. In W. H. Norman & T. J. Scaramella, (Ed.), *Mid-Life: Developmental and clinical issues* (pp. 85–109). New York: Brunner/Mazel.

Oliver, R. (1977). The "empty nest syndrome" as a focus of depression: A cognitive treatment model, based on rational emotive therapy. *Psychotherapy: Theory, Research and Practice, 14*(1), 87–94.

Oliver, R. (1982). "Empty nest" or relationship restructuring? A rational-emotive approach to a mid-life transition. *Women and Therapy, 1*(2), 67–83.

Peth, P. R. (1974). Rational-emotive therapy and the older adult. *Journal of Contemporary Psychotherapy, 6*(2), 179–184.

Rindskopf, K. D., & Gretch, S. E. (1982). Women and exercise: A therapeutic approach. *Women and Therapy, 1*(4), 15–26.

Roberts, C. L., & Lewis, R. A. (1981). The empty nest syndrome. In J. G. Howells, (Ed.), *Modern perspectives in the psychiatry of middle age* (pp. 328–336). New York: Brunner/Mazel.

Rubin, L. B. (1979). *Women of a certain age: The mid-life search for self*. New York: Harper & Row.

Sontag, S. (1972, September 23). The double standard of aging. *Saturday Review*.

14

Rational Living with Dying

HARRY J. SOBEL

This will be my final word on the topic of death for some time to come, so it is fitting that I should conclude this volume with a chapter on thanatology and rational-emotive psychotherapy.

For quite some time now, I have spent a significant portion of my clinical and research time working with cancer patients, counseling the dying, assessing the plight of patients confronting life-threatening illnesses, and generally attempting to make rational sense of how, as mortal men and women, we perceive and integrate the fact of our finiteness. I have been exposed to a wide assortment of personal coping strategies, and observed dying patients and their families reaching for a multitude of explanations that might ease the psychological pain of saying goodbye to a life cherished and enjoyed.

All too often patients are bolstered by clinical interventions that provide them with little comfort and not much training in how one can maintain self-control, self-respect, and morale in the face of one's inexorable dying. Therefore as I write one last statement on our need to confront dying and death as a normal dimension of the life process, it is appropriate that rational-emotive therapy be discussed. The philosophies and clinical theories of RET provide a most humanistic and pragmatic approach for clinicians, families of the dying, and all of us who understand that even the best of denial mechanisms will not excuse us from the final task of life, namely a clear, cognitive, and affective interaction with our eventual death.

In this chapter I intend first to review some problems with traditional approaches in clinical thanatology, and then to suggest how an RET

HARRY J. SOBEL • Department of Psychiatry, Harvard Medical School, Boston, Massachusetts 02138.

perspective might function and what advantages exist for implementing its basic premises into our counseling practices. For those who have been trained in traditional methods and are accustomed (if not conditioned) to walking lightly and quietly around the dying, this chapter might prove, at least initially, as a cold, overly pragmatic, unemotional or even antispiritual document. This need not be the case. Rational-emotive concepts, and cognitive-behavioral methods in general, are not aimed at an Orwellian world of totalitarian rule where emotions and thought "must" or "should" be controlled at all costs (Ellis, 1973; Mahoney, 1974). On the contrary, we who have witnessed a Western preoccupation and simultaneous phobic avoidance of dying, also view RET as uniquely personal, emotional, and in the service of individual choice. My colleague Avery Weisman, truly a pioneer in the thanatological arts and sciences, noted that an "appropriate death" is a death that one might choose if you had the choice (Weisman, 1972). Choice, freedom, flexibility, and control are the essence of RET's contribution to thanatology. Simply stated, RET can help us die without undue whining and wailing!

The Rise of the Western Death Culture

It is no longer a profound observation to state that death, and the dying process, were dehumanized by the scientific revolution. In our quest for experimental control and dominance over nature, traditional twentieth-century Western cultures have been uncomfortable with any phenomenon that could not be predicted, controlled, or replicated through industrial or empirical means. Death has always been a glaring reminder of the limits of a scientific world view, albeit a process that is at once both natural and guaranteed for all. In the last 20 years our preoccupation, perhaps even obsession, with control has reached new heights. The word itself infiltrates thinking and perception, appearing in our language as a symbol of mastery: wage and price controls, diet control, air traffic control, control data systems, arms control, birth control, temperature control, self-control, behavioral control, mind control, and so forth. For the most part, our striving for mastery and control has led to great achievement; however there is a point when letting go of control as a desired goal actually, and paradoxically, gives the individual more control. The fact that I might be able to tell myself that Goal A is unreachable and foolish at a specific point in time reinstates a sense of mastery in the present.

How all of this relates to the rise of the Western death and dying culture is quite simple. As interest in death and dying increased around the time that Kübler-Ross (1969) first published her book *On Death and Dying,* a polarizing process began. On one side we could observe those who insisted on transfering the *control-at-all-costs* empirical approach to clinical work with the dying patient. The opposite end was (and still is to a great extent) filled with the spiritualists and mystics who preferred to make death and dying a cult. In both cases, the insistence on total control hindered a more humanistic and rational position. The intentions were obviously good, but the resulting effects were detrimental for anyone interested in rehumanizing the normality and inevitability of death.

Let us briefly examine these two popular positions from a clinical and philosophical perspective.

The control-at-all-costs thanatologists are those clinicians who did not and have not challenged one assumption feeding their clinical pursuits; namely, that human beings should and must gain total control over all events in the universe and without doing so will find it almost impossible to thrive, adjust, and be happy. This belief system goes far beyond the drive for exploration and scientific understanding through experimentation. It is an insidious and subtle world view that constantly runs up against our mortality. And each time we are reminded of this fact, whether it be through loss, temporary sickness and vulnerability, accident, or limitation of faculties, we are led to self-devaluation, rationalization, and symbolic manifestations of our denial of death (Becker, 1974).

I do not want to suggest that at the early phases of her career, Kübler-Ross wanted to humanize death through dehumanized demands for total control. Any reading of her work will prove the contrary. But as is the case with so many pioneers, it is the disciple and the "groupies" who stray into inappropriate directions and thus taint the original notions. Such is the case with the controllers; they are clinicians and counselors who, in their fervent desire to control death, rather than "realize" (Weisman, 1974) its existence, began to promote dogmatic and rigid interventions. In the end, they are left exactly in the position they attempted to avoid: death and dying become falsely controlled, their realities denied through techniques, stages, and excessive intervention.

Kastenbaum (1978) summarizes an aspect of this position quite succinctly:

> To put it differently, many of us are bad losers, and death in our contemporary society is often interpreted as total loss. There is a distinctly practical side to this proposition. The psychology of learning and conditioning tells us that in times of stress we are most likely to fall back upon our most overlearned responses. We have been practicing to stay in control all of our lives. The stress of the dying situation potentially arouses in everyone in-

> volved a massive response to control, control and control again. If one cannot control by changing the outcome, perhaps one can control by controlling the behavior of others, by leaving the scene, or by employing a well-rehearsed strategy to control one's own thoughts and feelings. (p. 238)

As is obvious, I am implying that there exists an important difference between reality-based, humanistic interventions aimed at reinstating some sense of self-control in a patient, and the control-at-all-costs philosophy that mainly denies mortality and the limits to human cognitive or behavioral powers. This differentiation is vital to make when visualizing rational-emotive therapy as a type of cognitive control procedure.

The subtle insistence on total control is manifest on the other end of the spectrum as well, and those who have rested comfortably here run the same risk of circularity. Keep in mind that these clinicians also originated from a point that perceived our Western culture as a death phobic one, and a culture that desperately required a rehumanizing of dying. The problem, however, was that they too were unable to confront a very rational belief prior to beginning their journey of helping patients. Here it is, simply and plainly stated: we all die, and for all intents and purposes, it is the end as we know it. To accept this fact would lead to a lifestyle based on much of what this entire volume describes. To feel terribly uncomfortable with it, or to refuse, firmly and stubbornly, to accept it, leads the irrational thanatologist to one of the two positions that I am describing. Ironically, position two tells the patient that death is a normal dimension of life, but then proceeds to make it mystical, overly spiritual, enchanting, and cult-like (Agena, 1983).

The mystical thanatologists have returned to Middle Ages conceptualizations in which people are given pseudocontrol through rite and ritual. There is much evidence for this, a mainly American phenomenon, which Rosenbaum (1982) called the "turn on, tune in, drop dead" pro-death movement! There is no question in my mind that such things as hospice centers and family workshops are appropriate and practical. There are, however, many developments from the so-called pro-death movement that are quintessentially irrational because they demonstrate people's basic refusal to accept finality and the fact that we all die, without any exceptions. My personal confrontations with certain gurus and disciples of position two have taught me that in many circumstances they worship death, dying, death encounters, stages of termination, home dying, dying centers, euthanasia, suicide, video death recording, out of body experiences, and so forth, because they fear life and living.

A devotion to death, or to schemes of dying properly, right, in control, or actualized perfectly, are irrational devotions to denial and not to living to the fullest. When, at some point in time, I begin to die the death that is the only life warranty I received, there will be a sign on my door stating: Death and Dying Groupies Go Home—Helping Junkies Not Wanted!

By analyzing both types of responses, it has been my purpose to underline some of the negative responses to our long standing dehumanization of dying and death. Unfortunately, the polarizing effect responding to the need for new approaches to the dying, has redirected a certain amount of intellectual and clinical energy away from practical, rational, and life-enriching approaches. The rise of the death culture (death *chic* if you will) had great intentions of opening our thoughts to the reality and normality of dying. It all too often backfired when the clinician and the potentially vulnerable patient became preoccupied with death *per se.* And so it should not surprise any of us to hear about patients who were bombarded with books to read, tapes to hear, fantasies to practice, vitamins to eat, hypnotic techniques to use, chants to sing, and stages to go through, as some well-intentioned counselor reported to staff that "poor Mrs. Jones in Room 201 is about to die and we can't let her because she never made it through stage 4 of good dying!"

This type of control coming from both positions reflects our stubborn refusal to accept the obvious: eventually we all just die and are finally, despite even glorious clinical paraphanelia, *dead.* As Ellis (1981) states:

> Death, at the present time, is also inevitable. The mere fact that we are born and continue to live means that, like all forms of contemporary life, we will definitely die. To be accorded the boon of life, we have to (until the fountain of youth is someday—perhaps—discovered) suffer the fate of dying. Some of us will die sooner, some later, but we all (yes, all!) will die. (p. 169)

Integrating this blatant notion, whether one be spiritually inclined or more secular in viewpoint, leads to rational control; a psychological position that acknowledges death's inevitability without subtle denial, and once accepting such, can proceed to focus on practical and reasonable living with dying. Philosophies and methods of rational-emotive psychotherapy serve this goal in an exemplary manner, without performing a so-called "Roto-Rooter of the mind."

Irrational Thanatology and the Irrational Death Counselor

Many of my perspectives on clinical myths that lead to misguided and irrational interventions with those facing life-threatening illnesses were derived from interviews with patients such as Ellen, a woman who was certainly more enlightened than many of the helpers who swarmed her room as she faced death. Here is an excerpt from one of Ellen's first talks with me back in 1979:

> I've been in this room for weeks now watching nurses and doctors and technicians, and family and friends, come and go. You know everyone seems to have a look of doom and despair, even when I feel like cherishing a few moments about my life or when I may become a bit reflective, maybe melancholic is the better word, you know. They all want me to be a certain way, you know. I think this place must tell everyone "Hey, get those dying ladies in shape for the final act." It sometimes seems scripted, Dr. Sobel. I wonder if they expect me to die the way all patients on this ward have died in the past, you know, the Ward Three Approach and all that stuff. There's a nurse here who keeps asking me if I'm depressed and after awhile, I started wondering if that's the way I'm supposed to be. I've spent most of my life trying to be the way you're supposed to be. Maybe you can't die your own way anymore either. I don't know, it just seems spooky the way these people stare at me. They're more afraid than I've been for the past six months. I'll tell you one thing, Dr. Sobel, I'm sick and tired and bored with people trying to tell me how to die. They've never died and neither have you or I. I saw a movie recently about some poet who died. He summed it up for me real well. He said: "Dying is a drag, it's a bore . . . so people, please let me live a few more hours without all that pressure."

Ellen always stands out in my mind when I reflect on how irrational the many parts of thanatology have become in recent years. One has to ask the question whether it is the majority of the patients or the substantial number of denying, control-at-all-cost therapists who are experiencing the actual stress and vulnerability of death as a normal life process?

Before we examine some specific aspects of RET in practice with the dying patient, it seems worthwhile to review some basic tenets of Irrational Emotive Thanatology (IET) and how these premises affect the counselor. I have written elsewhere (Sobel, 1981) about myths of cancer counseling and how clinical prescriptions often interfere with the humane treatment of patients. Consider some of these myths restated in terms of principles for an Irrational Emotive Therapist.

IET Principle #1

Good solid psychosocial care of the dying involves helping the patient or family reach deep and profound insights into character and personality. An irrationally-based therapist/counselor therefore will insist that a patient not die until self-analysis is complete, problems with others all completely resolved, and death, as a definite existential crisis, is integrated perfectly! In other words, a patient *must* and *should* be pushed to confront all life concerns and achieve a TRD—Totally Resolved Death. The clinician can be expected to be heard muttering such subvocal self-statements as "Don't die on me yet" or "She must learn to let go of her anger towards her father, she just must."

IET Principle #2

A competent thanatologist is an individual who can always teach a dying patient how to die correctly, with little ambiguity. Dying correctly is somehow an agreed on process. Therefore should any patient engage in creative and self-enhancing methods that do not fit into the prepared D.C. ("dying correctly") script, it behooves the helper to intervene and describe what will occur. One can expect to hear the counselor impersonating Carl Rogers with such tailored empathic responses as "I know what it's like" or "I've been there before and it's painful."

IET Principle #3

One must always assume that a dying patient is terribly depressed, vulnerable, miserable, and precariously near the zone of psychological decompensation. Once you assume this clinical belief, then it is quite obvious that *all* patients and their families *should* be approached with great caution and prudence. Furthermore, the IE therapist accepts it as proven fact that dying, and thoughts or images of death itself, are the most frightening, tragic, and catastrophic dimensions of the patient's life; or as I have stated previously, these helpers will always acknowledge that "fear of death reigns supreme over fears of other biopsychosocial events, such as pain, bodily disfigurement, and isolation" (Sobel, 1981).

IET Principle #4

Clinical sessions with the dying and their friends and family should always aim for the profound existential concerns that *always* lie at the core of observable stress. Thus, a here-and-now clinical orientation, or one that seeks to teach problem solving, active coping with real life dilemmas, and cognitive self-instruction taught by those evil and dehumanized behaviorists, *must* be viewed as countertherapeutic, if not downright unprofessional and unfeeling.

Should the patient begin to confront reality with a degree of practicality and resourcefulness, I suggest that the IET immediately find something stress-producing to utter so that the patient can begin a catharsis. For example, (and this is especially relevant for the IET who believes that intense emotional release is the *sine qua non* of effective thanatological care and a TRD), the counselor can say the following: "I bet you must be feeling awfully sad, lonely, depressed, isolated, dejected, scared, and frightened because you're going to die soon and then you'll never be able to speak with all the people you love so much." This approach is extraordinarily effective in stimulating an emotional response.

IET Principle #5

The IE therapist assumes that people cope poorly with such life-threatening illnesses as cancer, and that dying patients *must* and *should* have professional counseling because denial is always bad. Here is our chance to actualize the belief that anxiety and even moderate amount of depression can never be positive motivating factors in adjustment. Therefore the IE therapist will search for any means available to extinguish normal despair or periodic anxiety, even going to great lengths to design compulsive behavioral programs that force the patient to relax, meditate, chart, count, self-instruct, sing, hum, dance, eat yogurt, imagine, covert condition, and model, all day, without stop, just so that predictable effects are avoided. The clinician typically mutters the following: "I cannot allow the patient to stand any anxiety. I cannot permit him to lose any control. I cannot let the patient realize that she will actually be dead, and I cannot let her deny the fact that she will die." Furthermore, the helper will accept the notion that all patients go through orderly stages of dying and follow precise psychological processes. And to the degree that patients demonstrate creative coping and innovation not appearing as part of Kubler-Ross stages, the helper is justified in becoming angry at the one being helped and certainly entitled to feel like an incompetent clinician.

IET Principle #6

A concerned and competent irrational-emotive thanatologist *should* always like and love each patient he or she works with because the patient is nearing death. Whatever the patient or family might do, regardless of how self-defeating they become or how truculent and cantankerous they are, the good and perfect helper (family member included) continues to present genuine warmth and never, under any circumstances, confronts the patient about rude and alienating behavior.

Remember, dying is not part of life, and thus we helpers should be perfectly understanding of all deviant behaviors, convincing ourselves that "we like and love all our patients, regardless!" The act of "just being there existentially" will guarantee a highly successful therapeutic outcome, even if the patient expects everything to go his or her own way, complains incessantly, and reminds us consistently that this [the fact of dying] should not be happening.

There was the case of a patient named Michael S. that demonstrates what can occur when a more humanistic, rational therapist entered the scene following weeks of IE therapists handling the intervention:

> Michael was admitted to the hospital following his second recurrence of cancer originally diagnosed as malignant melanoma five years before. The disease had metastasized and Michael was fully aware of the process, especially given the fact that he was a physician. Right from the outset of the current admission, the patient engaged in continuous complaining, always arguing with members of his family and the hospital staff. The family had spent many hours with a pastoral counselor who kept reassuring everyone that Michael was dealing with his terminal condition "in his own way and required acceptance of his long and painful angry stage." The counselor was brought into the hospital to consult with the medical staff, all of whom were seemingly pleased to have someone direct the encounters with Michael. The patient continued his very childlike demands, constantly complained about everything from the food to the reception on the television, yet all through these behaviors, the staff and Michael's family were instructed to refrain from stopping his rage. Fearful of engaging in assertive behaviors, the family grew increasingly reserved and nonverbal, and Michael became more demanding. Finally, Michael's sister convinced the family to invite a young clinical psychologist into the case management. At the initial family session, without Michael present, the psychologist learned that the staff and the family were frightened of confronting Michael "because he's dying." The new therapist entered Michael's room shorly thereafter, alone, and with great caring and obvious empathy stated: "Hello Michael, I'm Dr. John S. and I'm here at the request of your family. They tell me that you are dying and that you have been engaging in behavior that is a pain in the ass. I'm here to help you stop this and to begin enjoying your current life with people that you love."

Family relations improved considerably following the intervention.

IET Principle #7

Here the therapist assumes that dying, and the eventual death (or grieving and loss for that matter) are awful, horrible and terrible, and because they are such, this implies that dying and death *should not* and *must not* exist. Once the irrational therapist assumes this cognitive stance, then it is quite simple to justify bolstering pathological denial by either mystifying the dying process, or spending an inordinate amount of time "working through" the final demise. Thus intervention will be death enhancing, not life enhancing, and one can feel pleased as the patient dedicates his or her final life energies to worshiping death and gaining pseudo-self-control. As Albert Ellis (1981) noted, the irrational emotive therapist should reinforce the list of "typical musts":

> (1) "I *must* not die (or must not die so young or must not die so painfully)!"; (2) "Because I have led such a good life, I *should* not suffer!"; (3) "It is terribly unfair that I (or so and so) should die; and things *must* not be so unfair!"; and (4) "This treatment for my serious illness *must* not be so gruesome." (p. 157)

Mastering principle #7 can often involve doing something as simple as doing nothing but nodding one's head and reflecting disruptive affects when facing the patient!

Taken together, principles one through seven of irrational emotive thanatotherapy that I have described above will insure the strategic failures that have become all too common in counseling dying patients and their families. The acceptance of these principles as a *modus operandi* for clinical intervention is far more common than any of us would care to believe. In many respects, they were, and are, an inevitable result of the polarizing trends in the rise of the Western death and dying cult.

Toward a Rational Thanatology

In a recent *U.S. News and World Report* feature on death (July, 1983) a headline proclaimed the following:

> A NEW UNDERSTANDING ABOUT DEATH
> Living Wills, Thanatology Courses, Self-help Groups, the Hospice Movement—All Are Part of a Widespread Yearning to Make Sense out of Life's Ultimate Mystery.

This headline dramatizes the predicament that those of us practicing RET face as we confront colleagues from many different disciplines. Whereas we aim in the direction of helping people see death as inevitable, and accept that its mystery, in all likelihood, will remain forever, the traditional thanatologist is often motivated compulsively to "make sense" out of something that we are incapable of making sense out of, given the limits of our very human brains.

This so-called widespread yearning is but a game that too often reinforces denial while keeping patients on track with demands that their deaths *should* and *must* not approach because death does not make sense. Herein lies an important and quite unprofound premise for the rational-emotive therapist who specializes in thanatology: death is only a mystery insofar as we demand that we should know why we die, when we will die, and where we go once we are pronounced dead! We cannot make sense out of life's "ultimate mystery," and the more we attempt such self-defeating goals, the more we lose touch with our current life options. In the final analysis, RET helps an individual perceive feasible life options despite the most horrendous of circumstances. It does not attempt to make sense of something that is not within our capacity to understand. We are imperfect and fallible and do not understand all of nature's ways.

Practicing RET with terminal cancer and dying patients turns out to be much easier than most things that I have had to do as a therapist. When I accept a patient's insistence on knowing everything and accept a patient's demand that something "*should* not be" precisely the way it is, then I become trapped. The result is professional burnout (Kolotkin, 1981; Maslach, 1976) stemming from all sorts of untenable and irrational beliefs: (1) I, as a thanatology expert, must help all my patients understand and "make sense" of death, suffering, pain, and loss of faculties; (2) I must glorify this or that dying process or it will seem a total waste of time; (3) somehow there must be a way to "cure" death for this warm, bright, and lovable young patient who is dying from a horrible illness; and (4) I am responsible for all the hard work that precedes altering cognitions to affect emotional responses. None of these will lead to an effective psychotherapy process or outcome.

In the preceding chapters of this volume you have been exposed to the many principles of RET, as well as new and highly innovative techniques that can be used to alter a person's interpretation of any event *A*. The simple fact of the matter (and I fully realize that we have not been trained to think in this fashion) is that RET is not altered just because activating event *A* is the patient's approaching death. To the extent that we perceive this as the most horrible and catastrophic event imaginable, then naturally the counseling process becomes illogical and unmanageable. Because you as the therapist cannot ever expect to change the patient's dying process, you are stuck in the position of believing, along with the patient, that "death should not occur" and that "it is unfair and unnatural" even though it happens to everyone.

For some odd reason, people do not see that dying is perfectly predictable. It will happen to every single human being and animal on the face of the earth, yet we insist on inserting a self-defeating belief that says "it should not be this way for me or my loved one, and I will not let it happen because it is unfair and terribly sad and makes me feel lonely and fearful." For the rational-emotive therapist, the activating event at point *A* is still the irrefutable fact that we all die. The effect of this lies in the nature of our own cognitions and coping potency (Mechanic, 1977). The patient has the power, and certainly through our assistance after we accept the fact as well, to work extremely hard in changing how the inevitability of death is perceived and interpreted. In this sense, the process is simple, and no different from helping, for example, a phobic patient. The biggest trap is the ease with which therapists themselves become entrenched in irrational beliefs regarding the nature of death and dying.

I labeled this section "toward a rational thanatology." This is actually an imprecise heading, for it implies that the tools and techniques are not currently available to assist dying patients via RET. Despite arguments of the few who will claim that I preach a cold and cruel science, it is my contention that all the principles of RET (Ellis & Grieger, 1977) can be appropriately and humanistically applied to the dying patient. The same common irrational assumptions that lead healthy patients into emotional difficulty appear in the thinking of people coping with life-threatening illnesses. The same predispositions to distort reality, to whine against things that we cannot change, and to refuse to search for feasible options within a current life position are commonly observed among those approaching their final days. The practice of RET entails hard work, directed at specific and concrete (not mystical and magical) interventions that reinforce life options existing in the here-and-now, not the hereafter.

Rational thanatology assists the patient in bolstering his or her overall coping capacity, without falling prey to self-defeating cognitions. Coping, choice, and realistic control are invariably related. By reinstating a sense of realistic personal control, and thus hoping to prevent future distress, the rational-emotive therapist can guide the patient to an awareness of how many things can indeed be altered, modified, or preserved despite the reality of death. Even the simple act of teaching a patient how to reduce bodily anxiety through progressive muscle relaxation is a first step in helping to fortify personal control and morale (Sobel & Worden, 1982). Intervention becomes a learning process for the patient as he or she begins to recognize how one can control and choose, within limits, specific responses in the internal and external environments. Many irrational self-statements will blind the dying patient from perceiving the potential for self-control and life options that do in fact exist. Self-control strategies, not mystical "control-at-all-costs" theologies or ideologies, serve the practical clinical demands for assuring safe conduct, an appropriate death, and dignified dying:

> Dignified dying is not an exotic concept; it simply means that one continues to regard a dying patient as a responsible person, capable of clear perceptions, honest relationships, and purposeful behavior, consistent with the inroads of physical decline and disability. (Weisman, 1980, p. 1756)

It is the meaning and type of control imposed by the patient that becomes the blueprint for the eventual effectiveness of a particular intervention, whether that be behavioral or cognitive.

It is my clinical impression, supported by the longitudinal empirical work that I completed as part of Harvard's Project Omega (Sobel & Worden, 1979; Sobel & Worden, 1982; Weisman & Sobel, 1979; Weisman, Worden, & Sobel, 1980) that rational coping with death and dying (or life and living) almost always occurs within the confines of active, flexible, and practical problem solving. Adaptive and creative control that reinforces life options in the face of death, will develop in direct relation to a patient's willingness to make decisions while disputing irrational assumptions. Three aims, then, of short-term intervention are (1) to assess deficits in decision making along with the patient, (2) to teach self-observation, and finally (3) to reinforce a vigilant (Janis & Mann, 1977) style of problem solving. My work with highly distressed cancer patients, who so often insist that their illness *should not* have occurred and thus refuse to make any concrete decisions that might combat destructive emotions at point C, has led me to employ a step-by-step decision process as applied to one specific problem at a time: (1) identify primary affects; (2) define uppermost problems and subsidiary concerns; (3) generate alternatives and observe covert structures; (4) imagine how others might respond if asked to solve similar problems; (5) consider pros and cons of each proposed solution; (6) rank order all possible solutions; (7) select the most acceptable or feasible solution; and (8) reexamine and redefine the original problem in light of the assessment (Sobel, 1981). As the patient confronts and resolves successive problems, we begin to see the need for denial decrease and see surface the desire for living with an approaching death.

Conclusion

Throughout this chapter I have tried to suggest that rational-emotive therapy can make a great contribution to how we confront our own dying and how we help others who feel overwhelmed with sadness and dysphoria. Perhaps more than any other problem or hassle of contemporary life discussed in the present volume, the reality of death and dying brings along centuries of paradox, irrelevant baggage, and harmful metaphor. There is no question in my mind that rational-emotive therapists will confront a significant number of obstacles within institutional settings as they attempt to practice the modality. Those who have been traditionally entrusted to help us die are unaccustomed to rehumanizing while concomitantly demystifying. At least obtrusively, most thanatologists and counselors want patients to feel better about saying goodbye, and finally dying. Our task as practitioners of RET is to understand the perspectives that lie at the motivating center of much of their clinical methods. We certainly cannot understand this by dismissing it arrogantly or by devaluing all that has developed in thanatology. The rational-emotive therapist does not practice RET because it *should* or *must* be done, but because it seems highly effective in facilitating problem solving and personal dignity.

The dying process, especially when it involves an illness such as cancer, is a biopsychosocial process. As such, patients find themselves interacting with social systems and supports, family, medical personnel, physical facts, helping professionals, treatment consequences, and unknown aspects of personal consciousness. As a process, dying changes at various points for the patient and leads to dynamic beliefs about overt and covert events. RET may in fact focus heavily on personal beliefs and how these cognitions distort events, leading to unpleasant consequences. But we run the risk of oversimplication if we ignore the biopsychosocial system. A patient is a consumer, who has the right to express what he or she wants, yet the requests occur in multiple contexts. The flexible and resourceful therapist attempts to modify patient beliefs while observing the shifting of contexts, social supports, and temporal restraints on dying. If we keep this in mind and recognize that the individual patient does not always, and will not always, have the power to change everything or everyone, then RET cannot but achieve a major position in helping people live peacefully and practically with their dying.

In our dying we have the option for one final self-enhancing experiment with life. As a rational therapist I underscore the benefits of an experiment that results in creative coping and social connectedness; not creative misery and isolation. In the end, as Kurt Vonnegut states: "it's all doodley squat." But until the end, life is all I have; nothing more and nothing else. And so it goes. . . .

References

Agena, K. (1983, November 27). The return of enchantment. *New York Times Magazine*, pp. 66–80.

Becker, E. (1974). *Denial of death.* New York: Free Press.

Ellis, A. (1973). *Humanistic psychotherapy.* New York: McGraw-Hill.

Ellis, A. (1981). The rational-emotive approach to thanatology. In H. Sobel (Ed.), *Behavior therapy in terminal care: A humanistic approach* (pp. 151–176). Cambridge, MA: Ballinger.

Ellis, A., & Grieger, R. (1977). *Handbook of rational-emotive therapy.* New York: Springer.

Janis, I., & Mann, L. (1977). *Decision-making: A psychological analysis of conflict, choice and commitment.* New York: MacMillan.

Kastenbaum, R. (1978). In control. In C. Garfield (Ed.), Psychosocial care of the dying patient (pp. 227–240). New York: McGraw-Hill.

Kolotkin, R. (1981). Preventing burn-out and reducing stress. In H. Sobel (Ed.), *Behavior therapy in terminal care: A humanistic approach* (pp. 229–252). Cambridge, MA: Ballinger.

Kübler-Ross, E. (1969). *On death and dying.* New York: Macmillan.

Mahoney, M. (1974). *Cognition and behavior modification.* Cambridge, MA: Ballinger.

Maslach, C. (1976). Burn-out. *Human Behavior, 5,* pp. 16–22.

Mechanic, D. (1977) Illness behavior, social adaptation, and the management of illness. *Journal of Nervous and Mental Diseases, 165,* pp. 74–87.

Rosenbaum, R. (1982, July). Turn on, tune in, drop dead. *Harper's,* pp. 32–42.

Sobel, H. (Ed.) (1981). *Behavior therpay in terminal care: A humanistic approach.* Cambridge, MA: Ballinger.

Sobel, H., & Worden, J. (1979). The MMPI as a predictor of psychosocial adaptation to cancer. *Journal of Consulting and Clinical Psychology, 47,* pp. 716–724.

Sobel, H., & Worden, J. (1982).*Helping cancer patients cope: A problem-solving intervention program.* (A manual and cassette recording). New York: Guilford Publications and BMA.

A new understanding about death. (1983, July 11). *U.S. News and World Report.*

Weisman, A. (1972) *On dying and denying.* New York: Behavioral Publications.

Weisman, A. (1974). *The realization of death.* New York: Jason Aronson.

Weisman, A. (1980). Thanatology. In H. Kaplan, A. Freedman, & B. Sadock (Eds.), *Comprehensive textbook of psychiatry.* (pp. 1748–1759). Baltimore: William & Wilkins.

Weisman, A., & Sobel, H. (1979). Coping with cancer through self-instruction: A hypothesis. *Journal of Human Stress, 5,* pp. 3–8.

Weisman, A., Worden, J., & Sobel, H. (1980). *Psychosocial screening and intervention with cancer patients.* Boston, MA: A Project Omega-Harvard University Research Monograph.

Index

GPSR Compliance

The European Union's (EU) General Product Safety Regulation (GPSR) is a set of rules that requires consumer products to be safe and our obligations to ensure this.

If you have any concerns about our products, you can contact us on ProductSafety@springernature.com

In case Publisher is established outside the EU, the EU authorized representative is:

Springer Nature Customer Service Center GmbH
Europaplatz 3
69115 Heidelberg, Germany

Batch number: 10844655

Printed by Printforce, the Netherlands